HOW to
Bankrupt Your Student Loans
and Other Discharge Strategies

By Chuck Stewart, Ph.D.

July 2023 All rights reserved©.

Includes 34 case studies where the debtor won!

Learn the inside tips from the author who successfully bankrupted $72,000 in student loans!

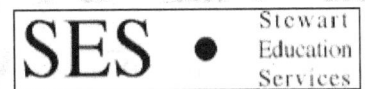

Publisher's Page

How To Bankrupt Your Student Loans and Other Discharge Strategies

Typeset and printed in the United States of America.

Published by Stewart Education Services
www.StewartEducationServices.com

Distributed by Stewart Education Services.
E-mail: info@StewartEducationServices.com

First edition, first printing: July 2023

Stewart, Chuck. 1951-
How to bankrupt your student loans and other discharge strategies / by Chuck Stewart, Ph.D.
       p. cm.
    Includes index
        1. Bankruptcy—United States—Popular works. I. Stewart, Chuck.

ISBN 0-97809764154-6-6

Library of Congress Control Number:

All Rights Reserved. Printed in the U.S.A. Copyright © 2023 by Chuck Stewart, Ph.D. No part of this publication may be reproduced, stored in a retrieval system, or transmitted in any form or by any means, electronic, mechanical, photocopying, recording or otherwise without the prior written permission of the publisher and the authors. Reproduction prohibitions do not apply to the forms contained in this product when reproduced for personal use.

Academic books by Stewart Education Services are available at: www.StewartEducationServices.com

Dedication

This book is dedicated to honest debtors who have the fortitude to assert their right to bankruptcy as assured in the U.S. Constitution.

— C.S.

Acknowledgments

The author gratefully acknowledges Bonnie Bell, Ph.D., for her insightful editing and attention to details in the production of this book; and to Jim Dochterman, Esq., for his help and support.

About the Author

Chuck K. Stewart, Ph.D., is an independent researcher and writer on many topics. His published works at ABC-CLIO include: *"Gender and Identity Around the World"* (2020), *"Documents of the LGBT Movement"* (2018); *"Lesbian, Gay, Bisexual, and Transgender Americans at Risk"* (2018) (*WINNER* of the 2018 American Book Fest best book award in the category of LGBTQ Non-fiction) ; *"Proud Heritage: People, Issues, and Documents of the LGBT Experience"* (2014); *"Greenwood Encyclopedia of LGBT Issues Worldwide"* (2009); *"Issues in Focus— Understanding Controversy and Society"* (2006, 2010); *"Gay and Lesbian Issues— A Contemporary Resource"* (2003); and *"Homosexuality and the Law"* (2001). For SAGE Publications, he wrote *"Sexually Stigmatized Communities— Reducing Heterosexism and Homophobia: An Awareness Training Manual"* (1999) that was used to create training programs used by the Los Angeles Police Academy and many other police departments. Stewart also publishes the legal self-help book— *"How to Bankrupt Your Student Loans and Other Discharge Strategies"* (2023)— besides books and training manuals on environmental issues in residential real estate. He won the David Cameron Legal Research Award besides many other grants. Stewart holds a doctorate in Education with certificate in Women's Studies from the University of Southern California. His first degrees were in physics, math, and engineering, and worked for many years in aerospace. He has taught at all levels of education and currently teaches math and statistics courses for National University. Surprisingly, he was a classical ballet dancer for twenty-five years and for the past twenty years has taught ballroom and western dancing to the gay and lesbian community. He founded and guided *Out Dancing Ballroom* from 2000 to 2006; a L.A. dance troupe dedicated to same-sex couple ballroom dancing.

Additional materials and instructional videos are available at–
www.HowToBankruptYourStudentLoans.com.

If you have comments or questions about this book, you are welcome to contact Chuck Stewart via email at: info@HowToBankruptYourStudentLoans.com. Please be courteous. Realize that hundreds of emails each week are submitted to *HowToBankruptYourStudentLoans.com,* mostly from people asking for legal advice. Chuck Stewart is not an attorney and provides legal information, not legal advice. Please don't ask specific questions about your own situation. But, if you have a unique question or slant on the student loan problem and suggested solutions that could benefit others, do write. This book is, in many ways, a community outpouring on the topic since the legal profession and Department of Education actively discourage an honest discussion on the student loan problem.

Chuck Stewart's bankruptcy case is public information and can be found at the California Central Bankruptcy Court case LA04-19681ER, reported August 2004. This is provided to you since, unfortunately, there are still critics who claim it is impossible to bankrupt student loans.

This is the documentation related to the bankruptcy and adversarial filing for Chuck Stewart, author of *How to Bankrupt Your Student Loans*. At one time, court cases were easily obtained by a search of court records. Now, they can only be made with PACER service through the courts. It is free to register and search. You are welcome to visit their website and register: https://pacer.uscourts.gov

Case Summary
2:04-bk-19681-ER Chuck Klenzing Stewart
Case type: bk **Chapter:** 7 **Asset:** No **Vol:** v **Judge:** Ernest M. Robles
Date filed: 04/28/2004 **Date of last filing:** 08/25/2004 **Date discharged:** 08/09/2004
Date terminated: 08/25/2004

Office: Los Angeles
County: LOS ANGELES-CA
Fee: Paid
Current chapter: 7
Disposition: Standard Discharge
Nature of debt: consumer
Related adversary proceedings: 2:04-ap-02232-ER
Trustee: Alberta P Stahl (TR)**City:** Los Angeles **Phone:** (213) 580-7977**Email:** trusteestahl@earthlink.net
Party 1: Stewart, Chuck Klenzing (Debtor)
SSN / ITIN: xxx-xx-8233
Location of case files:
Volume: CS1
The case file may be available.

Filed: 04/28/2004
Terminated: 08/25/2004
Discharged: 08/09/2004

U.S. Bankruptcy Court, Central District of California (Los Angeles)
Adversary Proceeding #: 2:04-ap-02232-ER

Assigned to: Ernest M. Robles
Lead BK Case: 04-19681
Lead BK Title: Chuck Klenzing Stewart
Lead BK Chapter: 7
Show Associated Cases
Demand: $55000 (adjusted to $72,000 in 2023 dollars)

Date Filed: 08/02/04
Date Terminated: 04/27/05

Nature[s] of Suit: 426Dischargeability 523

Plaintiff	V.	**Defendant**
Chuck K Stewart 3722 Bagley Ave #19 Los Angeles, CA 90034-4113		**United States Dept Of Education** Po Box 4609 Utica, NY 13504-4609 represented by **Catherine E Bauer** 300 N Los Angeles St Rm 7516 Los Angeles, CA 90012-9834 213-894-3038 Email: Catherine.Bauer@usdoj.gov

FOREWORD

July 2023

A PERSONAL LETTER FROM THE AUTHOR,

I want to personally thank you for buying *How to Bankrupt Your Student Loans and Other Discharge Strategies*. You made a wise choice to educate yourself on this crucial topic.

You are embarking on a very difficult and personal struggle. I have been there. I was faced with overwhelming financial debt, of which student loans seemed an insurmountable problem. I was told it was impossible to bankrupt my student loans. Attorneys actually laughed at me and wanted exorbitant amounts of money to represent me– and then predicted I would lose. When the U.S. Attorney laughed at me for asking how to bankrupt my student loans, I felt I had nothing to lose by representing myself. But the problems were daunting. There simply were no books or resources revealing how to go about this.

I wrote this book to help honest debtors, like you, to have the best chance at representing yourself in attempting to bankrupt, or have discharged, your student loans. Not everyone buying this book should consider bankruptcy. There are other means to discharging student loans. The book covers a multitude of options. Perhaps one of them will work for you.

I hope you visited our website– www.HowToBankruptYourStudentLoans.com. Not all debtors qualify to attempt to discharge their student loans through the bankruptcy "undue hardship" exemption. However, the book also gives information and strategies for direct negotiations with the Department of Education. Even if you cannot bankrupt your student loans, perhaps you can strongly negotiate with the Department of Education for better loan terms or the discharge of part, or all, of your student loans. The book can help with those negotiations.

Once you complete the process or decide not to go forward, may I suggest that you donate the book to your local library. If the book is unblemished, they can put it in their reference section. You will be helping future debtors with their problems.

I want to share that during the adversary proceeding process, there were times I felt angry, overwhelmed, under attack, like giving up, confused, and more. It is a very emotional journey made difficult by attorneys who are paid not only to defend the government but to attack you. My heart goes out to you.

You are welcome to contact me with questions about the book. However, <u>I cannot help you with your particular case since I am not an attorney or your attorney</u>. This book is for educational purposes only. I would like to hear about your case, along with any new insights to add to future editions of the book.

I first published a similar book on this topic in 2005. This 2023 revision is more than 90 percent new, with almost 100 more pages. In the intervening fifteen years, hundreds of people have contacted me with their plight. Some frequent questions have come up and changes to the law that made it necessary to rewrite the book completely. The most common question comes from those who have already been through bankruptcy to only learn that it may have been possible for them to include their student loans. I have heard the pain and anger in their emails at being told (or better yet "duped" into believing) it was impossible to bankrupt their student loans. It is possible to reopen a bankruptcy and pursue an adversary proceeding. You will read of a few cases where people have reopened their bankruptcy and successfully mounted an adversary proceeding and won. I've included a generalized petition they are using for this purpose. It seems to be a strategy worth pursuing since tens of millions of people who have been through bankruptcy are still struggling with the burden of student loans. I hope it opens the floodgates of litigation.

Besides many legal updates, this edition contains:
- Discussion and forms related to reopening a bankruptcy for the purpose of including student loans and filing an adversary proceeding.
- Extended discussion on the Compromise and Write-Off procedures. There seems to be many people

who are not considering bankruptcy but live under crushing student loan debt and need to do something to make life more bearable. Here I discuss more the psychology behind these two discharge strategies.
- Updated forms reflecting recent changes in the law.
- A listing of major cases where debtors won against the Department of Education. The book now reviews 45 cases in detail including 34 where the debtor won against the DOE.

A website— www.HowToBankruptYourStudentLoans.com— has been created, specifically on this topic and book. Please visit the website for updated information.
- Gain access to all forms in downloadable format
- Have access to many videos explaining specific aspects of the adversary proceeding, including discussions on the overall problem and strategies.

I revised this book during the lockdown caused by the Covid-19 pandemic. These are trying times, and unfortunately, massive numbers of people will seek protection under the United States' bankruptcy laws. It is my hope that those of you who are entering bankruptcy and have student loans take the additional step to file an adversary against the Department of Education. If just 10 percent of you in this situation were to file an adversary, it would swamp the DOE so badly that it would come to a screeching halt. They simply don't have enough attorneys or courts to fight against tens of thousands of cases. I believe this is the only way to bring this daunting problem of student loans to Congress's attention and make rational changes to the bankruptcy code. It costs nothing to file an adversary proceeding.

As you read the book, you may come to understand that besides your specific situation, there is a need for a complete revision of the student loan discharge options. A national political movement of debtors, attorneys, and community activists is needed to address the growing student loan problem. One purpose of the website is to become a center for this political movement. The website contains links to various student loan activists' groups. Hopefully, attorneys who believe in the cause will join in and help develop a nationwide resource of legal centers and attorneys willing to work with debtors on this problem.

Ultimately, I would like to see class action suits attack the inherent unfairness of the adversary proceeding. I believe that student loan debt needs to be reclassified back to being unsecured debt and dischargeable through the standard bankruptcy process, as they were before. In the future, there should be no need for this book. Let's work to make this happen.

Best of luck.

Chuck Stewart (*See* About the Author for contact information.)

Table of Contents

CHAPTER 1 You Can Do It! 1
What This Book Covers 2
Why You Should Use This Book 2
Who Qualifies for an Adversary Proceeding, Compromise, or Write-Off and When are they Applied? 3
How to Use this Book 4
Reopening a Bankruptcy 6

CHAPTER 2 Taking Control 9
Postponement and Repayment Options 9
    Deferment 10
    Forbearance 10
    Consolidation 10
Repayment and Forgiveness Plans 11
    Standard Repayment Plan 11
    Graduated Repayment Plan 11
    Extended Repayment Plan 12
    Income-Driven Repayment ("IDR" plans) 12
Typical Discharge Options 14
Specific Forgiveness, Cancellation, or Discharge Programs 15
Ask for Relief— Compromise and Write-Off 16
    Compromise Your Loans 16
    Write-Off Your Loans 17
Default and Collections 17
Other Legal Considerations 18
    Federal Benefits 18
    Being Sued 18
    Legal Defenses That Will Not Work 19
Should I Go Forward with an Adversary Proceeding or Compromise or Write-Off? .. 19
Summary 20

CHAPTER 3 DOE Programs Details: Forgiveness, Cancellation, or Discharge of Student Loans 21
Public Service Loan Forgiveness (PSLF) 21
Teacher Loan Forgiveness 23
Closed School Discharge 26
Perkins Loan Cancellation 27
and Discharge 27
Total and Permanent Disability Discharge 31
Discharge Due to Death 33
Discharge in Bankruptcy 34
Borrower Defense to Repayment 34
False Certification Discharge 36
Unpaid Refund Discharge 37
Eligibility for Parent Borrowers 37
Summary 37

CHAPTER 4 History of Bankruptcy and the Student Loan Program 39

SECTION 1: Bankruptcy is a "Right" included in the U.S. Constitution 39
Types of Bankruptcies 41
Debts that are Excluded from Bankruptcy 42
SECTION 2: The Development of Student Loans 42
GSLP 1965 (Stafford Loans) 42
Middle Income Student Assistance Act 1978 43
Media Hype of Abuse 43
Compromise Bill Results in Nondischargeability of Student Loans 44
1978 Bankruptcy Reform Act Section 523(a)(8) 45
1990 Crime Control Act 1991 Higher Educational Technical Amendments 45
1998 Higher Education Amendments 45
2005 Bankruptcy Abuse Prevention and Consumer Protection Act 46
Student Loan Debt and Default Statistics 46
Summary 47

CHAPTER 5 Court Opinions and Tests 51

"Undue Hardship" 51
Court Tests for "Undue Hardship" 52
The Johnson Test 52
The Bryant Poverty Test 53
The Totality of the Circumstances Test 53
The *Brunner* test 54
Summary 55

CHAPTER 6 "Undue Hardship" Arguments 57

Characteristics Common to Undue Hardship Tests 57
Characteristic A—Current Living Condition and the Impact of Repaying Loan on "Minimal Living" Standard 58
Characteristic B—Prospects for Repaying the Loans 58
Characteristic C—Good Faith and Loan Repayment 63
Summary 64

CHAPTER 7 Example Court Cases With Analysis 67

1987 Case: In re Courtney 67
1988 Case: In re Conner 68
1989 Case: In re Gravante 68
1993 Case: In re Healey 68
1993 Case: In re Ford 69
1993 Case: In re Kraft 70
1993 Case: In re Myers 70
1993 Case: In re Roberson 70
1994 Case: In re Cheesman 71
1994 Case: In re Stebbins-Hopf 72
1995 Case: In re Walcott 72
1996 Case: In re Skaggs 72
1996 Case: In re Wetzel 73
1997 Case: In re Rivers 73
1997 Case: In re Innes 74
1998 Case: In re Lehman 75

1998 Case: In re Pena 76
2002 Case: In re Goulet 76
2006 Case: In re Lorna Nys 77
2007 Case: Mendoza v. Educational Credit 78
2007 Case: Carnduff v. DOE 79
2007 Case: In re Barrett 79
2009 Case: In re Scott 80
2011 Case: Johnson et al v. ECMC 81
2012 Case: Shaffer v. U.S. DOE 81
2013 Case: In re Roth 83
2013 Case: Krieger v. Educational Credit 83
2013 Case: Hedlund v. The Educ. Res. 84
2013 Case: In re Wolfe 84
2014 Case: Conway v. National Collegiate 85
2014 Case: In re Lamento 86
2014 Case: Blanchard v. New Hampshire 87
2015 Case: Abney v. U.S. Dept. of Educ. 87
2015 Case: Acosta-Conniff v. ECMC 88
2015 Case: DeLaet v. National Collegiate Trust 89
2015 Case: In Re Nightingale 89
2015 Case: Kelly v. ECMC 90
2016 Case: Fern v. FedLoan 90
2016 Case: McDowell v. ECMC 91
2016 Case: Murphy v. ECMC 92
2016 Case: Precht v. U.S. DOE 93
2017 Case: In Re Murray 93
2018 Case: In Re Metz 94
2020 Case: Bukovics v. ECMC 95
2020 Case: In Re Rosenberg 95
Summary 97

CHAPTER 8 Advocacy 103
Rate of Success at Discharging Student Loans Through Bankruptcy 104
Challenges to 11 U.S.C.A. §523(a)(8) 105
The Law Is, and Was, Unnecessary 105
Law Violates Equal Protection Clause of the U.S. Constitution 106
Unintended Impact on the Poor and Minorities 108
Violates Bankruptcy's "Fresh Start" Concept 109
Congress Failed to Clearly Define the Law 111
Challenges to *Brunner Test* 116
Challenges to Income-Driven Repayment ("IDR" plans) 117
DOE Claims IDR Plans Make it Impossible to Satisfy the Brunner First and Third Prong 117
Trading One Nondischargeable Loan for Another 118
Emotional Hardship Having Loan for Twenty-Five Years 118
Not Participating in IDR Plan is Tantamount to Violating "Good Faith Effort" 118
Tax Consequences to Forgiven Loan Are a Hardship 118
Courts Have Recommended Abolishing Brunner Third Prong 118
Paying "Something" on the Loans Should Reduce the Debt 119
"Good Faith" Argument to Repay Loan Makes Bankruptcy Impossible 119
The Repayment Period is Over Once a Loan is in Default 119
2005 Changes to Bankruptcy Code 119
Chapter 13 Bankruptcies 119
Summary 120

CHAPTER 9 Preparing for the Adversary Proceeding ... 127
The Adversary Proceeding ... 127
   PRE-INFO— Undue Hardship Test and Student Loan History ... 127
   CHARACTERISTIC A— Current Living Condition and the Impact of Repaying Loan on "Minimal Living" Standard ... 128
   CHARACTERISTIC B— Prospects for Repaying the Loans ... 130
   CHARACTERISTIC C— Good Faith and Loan Repayment ... 131
   INCOME-DRIVEN REPAYMENT (IDR) PLANS ... 131
Review ... 132

CHAPTER 10 Step-By-Step Procedures for The Adversary Proceeding ... 135
The Adversary Proceeding ... 135
   Before Filing the Complaint ... 135
   Filing and Serving the Complaint ... 138
   Status Hearing ... 141
   Mediation ... 142
   Pretrial Hearing and Trial ... 147

CHAPTER 11 Preparing Your Case for *Compromise* or *Write-Off* 149
   PRE-INFO— Student Loan History ... 149
   CHARACTERISTIC A— Current Living Condition and the Impact of Repaying Loan on "Minimal Living" Standard ... 149
   CHARACTERISTIC B— Prospects for Repaying the Loans ... 151
   CHARACTERISTIC C— Good Faith and Loan Repayment ... 152
   INCOME DRIVEN REPAYMENT (IDR) PLAN ... 152
Review ... 153

CHAPTER 12 Step-By-Step Negotiations for *Compromise* or *Write-Off* ... 155
Compromise ... 155
Write-Off ... 155
Contacting the Agency ... 156
Writing the Agency ... 157
Stronger Negotiations ... 158
Proposing a Settlement ... 159
Just Who Does the Negotiations at DOE? ... 159

APPENDIX ... 161

APPENDIX A Department of Education Repayment Plans and Discharge Options ... 163
Repay Your Direct Loans and Federal Family Education Loan (FFEL) Program Loans ... 163
   Summary Table ... 163
Postponing Repayments ... 167
   Deferments ... 167
   Cancer Treatment Deferment ... 167

Economic Hardship Deferment	167
Graduate Fellowship Deferment	167
In-School Deferment	167
Military Service and Post-Active Duty Student Deferment	168
Parent PLUS Borrower Deferment	168
Rehabilitation Training Deferment	168
Unemployment Deferment	168
Forbearances	169
Forbearances Request Form—General 2021	171
Forbearances Request Form—Mandatory 2021	175
Loan Delinquency and Default	**180**
Delinquency and Default	180

APPENDIX B Laws and Legal Guidelines 183

Rules and Regulations	**183**
31 U.S.C.A. §3716 — Administrative Offset of Federal Benefits	183
Standardized Compromise and Write-Off Procedures	186
Standardized Compromise and Write-Off Authorization Letter 1994	193
Standardized Compromise and Write-Off Guidelines 1993	196
Interrogatories— Kentucky	199
Interrogatories Kentucky—Request for Documents	204
IRS Collection Financial Standards	206
Federal Poverty Guideline	**222**
HHS Poverty Guidelines for 2023	222
Federal Department of Education Poverty Guidelines (2023)	225
11 U.S.C.A. § 523 (a) (8)	**226**

APPENDIX C Bankruptcy Forms 231

Chapter 7 Bankruptcy	**231**
U.S. Bankruptcy Forms 2023	231
Voluntary Petition for Individuals Filing for Bankruptcy	237
Application to Have the Chapter 7 Filing Fee Waived	246
Chapter 7 Income	250
Chapter 7 Creditors	252
Chapter 7 Expenses	258
Reopening a Bankruptcy	**261**
Motion to Reopen Bankruptcy Sample 1	261
Motion to Reopen Bankruptcy Sample 2	263
Amendment to Schedule F Sample	263
Amendment to Schedule F Blank Form	265

APPENDIX D Worksheets 267

Worksheets	**267**
Student Loan History	267
Current Income Status	268
Current Expenditure Status	269
Work Time Accounting Table	271
Income and Student Loan Payment	272
Worksheet Samples	**274**
Current Income and Family Status	274
Current Expenditures and Minimalized Living	275

Work Time Accounting Statement 276
Personal Limitations Statement 277
Good Faith and Loan Repayment Statement 278
Income-Driven Repayment (IDR) Plans 281

APPENDIX E Forms for Adversary Proceeding 283

Forms—Instructions 284
Blue Back 285
Who Handles My Loans? 286
Adversary Proceeding Cover Sheet 289
Adversary Proceeding Complaint 292
Summons 298
Proof of Service with Mail Matrix and Cover 300

Forms—Samples 305
Adversary Proceeding Sheet (Cover) (Sample) 306
Adversary Proceeding Complaint (Sample-simple) 308
Adversary Proceeding Complaint (Sample-Full) 311
Summons (Sample) 329
Proof of Service (Sample) 330
Mail Matrix (Sample) 331
Proof of Service Cover (Sample) 332
Joint Status Report (Sample) 333
Request for Documents from Department of Education (Sample) 337
Stipulation (Sample) 340

Forms—Blank 344
Blank Legal (Pleading) Paper 345
Adversary Proceeding Cover Sheet 346
Summons and Notice of Status Conference (CA Central District) 348
Proof of Service 349
Joint Status Report 350

APPENDIX F Academic Articles 355

Almost Two-Thirds of All Bankruptcies Due to Medical Bills 356
The Consequences of Age on the Ability to Repay 357
Discrimination Based on Age 359
Discrimination Against the Highly Educated 362
Discrimination Based on Sexual Orientation 364
Reverse Discrimination Based on Gender or Race 365
U.S. Economy (2023) 366

APPENDIX G Resources 369
U.S. Bankruptcy Court Contacts 369

Glossary 373

Index 375

Notes 379

CHAPTER 1
You Can Do It!

You have been told that it is impossible to bankrupt your student loans. Attorneys tell you this, the Department of Education tells you this, and it is common knowledge. But it is not true.

You can bankrupt your student loans or discharge them through other means.

Chuck Stewart, Ph.D., author of this book, successfully bankrupted over $72,000 in student loans as part of a Chapter 7 bankruptcy (this is documented in the Preface of this book). Like many of you, after receiving his college degree, he experienced years of difficulty getting employment. Either the job market was tight, or his degree was in a field that had too many other job seekers, or he lived in the wrong place with few jobs or the company he worked for downsized, and he lost his job, and more. If he tried to get "any" job, including ones well below his education, he was not hired because he was "over-qualified." As he got older, ageism became a real barrier to employment. Years of part-time employment took its financial toll. Credit card debt mounted. He lost his house. He supported his very ill partner, who eventually died. After 10-years of struggle, he had large debts, no retirement, no savings, no medical insurance, and little hope of ever finding a decent job. He subsisted at the poverty level.

Many of you have experienced similar problems: loss of job, years of part-time employment, never getting ahead. Many of you have your own medical illnesses— not bad enough to get you permanent disability (for which you could have your student loans discharged) — but bad enough to push you into poverty and keep you there. Or maybe you are taking care of someone with medical needs, and that is pushing you over the financial and emotional edge. Medical problems are the number one cause of bankruptcy. It is estimated that two-thirds of all bankruptcies are precipitated

> **Overruled!**
>
> Jonathan G, 46, had $100,000 in student loans incurred while earning a degree from the New England Conservatory of Music. He performed with two city orchestras and finally won a position with the Louisiana Philharmonic Orchestra in New Orleans. Even after reaching this high level of professionalism, he taught cello at Tulane University to earn a paltry $20,000 a year. He filed for bankruptcy to try and get out from under the crushing debt.
>
> Attorneys from the Department of Education and a guarantee agency that held some of the loans scrutinized his living expenses and argued that he could trim his expenses if he canceled his internet services ($23.90/m), gym membership ($48.51/m) and got rid of his cat ($20/m). The bankruptcy judge sided with Mr. G, saying that the Internet service was needed to look for work, the gym membership to work out the pain in his back caused from playing the cello, and the expenses related to the cat were not "luxuries" considering Mr. G was single and living alone. The judge ruled the loans caused an "undue hardship" and were discharged.
>
> The Education Department appealed, and Mr. G lost. The federal appellate court suggested Mr. G find a job as a music-store clerk.
>
> Hechinger, J. (January 6, 2005) U.S. Gets Tough on Failure to Repay Student Loans, *Wall Street Journal*, v.CCXLV n.4, p.1

by crushing medical bills. For some of you, either you did not finish your education, or the training program you paid for was of such low quality or with outdated skills that you never landed a better paying job. In either case, education did not lead to a better life and participation in the American dream. Now you are saddled with student loan debts for an education that did not benefit you. How aggravating!

Of course, the recent catastrophic decline in the economy caused by the Covid-19 pandemic is devastating many families. Up to 40-million Americans have lost their jobs. Businesses after businesses have shuttered their doors; many permanently. The old jobs are not coming back. Bankruptcy looms to which student loans add an extra burden.

This book is for you.

What This Book Covers

This book discusses many strategies for discharging your student loans. The focus of the book is to help you discharge your student loans through either bankruptcy OR direct negotiation with the Department of Education (what is termed *Compromise* or *Write-Off*).

Bankruptcy: This book gives the step-by-step procedure for filing, mediating, and arguing an adversary proceeding as part of a bankruptcy. *Student loans are not dischargeable in a straightforward bankruptcy.* Student loans are listed as part of the overall debt in bankruptcy, and then, usually within 60 days of the creditor meeting, an adversary proceeding is filed with the bankruptcy court against the U.S. Department of Education to prove that repaying the student loans will create an "undue hardship." If you prevail, the court will discharge all or a portion of your student loans as part of your bankruptcy.

Many people have already been through bankruptcy. Most were told it was impossible to include their student loans in bankruptcy or that it was very very "difficult" and shouldn't be tried. As such, they did not file an adversary proceeding in conjunction with their bankruptcy filing. Some debtors have sought to reopen their previous bankruptcy to attempt an adversary proceeding. This strategy is discussed in detail later in this chapter.

Negotiating a Discharge: If you are not planning a bankruptcy, this book can still provide valuable information on other discharge strategies and for negotiating a reduction or discharge of your student loans through the *Compromise* or *Write-Off* procedures.

No other book provides the information or guidance needed to help you discharge student loans through bankruptcy or negotiation. This book provides:

- Step-by-Step process for filing an adversary proceeding or negotiating a Compromise or Write-Off; and, if needed, reopening a bankruptcy
- All forms
- Sample forms
- History and Analysis of the student loan program and its enforcement to help you prepare your own arguments.
- Mediation strategies
- Many more resources

Why You Should Use This Book

When the author of this book first contemplated bankrupting his student loans as part of his Chapter 7 bankruptcy, he sought the advice of several attorneys. All of them said it was virtually impossible to win an adversary proceeding but that they would take on the case for $10,000 upfront and $550 per hour with court fees. Even still, they warned him that he most likely would not win. The author was broke, down to his last $300, and could not possibly pay the attorney fees. So, he thought he had nothing to lose by representing himself. Being an academic with several published books (including a law dictionary), he researched the problem.

First, he discovered that people who represent themselves in an adversary proceeding are more likely to win. Judges are aware that if you can afford a high-priced lawyer, you are obviously not in terrible financial need. Also, you know your situation better than any hired attorney. You can argue your case with greater fervor and conviction.

Second, until the release of this book, there was no concise information that addressed the problem of bankrupting student loans through an adversary proceeding or negotiating a discharge through Compromise or Write-Off. The author researched many law journals, cases, and books to pull together everything that is needed to attack this problem. He also spoke with a number of people who have gone through the process, gleaning from them bits of information that is never written in law journals.

Third, this is a very personal journey. There are many self-help law books that describe the bankruptcy process. When it comes to student loans, they devote less than a page to the problem and refer you to an attorney. These books are well written but very impersonal. An adversary proceeding is very different. The courts will pry deeply into your life, making judgments every step along the way. They will question your purchasing decisions, e.g., did you minimize living expenses by getting rid of your pet to free up $20 more a month to make payments to the government (see the box at the beginning of this chapter describing the ordeal of Mr. Jonathan G). They will question your inability to find work and much more. You will feel besieged and belittled. The author of this book has been through this process and shares his experience about how to minimize the government's efforts to beat you down and, thus, win your case. No attorney isolated in a glass office, living in the upper levels of income, can possibly understand this.

And **fourth**, there is a track record of success by people who have used this book. Of the people who have corresponded with the author about their experiences, everyone has expressed their gratitude for the help received from the book. Many have either renegotiated their loans for much better terms or have successfully bankrupted all or most of their student loans. Many people have been successful at having hundreds of thousands of dollars in student loans discharged.

Although the author cannot provide legal advice, he would like to hear your stories to improve future updates of this book. See the contact information on the "About the Author" page. Let's make it better for honest debtors to legitimately discharge student loans.

Who Qualifies for an Adversary Proceeding, Compromise, or Write-Off and When are they Applied?

You may qualify to file for an Adversary Proceeding, Compromise, or Write-Off if:

- You have student loans backed or issued by the U.S. Department of Education that you want to have discharged. This now includes "private" loans designated as "student loans." With the changes in the law, virtually all loans used for education, even private loans, are protected from simple bankruptcy.
- You cannot maintain your current living standard if forced to repay your outstanding debt, including your student loans.
- There are circumstances that will prevent you from obtaining sufficient income in the future to repay your student loans.

Considering Bankruptcy:

- You are ready to file, or have filed, a Chapter 7, 11, 12 or 13 Bankruptcy.
- It has not been more than 60 days since your meeting with your creditors.

Previous Bankruptcy:

- Have already completed bankruptcy and want to reopen the bankruptcy for the purpose of including your student loans.

Not considering Bankruptcy:

- There are circumstances that will prevent you from obtaining enough income in the future to repay your student loans. These include the job market; familial obligations; discriminatory factors such as age, race, sexual orientation, gender; and other.

The courts have developed several comprehensive tests that delve much deeper into your living and financial conditions than the usual bankruptcy courts. These tests have revealed several rule-of-thumb guidelines that if you do not meet the conditions, it will be very difficult to explain away. Not that they are impossible to overcome, but it will be very difficult. These conditions include:

- Your student loans should not make up more than 50 percent of your total debt.
- You should be living at or near the Federal Poverty Guideline.
- More than seven years should have passed since obtaining your last student loan.
- You have been diligent in making payments on your student loans. When you were unable to make loan payments, you showed diligence by delaying payment through the proper use of forbearances and deferments, or, negotiated alternative repayment plans.
- There should be a sense of *"hopelessness"* with the circumstances of your case.

Even though these are guidelines many courts have adopted, they are not set in stone. It is our hope that with the onslaught of adversary proceedings generated through the use of this book, the guidelines will be challenged and changed. Many of the guidelines are not logical and were never specified by Congress. For example, as you will read in this book, the adoption of the Federal Poverty Guideline to determine "undue hardship" was arbitrary. There are many other federal measures of poverty. Why was this one– which is the most restrictive and not based on poverty but on survival– adopted by the courts? Easy, the Department of Education used it in one of the earliest cases, and it stuck. It is arbitrary and abusive. It needs to be challenged and changed. A few courts have decided that a standard of living below middle-class is an "undue hardship," thereby overruling the accepted practice of using the Federal Poverty Guideline. It will take many more cases ruling for a middle-class standard for it to become an adopted practice.

Here is another way to think of your debt situation: If you don't attempt to discharge your student loans, you probably will be stuck with them for the rest of your life, which will prevent you from ever owning a home or achieving the American Dream. So, what do you have to lose? Filing an adversary proceeding does not make your financial situation any worse.

How to Use this Book

If you have filed a Chapter 7 bankruptcy, you have discovered how relatively easy it is. Many free legal clinics can help with bankruptcy, and there are many fill-in-the-blanks books on the topic. Really, it is easy to file a Chapter 7 bankruptcy. Although the recent changes in the bankruptcy laws require a preliminary step of court oversight, it doesn't change that most (over 90 percent) people will proceed to the traditional Chapter 7 process. The meeting with the creditors is a non-event. The meeting lasts a few minutes if there are no challenges to the debts of your case (which is usually the situation). The judicial representative looks over your forms to see that they are complete. That's it. No drama. Usually, there are no questions. If you visit the court a few days or hours before your meeting, you will be able to watch the process and be amazed by how fast they conduct each case. Maybe one case in thirty has a creditor show up to challenge some aspect of the bankruptcy. So, relax. Within three months after the meeting of the creditors, your common debt will be discharged.

An *Adversary Proceeding* is very different. This is a full-blown lawsuit against the government and its attorneys. They have thirty years of litigating this problem. As such, it is paramount that you educate yourself thoroughly on the topic. You are not expected to be an expert, but you must be able to hold your own. This book is for you.

If you plan to file a *Compromise* or *Write-Off*, this book provides everything you need to prepare your arguments and negotiate with the Department of Education— so much hinges on understanding the psychology of those who work for the Department of Education.

You are strongly advised to read every chapter thoroughly. Not just skim them but read them in-depth. Take your time. Take a couple of days, and then revisit a chapter. As you begin preparing your case, reread sections that come to mind. Don't let your anger overwhelm you. You must become fully knowledgeable on this topic if you are to win. It usually takes months between each action in court, so you have time to prepare.

Chapter 2—Taking Control: Helps you evaluate your student loan situation. Perhaps bankruptcy is not the right action for you to take? There are many other ways to discharge student loans if you qualify. This chapter presents some of the alternatives to bankruptcy.

Chapter 3— DOE Programs Details: Forgiveness, Cancellation, or Discharge of Student Loans: Presents the details of the various DOE programs used to forgive, cancel, or discharge student loans. These include:

- Public Service Loan Forgiveness (PSLF)
- Teacher Loan Forgiveness
- Closed School Discharge
- Perkins Loan Cancellation and Discharge
- Total and Permanent Disability Discharge
- Discharge Due to Death
- Discharge in Bankruptcy
- Borrower Defense to Repayment
- False Certification Discharge
- Unpaid Refund Discharge
- Eligibility for Parent Borrowers

Chapter 4—History of Bankruptcy and the Student Loan Program: Gives a historical background to the implementation of student loan programs backed or issued by the U.S. Department of Education. It is important for readers to understand how these programs came about and the concerns the public, and many in Congress had over the increasing number of students defaulting on their government loans. Congress slowly amended the laws to make it more difficult for debtors to bankrupt their student loans. It is this Congressional debate that molded many court decisions. People planning to defend their adversary proceeding must be familiar with this debate as they, too, will have to use the same language and concepts.

Chapter 5—Court Opinions and Tests: Briefly examines the U.S. bankruptcy system as related to the concept of "undue hardship." Ultimately, to have student loans discharged, a debtor must present a strong case proving that repaying the student loans would create an undue hardship for them. Unfortunately, Congress failed to define "undue hardship," leaving it to courts to construct. This chapter describes in great detail the four major tests used by a majority of United States courts to determine undue hardship and the dischargeability of student loans.

Chapter 6—"Undue Hardship" Arguments: Develops a set of characteristics common to all undue hardship tests and reviews some of the arguments you will use to meet the tests.

Chapter 7—Example Court Cases with Analysis: Presents forty-five bankruptcy cases and analyzes why they succeeded or failed. Special attention is given to the thirty-four cases where the debtor won a full or partial discharge. You will gain a better understanding of the capricious nature of the courts and the overt aggressiveness displayed by the Department of Education. You will also learn how to evaluate your own case to increase the possibilities of success. There is plenty to learn from all the cases where the debtor won.

Chapter 8—Advocacy: The bankruptcy code that governs the discharge of student loans is bad law. The Department of Education and courts have mostly taken a very narrow interpretation of the law. As a result, few debtors are successful at having their student loans discharged through bankruptcy. This chapter discusses many of the limitations of the law and the poor application by the courts. You may want to engage in advocating for rescinding or overturning this law. If you are successful at having the law rescinded, then your student loan debt becomes just like any other unsecured debt and bankrupted through a standard bankruptcy proceeding.

Chapter 9—Preparing for the Adversary Proceeding: This chapter helps you gather all the personal and financial information necessary to present a solid case for the discharge of your student loan debt. Forms and worksheets were developed and are included in the Appendix.

Chapter 10—Step-By-Step Procedure for the Adversary Proceeding: This chapter gives the exact steps required to file an adversary proceeding, strategies for effective mediation, and presentation in court (if needed).

Chapter 11— Preparing Your Case for Compromise or Write-Off: This chapter helps you gather all the documents and personal information needed to prove during a Compromise or Write-Off negotiation that repaying your student loans would be impossible.

Chapter 12— Step-by-Step Negotiations for Compromise or Write-Off: Provides effective strategies for engaging the Department of Education in tough negotiations to discharge all or part of the student loans during Compromise or Write-Off proceedings.

(If you do not need to reopen a bankruptcy, you may skip the next section and proceed to Chapter 2).

Reopening a Bankruptcy

Since the publication of the first edition of this book in 2005, the most frequently asked question comes from people who have already completed a bankruptcy. They are interested in knowing if it is possible to still bankrupt their student loans. Their correspondence is usually filled with despair and anger. Bankruptcy relieved them of some personal debt but not their student loans. Upon learning it was possible for them to have included their student loans in their bankruptcy, they feel duped by a system upheld by attorneys and the Department of Education.

A few of these people have recently attempted to reopen their bankruptcy to address their student loans. Some have met with success. They have shared their experiences and documents with the author. The information is presented here as a starting point. If you proceed with this course of action, please keep the author abreast of the case development. We would like to provide accurate information to others needing to take this course of action. Pleases check our website– www.HowToBankruptYourStudentLoans.com– for updates on this strategy.

Recommendation: When other legal self-help books broach the topic of reopening a bankruptcy, they recommend that you seek the advice of an attorney. The author of this book also encourages you to seek the help of an attorney to reopen a bankruptcy.

Bankruptcy Code [Section 11 U.S.C. § 350(b)] authorizes bankruptcy courts to allow for the reopening of bankruptcy cases for several reasons. The decision to allow a case to be reopened is at the discretion of the court— meaning that the court is not required to reopen a case.

There are three steps to the process:
(1) bring a motion to reopen the case,
(2) amend your original petition by modifying the form found in Appendix C (this assumes you did not originally list your student loans), and
(3) send notice to the creditors, trustee, and the U.S. Trustee of the amendment.

The fees for reopening and amending the original petition vary according to local law, often costing as much as $1,000 and varies depending on if you are reopening a Chapter 7, Chapter 11, or Chapter 13. One person who reopened his bankruptcy found that once the court was clear, the purpose was to file an adversary proceeding to determine the dischargeability of student loans, the filing fees were waived.

Step 1 — Gather all your bankruptcy documents so that you can pull the necessary information.

Step 2 — Contact the court where your bankruptcy was processed to ask for guidance for filing a motion to reopen your bankruptcy. Forms, fees, timing, and exact procedures vary from state to state. Some courts are providing forms that can be filled in and filed through the Internet. The forms and fees vary by court.

Step 3 — Prepare your Motion to Reopen Bankruptcy and file with the court. Examples and blank forms are provided in the Appendix. This shows how they vary depending on location. Remember, these forms are just a suggestion, and their exact form may be different at your local court. You must check with your bankruptcy court first to find out what form they use.

Step 4 — Amend Bankruptcy Forms. When you filed your original bankruptcy forms, you did not include your student loans under the section for unsecured debt. If this is so, then the forms need to be amended. In a Chapter 7 Bankruptcy, Schedule 106E/F is where your student loans should have been listed. Once your Motion to Reopen Bankruptcy is approved, an Amendment to Schedule F needs to be filed with the court. An example and blank form are provided in the Appendix. If you did include your student loans in the original bankruptcy, you do not need to perform this step.

Step 5 — Notify the creditor, trustee, and the U.S. Trustee. Here, you notify the creditor (Department of Education) that the bankruptcy has been reopened and the list of creditors modified. Notification details are given in Chapters 9 and 10.

You will have 30 or 60 days from the date the judge approves the Motion to Reopen Bankruptcy to complete these steps and file the adversary proceeding. Check with your local court to be sure. For details on preparing, filing, and representing yourself in an adversary proceeding, see Chapters 9 and 10.

We hope the best for you. If you have insight on this process, please contact the author so that better information can be provided to future debtors having to engage in this process.

*

Disclaimer

There is no guarantee that by using this book, you will achieve a discharge of your student loans.

This book is based on the personal experiences of the author, the experiences of other debtors who have gone through the process, and the author's research into the topic. Your experiences may be different.

<u>The author is not an attorney and makes no claims concerning the legal accuracy of this book.</u>

No part of this book should be construed as being legal advice. If in doubt, consult an attorney in your area. Be aware, though, that very few attorneys are knowledgeable in this field. By reading this book, you will be able to assist better any attorney you consult. An attorney or paralegal may be useful in helping you construct the legal document needed to file with the courts.

The author is providing legal information. Legal knowledge is not legal advice.

CHAPTER 2
Taking Control

This book assumes you plan to discharge your student loans through either bankruptcy or a Compromise or Write-Off.

Perhaps bankruptcy is not the best solution for you? Let's evaluate the situation and, by doing so, take control of the problem. Remember, trying to bankrupt your student loan should be viewed as your last possible option. Although the specific steps are easy, the outcome is uncertain, and the process is emotionally very difficult.

An excellent book for helping you manage your student loans is Robin Leonard and Deanne Loonin, 2001, *Take Control of Your Student Loan Debt*, from NOLO Press.

Postponement and Repayment Options

If you are struggling to make your student loan payments, one option is to delay or postpone payment until you are in better financial condition. Another option is to change to a different repayment plan. Loan holders and the Department of Education have many different plans to accommodate most debtors.

It is important to visit the DOE website since the details of repayment plans constantly change due to politics, even the well-established standard plans. For example, this book was written during the COVID-19 pandemic. On August 8, 2020, President Trump issued an executive order to suspended student loan payments and interest until December 31, 2020. Many things are not clear with the order. The was order extended— or how this affects the student loan benefits contained in the Cares Act. It does not clarify if the order applies to loans in debt collection or litigation, and other questions. Politics play a prominent role in determining all student loan repayment options. Please see Appendix A for greater details of these

If You Ignore It, They Will Come

At one time, students who ignored repaying their student loans often never heard from the government, or if they did, it occurred after the time limit the government had in which to collect. Some students thought that if they stayed out of sight, they could get out of repaying their student loans.

Changes in law and an increased effort in debt collection have made such a strategy unworkable. Now, if payments are missed, you will probably hear from the loan holder immediately. Miss a few more and your account will be sent to collection where the government has the right to intercept your federal and state income tax refund check, garnish your wages and social security check, add hefty collection fees, and more. Further, there is no time limitation on how long the government can track you down to get payment!

It is important for you to show diligence by staying current with your loan. In times of financial stress, contact your loan holder and negotiate a delay in repayment, or a new repayment plan, or some other option. Do not ignore your responsibility!

plans.

Deferment

Deferment is a postponement of repayment of student loans under various and specific circumstances. In some cases, you don't have to pay principal or interest during deferment. In other cases, interest still accrues during the time no payments are made on the loan. In general, you are allowed up to a maximum of three deferments (of one year each). You must apply for deferments directly through the Department of Education. The general status qualifying for deferment is:
- Enrollment in school
- Temporary total disability
- Unemployment
- Economic hardship
- Enrollment in a rehabilitation program for the disabled
- Parents with young children

The conditions for deferment change constantly. Contact the Department of Education for requirements concerning deferments. For plan details, see Appendix A or visit the Department of Education website.

Forbearance

If you are not eligible for a deferment and still need debt relief, you might be granted forbearance for a limited and specified period. During forbearance, your payments are temporarily postponed or reduced, but interest will still be charged. The interest will be capitalized (added to the loan amount) if you are unable to pay it during the forbearance period.

You must formally apply for forbearance from your loan holder just as you would for a deferment. The two most common reasons forbearances are granted include:
- inability to pay due to poor health, extended unemployment, or other unforeseen personal problems.
- you are serving in a medical or dental internship or residency serving in a position under the National Community Service Trust Act of 1993

This is not a complete list of conditions that might qualify you for forbearance. As with deferments, you are allowed up to a maximum of three forbearances (of one year each) on any particular loan. Contact the Department of Education for requirements concerning forbearances. For plan details, see Appendix A or visit the Department of Education website.

Consolidation

If you have used up all your available deferments and forbearances, consolidation may work for you. Not only can consolidation lower your monthly payments, but it also restarts the clock for all deferments and forbearances— thus postponing when you must begin repaying your student loans. For example, if you have already used three years of deferments and three years of forbearances for a particular set of loans, by consolidating them into one loan, you can get up to three more years of forbearances.

Consolidation allows you to simplify the repayment process by combining several types of federal education loans into one loan, thereby making just one payment each month. Also, that new monthly payment might be lower than what you are currently paying because interest rates may be lower and repayment time has been extended from ten to thirty years. Consolidated loans are available from private lenders (Federal Family Education Loan, FFEL) or Direct Consolidation Loan Program offered by the Department of Education. You may want to consider consolidation if:
- You have used up all your deferments and forbearances, don't qualify for any of the low-payment plans, and cannot afford your monthly payment.
- You want a lower interest rate even though you can afford your current repayment plan.
- Your loans are in default. Under the Direct Consolidation Loan Program, loans that are in default may be consolidated with the government. Loans in default with private lenders may be consolidated, but with greater effort. Often, with private lenders, you must make three consecutive months of payments before they will consider allowing your loans

to be consolidated.

You may think getting a loan consolidation is a no-brainer since it usually results in a lower interest rate loan with lower payments. However, there are some details that may change your mind.

- First, like all low-payment plans, extending payments over a much longer time results in much more money being paid in interest. Thus, the loan cost more over its lifetime—often two to three times greater.
- Second, if you are married, you can consolidate your loans jointly but only if both you and your spouse agree to the repayment of the entire loan—even if you divorce. That seems unwise considering most couples divorce within five years of marriage. Further, if you consolidate jointly and one of you dies, the surviving spouse is still responsible for repayment on the entire consolidated loan; unlike if the loans are separate and one person dies, then his or her loans are canceled.

Once made, consolidation loans can't be unmade because the loans that were consolidated have been paid off and no longer exist. Contact the Department of Education for requirements concerning consolidation. For plan details, see Appendix A or visit the Department of Education website.

Repayment and Forgiveness Plans

If you are having difficulty making payments with the Standard Repayment Plan, perhaps another repayment plan may work for you and keep you out of default. There are many repayment plans available:

- Standard Repayment Plan
- Graduated Repayment Plan
- Extended Repayment Plan
- Income-Driven Repayment Plans ("IDR" plans)
    - Income-Based Repayment (IBR)
    - Pay As You Earn (PAYE)
    - Revised Pay As You Earn (REPAYE)
    - Income-contingent Repayment (ICR)
    - Income-sensitive Repayment Plan

There are also several loan forgiveness programs that constantly change depending on political dynamics in the federal government. One such program is The Public Service Loan Forgiveness (PSLF); there are many others, each with their specific criteria. These plans are described below and in much greater detail in the next chapter. Eventually, you should contact the Department of Education or visit their website for updated information.

Standard Repayment Plan

Under Standard Plan, you pay a fixed amount each month until your loans are paid in full. You pay a minimum of $50 a month with up to ten years to completely repay the loans (ten to thirty years for Consolidated Loans). By setting higher payments, the Standard Plan allows you to repay your loans more quickly and with lower total interest. All borrowers are eligible. Standard Repayment Plan with a ten-year repayment period is not a good option for those seeking Public Service Loan Forgiveness (PSLF). Also, Standard Repayment Plan for Consolidation Loans is not a qualifying repayment plan for PSLF. May be used for:

- Direct Subsidized and Unsubsidized Loans
- Subsidized and Unsubsidized Federal Stafford Loans
- all PLUS loans
- all Consolidation Loans (Direct or FFEL)

Graduated Repayment Plan

With this plan, payments begin low and increase every two years with the goal of paying off the loan within ten years. The repayment period is calculated based on the total amount owed when the loans go into repayment. This plan may be the right choice for you if you anticipate your income increasing steadily over the years. All borrowers are eligible. Generally, graduated repayment plans are not a qualifying plan for PSLF. May be used for:

- Direct Subsidized and Unsubsidized Loans
- Subsidized and Unsubsidized Federal Stafford Loans
- all PLUS loans
- all Consolidation Loans (Direct or FFEL)

Extended Repayment Plan

Under the Extended Repayment Plan, you make minimum monthly payments of at least $50 but for an extended time: usually from twelve to twenty-five years. The length of the repayment period depends on the total amount owed at the point the loans go into repayment. Payments may be fixed or graduated. Because the time is extended and payments are lower, you pay more interest. If you are a Direct Loan borrower, you must have more than $30,000 in outstanding Direct Loans. These plans are not a qualifying repayment plan for PSLF. May be used for:
- Direct Subsidized and Unsubsidized Loans
- Subsidized and Unsubsidized Federal Stafford Loans
- all PLUS loans
- all Consolidation Loans (Direct or FFEL)

Income-Driven Repayment ("IDR" plans)
(herein, all these plans will be lumped under "IDR" plans)

The U.S. Department of Education has developed several plans based on the ability to pay (also called "income-sensitive repayment plans"). These include:
- Income-Based Repayment (IBR)
- Pay As You Earn (PAYE)
- Revised Pay As You Earn (REPAYE)
- Income-contingent Repayment (ICR)
- Income-sensitive Repayment

All of them require the borrower to file family and income information every year. The monthly payment is calculated based upon annual Adjusted Gross Income, family size, and loan amount. Some plans compare the borrower's income against the Federal Poverty Guidelines of the state of residence to determine the ability to pay. All of these plans cap your monthly federal student loan payment at 10-20 percent of your monthly discretionary income. After twenty to twenty-five years, the remaining balance is "forgiven." Be aware; the "forgiven" loans are considered income by the IRS and there is a tax liability on this "gift." To participate in the program, borrowers are required to sign a form allowing the IRS to verify income information.

There are some disadvantages to IDR plans. You most likely will pay much more on your loan than originally agreed in a Standard Repayment Plan, and the interest rate is fixed with no allowances for renegotiation for a lower rate. You must recertify each year by providing IRS documentation of your income and expenses. To obtain loan forgiveness, you must make on-time payments for the entire twenty to twenty-five years of the loan repayment schedule. If you miss a payment, are late, or default on the loan, the remaining balance is not forgiven, and the debt will probably hang over your head for the rest of your life. If you face missing a payment, contact your loan provider. With IDR plans, you can have your monthly payment dropped to zero if you qualify.

Income-Based Repayment (IBR)

The *College Cost Reduction and Access Act of 2007* established an Income-Based Repayment (IBR) plan for both the direct federal loan and the Federal Family Education Loans (FFEL). Your monthly payments will be either 10 percent or 15 percent of your discretionary income, but never more than what you would have paid under the ten-year Standard Repayment Plan. You must update your income and family size information each year, even if they haven't changed, and payments are recalculated each year based on this information. If you are married, your spouse's income or loan debt will be considered only if you file a joint tax return. Any outstanding balance on your loan will be forgiven if you had not repaid your loan in full after twenty or twenty-five years, depending on when you received your first loan— a good option for those seeking PSLF. However, you may have to pay income tax on the amount that is forgiven. You may face a large tax liability with IBR. May be used for:
- Direct Subsidized and Unsubsidized Loans
- Subsidized and Unsubsidized Federal Stafford Loans
- all PLUS loans made to students
- Consolidation Loans (Direct or FFEL) that do not include Direct or FFEL PLUS loans made to parents

Pay As You Earn (PAYE)

The *Health Care and Education Reconciliation Act of 2010* modified the IBR by reducing the amount of discretionary income to 10 percent and shorten the repayment period to twenty years for new borrowers as of July 2014. Under PAYE, you will not pay more than the 10-Year Standard Repayment Plan amount. You must update your income and family size information each year, even if they haven't changed, and payments are recalculated each year based on this information. If you are married, both you and your spouse's income or loan debt will be considered, whether taxes are filed jointly or separately (with limited exceptions). Most borrowers who qualify for PAYE cannot afford their student loan payments and started college after 2007. If you enrolled before 2007, you may still qualify for PAYE if:

- You borrowed federal student loans after October 1, 2007
- You didn't have a federal student loan balance when you borrowed federal student loans after October 1, 2007
- You received a Direct Loan on or after October 1, 2011.

This is a good option for those seeking PSLF. However, you may have to pay income tax on the amount that is forgiven. You may face a large tax liability with PAYE. May be used for:

- Direct Subsidized and Unsubsidized Loans
- Direct PLUS loans made to students
- Direct Consolidation Loans that do not include PLUS loans (Direct or FFEL) made to parents

Revised Pay As You Earn (REPAYE)

Launched in 2015 as a revision of the PAYE repayment plan, the *Revised Pay As You Earn* (REPAYE) plan became available to borrowers who first took out a federal loan on or after October 1, 2007, and who received loan funds on or after October 1, 2011. Because of some of the restrictions with PAYE, the program was revised to allow a broader range of borrowers. Your monthly payments are still capped at 10 percent of your discretionary income, but it offers a twenty-year repayment period. You must update your income and family size information each year, even if they haven't changed, and payments are recalculated each year based on this information. If you are married, both you and your spouse's income or loan debt will be considered, whether taxes are filed jointly or separately (with limited exceptions). Any outstanding balance on your loan will be forgiven if you have not repaid your loan in full after twenty years (if all loans were taken out for undergraduate study) or twenty-five years (if any loans were taken out for graduate or professional study). This is a good option for those seeking PSLF. However, you may have to pay income tax on the amount that is forgiven. You may face a large tax liability with REPAYE.

Unlike IBR and PAYE, the REPAYE plan has a marriage penalty and no cap on the monthly loan payments. REPAYE bases the monthly payments on joint income, regardless of tax filing. May be used for:

- Direct Subsidized and Unsubsidized Loans
- Direct PLUS loans made to students
- Direct Consolidation Loans that do not include PLUS loans (Direct or FFEL) made to parents

---

—*WARNING*—
IDR Tax Liability

If you are experiencing dire financial problems, the Department of Education will try to force you into one of the Income-Driven Repayment Plans. They will argue that anyone can make "zero dollar payments" as allowed under the IDR. The tax liability at the end of the program can be huge! Imagine being 65, 70, 80-years old, having just finished an IDR Plan, and faced with the tax liability on $100,000 income or more? At a tax rate of 25%, you would owe $25,000 in taxes. Can you imagine being hit with that bill after a lifetime of financial struggle? That is definitely an undue hardship. More information is written about the IDR Plans in later chapters.

Income-contingent Repayment (ICR)

The *Higher Education Amendments of 1992* established the Income-contingent Repayment (ICR) plan. ICR bases your monthly payments on the ability pay. The monthly payments will be the lesser of: (a) 20 percent of discretionary income, or (b) the amount you would pay on a repayment plan with a fixed payment over twelve years adjusted to your income. Because it is based on your income, it is possible for monthly payments to be as low as zero dollars. Payments rates are recalculated each year based on updated income, family size, Federal Poverty Guidelines, and the total amount of your Direct Loans. If you are married, your spouse's income or loan debt will be considered only if you file a joint tax return. Any outstanding balance on your loan will be forgiven if you had not repaid your loan in full after twenty-five years, depending on when you received your first loan. However, you may have to pay income tax on the amount that is forgiven. You may face a large tax liability with ICR. This is a good option for those seeking PSLF. Parent borrowers can access this plan by consolidating their Parent PLUS Loans into a Direct Consolidation Loan. May be used for:
- Direct Subsidized and Unsubsidized Loans
- Direct PLUS Loans made to students
- Direct Consolidation Loans

Income-sensitive Repayment

Similar to the other IDR plans discussed in this section, except that it is only available for FFEL Program loans, which are not eligible for PSLF. The monthly payment is based on your income with the goal of paying it off within fifteen years. The formula for determining monthly payments vary from lender to lender. May be used for:
- Direct Subsidized and Unsubsidized Federal Stafford Loans
- FFEL PLUS Loans
- FFEL Consolidation Loans

Typical Discharge Options

What situations can discharge student loans? Here are basic discharge options for *Direct Loan* and *FFEL*:
- Borrower's total and permanent disability or death (100 percent forgiven)
- Full-time teacher for five consecutive years in a designated elementary or secondary school serving students from low-income families (up to $5,000)
- Bankruptcy (up to 100 percent forgiven)
- School closure (before the student could complete a program of study) or false loan certification (100 percent forgiven)
- School does not make the required return of loan funds to the lender (Total amount the school was required to return).

Here are basic discharge options for *Perkins Loans*:
- Borrower's total and permanent disability or death (100 percent forgiven)
- Full-time teacher in a designated elementary or income families (up to 100 percent forgiven)
- Full-time special education teacher (includes teaching children with disabilities in a public or other nonprofit elementary or secondary schools—up to 100 percent forgiven)
- Full-time qualified professional provider of early intervention services for the disabled (up to 100 percent forgiven)
- Full-time teacher of math, science, foreign languages, bilingual education, or other fields designated as teacher shortage areas (up to 100 percent forgiven)
- Full-time employee of a public or nonprofit child or family services agency providing services to high-risk children and their families from low-income communities (up to 100 percent forgiven)
- Full-time nurse or medical technician (up to 100 percent forgiven)
- Full-time law enforcement or corrections officer (up to 100 percent forgiven)
- Full-time staff member in the education component of a Head Start Program (up to 100 percent forgiven)
- Vista or Peace Corps volunteer (up to 70 percent forgiven)
- Service in the U.S. Armed Forces (up to 50 percent forgiven)
- Bankruptcy (up to 100 percent forgiven)

- School closure (before the student could complete the program of study) (up to 100 percent forgiven)

The details of these discharge options are continually changing. For FFEL loans, contact the lender or agency that holds your loan. If you have a Federal Perkins Loan, contact the school that made you the loan. For plan details, see Appendix A or visit the Department of Education website.

Specific Forgiveness, Cancellation, or Discharge Programs

There are several other special programs that will eliminate student loans through *forgiveness*, *cancellation*, or *discharge*. These programs are constantly changing due to politics.

The terms *forgiveness*, *cancellation*, and *discharge* mean nearly the same thing, but they are used in different ways by the Department of Education. If you are no longer required to make payments on your loans due to your job, this is generally called *forgiveness* or *cancellation*. If you are no longer required to make payments on your loans due to other circumstances, such as a total and permanent disability, or the school's closure where you received your loans, this is generally called *discharge*.

Forgiveness, cancellation, and discharge all refer to the cancellation of a borrower's obligation to repay all or a portion of the remaining principal and interest owed on a student loan but are generally used in different contexts.

"Loan cancellation" and "loan forgiveness" generally refer to the cancellation of a borrower's obligation to repay some or all of the remaining amount owed on a loan if the borrower works full-time for a specified period of time in certain occupations or for certain types of employers. "Loan cancellation" is usually used in reference to the various Perkins Loan Program cancellation benefits. "Loan forgiveness" is usually used in reference to the Direct Loan and FFEL Teacher Loan Forgiveness Program or the Direct Loan Public Service Loan Forgiveness Program. Borrowers are not required to pay income tax on loan amounts that are canceled or forgiven based on qualifying employment.

"Loan discharge" generally refers to the cancellation of a borrower's obligation to repay some or all of the remaining amount owed on a loan due to circumstances such as school closure, a school's false certification of a borrower's eligibility to receive a loan, a school's failure to pay a required loan refund, or the borrower's death, total and permanent disability, or bankruptcy. In some cases, a discharge may also entitle a borrower to receive a refund of payments previously made on a loan. Depending on the type of discharge, the amount of a loan that is discharged may be treated as taxable income. As of 2023, these are the programs available for loan forgiveness, cancellation, or discharge:

- Public Service Loan Forgiveness (PSLF)
- Teacher Loan Forgiveness
- Closed School Discharge
- Perkins Loan Cancellation and Discharge
- Total and Permanent Disability Discharge
- Discharge Due to Death
- Discharge in Bankruptcy
- Borrower Defense to Repayment
- False Certification Discharge
- Unpaid Refund Discharge
- Eligibility for Parent Borrowers

These programs are reviewed in detail in the next chapter of this book. There are also special programs sponsored by states and other government agencies that will discharge student loan debt. They may include:

- <u>Teaching service</u> cancellation/deferment options can be found at www.studentaid.ed.gov. At the site, click on "Repaying," then on "Cancellation and Deferment Options for Teachers."
- Your <u>state</u> might offer programs that cancel or reduce part of your loan for certain types of service you perform (such as teaching or nursing). Contact your state agency for postsecondary education to see what programs are available in your state. For the address and telephone number of your state agency, call the Federal Student Aid Information Center. You can also find this information at http://www.studentaid.ed.gov. At the site, click on the "Funding" tab, and then go to "State Aid."

- You should also contact professional, religious, or civic organizations to see if any benefits would be available to you for loan repayment.
- Some branches of the military offer loan repayment programs as an incentive for service. Check with your local recruiting office for more information.
- Another type of repayment assistance (again, not a discharge) is available through the Nursing Education Loan Repayment Program (NELRP) to registered nurses in exchange for service in eligible facilities located in areas experiencing a shortage of nurses. For more information, call NELRP, toll-free, at 1-866-813-3753 or visit http://www.bhpr.hrsa.gov/nursing/loanrepay.ht
- The AmeriCorps Program allows participants to earn education awards— including money to repay student loans—in return for national service. For more information, contact the Corporation for National Service, which administers the AmeriCorps Program.

For details, visit the Department of Education website.

Ask for Relief— Compromise and Write-Off

Ask the government to forgive your guaranteed student loan debt. This may sound crazy, but some debtors have been successful at having their loans reduced or discharged by this method.

Who would do this? — Debtors who do not qualify for any of the discharge plans listed in this chapter and are not planning a bankruptcy and whose only real debt is their student loan. For example, let's say you live modestly, but your student loan payments are so large that they place a severe burden on you and your family. You don't want to file for bankruptcy because you have no real debt except the student loans (i.e., student loans account for more than 70 percent of your total debt load). There are two conditions under which the Department of Education is authorized to forgive the debt. These are *Compromise* and *Write-Off*.

Compromise Your Loans

The Department of Education regulations allow for a guarantee agency to compromise student loans. That means that they are allowed to accept less than the total amount due to fully satisfy the conditions of the loan (and end a default status). This policy was specified in a regulation the Director of the U.S. Department of Education, Policy Development Division, approved on 12/23/93. (*See* Appendix B for *Standardized Compromise and Write-Off Procedures*.)

The collections supervisor at a guarantee agency may reduce ("compromise") your loan under these conditions :

- If you agree to pay the full amount of the loan— principal and interests owed on defaulted loans— then all collection costs, including the standard 25 percent collection fee, may be waived.
- If you agree to pay the remaining principal and interest owed on a defaulted loan, then up to 30 percent of the principal and interest may be waived.
- If you are in dire conditions and it looks like you won't be able to service your loans in the future, the agency's director has the authority to waive even more than 30 percent of the principal and interest of your defaulted loans.
- If you agree to pay off the entire principal (with certified check) of your defaulted loans within 30 days of negotiating the compromise, then all interests' charges may be waived.

The letter authorizing *Compromise* along with Guidelines are included in Appendix B of this book

---

Strategy Tip

Compromise works best for old loans where most of the principal has been paid and has been in default for a while. If you can afford to pay the remaining principal in one lump sum, they are most likely to cancel the interest and collection fees.

because few people in the Department of Education even know the existence of these options. If you can afford to pay a substantial lump sum to pay off your student loan debt, then contact the guarantee agency and ask about a Compromise. Most likely, you will be directed to the head of the collections department.

The agency determines if the compromise represents the best interest of the government. Obviously, this is very subjective open to the judgment of the agency director. If you can show that you have very limited income and that it will not change in the future, they may accept your request. The only alternative for the government is to sue, which is an expensive process for the government.

Write-Off Your Loans

Another idea is to ask the guarantee agency of the Department of Education to *Write-Off* your loans. This works only if you are in dire financial straits, do not believe you will ever be able to repay your loans, and you don't qualify for Discharge or Compromise. The three conditions most likely to be written-off include:

- The balance on your principal is $100 or less.
- The total balance of your loans does not exceed $1000.
- The balance of your loans is for interest, court fees, collection costs, and costs other than the principal, regardless of the total loan amount.

If you can convince the Department of Education that your situation is hopeless, it can write-off much larger loans and end collection efforts. *If you receive a Write-Off, you may never again seek a federal school loan. If you do go back to school and seek education loans, your old loans will be revived, and you will be responsible for paying them back.*

Convincing the Department of Education that your situation is hopeless is similar to proving "undue hardship" (discussed at length in this book). We suggest that if you attempt to obtain a Write-Off of your loans, to read this book carefully and use Chapters 11 and 12 to help prepare and guide your negotiations with the Department of Education. We hope you the best in your negotiations.

Default and Collections

Default occurs with *Federal Perkins Loan* when you don't make an installment payment when due or don't comply with the promissory note's other terms. Default for a *FFEL* or *Direct Loan* occurs if you become 270 days delinquent (if you are making monthly payments) or 330 days delinquent if payments are made less than monthly.

The consequences of default are severe:

- Your entire loan balance (principal and interest) can be immediately due and payable.
- You'll lose your deferment options.
- You won't be eligible for additional federal student aid.
- Your account might be turned over to a collection agency. If so, you'll have to pay additional interest charges, late fees, collection costs, court costs, and attorney fees.
- Your account will be reported to national credit bureaus resulting in damage to your credit rating. You might find it very difficult to receive other types of credit, such as credit cards, car loans, or mortgages. Many landlords do credit checks, and a negative student loan report may make it difficult even to rent an apartment. Similarly, some employers check to see if you are "responsible" by looking at your credit rating, and a negative one may affect your ability to get a job. Additionally, your default will remain on your credit report for up to seven years.
- Without having to go to court, the government can seize your federal income tax refunds (and in some states, your state income tax refunds as well).
- Without having to go to court, your wages may be withheld (garnished).
- You might be unable to obtain a professional license in some states.

These are serious consequences; so, don't fall into default. Make sure to contact your lender as soon as you think you might have trouble making payments. Don't ignore calls or letters from your lender or servicer, either. Putting things off is never the answer because these loans won't go away. Talk to your lender and discuss all the options for making payment easier. Get the details from your lender/servicer on how you can benefit from the various options. Contact the Department of Education before you default. For details, see Appendix A.

Other Legal Considerations

Federal Benefits

If you receive federal benefits, read this section closely.

The 1996 Debt Collection Improvement Act (DCIA) (31 U.S.C. § 3720D) allows federal agencies (including the Department of Education) to take certain federal benefits to pay federal non-tax debts. Taking some of your federal benefits to satisfy government debt is called "*offset*." This means that instead of receiving your full benefits check, a portion of it is kept ("offset") by the government to pay toward your student loan debt. The government may offset benefits originating from:
- Social Security Retirement
- Social Security Disability (SSDI)
- Black Lung (part B only)
- Railroad Retirement Benefits (other than tier 2 benefits)

Benefits that may not be offset include:
- Supplemental Security Income (SSI)
- Black Lung (other than part B)
- Railroad Retirement Benefits (tier 2 benefits)

(*See* Appendix B for 31 USCA 3716 at (c)(3)(a)(i) for details.)

The government did not begin using offset until March 2001. What is still unclear is how to challenge an offset when it occurs. If you are subject to an offset of your federal benefits, and you believe the offset is incorrect or misplaced, contact the agency listed on the offset letter. You may need to contact a consumer protection agency for help.

Student Loans Less Than 10-Years Old

For persons receiving income from which offset may be applied, and with student loans that are less than 10-years old, the first $9,000 (or $750 per month) cannot be seized. If you have federal benefits greater than this amount, the government cannot take more than 15 percent of that income. For example, if your federal benefit income is $950 per month, the government is allowed take the lesser of 15 percent of that income (15 percent of $950 is $142.90) or the amount over $750 per month ($950-$750 is $200). In this example, the lesser amount, and the most the government could offset from your federal benefits, would be $142.90. (*See* Appendix B for 31 USCA 3716 at (c)(3)(a)(ii).)

Student Loans More Than 10-Years Old

~~If your government guaranteed student loans are more than 10-years old, the federal government may not apply offset against your federal benefits [31 U.S.C. §3716(e)(1)] regardless of how large the benefits are.~~

We have left the above language in this book but as "strikeout" so you can see what used to be true in case someone mentions this issue to you. The U.S. Supreme Court in December 2005 declared that the government may seize a person's Social Security benefits to pay old student loans. Justice Scalia wrote that Congress "unambiguously authorized, without exception, the collection of 10-year-old student loan debt . . ." In doing so, it flatly contracted and thereby effectively repealed part of the Social Security Act. Thus, the claim that student loan debt more than 10-years-old cannot be collected from Social Security is no longer valid. See *Lockhart v. U.S., 04-881*.

Remember, if you have other assets or other sources of income not related to federal benefits, the government may sue you to recover on the student loan debt, regardless of the protected status of your federal benefits.

Being Sued

At one time, there was a statute of limitations that applied to student loans. On April 9, 1991, President Bush signed into law the Higher Education Technical Amendments that did away with the limitation retroactively, back to 1965 when student loans were first issued. Thus, there is no statute of limitation preventing the government from finding default debtors and suing them.

Legal Defenses That Will Not Work

Over the years, debtors have tried raising certain legal arguments in the hope of having their student loans discharged. In case you hire an attorney to represent you, here are the arguments that cannot succeed, so you don't waste time and money trying these legal defenses:
- Statute of Limitations
- Laches
- Infancy
- Truth-in-Lending

Statute of Limitation
In general, the government has up to six years to sue someone for breach of contract or default on government loans (such as Federal Housing or Small Business Administration loans). As noted above, President Bush specifically rescinded the statute of limitations for student loans in 1991 and extended it back to the very first student loans issued by the government in 1965. Thus, you cannot raise the statute of limitation argument to have your student loans discharged.

Laches
Since the statute of limitation arguments are no longer valid, some debtors have tried to argue that the government was unreasonably delayed in initiating a lawsuit, and it would be prejudicial to the debtor being sued to defend the case. This is the legal concept of laches. In general, the laches argument cannot be used against the government and almost every court that has considered this argument in relation to student loans has concluded that the laches defense may not be raised.

However, in one extreme case, the court ruled in favor of laches. Here the government did not attempt to sue the student debtor until seventeen years after the loans came due. In the intervening years, the school closed, and the student could not obtain his records. Further, the borrower had evidence that he did, indeed, pay back the loan. The court allowed the laches defense simply because the case was so extreme (*United States v. Rhodes*, 788 F. Supp. 339 (E.D. Mich. 1992)). Just one year later, this same court was faced with a much more ordinary case and disallowed the laches defense (*United States v. Robbins*, 819 F. Supp. 672 (E.D. Mich. 1993)).

Infancy
Some debtors had tried to argue that, since they were under age 18 when they signed the loan documents, they were not competent to enter into a contract. Although this defense, called *infancy*, can be used with consumer contracts, it was eliminated in 1991 at the same time the statute of limitations was repealed.

Truth-in-Lending
The federal Truth in Lending Act (15 U.S.C. § 1638) requires lenders to disclose the terms of the loan, including the interest rate, payment schedule, and more. Failure to provide this information is grounds for having the loan canceled. Although the defense is applicable in consumer contracts, federal law specifically states that it is not a defense in cases of student loan default.

Should I Go Forward with an Adversary Proceeding or Compromise or Write-Off?

Hopefully, the information in this chapter helped you to better evaluate your situation. Perhaps simply delaying payment on your loans will give you the time to catch up and begin repayment at a later time. Possibly one of the other repayment plans would work for you; or, you qualify to have your loans discharged through one of the discharge options. With almost two-thirds of all bankruptcies related to medical illness and the resulting unemployment and medical bills, perhaps you qualify for a medical disability discharge.

If none of these standard discharge options work for you, then you may choose to file bankruptcy with an *Adversary Proceeding* or to pursue a *Compromise* or *Write-Off*. This is discussed later in the book.

Summary

- Payment for student loans may be delayed by:
  - Deferment
  - Forbearance
- Consolidation
  - May yield lower payments and interest but higher overall costs
  - Restarts clock for deferments and forbearances
- Repayment plans include:
  - Standard Repayment Plan
  - Graduated Repayment Plan
  - Extended Repayment Plan
  - Income-Driven Repayment Plans
    - Income-Based Repayment (IBR)
    - Pay As You Earn (PAYE)
    - Revised Pay As You Earn (REPAYE)
    - Income-contingent Repayment (ICR)
    - Income-sensitive Repayment Plan
- Student loans may be discharged (in general):
  - Borrower death
  - Borrower total and permanent disability
  - <u>Bankruptcy</u> (very difficult)
  - School closure or false loan certification
  - Very specific conditions of service (teaching, law enforcement, armed forces, and others)
  - Student loans may be paid off under some very specific conditions
  - Ask to relieve the debt through <u>Compromise</u> or <u>Write-Off</u>
- Specific Programs used to forgive, cancel, or discharge student loans (which are discussed in detail in the next chapter):
  - Public Service Loan Forgiveness (PSLF)
  - Teacher Loan Forgiveness
  - Closed School Discharge
  - Perkins Loan Cancellation and Discharge
  - Total and Permanent Disability Discharge
  - Discharge Due to Death
  - Discharge in Bankruptcy
  - Borrower Defense to Repayment
  - False Certification Discharge
  - Unpaid Refund Discharge
  - Eligibility for Parent Borrowers
- Default on loans may result in:
  - Entire loan balance coming due and payable
  - Loss of deferment options
  - No longer eligible for additional student loans
  - Collection agency with additional expenses
  - Credit standing impacted
  - Without a court order, the seizure of federal income tax refunds, wages garnished, and more.
- Other arguments:
  - In general, receiving various federal benefits that do not exceed $9,000 a year makes student loans uncollectible.
  - ~~If student loans are more than 10-years old, most federal benefits cannot be "offset" to pay for them.~~
  - Statute of limitations no longer apply to student loans
  - Laches defense generally does not apply to student loans
  - Infancy defense exempted from student loans
Truth-in-Lending arguments exempted from student loans

CHAPTER 3
DOE Programs Details: Forgiveness, Cancellation, or Discharge of Student Loans

In the last chapter, many of the repayment plans were briefly reviewed. Perhaps one of them would apply to you. In this chapter, we look at several of the loan forgiveness programs in greater detail. Each of the DOE programs or situations can eliminate student loan debt. If, after reviewing these programs, you still feel bankruptcy is your best option, proceed to the next chapter. Visit the DOE website for current information since politics are constantly changing the exact conditions of these programs: https://studentaid.gov/manage-loans/forgiveness-cancellation.

Public Service Loan Forgiveness (PSLF)
Available for Direct Loans

If you are employed by a government or not-for-profit organization, you may be able to receive loan forgiveness under the Public Service Loan Forgiveness (PSLF) Program.

PSLF forgives the remaining balance on your Direct Loans after you have made 120 qualifying monthly payments under a qualifying repayment plan while working full-time for a qualifying employer.

Federal Family Education Loan (FFEL) Program loans and Perkins Loans may become eligible for Public Service Loan Forgiveness if they are consolidated into the Direct Loan Program.

To qualify for PSLF, you must
- be employed by a U.S. federal, state, local, or tribal government or not-for-profit organization;
- work full-time for that agency or organization;
- have Direct Loans (or consolidate other federal student loans into a Direct Loan);
- repay your loans under an income-driven repayment plan, and make 120 qualifying payments.

Qualifying Employment:

Qualifying employment for the PSLF Program isn't about the specific job that you do for your employer. Instead, it's about who your employer is. Employment with the following types of organizations qualifies for PSLF:
- Government organizations at any level (U.S. federal, state, local, or tribal)
- Not-for-profit organizations that are tax-exempt under Section 501(c)(3) of the Internal Revenue Code

Serving as a full-time AmeriCorps or Peace Corps volunteer also counts as qualifying employment for the PSLF Program.

The following types of employers do not qualify for PSLF:
- Labor unions
- Partisan political organizations
- For-profit organizations, including for-profit government contractors

A qualifying employer must directly employ contractors for your employment to count toward PSLF. If you are employed by an organization that is doing work under a contract with a qualifying employer, it is your employer's status—not the status of the organization that your employer has a contract with—that determines whether your employment qualifies for PSLF. For example, if you are employed by a for-profit contractor that is doing work for a qualifying employer, your employment does not count toward PSLF.

Other types of not-for-profit organizations: If you work for a not-for-profit organization that is not tax-exempt under Section 501(c)(3) of the Internal Revenue Code, it can still be considered a qualifying employer if it provides certain types of qualifying public services. However, in our experience, few organizations meet these criteria.

Full-Time Employment:

For PSLF, you are generally considered to work full-time if you meet your employer's definition of full-time or work at least thirty hours per week, whichever is greater.

If you are employed in more than one qualifying part-time job at the same time, you will be considered full-time if you work a combined average of at least thirty hours per week with your employers.

If you are employed by a not-for-profit organization, time spent on religious instruction, worship services, or any form of proselytizing may not be counted toward meeting the full-time employment requirement.

Eligible Loans:

Any loan received under the William D. Ford Federal Direct Loan (Direct Loan) Program qualifies for PSLF.

Loans from these federal student loan programs don't qualify for PSLF: The Federal Family Education Loan (FFEL) Program and the Federal Perkins Loan (Perkins Loan) Program. However, they may become eligible if you consolidate them into a Direct Consolidation Loan.

Student loans from private lenders do not qualify for PSLF.

If you consolidate your loans, only qualifying payments that you make on the new Direct Consolidation Loan can be counted toward the 120 payments required for PSLF. Any payments you made on the loans before you consolidated them don't count.

Qualifying Payments:

A qualifying monthly payment is a payment that you make:
- after October 1, 2007;
- under a qualifying repayment plan;
- for the full amount due as shown on your bill;
- no later than fifteen days after your due date; and
- while you are employed full-time by a qualifying employer.

You can make qualifying monthly payments only during periods when you are required to make a payment. Therefore, you cannot make a qualifying monthly payment while your loans are in:
- an in-school status,
- the grace period,
- a deferment, or
- a forbearance.

If you want to make qualifying payments, but you are in a deferment or forbearance, contact your federal student loan servicer to waive the deferment or forbearance.

Your 120 qualifying monthly payments do not need to be consecutive. For example, if you have a period of employment with a nonqualifying employer, you will not lose credit for prior qualifying payments you made.

The best way to ensure that you are making on-time, complete payments is to sign up for automatic debit with your loan servicer.

You may make a monthly payment for more than the amount you are required to pay; you should keep in mind that you can receive credit for only one payment per month, no matter how much you pay. You cannot qualify for PSLF faster by making larger payments.

If you want to pay more than your required monthly payment amount, you should contact your servicer and ask that the extra amount not be applied to cover future payments. Otherwise, you may end up being paid ahead, and you cannot receive credit for a qualifying PSLF payment during a month when no payment is due.

There are special rules that allow borrowers who are AmeriCorps or Peace Corps volunteers to use their Segal Education Award or Peace Corps transition payment to make a single "lump-sum" payment that may count for up to 12 qualifying PSLF payments.

In addition, borrowers who have lump-sum payments made on their behalf under a student loan repayment program administered by the U.S. Department of Defense may also receive credit for more than one qualifying PSLF payment.

Qualifying Repayment Plans:

Qualifying repayment plans include all of the income-driven repayment (IDR) plans (plans that base your monthly payment on your income).

While payments made under the 10-year Standard Repayment Plan are qualifying payments, you would have to change to an IDR plan to benefit from PSLF. Under the 10-year Standard Repayment Plan, your loans will be paid in full once you have made the 120 qualifying PSLF payments, and there will be no balance to forgive. Before you change to an IDR plan, however, you should understand that your payment may increase under these plans depending on your income and the amount that you owe. If this is the case for you, and you do not wish to pay this higher amount, then the PSLF Program may not benefit you.

The following repayment plans do not qualify for PSLF:
- Standard Repayment Plan for Direct Consolidation Loans
- Graduated Repayment Plan
- Extended Repayment Plan
- Alternative Repayment Plan

Teacher Loan Forgiveness

Available for Direct Loans and FFEL Program loans.

If you teach full-time for five complete and consecutive academic years in a low-income elementary school, secondary school, or educational service agency, you may be eligible for forgiveness of up to $17,500 on your Direct Loan or FFEL Program loans.

Note: You may not receive a benefit for the same qualifying payments or period of service for Teacher Loan Forgiveness and Public Service Loan Forgiveness.

If you have a Direct Consolidation Loan or a Federal Consolidation Loan, you may be eligible for forgiveness of the outstanding portion of the consolidation loan that repaid an eligible Direct Subsidized Loan, Direct Unsubsidized Loan, Subsidized Federal Stafford Loan, or Unsubsidized Federal Stafford Loan.

The eligibility requirements are:
- You must not have had an outstanding balance on Direct Loans or Federal Family Education Loan (FFEL) Program loans as of October 1, 1998, or on the date that you obtained a Direct Loan or FFEL Program loan after October 1, 1998.
- You must have been employed as a full-time, highly qualified teacher for five complete and consecutive academic years, and at least one of those years must have been after the 1997–98 academic year.
- You must have been employed at an elementary school, secondary school, or educational service agency that serves low-income students (a "low-income school or educational service agency").
- The loan(s) for which you are seeking forgiveness must have been made before the end of your five academic years of qualifying teaching service.

If you were unable to complete a full academic year of teaching, that year may still be counted toward the required five complete and consecutive academic years if:
- you completed at least one-half of the academic year; and
- your employer considers you to have fulfilled your contract requirements for the academic year for the purposes of salary increases, tenure, and retirement; and
- you were unable to complete the academic year because;
  o you returned to postsecondary education, on at least a half-time basis, in an area of study directly related to the performance of the teaching service described above;

- you had a condition covered under the Family and Medical Leave Act of 1993 (FMLA); or
- you were called or ordered to active duty status for more than thirty days as a member of a reserve component of the U.S. armed forces.

Teacher clarification: A teacher is a person who provides direct classroom teaching, or classroom-type teaching in a non-classroom setting. Special education teachers are considered teachers.

There are basic requirements that all teachers must meet to be considered highly qualified. There are also additional requirements that you must meet depending on whether you are an elementary or secondary school teacher and whether you are new to the teaching profession.

Basic Requirements for All Teachers—To be a highly qualified teacher, you must have:
- attained at least a bachelor's degree;
- received full state certification as a teacher; and
- not had certification or licensure requirements waived on an emergency, temporary, or provisional basis.

You are considered to have received full state certification even if you received your certification through alternative routes to certification or by passing the state teacher licensing examination.

If you are a teacher at a public charter school, you are considered to have received full state certification as a teacher if you meet the requirements set forth in the state's public charter school law.

Additional Requirements for Elementary School Teachers Who Are New to the Profession: To be considered highly qualified as an elementary school teacher who is new to the profession, you must also have demonstrated subject knowledge and teaching skills in reading, writing, mathematics, and other areas of the basic elementary school curriculum by passing a rigorous state test.

The rigorous state test may be a state-required certification or licensing test or tests in reading, writing, mathematics, and other areas of the basic elementary school curriculum.

Additional Requirements for Middle or Secondary School Teachers Who Are New to the Profession: To be considered highly qualified as a middle or secondary school teacher who is new to the profession, you must also have demonstrated a high level of competency in each of the academic subjects in which you teach. To demonstrate a high level of competency, you may either:
- pass a rigorous state academic subject test in each of the academic subjects in which you teach or
- successfully complete an academic major, a graduate degree, course work equivalent to an undergraduate academic major, or an advanced certification or credential in each of the academic subjects in which you teach.

The rigorous state test may be a state-required certification or licensing test or tests in each of the academic subjects in which you teach.

Additional Requirements for Elementary, Middle, or Secondary School Teachers Who Are Not New to the Profession: To be highly qualified as an elementary, middle, or secondary school teacher who is not new to the profession, you must also:
- meet the applicable requirements for an elementary, middle, or secondary school teacher who is new to the profession or
- demonstrate competence in all the academic subjects in which you teach based on a high, objective, uniform state standard of evaluation.

The uniform state standard of evaluation may involve multiple, objective measures of teacher competency and must:
- be set by the state for both grade-appropriate academic subject matter knowledge and teaching skills;
- be aligned with challenging state academic content and student academic achievement standards and developed in consultation with core content specialists, teachers, principals, and school administrators;
- provide objective, coherent information about your attainment of core content knowledge in the academic subjects in which you teach;
- be applied uniformly to all teachers in the same academic subject and the same grade level throughout the state;
- take into consideration, but not be based

primarily on, the time you have been teaching in the academic subject; and
- be made available to the public upon request.

How do I know if I'm teaching at a low-income school or educational service agency? The school or educational service agency must be listed in the Teacher Cancellation Low Income (TCLI) Directory, which is published by the U.S. Department of Education (ED) each year. To find out if your school or educational service agency is classified as low-income, search the directory database for the years you have been employed as a teacher. If the TCLI Directory is not available before May 1 of any year, the previous year's directory may be used for that year.

Any questions about the inclusion or omission of a particular school must be directed to the state education agency contact in the state where the school is located and not to ED. State education agencies are responsible for determining which schools or educational service agencies are eligible to be reported to ED for inclusion in the TCLI Directory.

If your school or educational service agency is included in the TCLI Directory for at least one year of your teaching service, but is not included during subsequent years, your subsequent years of teaching at the school or educational service agency will still be counted toward the required five complete and consecutive academic years of teaching. For example, if you taught at the same school for five complete and consecutive academic years from 2011–12 through 2015–16, but the school was included in the TCLI Directory only for the 2011–12 academic year, your subsequent four academic years of teaching at that school can still be counted toward the required five complete and consecutive academic years.

Teaching service performed at an educational service agency may be counted toward the required five years of teaching only if the consecutive five-year period includes qualifying service at an eligible educational service agency performed after the 2007–08 academic year.

All elementary and secondary schools operated by the Bureau of Indian Education (BIE)—or operated on Indian reservations by Indian tribal groups under contract with BIE—qualify as schools serving low-income students. These schools are qualifying schools for the purposes of this loan forgiveness program, even if they are not listed in the TCLI Directory.

The maximum forgiveness amount is either $17,500 or $5,000, depending on the subject area taught. If you have eligible loans under both the Direct Loan Program and the FFEL Program, $17,500 or $5,000 is a combined maximum forgiveness amount for both programs. You may receive up to $17,500 in loan forgiveness if you were:
- a highly qualified full-time mathematics or science teacher who taught students at the secondary school level; or
- a highly qualified special education teacher (at either the elementary or secondary level) whose primary responsibility was to provide special education to children with disabilities, and you taught children with disabilities that corresponded to your area of special education training and demonstrated knowledge and teaching skills in the content areas of the curriculum that you taught.

If you didn't teach mathematics, science, or special education, you may receive up to $5,000 in loan forgiveness if you were a highly qualified full-time elementary or secondary education teacher.

You can potentially receive forgiveness under both the Teacher Loan Forgiveness Program and the Public Service Loan Forgiveness Program, but not for the same period of teaching service. For example, if you complete five consecutive years of qualifying teaching and receive forgiveness of your Direct Loans under the Teacher Loan Forgiveness Program, any payments you made on your Direct Loans during that five-year period cannot be counted toward the required 120 monthly payments for the Public Service Loan Forgiveness Program. To receive Public Service Loan Forgiveness, you would need to make 120 more qualifying monthly payments.

If you are an AmeriCorps Program volunteer, a period of teaching that qualifies you for a benefit through the AmeriCorps Program cannot be counted toward the required five consecutive years of teaching for the Teacher Loan Forgiveness Program.

PLUS loans for parents and graduate or professional students aren't eligible for this type of forgiveness.

Federal Perkins Loans aren't eligible for this type of forgiveness. However, you may be eligible to have all or a portion of your Federal Perkins Loan canceled (based on your employment or volunteer service) or discharged (under certain conditions).

If you are in default on a loan, you are not eligible for forgiveness of that loan unless you have made satisfactory repayment arrangements with the holder of the defaulted loan. However, recent court cases have viewed "defaulted" loans as meeting the *Brunner* test and have been discharged. So, the court interpretation of this policy is conflicted.

You apply for teacher loan forgiveness by submitting a completed Teacher Loan Forgiveness Application to your loan servicer after you have completed the required five consecutive years of qualifying teaching.

The chief administrative officer of the school or educational service agency where you performed your qualifying teaching service must complete the certification section. If you are applying for the forgiveness of loans that are with different loan servicers, you must submit a separate form to each of them.

Closed School Discharge

Available for Direct Loans, FFEL Program loans, and Perkins Loans.

If your school closes while you are enrolled or soon after you withdraw, you may be eligible for discharge of your federal student loan.
You may be eligible for a 100 percent discharge of your William D. Ford Federal Direct Loan (Direct Loan) Program loans, Federal Family Education Loan (FFEL) Program loans, or Federal Perkins Loans if you were unable to complete your program because your school closed, and if:
- you were enrolled when your school closed;
- you were on an approved leave of absence when your school closed; or
- your school closed within 120 days after you withdrew.

You are not eligible for discharge of your loans if your school closes and any of the following is true:
- Except in exceptional circumstances, you withdrew more than 120 days before the school closed.
- You are completing a comparable educational program at another school:
  o through a teach-out,
  o by transferring academic credits or hours earned at the closed school to another school,
  o or by any other comparable means.
- You completed all the coursework for the program before the school closed, even if you did not receive a diploma or certificate.

If you meet the eligibility requirements for a closed school discharge of your loans obtained to attend a school that closed on or after November 1, 2013, and you have not enrolled at another school that participates in the federal student aid programs within three years of the date your prior school closed, you will receive an automatic closed school discharge. This discharge will be initiated by the U.S. Department of Education (ED), and your loan servicer will notify you.

Although this closed school loan discharge is granted automatically after three years have passed since your school's closure, nothing prevents you from applying for and receiving a closed school discharge as soon as your school's official closure date is confirmed by ED. If you 1) attended a school that closed less than three years ago, 2) meet the eligibility requirements for a closed school discharge, and 3) want your loans discharged, contact your loan servicer about applying for a closed school discharge now instead of waiting for three years to receive an automatic closed school discharge.

By receiving a closed school loan discharge, you receive:
- you have no further obligation to repay the loan,
- you will receive reimbursement of payments made voluntarily or through forced collection, and
- the record of the loan and all repayment history associated with the loan, including any adverse history, will be deleted from your

credit report.

You will need to contact the private lender that made the loan to get that information.

Only loans you received for a program that you were unable to complete because of the school's closure are eligible for discharge.

For example, if you initially enrolled in Program A, but decided not to continue with that program and transferred to Program B, and you were then unable to complete Program B because the school closed, only loans you received for Program B could potentially be discharged.

In the example, you would not be eligible for discharge of any loans you received for Program A, because the school's closure did not prevent you from completing that program.

Before closing, some schools may issue a diploma or certificate to students who did not complete the program of study. If you did not complete your program of study, the fact that the school gave you a diploma or certificate does not disqualify you for discharge.

Transfer of credits from the closed school to a completely different program of study at the new school does not disqualify you for discharge. I attended a school that is now closed.

To obtain copies of your loan payments, contact the state licensing agency in the state where the school was located to find out if the state has the records.

A teach-out is a written agreement between schools that provides for the equitable treatment of students and a reasonable opportunity for students to complete their program of study if a school ceases to operate before all students have completed their program of study.

If you completed or are in the process of completing a comparable program of study at another school through a teach-out, by transferring academic credits or hours from the closed school, or by any other comparable means, you are not eligible for a closed school discharge.

However, you may be eligible for discharge if you completed or are in the process of completing a comparable program at another school, but you did not participate in a teach-out, transfer credits or hours from the closed school, or benefit from the training you received at the closed school by any other comparable means, and if you otherwise meet the eligibility requirements for a closed school discharge.

Perkins Loan Cancellation and Discharge

Available only for Federal Perkins Loans.

You may be eligible to have all or a portion of your Perkins Loan canceled (based on your employment or volunteer service) or discharged (under certain conditions). This includes Perkins Loan Teacher Cancellation.

You may qualify for cancellation of up to 100 percent of a Federal Perkins Loan if you have served full-time in a public or nonprofit elementary or secondary school system as a:

- teacher in a school serving students from low-income families;
- special education teacher, including teachers of infants, toddlers, children, or youth with disabilities; or
- teacher in the fields of mathematics, science, foreign languages, or bilingual education, or in any other field of expertise determined by a state education agency to have a shortage of qualified teachers in that state.

Eligibility for teacher cancellation is based on the duties presented in an official position description, not on the position title. To receive a cancellation, you must be directly employed by the school system. There is no provision for canceling Federal Perkins Loans for teaching in postsecondary schools.

Note that you also qualify for deferment while you are performing teaching service that qualifies for cancellation. Contact your college or your college's Perkins Loan servicer for information on applying for deferment.

A teacher is someone (including, for example, a school librarian or guidance counselor) who provides elementary or secondary school students with direct services directly related to classroom teaching.

You do not need to be certified or licensed to receive cancellation benefits. However, your employing school must consider you to be a full-time professional for the purposes of salary, tenure, retirement benefits, etc. If you are a supervisor, administrator, researcher, or curriculum specialist, you are not considered a teacher unless you primarily provide direct and personal educational services to students.

For each full academic year (or its equivalent) of full-time teaching service, you are eligible to have a portion of your loan canceled. There is no requirement that you must teach a given number of hours a day to qualify as a full-time teacher; the employing school is responsible for making that decision.

An "academic year or its equivalent" for cancellation purposes is defined as one complete school year or two half-years that are from different school years. The two half-years must be complete and consecutive, excluding summer sessions, and must generally fall within a 12-month period.

The loan may be canceled if you are simultaneously teaching part-time in two or more schools if an official at one of the schools where you taught certifies that you taught full-time for a full academic year.

Your loan can be canceled for services performed in a private school if the private school has established its nonprofit status with the Internal Revenue Service, and if the school is providing elementary and/or secondary education according to state law.

Your loan can be canceled only if the state considers such a program to be a part of its elementary education program. A low-income-school-directory designation that includes prekindergarten or kindergarten does not suffice for a state determination of program eligibility.

A cancellation based on teaching in a school serving students from low-income families will be granted only if you taught in an eligible school as determined by the state education agency. To be considered a "low-income school," the school must be in a school district that qualified for federal Title I funds in the year for which the cancellation is sought. Also, more than 30 percent of the school's enrollment must be made up of children in the Title I program.

Each year, the U.S. Department of Education (ED) publishes a list of low-income elementary and secondary schools. To find out if a school is classified as a low-income school, check our online database for the year(s) you have been employed as a teacher. Questions about the inclusion or omission of a particular school must be directed to the state education agency contact in the state where the school is located and *not* to ED.

All elementary and secondary schools operated by the Bureau of Indian Education (BIE)—or operated on Indian reservations by Indian tribal groups under contract with BIE—qualify as schools serving low-income students.

NOTE: If you have had a portion of your loan canceled for teaching at a low-income elementary or secondary school in one year, you can continue to have portions of your loan canceled for teaching at that school even if it is not listed as a low-income school in later years. Under certain circumstances, the institution that holds your Perkins Loan may permit retroactive cancellation if you can demonstrate that you qualified for cancellation in a prior year. However, the institution may not refund payments made during such a retroactive period.

If you teach at an educational service agency, your teaching service may qualify for cancellation if the period of qualifying service includes August 14, 2008, or begins on or after that date.

You must have an official at the public or other nonprofit elementary or secondary school certify that you are a full-time special education teacher of infants, toddlers, children, or youth with disabilities either on the deferment/cancellation form or on an official letter from the school bearing the school's seal or letterhead.

If you provide one of the services listed below, you qualify as a teacher only if you are licensed, certified, or registered by the appropriate state education agency for that area in which you are providing related special educational services, and the services you provide are part of the educational curriculum for handicapped children.

The services are:
- speech and language pathology and audiology,
- physical therapy,
- occupational therapy,
- psychological and counseling services, and

- recreational therapy.

This cancellation is based on full-time teaching if there is a shortage of teachers in your subject area. Each year the state education agency determines any subject shortage areas in the elementary and secondary schools within the state. Check with your local school system or state education agency to find out if your subject-matter area has been so designated. If you teach full-time in science, mathematics, foreign language, or bilingual education, you qualify for cancellation even if the state has not designated one of these subject areas as a shortage area. For a borrower to be considered as teaching in a field of expertise, the majority of classes taught must be in that field of expertise.

You may download the list of teacher shortage areas:
- PDF: Teacher Shortage Areas Nationwide Listing
- Word file: Teacher Shortage Areas Nationwide Listing

If you are eligible for cancellation under any of the categories listed above, up to 100 percent of the loan may be canceled for teaching service in the following increments:
- 15 percent canceled per year for the first and second years of service
- 20 percent canceled for the third and fourth years
- 30 percent canceled for the fifth year
- Each amount canceled per year includes the interest that accrued during the year.

In addition to teaching, the following employment or service may qualify you for a full or partial Perkins Loan cancellation depending on the type of loan you have and the date of the loan:
- Early childhood education provider
- Employee at a child or family services agency
- Faculty member at a tribal college or university
- Firefighter
- Law enforcement officer
- Librarian with a master's degree at Title I school
- Military service
- Nurse or medical technician
- Professional provider of early intervention (disability) services
- Public defender
- Speech pathologist with a master's degree at Title I school
- Volunteer service (AmeriCorps VISTA or Peace Corps)

Under certain conditions, your Perkins Loan may be discharged. When your loan is discharged, it means that you are no longer obligated to pay back your loan. Conditions that may lead to discharge include the following:
- Bankruptcy
- Death
- School closure
- Service-connected disability (veterans)
- Spouse of a victim of the events of 9/11
- Total and permanent disability

Cancellation Chart

Unless otherwise noted in the chart, the cancellation rate per completed academic year of full-time teaching or for each year of otherwise qualifying full-time service is
- 15 percent of the original principal loan amount for each of the first and second years;
- 20 percent of the original principal loan amount for each of the third and fourth years; and
- 30 percent of the original principal loan amount for the fifth year.

Each amount includes the interest that accrued during each year of service.

Cancellation Chart

Unless otherwise noted in the chart, the cancellation rate per completed academic year of full-time teaching or for each year of otherwise qualifying full-time service is

- 15 percent of the original principal loan amount for each of the first and second years;
- 20 percent of the original principal loan amount for each of the third and fourth years; and
- 30 percent of the original principal loan amount for the fifth year.

Each amount includes the interest that accrued during each year of service.

Cancellation Conditions	Amount Canceled
Teacher cancellation	Up to 100 percent for five years of eligible service
Full-time nurse or medical technician cancellation	Up to 100 percent for five years of eligible service
Full-time firefighter cancellation (for service that includes Aug. 14, 2008, or began on or after that date)	Up to 100 percent for five years of eligible service
Full-time qualified professional provider of early intervention services for the disabled cancellation	Up to 100 percent for five years of eligible service
Full-time faculty member at a tribal college or university cancellation (for service that includes Aug. 14, 2008, or began on or after that date)	Up to 100 percent for five years of eligible service
Full-time speech pathologist with master's degree working in a Title I-eligible elementary or secondary school cancellation (for service that includes Aug. 14, 2008, or began on or after that date)	Up to 100 percent for five years of eligible service
Librarian with a master's degree working in a Title I-eligible elementary or secondary school or in a public library serving Title I-eligible schools' cancellation (for service that includes Aug. 14, 2008, or began on or after that date)	Up to 100 percent for five years of eligible service
Full-time law enforcement or corrections officer cancellation	Up to 100 percent for five years of eligible service
Full-time attorney employed in a federal public or community defender organization cancellation (for service that includes Aug. 14, 2008, or began on or after that date)	Up to 100 percent for five years of eligible service
Full-time employee of a public or nonprofit child- or family-services agency providing services to high-risk children and their families from low-income communities cancellation	Up to 100 percent for five years of eligible service
Full-time staff member in the education component of a Head Start program cancellation	Up to 100 percent for seven years (at a rate of 15 percent per year for the first six years and 10 percent for the seventh year) of eligible service
Full-time staff member in the education component of a prekindergarten or childcare program that is licensed or regulated by a state cancellation (for service that includes Aug. 14, 2008, or began on or after that date)	Up to 100 percent for seven years (at a rate of 15 percent per year for the first six years and 10 percent for the seventh year) of eligible service
Military service in the U.S. armed forces in a hostile fire or imminent danger pay area cancellation	Up to 100 percent for five years of eligible service for borrowers whose active duty service includes or began on or after Aug. 14, 2008
AmeriCorps VISTA or Peace Corps volunteer cancellation	Up to 70 percent for four years (at a rate of 15 percent for the first and second years and 20 percent for the third and fourth years) of eligible service

Note: As of Oct. 7, 1998, all Perkins Loan borrowers are eligible for all cancellation benefits regardless of when the loan was made or the terms of the borrower's promissory note. However, this benefit is not retroactive to services performed before Oct. 7, 1998.

Total and Permanent Disability Discharge

Available for Direct Loans, FFEL Program loans, and Perkins Loans.

If you are totally and permanently disabled, you may qualify for a discharge of your federal student loans and/or Teacher Education Assistance for College and Higher Education (TEACH) Grant service obligation. A total and permanent disability (TPD) discharge relieve you from having to repay a William D. Ford Federal Direct Loan (Direct Loan) Program loan, a Federal Family Education Loan (FFEL) Program loan, and/or a Federal Perkins Loan or to complete a TEACH Grant service obligation.

To qualify for a TPD discharge, you must complete and submit a TPD discharge application, along with documentation showing that you meet our requirements for being considered totally and permanently disabled, to Nelnet, the servicer that assists the U.S. Department of Education with the TPD discharge process.

You can show that you qualify for a TPD discharge by providing documentation from one of three sources:
- the U.S. Department of Veterans Affairs (VA)
- the Social Security Administration (SSA)
- a physician

There are specific requirements for each type of supporting documentation that you can submit to show your eligibility.

If you are a veteran, you can qualify for a TPD discharge by providing documentation from the VA that shows you have received a VA disability determination because you: (1) have a service-connected disability that is 100 percent disabling; or (2) are totally disabled based on an individual unemployability rating.

If you are eligible for Social Security Disability Insurance or Supplemental Security Income, you can qualify for a TPD discharge if you provide a copy of your SSA notice of award or Benefits Planning Query showing that your next scheduled disability review will be five to seven years or more from the date of your last SSA disability determination.

You also can qualify for a TPD discharge by having a physician certify on the TPD discharge application that you are unable to engage in any substantial gainful activity due to a physical or mental impairment that
- can be expected to result in death;
- has lasted for a continuous period of at least 60 months; or
- can be expected to last for a continuous period of at least 60 months.

Substantial gainful activity is a level of work performed for pay or profit that involves doing significant physical or mental activities or a combination of both.

The physician who certifies your TPD discharge application must be a doctor of medicine (M.D.) or doctor of osteopathy/osteopathic medicine (D.O.) who is licensed to practice in the United States.

To apply for a TPD discharge, you need to complete a TPD discharge application and send it, along with any required documentation of your eligibility for discharge, to Nelnet, the TPD discharge servicer. The TPD discharge application applies to all of your federal student loans and TEACH Grant service obligations. Nelnet assists us in administering the TPD discharge process and communicates with borrowers and TEACH Grant recipients on our behalf concerning TPD discharge requests.

You can designate an individual or organization to complete and submit your TPD discharge application on your behalf and assist you throughout the discharge process. To designate a representative, you and your representative must complete an *Applicant Representative Designation* form. Nelnet must receive and process this form before working with your representative. You must submit this form even if your representative already has a power of attorney to act on your behalf in other matters.

After your application is received, Nelnet will explain the process for the review of your application. You won't be required to make any payments on your loans while your discharge application is being reviewed.

If your TPD discharge is approved, various documentation is required.

VA Documentation: If it is determined that you are

totally and permanently disabled based on documentation from the VA, Nelnet will:
- notify you that your loans and/or TEACH Grant service obligation have been discharged and
- instruct your loan holders to return any loan payments received on or after the effective date of the VA's disability determination to the person who made the payments.

SSA Documentation or Physician's Certification
If it is determined that you are totally and permanently disabled based on SSA documentation or a physician's certification, Nelnet will:
- notify you that your loans and/or TEACH Grant service obligation have been discharged;
- instruct your loan holders to return any loan payments received after the date Nelnet received the SSA documentation or the date the physician certified your discharge application to the person who made the payments; and
- notify you that you will be subject to a three-year postdischarge monitoring period that begins on the date the discharge is approved and that your obligation to repay your loans or complete your TEACH Grant service obligation will be reinstated if you don't meet certain requirements at any time during this monitoring period.

Your obligation to repay your loans or complete your TEACH Grant service obligation will be reinstated if, at any time during the three-year postdischarge monitoring period, you receive
- annual earnings from employment that exceed the poverty guideline amount for a family of two in your state, regardless of your actual family size;
- a new federal student loan under the Direct Loan Program or a new TEACH Grant;
- another disbursement (payment) of a Direct Loan or a TEACH Grant that was first disbursed (paid out) before your discharge was approved, and the new disbursement has not been returned to the loan holder or (for a TEACH Grant) to us within 120 days of the disbursement date; or
- a notice from the SSA stating that you are no longer disabled or that your next scheduled disability review will no longer be five to seven years from the date of your last SSA disability determination.

Note: During the postdischarge monitoring period, Nelnet will require you to submit documentation of your annual earnings from employment on a form that Nelnet will provide. If you don't submit this form with the required documentation of your income, your obligation to repay your loans or complete your TEACH Grant service obligation will be reinstated.

The poverty guideline amounts are updated annually by the Department of Health and Human Services. Nelnet will notify you of the current poverty guideline amounts during each year of the postdischarge monitoring period.

For detailed information regarding the three-year postdischarge monitoring period requirements, visit the TPD Discharge website at disabilitydischarge.com and select "Monitoring Period."

If you are a veteran whose TPD discharge application is approved based on documentation from the VA, you are not subject to a postdischarge monitoring period.

If you applied for a discharge of loans, your loans would be returned to the status they were in before you applied for discharge. This means that if a loan was in default before you applied for a TPD discharge, it will be returned to default status.

If your obligation to repay your loans or complete your TEACH Grant service obligation is reinstated, Nelnet will explain the reason for the reinstatement and provide information about what you can do if you have questions about the reinstatement or if you believe the reinstatement was based on incorrect information.

If it is determined that you do not qualify for a TPD discharge, Nelnet will:
- notify you of the reason for the denial of your discharge application;
- explain that you may ask us to reevaluate your discharge application if you provide new information that supports your eligibility for discharge within 12 months of the date you are notified that your discharge application has been denied;

- explain that if you don't request a reevaluation of your discharge application within 12 months of the date you are notified that your discharge application has been denied, and you still want us to reevaluate your eligibility, you must submit a new TPD discharge application with new information about your disabling condition that was not provided with your prior discharge application;
- explain that you are again responsible for repaying your loans, and that your loan holder will notify you when your first payment is due; and
- explain that if you applied for a discharge of a TEACH Grant service obligation, you are again responsible for meeting the terms and conditions of the service obligation.

If you received a TPD discharge based on VA documentation, SSA documentation, or a physician's certification and want to return to teaching, you must:

- give your school a letter from a physician stating that you are once again able to engage in substantial gainful activity, and
- sign a statement acknowledging that you cannot get a TPD discharge of the new loan or TEACH Grant based on a disabling condition that already exists when you receive the new loan or TEACH Grant unless that condition substantially deteriorates in the future.
- If you received a TPD discharge based on SSA documentation or a physician's certification and your three-year postdischarge period hasn't ended, you must also resume repayment on your previously discharged loans or acknowledge that you are once again responsible for meeting the terms and conditions of your TEACH Grant service obligation.

If my loan is discharged due to TPD, you may owe taxes on the forgiven amount.

- Because of a change in federal law related to the taxability of loan amounts discharged due to TPD, the answer depends on when you received the discharge.
- If you received a TPD discharge of a loan before January 1, 2018, the loan amount discharged may be considered income for federal tax purposes under Internal Revenue Service (IRS) rules.
- If you received a TPD discharge of a loan during the period from January 1, 2018 to December 31, 2025, the discharged loan amount won't be considered income for federal tax purposes.

For purposes of determining whether a loan amount discharged due to TPD may be treated as taxable income for federal tax purposes, the date you are considered to have received the discharge is different depending on how you qualified for the discharge.

If you are a veteran who showed that you are totally and permanently disabled based on a disability determination by the VA, you are considered to have received the discharge for federal tax purposes on the date we approve the discharge.

If you showed that you are totally and permanently disabled based on documentation from the SSA or a physician's certification (meaning that you are subject to a three-year postdischarge monitoring period), you are considered to have received the discharge for federal tax purposes at the end of the postdischarge monitoring period. For example, if your discharge was approved in July 2017, you would not be considered to have received the discharge for federal tax purposes until July 2020, at the end of the three-year postdischarge monitoring period. Therefore, the IRS would not consider the discharged loan amount to be taxable income for federal tax purposes.

If you receive a Form 1099-C, you should keep the form for your records, but you do not need to include it when filing your federal tax return. For additional information, visit irs.gov.

Discharge Due to Death

Available for Direct Loans, FFEL Program loans, and Perkins Loans.

Federal student loans will be discharged due to the death of the borrower or of the student on whose behalf a PLUS loan was taken out.

If you die and still owe on student loans,

then your federal student loans will be discharged after the required proof of death is submitted. Likewise, your parent's PLUS loan will be discharged if your parent dies or if you (the student on whose behalf your parent obtained the loan) die.

The loan will be discharged if a family member or other representative provides the loan servicer acceptable documentation of the borrower's or parent's death. Acceptable documentation includes an original death certificate, a certified copy of the death certificate, or an accurate and complete photocopy of one of those documents. For more information about documentation requirements, contact your loan servicer.

Discharge in Bankruptcy
Available for Direct Loans, FFEL Program loans, and Perkins Loans.

In some cases, federal student loans can be discharged after declaring bankruptcy. However, discharge in bankruptcy is not an automatic process. You may have your federal student loan discharged in bankruptcy only if you file a separate action, known as an "adversary proceeding," requesting the bankruptcy court find that repayment would impose an undue hardship on you and your dependents.

This book presents, in complete detail, how to file and argue an adversary proceeding to have your student loans discharged in bankruptcy.

Borrower Defense to Repayment
Available for Direct Loans.*

You may be eligible for discharge of your federal student loans based on "borrower defense to repayment" if you took out the loans to attend a school and the school did something or failed to do something related to your loan or to the educational services that the loan was intended to pay for. The specific requirements to qualify for a borrower defense to repayment discharge vary depending on when you received your loan. **Federal Family Education Loan (FFEL) Program loans and Perkins Loans may become eligible for borrower defense discharge if they are consolidated into the Direct Loan Program.*

Borrowers who attended Corinthian Colleges (Everest, Heald, and WyoTech) with a first date of attendance between July 1, 2010, and September 30, 2014, and are seeking federal student loan forgiveness through borrower defense will complete a Corinthian-specific application. For more information about forgiveness of federal student loan(s) used to attend Corinthian Colleges, go to the Information about Debt Relief for Corinthian Colleges Students page.

All *other* borrowers applying for borrower defense must submit their application using one of the U.S. Department of Education (ED) borrower defense application forms provided in the sections below. Please read the instructions provided within the application before filling out the application form. Please note that the instructions also include information for parent PLUS borrowers.

To apply for federal student loan forgiveness based on borrower defense, complete an online application form. Within the online application form, you will be required to provide your signature digitally. It is helpful to include additional documentation as part of your application by uploading additional electronic documents (for example, scanned PDF documents). ED recommends you prepare the additional documentation prior to starting the application process.

If you choose to submit additional documents as part of your borrower defense application, the following types of documents are among those that may be helpful to your application:
- Documentation to confirm the school for which you are applying for borrower defense, your program of study, and your dates of enrollment—such as transcripts, enrollment agreements, and registration documents
- Promotional materials from the school
- Emails with school officials
- Your school's manual or course catalog

To apply via email or physical mail, complete a fillable PDF application form, print it, and sign it. Send your completed form to the U.S. Department of Education by email to BorrowerDefense@ed.gov or by regular mail to U.S. Dept. of Education – Borrower Defense to Repayment, P.O. Box 1854, Monticello, KY 42633. If you submit your PDF application by email, you are required to upload an electronic version of your signature. You can upload a picture file of your signature (for example, taken with a smartphone or digital camera). If you have additional documents that you would like to include as part of your emailed application, please include the documents with your email (for example, by attaching scanned PDF documents). ED recommends you prepare the additional documentation prior to starting the application process.

Under the law, you may be eligible for borrower defense to repayment forgiveness of the federal student loans that you took out to attend a school if that school misled you or engaged in other misconduct in violation of certain state laws. Specifically, you may assert borrower defense by demonstrating that the school, through an act or omission, violated state law directly related to your federal student loan or to the educational services for which the loan was provided. You may be eligible for borrower defense regardless of whether your school closed or you are otherwise eligible for loan forgiveness under other laws.

If you are eligible to receive federal student loan forgiveness, you may be able to have all or part of your outstanding federal student loan debt forgiven, and you also may be reimbursed for amounts you have already paid on those loans.

You will only be eligible for this type of federal student loan forgiveness if your school's misleading activities or other misconduct directly related to the loan or to the educational services for which the loan was provided. You will *not* be eligible for this type of forgiveness based on claims that are not directly related to your loan or the educational services provided by the school. For example, personal injury claims or claims based on allegations of harassment are *not* bases for a borrower defense application.

Please note that eligibility for federal student loan forgiveness is limited to federal student loans taken out for payment to the school relating to your borrower defense application. If you would like to apply for borrower defense against multiple schools that you attended and for which you took out federal student loans, you must submit separate applications for each school of attendance.

Within the application, you may select to have your federal student loans placed into forbearance or stopped collections status while your application is reviewed by ED. If you choose for your loans to be placed into forbearance or stopped collections status, shortly after we receive your application, your loans will be placed in forbearance, and collections will cease on any of your loans that are in default while your application is evaluated.

More information on forbearance and stopped collections is available immediately below in the "Common Questions and Answers Regarding Forbearance/Stopped Collections" section.

To provide relief to student loan borrowers during the COVID-19 national emergency, federal student loan borrowers are automatically being placed in an administrative forbearance, which allows you to temporarily stop making your monthly loan payments. In addition, interest is being temporarily set at 0 percent on federal student loans. This 0 percent interest and suspension of payments will last from March 13, 2020, until the program ends but you can still make payments if you choose.

Find out what loans qualify, and get additional information about the 0 percent interest period, administrative forbearance, and other student loan flexibilities due to the COVID-19 national emergency.

We strongly encourage readers to review the materials at DOE on this topic as the details are very nuanced and changing.

For example, in 2020, Education Secretary Betsy DeVos took an active stand against the courts to deny the rightful debt cancellations owed to people who attended predatory, for-profit colleges. DeVos attempted to delay the Obama-era update to this program. A judge found DeVos's delay to this rule to be "unlawful" and "arbitrary and capricious." In a related case, Massachusetts Attorney general Maura Healey previously applied to the DOE on behalf of 7,200 former students of Corinthian Colleges under this program, saying their debts were unlawful and therefore uncollectable. Yet DeVos illegally seized the tax refund of Massachusetts borrowers even though they had opened applications for debt cancellation.

DeVos rewrote the Borrower Defense regulations so dramatically that almost no borrower would ever qualify for debt cancellation. Her department estimated that only about three cents on every dollar borrowed would be forgiven under the new rules. The Senate passed legislation to revoke her rewrite, but a veto by President Trump kept her rewrite in place. In an Orwellian sleight of hand, DOE wrote to tens of thousands of defrauded borrowers to say that their claims had been approved but because there was "no evidence of harm," the debt relief would be zero dollars thereby requiring the borrower to fully repay their fraudulent loans.

False Certification Discharge

Available for Direct Loans and FFEL Program loans.

You might be eligible for a discharge of your federal student loan if your school falsely certified your eligibility to receive a loan. There are three categories of false certification through which you might be eligible for a discharge of your Direct Loans or FFEL Program loans:

1. Ability to benefit: The school falsely certified your eligibility to receive the loan based on your ability to benefit from its training, and you didn't meet the ability-to-benefit student eligibility requirements that were in effect at the time the school determined your eligibility.
2. Disqualifying status: The school certified your eligibility to receive the loan, but at the time of the certification, you had a status (physical or mental condition, age, criminal record, or other circumstance) that disqualified you from meeting the legal requirements for employment in your state of residence in the occupation for which the program of study was preparing you.
3. Unauthorized signature or unauthorized payment: The school signed your name on the loan application or promissory note without your authorization or the school endorsed your loan check or signed your authorization for electronic funds transfer without your knowledge, and the loan money wasn't given to you or applied to charges you owed to the school.

If you have a Direct Loan or FFEL Program loan and you are ready to apply for the false certification discharge, you must complete the loan discharge application that applies to your circumstance:

- Loan Discharge Application: False Certification (Ability to Benefit).
- Loan Discharge Application: False Certification (Disqualifying Status)
- Loan Discharge Application: False Certification (Unauthorized Signature/Payment)*

*Complete the *Loan Discharge Application: False Certification (Unauthorized Signature/Payment)* only if you believe that an employee of the school that determined your eligibility for the loan signed your name on the promissory note or other loan documents without your authorization. If you believe that someone else (other than a school employee) forged your signature on a loan document or a loan was made in your name as a result of the crime of identity theft, contact your loan servicer.

Find out whom your loan servicer is by logging in.

If you meet the eligibility requirements for a discharge, the entire remaining balance of your loan will be discharged, and any payments made on the loan will be refunded.

If your loan discharge is denied, you will remain responsible for repaying your loan. If you believe that your loan discharge application was denied in error or if you have additional information that you believe would support your eligibility for a false certification discharge, you may ask the U.S. Department of Education to review the denial.

Some or all of your parent PLUS loan might be discharged if:

- the school falsely certified the student's ability to benefit from its training,
- the student had a disqualifying status at the time the school-certified your eligibility to receive the parent PLUS loan, or
- the school signed your name on the promissory note or other loan documents without your authorization.

Unpaid Refund Discharge

Available for Direct Loans and FFEL Program loans.

If you withdrew from school and the school didn't make a required return of loan funds to the loan servicer, you might be eligible for a discharge of the portion of your federal student loan(s) that the school failed to return.

If you withdrew from school after receiving a loan made under the William D. Ford Federal Direct Loan (Direct Loan) Program or Federal Family Education Loan (FFEL) Program, the school may have been required under federal regulations to return some or all of the loan money to your loan servicer. If the school didn't make a required return of the loan funds after you withdrew, you might be eligible for a discharge of the portion of your loan that the school failed to return.

If the school that you attended is still open, you should contact that school and attempt to resolve the issue with the school before applying for an unpaid refund discharge. If the school that you attended has closed, you should first determine if you may be eligible for a closed school discharge instead. Contact your loan servicer for more information. Find out who your loan servicer is by logging in to "My Federal Student Aid."

If you are ready to apply for the unpaid refund discharge, you must complete the *Loan Discharge Application: Unpaid Refund* and send the completed form to your loan servicer.

Only the portion of your loan that your school should have returned will be discharged. Contact your loan servicer for more information.

If your child withdrew from school, but the school didn't make a required return of your parent PLUS loan funds, the amount of the loan that the school should have returned will be discharged. Contact your loan servicer for more information.

Eligibility for Parent Borrowers

As with loans made to students, a parent PLUS loan can be discharged if you die, if you (not the student on whose behalf you obtained the loan) become totally and permanently disabled, or if your loan is discharged in bankruptcy. Your parent PLUS loan may also be discharged if the child for whom you borrowed dies.

In addition, all or a portion of a parent PLUS Loan may be discharged in any of these circumstances:
- The student for whom you borrowed could not complete his or her program because the school closed.
- Your eligibility to receive the loan was falsely certified by the school.
- Your eligibility to receive the loan was falsely certified through identity theft.
- The student withdrew from school, but the school didn't pay a refund of your loan money that it was required to pay under applicable laws and regulations.

Contact your loan servicer for more information.

Summary

This chapter reviewed in greater detail the various DOE programs that provide loan forgiveness, cancellation, or discharge of student loans:
- Public Service Loan Forgiveness (PSLF)
- Teacher Loan Forgiveness
- Closed School Discharge
- Perkins Loan Cancellation and Discharge
- Total and Permanent Disability Discharge
- Discharge Due to Death
- Discharge in Bankruptcy
- Borrower Defense to Repayment
- False Certification Discharge
- Unpaid Refund Discharge
- Eligibility for Parent Borrowers

Perhaps one of these programs would better fit your needs?

CHAPTER 4
History of Bankruptcy and the Student Loan Program

Unlike a Chapter 7 bankruptcy in which you fill out a few forms and file with the bankruptcy court, to bankrupt student loans, you must first file a Chapter 7 bankruptcy <u>and</u> concurrently sue the U.S. government (called an *adversary*) and successfully argue your case. To do so, it is important to know the history of bankruptcy in the United States and the student loan program, including legislative language and court challenges. It is highly recommended that you read these next few chapters and become thoroughly familiar with the concepts and language.

SECTION 1: Bankruptcy is a "Right" included in the U.S. Constitution

In Article 1, Section 8, Clause 4, the U.S. Constitution authorized Congress in 1789 to "establish . . . uniform laws on the subject of bankruptcies throughout the United States."[1] The founders of the United States did not want to see debtor prisons flourish in the new government as they did in Europe and colonies. They believed that holding people responsible for debt that they can never pay back to be unproductive for society, particularly the practice of passing debt down to future family members. In those situations, the debt obligation is usually not repaid and only makes people desperate and more likely to engage in questionable and illegal activities for survival. The elimination of unserviceable debt through bankruptcy was so important that the founders included it in the very first article of the Constitution; it was not an afterthought like the later Amendments that people hold so dearly to their hearts.

In the early years of the burgeoning country, many colonies established their own bankruptcy systems since there was no national system. These legal proceedings were very pro-creditor that often led to imprisonment for the debtors and, sometimes, their families. Even after the establishment of the United States and the implementation of the Constitution, state debtor prisons remained in operation until 1849, when they were formally abolished.

Allowing the bankruptcy of debts serves important social and economic purposes. It frees hopeless debtors to become responsible consumers and producing members of society[2]. Congress enacted the bankruptcy laws along with a separate judiciary to administer the law.

Unfortunately, the Constitutional clause did not clearly define which kinds of debts were to be included in bankruptcy, nor which kinds of debtors. These clarifications and the process were left up to Congress to define. The first law on the subject was the *Bankruptcy Act of 1800,* which applied only to merchants and those involved in involuntary proceedings. There was no provision for individuals to file their own claims. This was later repealed in 1803 since it was unworkable due to extensive fraud. Many states continued administering their own bankruptcy courts during this time.

Bankruptcy Acts of 1841 was considered too pro-debtor and repealed in 1843. The economic aftermath of the Civil War encouraged Congress to try again with *The Bankruptcy Act of 1867*. This was the first-time involuntary bankruptcies for individuals were included. Unfortunately, this too failed for similar reasons, and the United States had no functioning federal bankruptcy system for more than a decade. Congress tried again and established a nationwide permanent comprehensive bankruptcy system in 1898. Although modified many times, it clarified modern debtor-creditor relations and the process of bankruptcy.

The Bankruptcy Act of 1898 (known as the *Nelson Act*) had two major goals: (1) to provide honest, hard-working debtors with a "fresh start" in which they are free of oppressive debt, and (2) to obtain fair and equitable treatment for debtors and creditors alike.[3] Congress made a concerted effort to ensure a balance between the interests of creditors and the needs of debtors. Congress recognized that "[a] bankruptcy system that does not balance the interests of creditors and the interests of debtors will have neither their confidence nor, of even greater importance, the confidence of the American people."[4]

Bankruptcy was expanded under the *Bankruptcy Act of 1938* (known as the *Chandler Act*) to include voluntary petitions, thereby attracting more debtors to the system. Under the Chandler Act, the Securities and Exchange Commission administered bankruptcy filings.

In the 1970s, Congress began a discussion about revamping the bankruptcy laws. Student loan default, farm bankruptcies, crushing medical debt, and credit card abuse became major controversies in the media and Congressional debate. Eventually, the Act of 1898 was replaced with the *Bankruptcy Reform Act of 1978*[5] (now known as the "Bankruptcy Code"). It provided additional avenues for debtors to file bankruptcy and obtain a fresh start besides granting increase power to bankruptcy judges. The Reform Act allowed debtors to file under Chapter 7, 11, 12, or 13 of the Bankruptcy Code. (See the next section for details of these four kinds of bankruptcies).

However, the 1978 Reform Act created some legal issues concerning the roles and authority of judges and courts. After much litigation and appeal to the U.S. Supreme Court, some of the Reform Act was declared unconstitutional. The decision was stayed until 1982 to give Congress time to fix the problems. Even after the stay expired and an "Emergency Rule" was adopted by district courts as "local rules," Congress failed to act until 1984 at which time Congress implemented corrections to the Act by enacting the *Bankruptcy Amendments and Federal Judgeship Act of 1984*. This was further amended by the *Family Farmer Bankruptcy Act of 1986,* which established a permanent United States trustee system.

Most important to this book, the *Higher Education Amendments of 1998* eliminated the seven-year waiting period for including student loans in bankruptcy, leaving the "undue hardship" adversary proceeding as the only way to bankrupt student loans.

In 2005, Congress passed the *Bankruptcy Abuse Prevention and Consumer Protection Act* (BAPCPA) after years of study by many fact-finding commissions. It introduced the idea of a "means test" to determine if an individual qualified for a Chapter 7 bankruptcy or needed to use a Chapter 13 to reorganize payments on the debt. BAPCPA made it mandatory for individual debtors to undergo mandatory credit counseling and mandatory financial education courses. Further, it lumped private student loans with government-backed student loans, excepting them from bankruptcy. Thus, even private loans were now protected from simple bankruptcy without proving "undue hardship."

BAPCPA achieved many of its stated goals. The number of bankruptcy filings decreased immediately after its passage and passed-through the savings to consumers in the form of lower borrowing costs. However, it was found that the means test had little impact as most debtors qualified for Chapter 7 bankruptcy. The benefits to creditors from BAPCPA were wiped away with the economic recession of 2008 and the following decade of economic struggle. The rate of bankruptcies exploded for the first few years after the start of the recession peaking in 2010 with over one million Chapter 7 filings each year. Since then, the rate of filings has reduced to about 500,000 annually. The Covid-19 pandemic is expected to cause a massive explosion of bankruptcy filings by the end of 2023 and for the next few years with so many people struggle with a loss of job or business failure. At the time of this writing, some politicians are proposing major revisions to the bankruptcy code. Some plans want to bring back the seven-year rule. Others propose wiping out all student loans completely thereby, ameliorating the need for bankruptcy. Even Republican representative of New York John Katko proposed his *Discharge Student*

Loans in bankruptcy Act of 2019 to drop the "undue hardship" requirement completely and restore full bankruptcy protections to student loans. We shall see how this plays out the next few years.

Types of Bankruptcies

Chapter 7 is full liquidation of debt within a fixed time (usually 120 days) of filing a motion to dismiss and can lead to the liquidation of nonexempt assets to pay back creditors. A "means" test is used to determine if the debtor is eligible to use Chapter 7 law. Chapter 11 bankruptcies are a business reorganization plan often used by large businesses to help them stay in business while restructuring their business practices and debts. Chapter 12 (for farmers and fishermen) and 13 (for individuals) bankruptcy eliminates qualified debt through a repayment plan over a specific time period (typically three to five years).

Born during the Great Depression, Chapter 13 (or Chapter 12 if a family farmer or fisherman) bankruptcy was enacted in 1938 to better represent the needs of creditors. Debtors choosing Chapter 12 or 13 bankruptcy submit a repayment plan and reorganize their finances to pay off some eventually, or all, of their debt under court supervision within three to five years. Chapter 12, 13 debtors agree to commit all of their disposable income to the repayment plan in exchange for keeping their possessions and paying the debt agreed by the court. Chapter 13 bankruptcy results in better long-term creditworthiness for debtors and collects more money for creditors.

Debtors filing under Chapter 7 obtain a quick and full discharge of debts. It is designed to offer rapid debt relief for honest but over-burdened debtors. A "means" test is used to determine legibility. Although the test was designed to limit the number of Chapter 7 filings, in reality, almost 90 percent of debtors qualify for Chapter 7 bankruptcy. The means test compares the debtor's household income to the median income of the state the debtor resides. If her or his monthly income over six months prior to filing for bankruptcy is below the state median for a similar household, or if the debtor's monthly disposable income falls below a threshold established by a statutory means test,

---

History of Bankruptcy Reform Acts Related to Education

1976
Congress modifies the Higher Education Act of 1965 (codified as 20 U.S.C.A §§ 1097-3) to include §439A, which states:
  (a) such loan, benefit, scholarship, or stipend overpayment first became due more than <u>five years</u> (exclusive of any applicable suspension of the repayment period) before the date of the filing of the petition; or
  (b) excepting such debt from discharge under this paragraph will impose an <u>undue hardship</u> on the debtor and the debtor's dependents;"

1978
§439A is repealed, and similar nondischargeability provisions language placed within the 1978 Bankruptcy Reform Act §523(a)(8). Student loans are presumptively nondischargeable in bankruptcy.

1990-1991
The five-year wait period extended to seven-years, made the law apply to both Chapter 7 and Chapter 13 bankruptcies, and lifted the statute of limitation on collecting student loans.

1998
Completely removed the number of years a debtor had to wait before filing bankruptcy and implemented the Income-Driven Repayment (IDR) plans. This leaves "undue hardship" as the only argument debtors can pursue to discharge student loans.

2005
A "means" test for filing for bankruptcy was implemented. If the debtor's income fell below his/her state's medium income, he/she could file for a Chapter 7 bankruptcy. All "educational" loans were now protected from simple bankruptcy regardless if they were government-backed loans or from private sources.

he/she qualifies to process a Chapter 7 bankruptcy. Nonexempt assets are relinquished to the trustee, who then sells the assets. Proceeds from the bankruptcy sale are distributed among the creditors. As such, the debtor receives an immediate "fresh start" as all remaining debt is discharged. Because of the automatic and expeditious discharge of debt, Chapter 7 bankruptcy is the preferred method of bankruptcy for many individual debtors.

Debts that are Excluded from Bankruptcy

The Constitution never specified what kinds of debts or kinds of debtors could be denied the right to bankruptcy; that was left up to Congress. Slowly, exceptions to dischargeability of debts were added to the bankruptcy laws. Currently, there are nineteen categories of debt excepted from discharge under chapters 7, 11, 12, and 13 bankruptcies. Some of the more common types include certain types of tax claims, debts for spousal or child support or alimony, debts to governmental units for fines and penalties, debts for personal injury caused by the debtor's operation of a motor vehicle while intoxicated, debts for willful and malicious injuries to person or property, debts for certain condominium or cooperative housing fees, debts owed to certain tax-advantaged retirement plans, and debts for most government-funded or guaranteed educational loans.

Also, a conviction of a financial or fraud-related crime resulting in a felony affects bankruptcy exceptions. In these cases, many of the exempted assets that otherwise would be retained after the bankruptcy would also be liquidated to pay down the debt.

Some academics and activists claim the ever-expanding list of exceptions to the right to bankruptcy is subverting the intent of the Constitution.

SECTION 2:
The Development of Student Loans

A great debate over the state of American higher education occurred after the successful launch of the first unmanned space vehicle, Sputnik, in 1957 by the USSR. In response, Congress passed the *National Defense Education Act* (NDEA) in 1958 to address perceived deficits in the national defense and educational systems. Among other provisions, NDEA established the *National Defense Student Loan* (NDSL) to provide low interest (5 percent) loans to qualified students. NDSL loans (also known as *Perkins Loans*) were the first federally funded higher education loan program, which continues to the present.

GSLP 1965 (Stafford Loans)

The success of the NDSL program led to the enactment of the *Guaranteed Student Loan Program* (GSLP) in 1965 as part of the *Higher Education Act.* The GSLP (later renamed the Stafford Loan Program) was aimed to help reduce financial barriers to postsecondary education for the poorest students. The program was based on the core principle that students without adequate financial resources should still be able to obtain higher education even though they may be viewed as an unacceptable credit risk.

Stafford Loans are primarily funded by private lenders and ultimately guaranteed by the U.S. government. Initially, only the neediest students qualified for a loan. To qualify, "borrowers [had to] demonstrate financial need in excess of other financial aid sources and family contributions."[6] Forbearance and deferment options allowed students to delay repayment of the loans. Several repayment plans helped accommodate fluctuations in student income. (*See* Appendix A for details on these options and repayment plans.) Today, the financial requirements have been significantly relaxed, and most students qualify for government-financed or guaranteed loans.

Before the adoption of the *Bankruptcy Reform Act* in 1978, student loans were treated as any other unsecured debt and could be directly discharged through bankruptcy. Very few students attempted to eliminate their student loan debt through bankruptcy. In 1968-70, there were only 760 bankruptcies nationwide that involved student loans. By 1976, these numbers jumped to 8,641 bankruptcies involving student loans for a total of $33.1 million in unpaid loans.

Middle Income Student Assistance Act 1978

The success of the *Higher Education Act of 1965* for the poorest students did little to help middle-income Americans. The cost of education increased by 75 percent between 1965 and 1975. Middle-class students who did not qualify for student loans were hard-pressed to pay for increased education costs. In 1978, Congress made federal loans available to virtually all students regardless of need through the *Middle Income Student Assistance Act*. Student borrowing increased rapidly, and federal loan expenditures skyrocketed. Between 1975 and 1979, new federal student loan volume increased by $2 billion. Ironically, as federal spending for higher education increased, state funding for higher education decreased in all fifty states.[7] As a consequence, students took on more and more debt.

The Department of Health, Education, and Welfare reported that in 1976, $500 million was paid to banks for nearly 350,000 student loan defaults. Congress became concerned about the high number of student loan defaults. The student loan programs responded to the increased level of loan defaults by tightening up requirements and implementing stricter collection procedures. The default rate plummeted. Yet, the media fixated on a handful of stories of student loan fraud and default that gave the impression that the student loan program was on the verge of collapse through massive abuse. The public believed loopholes in the student loan programs enabled substantial abuse by students defrauding the taxpayers.

Media Hype of Abuse

The media played up reports of students discharging their student loan debts immediately upon graduation, never once having made any payments, and subsequently accepting high-paying jobs. Two cases illustrate the problem. In 1973, a former New Jersey student filed for bankruptcy fourteen days after graduating from Stanford Law School for the sole purpose of discharging $17,272 of his student loans. He had already earned a business degree and a master's degree in engineering.[8] Similarly, a Massachusetts couple was successful at discharging $20,000 worth of student loans through bankruptcy immediately after graduation. The husband held a law degree, while the wife held a graduate degree. They never made a payment on the loans.[9]

Many in Congress found such actions reprehensible, unethical, and "tantamount to fraud."[10] Debate in Congress focused on this abuse of the liberal discharge provisions of the Bankruptcy Code. Representative Allen Ertel (D-Pa) observed that federal student loan defaults increased by more than 300 percent between 1972 and 1976. He explained, "These bankruptcies could easily destroy the federal student loan programs…This problem cannot be permitted to spread nationwide, because destruction of the student loan programs would operate to deny the benefits of higher education to many would-be students who are otherwise qualified for post-high school education or training… This destruction of student loan programs would represent a tremendous waste of one of this nation's greatest assets, the minds and skills of American youth."[11] Rep. Ertel later introduced the amendment that eventually became 11 U.S.C.A. Section 523 (a)(8).

The facts are very different. Very few students abused the Bankruptcy Code in discharging their student loans. The 1973 Bankruptcy Review Commission acknowledged that student loan abuse was "more perception than reality."[12] A 1976 General Accounting Office study concluded that only half to three-quarters of 1 percent of all matured educational loans had been discharged through bankruptcy[13]. Similarly, The House Report on the Bankruptcy Law Revision (1977) stated, "a high default rate has been confused with a high bankruptcy rate, and has mistakenly led to calls for changes in bankruptcy laws."[14] Further, the House Report on the Bankruptcy Law Revision noted that the "rise [in student loan defaults] appears not to be disproportionate to the rise in the amount of loans becoming due or to the default rate generally on educational loans."[15] It can be concluded that most people who resorted to bankruptcy did so because they needed to, not because they were attempting to defraud the government.

Yet, the media frenzy[16] created the impression that students habitually received discharges of their loans through bankruptcy immediately after graduation.

Some in Congress saw past the media hype. For example, Rep. Cornell stated, "We can all agree that the intent of [§523(a)(8)] is to prevent abuse of our student loan program by those who would use bankruptcy simply to avoid repayment of their student loans."[17] Fraud and abuse of the student loan program is what concerned many in Congress, not that some people had a legitimate need to seek bankruptcy.

Some thought implementing a waiting period for filing bankruptcy after graduation would stem most student loan defaults and bankruptcies. As one academic noted to Congress, the average time between the last student loan and filing for bankruptcy ranged between "thirty months and forty-one months."[18] Thus, implementing a waiting period from the time the last student loan is used, and filing bankruptcy should eliminate most fraud. Sheldon Steinbach, Assistant Director of Government Relations of the American Council on Education stated, "[b]aring educational debts from discharge during the in-school period and first five years of repayment will erect a necessary barrier to graduates and dropouts who deliberately seek to dissolve their repayment obligations at a time when their assets are at a minimum."[19] Similarly, Judge Edward York testified, "[o]ur purpose in proposing an amendment [§523(a)(b)] to the bankruptcy laws [was] to terminate the growing propensity of student loan borrowers to resort to bankruptcy immediately upon graduation."[20]

Rep. Ertel stated, "if a [student debtor] has a hardship he can go to the court and say: 'I have a difficulty' and ask for a discharge," or "[a]fter the five-year period, if he has not been able to accumulate assets, he can go into bankruptcy."[21]

Compromise Bill Results in Nondischargeability of Student Loans

The nondischargeability of student loans was not originally included in the House bankruptcy bill. The House Judiciary Committee did not find adequate evidence of abuse to warrant making student loans non-dischargeable. The House bill made no distinction between student loans and other dischargeable debt. The Senate bill, on the other hand, made student loans non-dischargeable with only two exceptions. Eventually, the final bill that passed in 1976 adopted the Senate version without change. This was word-for-word the same draft bill recommended by the Bankruptcy Review Commission in its 1973 report to Congress.

Instead of a blanket nondischargeability of student loan debt, Congress decided to include both a five-year waiting time and "undue hardship" exceptions. The five-year exception was intended to close the loophole by preventing abusive discharges. The "undue hardship" exception was intended to provide "the honest, financially-troubled debtor the opportunity for a fresh start."[22] The language of Section 523(a)(8) was taken directly from 439(A) of the *Higher Education Act of 1965*. Student loans were listed in Section 523 along with other non-dischargeable debts including, taxes; fraudulent income tax returns or invoices; money owed for negligent or unlawful acts such as drunk driving (resulting in manslaughter); money or assets fraudulently or unlawfully attained (e.g., embezzlement); debts provided for in any final judgment against the debtor; penalties and fines owed to the government; debts not listed by the debtor; and child support and alimony.

The growing list of exceptions was telling. As one congressman explained as to the type of debtor Section 523 was aimed at, "we only define groups of people or different statuses for three types of people who are exempted from discharging their claims under bankruptcy"[23]— felons, those convicted of fraud, and those who are indebted in alimony payments. Rep. James O'Hara of Michigan claimed that the regulation "…treats educational loans precisely as the law now treats loans incurred by fraud, felony, and alimony-dodging. No other legitimately contracted consumer loan…is subjected to the assumption of criminality which this provision applies to every educational loan."

The Report of the Committee on the Judiciary in 1977 provided what ultimately became Section 523 and "retains the provisions of current law governing when a discharge is granted and when it is denied. Most of the grounds for denial of discharge concern misconduct by the debtor in the events leading up to the bankruptcy or during the conduct of the case."[24]

The concern about fraud influenced the

Senate to include nondischargeability of student loans in Section 523 along with other crimes of moral turpitude. However, it was recognized that not all debtors seeking bankruptcy engaged in fraud. As such, the undue hardship exception was created as an appropriate safeguard.

1978 Bankruptcy Reform Act Section 523(a)(8)

In 1976, Congress modified the *Higher Education Act of 1965* (codified as 20 U.S.C.A §§ 1097-3) to enact §439A[25] which made student loans <u>non</u>-dischargeable in bankruptcy <u>unless</u>: (a) the debt first became due more than five years before the date of filing of the bankruptcy, or, (b) failure to discharge the debt would cause "undue hardship" to the debtor or to dependents of the debtor. Later, Congress repealed §439A of the Higher Education Act and placed the nondischargeability provisions and language within the 1978 Bankruptcy Reform Act §523(a)(8)[26]. This is the Act that guides the discussion of this book.

Most bankruptcy cases decided under §523(a)(8) involved the undue hardship exception. This is a difficult endeavor since the drafters of the Bankruptcy Code did not define "undue hardship."[27] The drafters explicitly stated that the bankruptcy courts must decide undue hardship on a case-by-case basis, considering all the debtor's circumstances.

By 1981, 3.5 million students borrowed $7.7 billion from the Guaranteed Student Loan Program (GSL) program. This represented a 52 percent increase in the number of students and 60 percent increase in the amount of money borrowed by students over the previous year. Year by year, more and more money was being borrowed by students for a college education— an education that cost more each year.

1990 Crime Control Act
1991 Higher Educational Technical Amendments

Congress extended the original five-year exception for discharging student loans to seven years[28] under the *Crime Control Act of 1990*. At the same time, the law was extended to apply to both Chapter 7 and Chapter 13 bankruptcy cases when previously it had applied only to Chapter 7 cases. Further, the 1985 statute of limitation on collection of defaulted loans (which had been six-years) was eliminated. The *1991 Higher Educational Technical Amendments* eliminated the statute of limitation on banks trying to collect on defaulted student loans.

Congress became concerned about the solvency of the federal loan program and wanted to protect it from bankruptcy challenges. The Reagan administration proposed reductions in federal aid to postsecondary education. This prompted a bitter and protracted political debate in Congress about the role of the federal government in educational loans. Yet, legislation was passed in 1992 that made it even easier for middle-class students to borrow federal money for higher education.[29] Borrowing increased by 57 percent between 1992 and 1996 with federal expenditures reaching an all-new high of $23.1 billion annually.[30]

By the late 1990s, the federal government was guaranteeing almost $50 billion a year of student loans. Loans were (and still are) easy to get. Students who would otherwise be deemed poor credit risks are able, if not encouraged, to borrow money for college. As expected, mounting student indebtedness has led to an increase in the number of discharges sought based on undue hardship.

1998 Higher Education Amendments

In 1984, *The Bankruptcy Amendments and Federal Judgeship Act* further tightened the rules on bankruptcy discharge by dropping "of higher education" from the wording of the legislation. This broadened the restrictions on discharge to include private loans backed by nonprofit institutions as well as government loans.

Finally, and most importantly for this book, the *Higher Education Amendments* passed in 1998 completely eliminated the ability to discharge student loans through bankruptcy without proving repaying the loans caused an "undue hardship." No longer were student loans dischargeable through standard bankruptcy after a seven-year waiting period.

2005 Bankruptcy Abuse Prevention and Consumer Protection Act

Seven years later, Congress passed the *Bankruptcy Abuse Prevention and Consumer Protection Act in 2005* (often referred to as the "New Bankruptcy Law") that excluded all qualified educational loans, including most private loans, from bankruptcy discharge. No longer was the nature of the lender important, and the student loan did have to be associated with a nonprofit institution. It also implemented a "means" test to see if the debtor's income exceeded their state median income.

At this time, the only avenue debtors have to discharge student loan debt government is to demonstrate their hopeless financial situation and prove that repayment would subject them and their dependents to "undue hardship." For many student loan debtors, this is virtually impossible to do.[31] (The next Chapter discusses in depth the judicial construction of "undue hardship.")

Student Loan Debt and Default Statistics

The student loan program has existed for over fifty years and has helped millions of students obtain a college education or professional certification that they otherwise could not have afforded. Many of these students were the first in their families to attend college and brought immense pride to their families. By 2023[32], more than $1.64 trillion had been lent by the government for student loans servicing more than 43 million students. It is estimated that 65 percent of all graduates have student loans. The average U.S. household with student debt owes about $47,000. Students with professional degrees typically incurred much large student loan debts: medical school—$200,000, dental school—$300,000, and pharmacy school graduates—$170,000.

Of these loans, 18.6 million borrowers are in repayment; 3.4 million borrowers are in deferment; 2.7 million borrowers are in forbearance; and 8 million borrowers are in default.[33] On top of that, about 8 million debtors are in one of the Income-Driven Repayment (IDR) plans, of which most are not making any headway on paying down the principal of their loans. Thus, their loans are negatively amortizing, with loan balances increasing with each passing month. Overall, almost 25 million people with student loans are unable to make regular loan payments.

Federal income-driven repayment plans cap monthly payments at 10 percent to 20 percent of discretionary income and forgive the balance remaining after twenty or twenty-five years, depending on the plan. There are 7.37 million borrowers participating in the income-driven repayment plans: 2.82 million borrowers on *Income-Based Repayment* (IBR) plans; 2.56 million borrowers on *Revised Pay As You Earn*; 1.31 million borrowers on *Pay As You Ear*n; and 680,000 borrowers on *Income-contingent Repayment* (ICR) plans (as of 2023).

DOE reports very low default rates. This is deceiving for two reasons: (a) DOE only review loans issued within the last three years and not those dating back years or decades—it is surprising there are any loans in default within the first six years of the last loan being issued since forbearance and deferment options would keep the loans "current" and not in default and the debtor not having to make any payments; and, (b) loans in forbearance, deferment, or in any of the IDR plans are technically not in default regardless that they may never be paid off. The long-term view of student loans is dreadful with some academics estimating that more than half of all student loans eventually being defaulted.

On July 7, 2015, the Department of Education issued guidelines for student–loan guarantors and educational institutions for determining when they should oppose bankruptcy discharge for students.[34] DOE's Deputy Secretary Lynn Mahaffie, author of the letter, wrote that "[t]he Department is providing this guidance to assist loan holders in fulfilling their regulatory duty to protect the integrity of taxpayer dollars provided through student loans while consenting to and/or not opposing undue hardship discharge of student loans where repaying the loan would impose an undue hardship on the debtor."[35] The eleven factors loan holders should consider:

- Whether a debtor who asserts undue hardship due to physical or mental

impairment may qualify for Total and Permanent Disability Discharge (TPD) and/or other administrative discharges available...
- Whether a debtor has filed for bankruptcy due to factors beyond his or her control and the impact of such factor(s) have on debtor's ability to repay the student loan...
- Whether a debtor pursued available income–driven repayment plans... If the monthly repayment under any available income–driven plan is within the debtor's means, the ability to prove undue hardship should be correspondingly more difficult, though not impossible...
- Whether a debtor had made any payments on his or her student loan debt when the debtor had the resources to do so...
- Whether a student loan debt is a debtor's only debt and/or whether the student loan debt has been owed for a long period of time, filing a bankruptcy adversary proceeding solely to obtain a discharge of student loans could be indicative of a preplanned fiscal management strategy aimed at avoiding repayment. Similarly, filing a bankruptcy adversary proceeding shortly after the debt enters repayment could be indicative of a preexisting lack of intent to repay...
- Whether a debtor has reaffirmed other debts that are dischargeable in bankruptcy, reaffirmation of dischargeable debt(s) indicates a borrower's belief that he or she possesses sufficient funds for at least partial student loan debt repayment, as any payment towards a reaffirmed debt could be applied toward a student loan debt.
- Whether a debtor is approaching retirement, taking into consideration the debtor's age at the time student loans were incurred, and resources likely to be available to the debtor in retirement to repay the student loan debt... Borrowers who choose to incur student loan debt at an older age, whether the debt is for themselves or a dependent (i.e., Parent PLUS loans), should not be able to rely on their age alone and/or their entrance into retirement to prove undue hardship.
- Whether a debtor's health has materially changed since the student loan debt was incurred...
- Whether significant time has elapsed since the debt was incurred...
- Whether a debtor's expenses are reasonable and indicate minimization of unnecessary expenses to provide funds for student loan repayment.
- Whether a debtor had the mental and/or physical capacity to pursue administrative discharge options and/or income–driven repayment plans if those options were not pursued, or whether a debtor had any physical or psychological factors that would have made the administrative process more burdensome to the borrower.

Mahaffie suggested that student-loan holders evaluate whether they think the debtor meets the challenges of conforming to the undue hardship criteria against the cost of opposing the discharge, the likelihood of winning the case, and the outstanding loan balance. Considering that DOE consistently tries to force debtors onto IDR plans regardless that the loans will never be paid off shows that Mahaffie's 2015 policy letter is insincere.[36]

Summary

- Student loans were initially treated as any other unsecured loan and dischargeable through a standard bankruptcy.
- The student loan default rose significantly in the 1970s, causing great alarm in Congress about the solvency of the student loan programs. Congress conflated the concept of "default" with "bankruptcy" and caste the bankruptcy of student loans as a moral turpitude warranting the changes in the law to make student loan debt non-dischargeable.
- A few high-profile cases made media headlines involving students using bankruptcy to obtain a discharge of their student loans immediately or soon after graduation.
- The Congressional discussion leading up to

the implementation of §523(a)(8) of the 1978 Bankruptcy Reform Act shows:
  - Congress was most concerned about student loan abuse. They wanted to prevent dishonest borrowers from procuring a free college education by filing for bankruptcy shortly before or immediately after graduation.
  - Congress was very aware that some form of bankruptcy relief was necessary for honest debtors who found themselves unable to service their student loan debt.
  - Implementing a five-year waiting time from the assumption of the last student loan to the use of bankruptcy to discharge the loans was thought to weed out most attempts at abuse. This was later increased to seven-years but eliminated altogether in 1998.
  - Implementing the "undue hardship" clause gave another avenue to students in financial difficulties to discharge the loans.
- By 1998, only the "undue hardship" exception could be used to discharge student loan debt and required the filing of an "adversary" against the U.S. government.

Many people have attempted to bankrupt their student loans. As stated above, the law requires the debtor to prove "undue hardship." This was not defined by Congress but left up to the courts to determine on a case-by-case basis. The next section of this book examines some of the approaches used by courts to determine "undue hardship." This will help guide you in your efforts to develop your own bankruptcy case.

[1] United States Constitution, Article 1, Section 8, cl. 4.

[2] Jackson, Thomas H. (1985). The fresh start policy in bankruptcy law. *Harvard Law Rev.* (98), 1393, 1420.

[3] King, Lawrence & Cook, Michael. (1996). *Creditors' rights, debtors' protection, and bankruptcy* (3rd Edition). New York, NY: Matthew Bender and Col., Inc.

[4] See *Bankruptcy: The next Twenty years: National Bankruptcy Review Commission Final Report*. (October 20, 1997). National Bankruptcy Review Commission. Ch 1.4.5.

[5] Bankruptcy Reform Act of 1978, Pub. Law No. 95-598, 92 Stat. 2549, 2591 (1978).

[6] Zackerman, Jeffrey L. (1997). (Note) Discharging Student Loans in Bankruptcy: The Need for a Uniform "undue hardship" Test. *U. CIN. L. REV.* (691). 65.

[7] The Mortenson Report (2001). The sorry state of the States: State Tax Fund Appropriations for Higher Education, FY 2001. *Postsecondary Education Opportunity*, (103), 12-16.

[8] See Bankruptcy Act Revision: Hearings on H.R. 31 and H.R. 32 before the Subcomm. On civil and Constitutional Rights of House Comm. On the Judiciary, 94th Cong. 1078 (1976) (testimony of Hon. Edward York, U.S. Deputy Commissioner, U.S. Office of Education).

[9] See Bankruptcy Reform Act: Hearings on S. 235 and S. 236 before the Subcomm. On Improvements n Judicial Machinery of the Senate Comm. On the Judiciary, 94th Cong. 220-21 (1975).

[10] *In re Pelkowski*, 990 F.2d 737, 742 (3rd Cir. 2993), quoting 124 CONG. REC. 1793.

[11] Representative Allen Ertel (D-Pa). H.R. No. 95-595, 95 Cong. 1st Session (1997), U.S. Code Cong. And Adm in. News, 1978. pp. 5759, 5963.

[12] National Bankruptcy Review Commission Report, Pub. L. No. 103-394, at 197 (established pursuant to the Bankruptcy Reform Act of 1994) (Oct. 20, 1997) (recommending in its final report that Congress eliminates §523(a)(8)).

[13] H.R. REP. NO. 595, 95th Cong., 1st Sess. 133 (1977). See infra note 23 and accompanying text.

[14] H.R. Rep. No. 95-595, at 133 (1977), reprinted in 1978 U.S.C.C.A.N 5963, 6094.

[15] H.R. Rep. No. 95-595, at 133 (1977), reprinted in 1978 U.S.C.C.A.N. 5963, 6094. See also A&P 124 Cong. Rec. 1794 (daily ed. Feb 1, 1978).

[16] The popular press argued that student loan default and bankruptcy rates were unacceptably high. *See:* Time of reckoning for student deadbeats. (July 18, 1977) *U.S. News & World Report,* 21; Study now, pay never. (March 7, 1977). *Newsweek,* 95; Student loan mess. (Dec. 8, 1975). *Time* 8.

[17] A&B 124 Cong. Rec. 1794 (daily ed. Feb. 1, 1978) (statement of Rep. Cornell).

[18] Kosel, Janice E. (1981). Running the gauntlet of "undue hardship"; The discharge of student loans in bankruptcy. Golden Gate U. L. Rev., (11), 457, 465. (citing statistics from H.R. Rep No. 595, at 142 (1977), reprinted in 1978 U.S.C.C.A.N 6103).

[19] Bankruptcy Reform Act: Hearings on S. 235 &236 before the Subcommittee On Improvements in Judicial Machinery of the Senate Comm. On the Judiciary U.S. Senate, 94th Cong. 217 (1975) (statement of Sheldon Steinbach).

[20] *See* supra notes 48-49; Bankruptcy Act Revision: Hearings on H.R. 31 and H.R. 32 before the Subcomm. On Civil and Constitutional Rights of the House Comm. On the Judiciary, 94th Cong. 1078 (1976) (testimony of Hon. Edward York, U.S. Deputy Commissioner, U.S. Office of Education)

[21] A&B 123 Cong. Rec. H457, H469 (daily ed. Feb. 1, 1978) statement of Rep. Ertel).

[22] Collins, Thad. (1990). Forging middle ground: Revision of student loan debts in bankruptcy as an impetus to Amend 11 U.S.C.A. § 523(a)8. *Iowa L. Rev.* (75), 742 (Note 67).

[23] A&P 123 Cong. Rec. H457, H467 (daily ed. Feb. 1, 1978) (statement of Rep. Dodd).

[24] H.R. Rep. No. 95-595, at 128 (1977), reprinted in 1978 U.S.C.C.A.N. 5963, 6089 (emphasis added). The "provisions of current law" being referred to in this quote are 14, and 17, as discussed above.

[25] Section 439A of the Education Amendments provided: A debt which is a loan insured or guaranteed under the authority of this part may be released by a discharge in bankruptcy under the Bankruptcy Act only if such discharge is granted after the five-years period (exclusive of any applicable suspension of the repayment period) beginning on the date of commencement of the repayment period of such loan, except that prior to the expiration of that five-years period, such loan may be released only if the court in which the proceeding is pending determines that payment from future income or other wealth will not impose an undue hardship on the debtor of his dependents.

[26] Bankruptcy Reform Act of 1978, Pub. Law No. 95-598, 92 Stat. 2549, 2591 (1978).

[27] *See* Report of the Commission on the Bankruptcy Law of the United States, H.R. DOC. NO. 137, 93d Cong., 1st Sess., Pt. II, 140 (1973).

[28] 11 U.S.C.A. Section 3007 (b), 104 Stat. At 1388-28 (1990).

[29] William, Ian. (Sept. 20, 1996). The indentured class: Student loans are robbing us of our future. Providence Phoenix, 8. Quote, "Colleges suddenly saw the government as this giant wobbling teat just waiting to be sucked and started a spastic race towards who could charge the most ludicrous tuition for four years. . . ."

[30] William, Ian, id.

[31] Huey, B.J. (2002). Undue hardship or undue burden: Has the time finally arrived for Congress to discharge Section 523(a)(8) of the Bankruptcy Code? *Texas Tech Law Review*, (34), 89.

[32] Nykiel, Teddy. (2019, Dec. 20). 2019 Student Loan Debt Statistics. Nerdwallet. https://www.nerdwallet.com/blog/loans/student-loans/student-loan-debt/

[33] Fuller, Andrea. (January 18, 2020). Student Debt Payback Far Worse Than Believed. https://2.bp.blogspot.com/-viyp9l2Juus/WIJh_Lqn7pI/AAAAAAAACR0/OXG6Enf0AicQ09UpjLnrS761asUZ7NdOwCLcB/s1600/Playing%2Bfor%2Btime.png

[34] Mahaffie, Lynn. Undue Hardship Discharge of Title IV Loans in Bankruptcy Adversary Proceedings. U.S. Dep't of Educ., July 7, 2015, DCL ID: GEN–15–13.

[35] Id

[36] Fossey, Richard and Robert Cloud. The U.S. Department of Education's 2015 Letter Outlining Guidelines for when Creditors Should not Oppose Bankruptcy Discharge for Student-Loan Debtors under the "Undue Hardship" Rule" What Does it Mean for Distressed Student-Loan Debtors. West's Education Law Reporter, June 16, 2016, 329 Ed. Law rep. 595.

CHAPTER 5
Court Opinions and Tests

This chapter reviews the tenants of U.S. bankruptcy law as related to "undue hardship" and the relevant court tests.

Student loans are no longer discharged in a Chapter 7 bankruptcy. Instead, the debts are listed in the Chapter 7 bankruptcy, and a subsequent adversary proceeding is initiated. Here, a separate court decision specifically rules on the dischargeability of student loans. The 11 U.S.C.A. Bankruptcy Reform Act (1998) §523(a)(8) requires debtors to prove "undue hardship" in order to have their student loans discharged as part of a bankruptcy.

"Undue Hardship"

Congress did not clarify in §523(a)(8) the meaning of "undue hardship." Considering all the debate over the dischargeability of student loans, it is surprising that Congress left it up to the courts to interpret what the phrase meant.[1] Legislative history provides little help in defining the undue hardship exception. Congress left it up to the various bankruptcy courts to "utilize their discretion in defining what [the] term means after an analysis of the statute and a review of applicable legislative history."[2] As noted in other court cases, "Congress wanted to save the student loan programs and bar the undeserving student borrower from abusing the bankruptcy process [but did] not directly identify how Congress intended the discharge to be granted in cases of undue hardship."[3]

Over the past quarter-century, courts have developed many tests to determine the existence of undue hardship. Although courts have made a concerted effort to accurately reflect and enforce Congressional policy and intent, there are significant differences between the tests and their outcomes. It is often said "that there are as many tests for undue hardship as there are bankruptcy courts."[4] Each test reflects a particular court and its goal of balancing congressional intent to limit loan discharges with bankruptcy debt relief. "While these tests have received varying degrees of acceptance, no particular test authoritatively guides or governs the undue hardship determination."[5] There is, however, a general agreement among courts that undue hardship means more than just temporary financial adversity.[6]

Currently, there are four tests that most courts use to determine the dischargeability of student loans under the undue hardship provision. These are:

- **"Johnson Test"**
  — *Pa. Higher Educ. Assistance Agency v. Johnson* (In re Johnson), 5 Bankr. Ct. Dec. 532 (Bankr. E.D. Pa. 1979)
- **"Bryant Poverty Test"**
  — *Bryant v. Pa. Higher Educ. Assistance Agency* (In re Bryant), 72 B.R. 913 (Bankr. E.D. Pa. 1987)
- **"Totality of the Circumstances Test"**
  — *Andrews v. South Dakota Student Loan Assistance Corporation*, 661 F.2d 702 (8th Cir. 1981).
- **"*Brunner* Test"**
  — *Brunner v. N.Y. State Higher Educ. Servs. Corp.* (In re *Brunner*), 831 F.2d 395 (2d Cir. 1987), aff'g 46 B.R. 752 (Bankr. S.D.N.Y. 1985)

It should be noted that even in courts that use the same test, the "subtleties" by which the tests are applied often produce inconsistent results.[7]

Many courts have harshly and narrowly ruled that debtors cannot discharge educational loans unless they can demonstrate "a certainty of hopelessness" about their long-term financial condition. Some academic writers have noted that "certainty of hopelessness" has become the unofficial standard[8] and common thread for these kinds of bankruptcies.

Below are discussed some of the tests used by bankruptcy courts in deciding student loan discharges. In each case, the specific District Courts where the test is applicable are noted.

Court Tests for "Undue Hardship"

The tests are presented in their historical context.

The Johnson Test

One of the first tests developed to determine the existence of undue hardship came from *Pennsylvania Higher Education Assistance Agency v. Johnson*. This 1970 case developed a 3-prong test that has been adopted by many courts but rejected by many other courts as being too "intricate." The **first prong** of the Johnson Test is a "mechanical analysis" of the debtor's current and future ability to repay the loan. This prong looks at the debtors' present employment and income, future employment and income, educational level and skills, marketability of skills, personal health, and dependents. Future expenses are evaluated by estimating the expenses of a comparably situated debtor plus any extraordinary expenses the debtor may have to pay in the future (such as medical expenses, tax liabilities, child support, alimony, etc.). These factors are compared against the official Federal Poverty Guideline to determine if the debtor can maintain a "subsistence or poverty standard of living"[9] while repaying the loan.

Note, there are many different Federal Poverty Guidelines created by different departments of the U.S. Government. You will read in later chapters that the poverty guideline used in the Johnson case and adopted by subsequent courts is the most restrictive of all poverty guidelines and represents a level of income required for temporary survival and not for sustained living. They were developed by the Social Security Administration in 1964. The basic assumptions used to develop the scale have never been adjusted to modern living. For example, rents often account for half a household budget today, whereas they accounted for only one-third of the household budget in 1964. The courts could have chosen less restrictive guidelines.

If repaying the loans pushes the debtor to or below the poverty level, then the second prong of the test is evaluated. If the debtor can maintain a minimal standard of living while repaying the loan, the analysis stops, and the case is dismissed without discharge of the debt.

The **second prong** of the test is known as the "good faith" analysis. Here, debtors must demonstrate that a good faith attempt was made to repay the student loan debt. The court measures the debtor's attempt to obtain employment, maximize income, and minimize expenses. Interestingly, the Johnson court held that making minimal payments on the loan was not, in and of itself, evidence of good faith. While making this analysis, the court also tries to determine if the debtor was culpable in causing his or her own poor financial condition. If the court determines that the debtor's irresponsible or negligent acts cause the debtor to fall below the poverty level while repaying the loan, there is a presumption against discharge and the case will be dismissed without discharge of the debt. However, the debtor may challenge this presumption by the third prong test.

A "policy analysis" makes up the **third prong** of the Johnson test. First, the court compares the debtor's total indebtedness against the student loan amount while estimating the probability of future employment. Next, the court asks two questions: (1) Did the debtor file bankruptcy for the primary purpose of discharging his or her student loans? (2) Did the debtor benefit financially from the education that was financed, in its entirety or partially, through the government loans seeking to be bankrupted? The Johnson court emphasized that debtors who gained financially from their education have a special responsibility to repay their debt. If the answer to both questions is "no," then the debt is normally discharged. If answers to either of the questions are "yes," then the debt is not discharged.

The Johnson Test is sequential. If the debtor qualifies under the first prong, then the second prong is evaluated, and so on to the third prong. If the debtor fails to meet any of the prongs, the test is stopped, and the debt is not discharged. Some courts that adopted the Johnson Test did not follow these procedures and subjected debtors to all three prongs even if they failed a lower level prong. As such, there was much subjectivity associated with the Johnson Test.

To many people, the Johnson Test seemed harsh. Yet, it influenced other courts to adopt its principles. Primarily, it suggested that "undue hardship" was to be measured against the official Federal Poverty Guidelines.

The Bryant Poverty Test

Eight years after the Johnson decision, the same court decided the *Bryant v. Pennsylvania Higher Education Assistance Agency* in 1987. The court acknowledged that its original test was too complicated and sought a more "objective" test—now known as the Bryant Poverty Test. Here, only debtors with after-tax net income near or below the federal poverty level are eligible for an undue hardship discharge. Student loans were presumed to be dischargeable if the debtor's income was not "significantly greater than the poverty level."[10] The court explained that it had discretionary authority to grant discharges when debtor income was close to the poverty level but failed to define the term "significantly greater." Lenders challenged this finding, e.g., by showing that the debtor failed to maximize resources or had apparent signs of increased future income.

If a debtor's income was above the poverty level, then the debtor must prove "unique" or "extraordinary" circumstances before the loan could be discharged. The court interpreted "unique" and "extraordinary" as situations where the debtor would experience more than mere "unpleasantness" if forced to repay the loans.

Most importantly, the Bryant Poverty Test formally established the Social Security Federal Poverty Guidelines as the primary means test for undue hardship. Although few courts rely solely on the Federal Poverty Guidelines for determining undue hardship, most courts include some consideration of the poverty level in their overall analysis.[11]

The Totality of the Circumstances Test
(Currently used in 8th Circuit Court.)

The Eighth Circuit Court in *Andrews v. South Dakota Student Loan Assistance Corp* (1981) took a different approach. The court was influenced by *In re Wegfehrt*[12], which held that each undue hardship determination must be examined on the specific set of facts and circumstances involved in that particular bankruptcy. The Eighth Circuit developed the "Totality of the Circumstances Test," which requires an analysis of: (1) the debtor's past, present, and reasonably reliable future financial resources; (2) calculation of the debtor's and his or her dependents' reasonable living expenses; and (3) any other relevant facts and circumstances related to that specific case. By examining all the circumstances on a case-by-case basis, the court believed it could better balance the need to determine undue hardship as specified in Section 523(a)(8) in light of the fresh start goal delineated in the Bankruptcy Code. As such, the Totality of Circumstances Test is viewed by many to be more equitable and fair than other undue hardship tests.

Some courts apply the Totality of the Circumstances Test from their own unique perspective. For example, the Seventh Circuit Court also considers whether a "certainty of hopelessness" exists regarding a debtor's financial future.[13] Some of the factors other courts have examined during the

---

Bryant Poverty Test Example

A law student graduated with $11,000 in student loan debt. He failed to pass the state bar exam five different times. Subsequently, he became certified as a substitute teacher and had a net annual income that exceeded the Federal Poverty Guidelines level for a single person by only $200. He sought to have his student loans discharged. The debtor suffered from diabetes and faced $700 in "unique" and "extraordinary" expenses for medical supplies (insulin and needles). The lender argued against discharging the loan, emphasizing that the debtor would eventually pass the bar exam and become an attorney. The court decided otherwise, believing the debtor's chances of becoming an attorney were highly unlikely.

Totality of the Circumstances Tests include: whether or not the debtor is permanently or temporarily disabled; the ratio of the student loan debt to the debtor's total indebtedness; determining if the debtor's hardship is long-term; whether or not the debtor made payments on the student loans or sought other relief such as deferment or forbearance; and other conditions. As court observer Jennifer Frattini noted, "the subjectivity inherent with this method, combined with numerous and varying factors different courts consider, can lead to unpredictable and inconsistent standards of undue hardship."[14]

The *Brunner* test
(Currently adopted and used in 2nd, 3rd, 6th, 7th, and 9th Circuit Courts. Not formally adopted, but has been used in the 5th, 10th, and 11th Circuit Courts.)

The *Brunner* test was developed in 1985 in a Second Circuit Court case of *Brunner v. New York State Higher Education Services Corp*. Maria Brunner attempted to discharge her student loans just seven months after accepting her last student loan. At the time, student loans could be discharged through a standard bankruptcy without the need for filing an adversary proceeding if more than five years passed from when the last educational loan was issued. Although she lost the case and was required to make payments on her student loans, the *Brunner Test* became the most widely used legal instrument for determining undue hardship. The *Brunner Test* was formally adopted on appeal by all courts of the Second Circuit in 1987.

In determining if *Brunner* was entitled to a debt discharge, the court explored the purpose and meaning of undue hardship. First, the court articulated the belief that student loans are different from other unsecured debt because there is little or no consideration given to the borrower's credit status. Further, student loans require no co-signers or collateral. For access to this easy money through federal loan programs, the government demands quid pro quo. In return for obtaining a government loan, students are denied access to bankruptcy and discharge of their student loans in all but the most hopeless of circumstances. The court concluded that student borrowers must decide for themselves whether the risk of future hardship outweighs the potential rewards in accepting the education loan.

To discharge student loans under the undue hardship rule as specified by *Brunner*, it must be shown: (1) that the debtor cannot maintain, based on current income and expenses, a "minimal" standard of living . . . if forced to repay the loans; (2) that additional circumstances exist indicating that this state of affairs is likely to persist for a significant portion of the repayment period of the student loans; and (3) that the debtor has made good faith efforts to repay the loans. *All three prongs must be satisfied for a student loan debt to be discharged.*

The **first prong** analyses contain two steps: (1) observe the debtor's "lifestyle attributes" to determine his or her current standard of living, and

---

The *Brunner* Test

Brunner obtained a master's degree in social work and owed $9,000 in student loan debt. Seven months after receiving her degree, she filed for bankruptcy, and her outstanding debts were discharged, but not her student loans. Prior to the hearing, she was unemployed and supported with the help of food stamps and Medicaid. She testified that she sent out over 100 resumes without any success in obtaining employment in her field of study. She was under the care of a therapist for the treatment of anxiety and depression related to her unemployment. She testified that she was capable of working.

The Court agreed that she met the first prong of the *Brunner Test,* showing that her student loan debt accounted for 80% of her total debt load and that she was on public welfare. But she failed to give any evidence indicating a total foreclosure of job prospects in her area of training and thus failed the 2nd *Brunner* Test prong. Also, she failed the 3rd *Brunner* Test prong because she filed for bankruptcy too soon after obtaining her degree, failed to make any loan repayments, and demonstrated a lack of "good faith."

Her loans were not discharged.

(2) determine if forcing the debtor to make loan repayments will prevent him or her from maintaining a minimal living standard. This standard does not require showing that making minimum loan payments would force the debtor to live at or below the poverty level but does require showing that the debtor is more than simply strapped for cash. The debtor is expected to make personal and financial sacrifices to repay the student loan. If the debtor is successful at proving the first prong, then the second prong is evaluated, otherwise, the process is stopped, and the loan is not discharged.

The **second prong** is the most difficult of the three prongs to prove. In essence, the debtor must convince the court that there is no hope for improvement in future income. The court recognized that this prong is similar to a finding of "certainty of hopelessness" accepted by other courts. However, as the *Brunner* court itself conceded, "[p]redicting future income is . . . problematic." Courts who have used the *Brunner* Test have looked for "unique" or "exceptional" circumstances that impact future employment and earnings. These circumstances include: "illness, lack of usable job skills, the existence of a large number of dependents, or a combination of [the three]."[15] The second prong takes into account any possibility that a debtor's financial situation could improve in the future, and as the Second Circuit noted on appeal, "more reliably guarantees that the hardship presented is 'undue'."[16]

The **third prong** of the test was created "in accordance with the legislative intent behind §523(a)(8) of preventing intentional abusers from filing [for] bankruptcy immediately after graduation and making no effort to find employment and to make payments on their student loans."[17] Here, the debtor must show a "good faith" effort was made to repay the loan. Factors considered by the court include, "the number of payments the debtor made, attempts to negotiate with the lender, proportion of loans to total debt, and possible abuse of the bankruptcy system."[18]

The *Brunner* Test has been adopted or used by a majority of courts. Although some courts view *Brunner* as an appropriate test for determining undue hardship, in reality, it often causes harsh consequences for debtors and fails to further the core goal of the Bankruptcy Code, which is to facilitate a "fresh start" for honest but unfortunate debtors. A number of courts have moved away from Brunner for determining undue hardship (see *Krieger* and *Roth*).

Summary

- The U.S. Constitution provides for uniform laws about bankruptcies.
- The Bankruptcy Act of 1898 had two goals:
- to provide honest, hard-working debtors with a "fresh start" in which they are free of oppressive debt
- to obtain fair and equitable treatment for debtors and creditors alike
- Student loans were initially treated as any other unsecured loan and could be discharged in Chapter 7 bankruptcy.
- §523(a)(8) of the 1998 Bankruptcy Reform Act allows student loans to be discharged only in cases of "undue hardship."
- "Undue hardship" was not defined by Congress
- courts have had to construct tests to determine when undue hardship exists
- There are 4 major tests used by most courts to determine undue hardship:
  - **Johnson Test** — 3 prongs
    - Prong 1— "Mechanical Analysis" evaluates the debtor's current and future ability to repay the loan.
    - Prong 2 — "Good Faith Analysis" requires debtors to demonstrate they made a good faith attempt to repay the loans.
    - Prong 3 — "Policy Analysis" tries to determine if the primary purpose of the bankruptcy is to discharge the loans and evaluate whether or not the debtor benefited from the education obtained through the loans.
  - **Bryant Poverty Test** was developed by the same court that created the Johnson Test and tried to make it simpler.
    - Debtors must have after-tax net incomes near the Federal Poverty

- Guidelines to be considered for discharging their loans.
  - This case established the Federal Poverty Guidelines as the criteria all courts would use to measure undue hardship.
- **Totality of the Circumstances** Test — By examining all the circumstances on a case-by-case basis, the court believed it could better balance the need to determine undue hardship as specified in Section 523(a)(8) in light of the fresh start goal delineated in the Bankruptcy Code.
  - the debtor's past, present, and reasonably reliable future financial resources
  - calculation of the debtor's and his or her dependents' reasonable living expenses
  - any other relevant facts and circumstances related to that specific case.
- ***Brunner*** **Test** — The test used by a majority of U.S. courts has three prongs.
  - Prong 1 — that the debtor cannot maintain, based on current income and expenses, a "minimal" standard of living . . . if forced to repay the loans
  - Prong 2 — that additional circumstances exist indicating that this state of affairs is likely to persist for a significant portion of the repayment period of the student loans
  - Prong 3 — that the debtor has made good faith efforts to repay the loans.
  - ***All three prongs must be satisfied for a student loan debt to be discharged.***

---

[1] See Taylor v. United Student Aid Funds, Inc. (*In re Taylor*), 223 B.R. 747, 754 (B.A.P. 9th Cir. 1998); § 523(a)(8); Brunner v. N.Y. State Higher Educ. Servs. Corp. (*In re Brunner*), 831 F.2d 395, 396 (2d Cir. 1987), aff'g 46 B.R. 752 (Bankr. S.D.N.Y. 1985).

[2] Fox v. Pa. Higher Educ. Assistance Agency (*In re Fox*), 163 B.R. 975, 978 (Bankr. M.D. Pa. 1993); See also *In re Kapinos*, 243 B.R. at 274 (stating that Congress preferred leaving the construction of undue hardship to the courts).

[3] See *In re Andersen*, 232 B.R. at 130 ("[T]he legislative history offers little to define the nature of the exception (undue hardship) to he exception (nondischargeability).")

[4] Salvin, Robert F. (1996). Student loans, bankruptcy, and the fresh start policy: Must debtors be impoverished to discharge educational loans? *Tul. L. Rev. (71)*, 149 Supra note 73, at 149.

[5] Collins, Thad. (1990). Forging middle ground: Revision of student loan debts in bankruptcy as an impetus to Amend 11 U.S.C.A. § 523(a)8. *Iowa L. Rev. (75)*, 733, 744.

[6] *In re Brunner*, 831 F.2d 395, 396 [42 E. Law Rep. [535]] (2d Cir. 1987); Douglas v. Great Lakes Higher Education Servicing Corp. (*In re Douglas*), 237 B.R. 652, 654 (Bankr. N.D. Ohio 1999).

[7] Salvin, Robert F. (1996). Student loans, bankruptcy, and the fresh start policy: Must debtors be impoverished to discharge educational loans? *Tul. L. Rev. (71)*, 149 Supra note 73, at 150.

[8] Fossey, Richard (1997). The certainty of hopelessness: Are courts too harsh toward bankrupt student loan debtors? *Journal of Law and Education, (26)*, 29, 36. According to Fossey, the term "certainty of hopelessness" is mentioned in more than 30 federal cases and has become the "unofficial standard" for granting discharges to student loans.

[9] 5 Bankr. Ct. Dec. 532 (Bankr. E.D. Pa. 1979) at 544.

[10] Bryant v. Pennsylvania Higher Education Assistance Agency, at 917.

[11] Salvin, Robert F. (1996). Student loans, bankruptcy, and the fresh start policy: Must debtors be impoverished to discharge educational loans? *Tul. L. Rev. (71)*, 149 Supra note 73, at 162.

[12] *In re Wegfehrt*, 10 B.R. 826, 830 (Bankr. N.D. Ohio 1981).

[13] See Roberson v. Ill. Student Assistance Comm'n (*In re Roberson*), 999 F.2d 1132, 1136 (7th Cir. 1993).

[14] Frattini, Jennifer. (2001). The dischargeability of student loans: An undue burden? (Note and Comment). *Bankr. Dev. J. (17)*, 537, 556 supra note 144, at 565.

[15] Briscoe v. N.Y. State Higher Educ. Servs. Corp. (*In re Brisco*), 16 B.R. 128, 131 (Bankr. S.D.N.Y. 1981) at 755.

[16] Brunner v. N.Y. State Higher Educ. Servs. Corp. (*In re Brunner*), 831 F.2d 395, 396 (2d Cir. 1987), aff'g 46 B.R. 752 (Bankr. S.D.N.Y. 1985).

[17] Frattini, Jennifer. (2001). The dischargeability of student loans: An undue burden? (Note and Comment). *Bankr. Dev. J. (17)*, 537, 556 supra note 144, at 563.

[18] United States Dept. of Educ. V. Wallace (*In re Wallace*), 259 B.R. 170, 185 (Bankr. C.D. Cal. 2000).

CHAPTER 6
"Undue Hardship" Arguments

UNBELIEVABLE

Ms. Carol Ann Race borrowed $20,000 to study theology and philosophy in the 1980s. She made $300 monthly payments for two and a half years before losing her job as a religious educator in 1994. During this time, she married and began to have children. Two of her five children are autistic, requiring her to devote full-time to working as an at-home mother.

Her husband worked as a nursing-home aid and earned $18,000 annually. The family of seven lives in Minnesota on $28,000, including government disability payments for the autistic children.

Ms. Race filed for bankruptcy in the hopes of canceling the student loans— which are the family's only debt. The bankruptcy judge ruled against her since he was sure an appellate judge would overrule him. The bankruptcy judge did not believe he could erase the debt unless it was determined that repayment of the loans would strip the family of "all that is worth living."

In the end, Ms. Race debt increased to $34,000 at 7% interest. She has been placed on an income-sensitive plan linked to the family's net income.

Hechinger, J. (January 6, 2005) U.S. Gets Tough on Failure to Repay Student Loans, *Wall Street Journal*, v.CCXLV n.4,p.1

In the previous chapter, we examined the major tests developed by the courts to determine "undue hardship" under Section 523(a)(8). Here, a general list of salient characteristics extracted from these tests is developed, then a wide range of arguments are presented that could be used to meet these characteristics. Some of the arguments are presented in greater depth as academic articles in Appendix F. *If you decide to use an article from Appendix F, **do not copy** it since courts will recognize where it comes from (this book), and this may prejudice the court. Instead, present it in your own words but use the footnotes to make it look authoritative.*

Characteristics Common to Undue Hardship Tests

The *Brunner* test is used by a majority of bankruptcy courts in the United States. It embodies much of the Johnson test. Here we review the court finding for the *Brunner*, Johnson, Bryant Poverty, and the Totality of the Circumstances Test, and summarize three broad conditions common to every test.

Every undue hardship claim is reviewed in three areas:

Characteristic A—Current Living Condition and the Impact of Repaying Loan on "Minimal Living" Standard

Characteristic B—Prospects for Repaying the Loans

Characteristic C—Good Faith and Loan Repayment

Characteristic A—Current Living Condition and the Impact of Repaying Loan on "Minimal Living" Standard

Characteristic A explores two conditions: (1) the debtor's current living condition, and (2) whether repaying the student loans will push the debtor to, or below, the poverty level.

Condition 1: Every court reviews the debtor's current living condition and evaluates it against the Social Security's Federal Poverty Guidelines. Rightly or wrongly (this is discussed at length in Chapter 8—Advocacy), debtors with incomes above poverty will be scrutinized by the courts to assure all expenses are "minimized." The court will challenge expenditures for gym or video membership, Internet service, pet expenses, child or adult care, beauty salon, and more. Expenditures will be compared to an "idealized" debtor of similar situation but at the official poverty level. Expenditures that deviate from this ideal must be explained in terms of being necessary and extraordinary (e.g., needles and insulin for debtors or dependents who are diabetic), related to finding work (e.g., need for the Internet service), or related to keeping work (e.g., buying tools required for work or a gym membership to relieve pain). (*See* Chapter 9— Preparing for the Adversary Proceeding, for details about creating a Financial Status.) Courts have typically held that the debtor need not "live in poverty in order to satisfy the first inquiry" of *Brunner*.[1] Rather, "a minimal standard of living is a measure of comfort, supported by a level of income, sufficient to pay the costs of specific items recognized by both subjective and objective criteria as basic necessities."[2] Many courts have denied undue hardship discharges in cases in which the debtor's expenses were excessive,[3] such as where the debtor lived in an "unnecessarily large" home,[4] dined too frequently in restaurants instead of cooking at home,[5] or spent money on inessential items like recreational boats.

Condition 2: Once the court is satisfied, the debtor has minimized living expenses, the court evaluates whether repaying the student loans will push the debtor down to or below the poverty level. If the debtor's net income drops below the poverty level, the debt may be discharged. Some courts have granted "partial discharges" in situations where repaying the entire loan would be too severe. Partial discharges are controversial and may not be legal under certain circumstances (*see* discussion in Chapter 8—Advocacy).

The Department of Education and courts have a long history of evaluating debtors' lifestyle against the Social Security's Federal Poverty Guidelines (formally established in the Bryant Poverty Test). We believe this is incorrect and describe our objections in the Chapter 8—Advocacy. Regardless, you must develop your personal case around this federal measure.

Characteristic B—Prospects for Repaying the Loans

Courts evaluate debtors' prospects for improved future income. Even though courts recognize that predicting future income is "problematic," it hasn't stopped the practice (this is discussed at length Chapter 8—Advocacy). In general, the debtor must show there are "additional," "unique," or "exceptional" circumstances that impact future

Strategy Tip
Account for Your Time

In so many cases, debtors make a strong showing for their situation only to have the court reject the claim and tell the debtor to get a part-time minimum-wage job and use that money to make loan payments. Regardless of how laughable or tragic this may seem, it happens frequently. Thus, the debtor needs to account for his or her time working or providing dependent care, or both. Debtors need to clearly point out to the court that asking the debtor to take on any more work would push him or her over a standard workweek, and that would be an undue hardship.

employment and earnings. Although, *In re Lorna Nys* (2006), the Bankruptcy Appellate Panel (BAP) court specifically addressed the misapplication of the word "exceptional." Instead, the court reverted to the wording found in the *Brunner* test that requires the debtor to show "additional circumstances" (note the difference between the words *exceptional* and *additional*) to prove her inability to pay in the present would likely persist for a significant portion of the loan's repayment period. To that end, the court developed a non-exhaustive list of "additional circumstances" that would qualify debtors for discharging student loans:

1. Serious mental or physical disability of the debtor or the debtor's dependents which prevents employment or advancement; *Brunner*, 831 F.2d at 396;
2. The debtor's obligations to care for dependents; Id.;
3. Lack of or severely limited education; *Pena*, 155 F.3d at 1114;
4. Poor quality of education; 9 Page 447
5. Lack of usable or marketable job skills; *Birrane*, 287 B.R. at 497;
6. Underemployment;10
7. Maximized income potential in the chosen educational field, and no other more lucrative job skills;
8. A limited number of years remaining in work-life to allow payment of the loan; *Brunner*, 831 F.2d at 396;
9. Age or other factors that prevent retraining or relocation as a means for payment of the loan;
10. Lack of assets, whether or not exempt, which could be used to pay the loan;
11. Potentially increasing expenses that outweigh any potential appreciation in the value of the debtor's assets and/or likely increases in the debtor's income;
12. Lack of better financial options elsewhere.

We divide these additional circumstances into two categories: (1) Personal Limitations and (2) Social Factors.

Category 1—Personal Limitations

Debtors need to address in detail any personal limitations that may impact the ability to obtain appropriate employment. Courts have enumerated three instances (or a combination thereof) of unique or exceptional personal circumstances and include: (a) medical limitations, (b) support of dependents (and their medical conditions, if applicable), and (c) lack of useable job skills. These need to be described in detail and with supporting documents.

(a) Medical Problems

If you have medical problems that contributed to your bankruptcy, there are three things you will want to show the court:

1. Your medical condition contributed to your bankruptcy. Here you need to give a complete history of your medical condition and subsequent loss of work and income. You need to have detailed medical records and not just your recollection.
2. The costs related to the medical condition are the primary cause of bankruptcy. Courts are often unaware of how devastating medical bills can be and how medical conditions can

---

Strategy Tip
Medical Strategy 1

The clearest and easiest way to discharge student loans is to be declared "permanently disabled." If you are declared permanently disabled due to severe medical conditions, then a disability discharge is filed, and you won't even need to go through the aggravation of an adversary proceeding. If you have a physician who will not declare you permanently disabled, look for a different physician. If necessary, find one who will declare you partially disabled and who will give documentation showing that this will last the rest of your life. Too many court cases have fallen apart at this step because it is difficult to prove the future.

push people into bankruptcy and continued poverty. Appendix F contains an article on the effect medical bill has on bankruptcy

3. Finally, that your medical condition will continue into the future, most likely become worse, and that it will be impossible to make payments on the student loans.

Most debtors make a good showing on the first two items above. The real problem is convincing the court that the medical problems will persist for at least ten years, thereby impacting the debtor's ability to make student loan payments. This is a fuzzy area in which courts are inconsistent when interpreting the law.

(b) Dependents

Courts are aware that dependents cause time constraints for debtors who otherwise could use the time for employment. Thus, the larger the number of dependents and the time involved in their care directly impacts the debtor's ability to repay student loans.

Children: Courts make the assumption that children will leave home at eighteen years of age. Thus, courts will calculate when the youngest child is expected to leave home and try to determine if the debtor would be capable of resuming payments on his or her student loans at that time. Extenuating circumstances would include a disabled child who continues to reside with the parent.

Many cases are lost because courts decide that once the children leave, the debtor can resume loan payments. This is often not true. The debtor will be ten- to thirty-years older once children leave home. Ageism becomes a real issue for debtors over fifty years of age. Thus, combining the problem of dependent children with getting older and being out of the workplace for so many years might actually work to your advantage.

Spouse, Civil Union, or Domestic Partner: Courts are sensitive to the situation where debtors provide financial and emotional support for medically ill spouses (whether by marriage, Civil Union, or Domestic Partnership). Unlike with children, there is no assumption the spouse will leave. Even still, we encourage you to combine the care of a medically ill spouse with other factors that will impact your future ability to make income.

Elderly or Medically Ill Parents or Siblings: There have been a number of cases where courts have shown themselves insensitive to debtors who take care of elderly or medically ill parents or siblings. The courts question why the debtor is taking care of these people. It may seem obvious to the debtor, but not to the court. Thus, debtors need to make a strong case as to why it is they, and not their siblings, parents, or government, who takes care of these people. If this is your situation, you may want to discuss your moral or religious convictions that have influenced you to be the caretaker of these persons. Too often, courts take the position that the debtor should not take on this responsibility and, instead, focus on paying back student loans. We encourage you to combine the care of medically ill parents or siblings with other factors that will impact your future ability to make income.

(c) Lack of Useable Job Skills

Many debtors filing bankruptcy have student loans from training programs they either did not complete, or the program was of such dubious value that the debtor gained no improved job skills. Courts have been sensitive to debtors who lack useable job skills. They are aware that without

---

> ### *Strategy Tip*
> ### **Medical Strategy 2**
>
> Let's say you are partially disabled and that it will continue into the foreseeable future but won't necessarily get worse. How do you convince the court that you will not be able to repay your loans? One approach is to combine this problem with another, e.g., ageism. Once you are over 50 years old, it becomes virtually impossible to obtain employment (*see* Appendix F). Argue with the court that your medical disability and age will preclude you from finding appropriate work in the future.

proper job skills, it is very difficult for debtors to obtain high-paying employment and, subsequently, be able to make student loan payments.

Quite the opposite problem are highly educated debtors who also find they are unable to find work. It is not

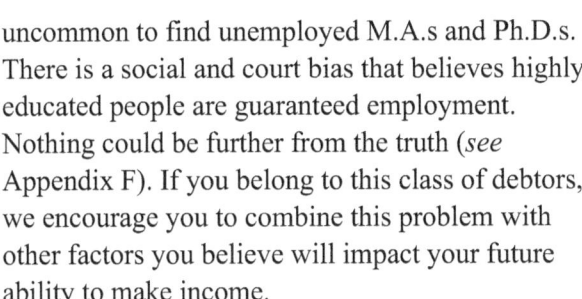

Strategy Tip
Lack of Useable Job Skills

Even though the court may agree with you that your lack of useable job skills is hurting your employment prospects, they may come back to you and ask why you don't educate yourself further to get a better job. A good answer is to explain the lack of time for furthering your education is due to the responsibilities of working and dependent care.

uncommon to find unemployed M.A.s and Ph.D.s. There is a social and court bias that believes highly educated people are guaranteed employment. Nothing could be further from the truth (*see* Appendix F). If you belong to this class of debtors, we encourage you to combine this problem with other factors you believe will impact your future ability to make income.

Category 2—External Factors Impacting Employability

Most debtors have had the challenge of showing "unique" or "exceptional" circumstances that prevent them from repaying their student loans. By focusing on unique or exceptional circumstances, courts end up evaluating personal limitations such as medical illness, dependents, or lack of useable job skills (described above). But there are also many external factors that affect employment opportunities. For example, if the economy is doing poorly, jobs are often scarce. If the debtor has been terminated from many jobs or was a whistleblower, future job interviewers may see him or her as a problem or troublemaker and not offer the job. Having a bankruptcy closes certain job opportunities. And, finally, discrimination plays a significant role in our society, placing many job environments out of reach of millions.

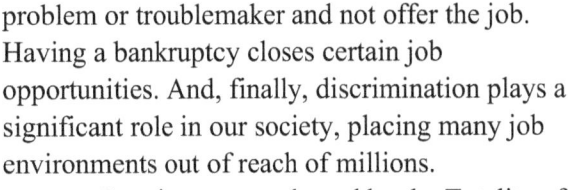

Certain cases evaluated by the Totality of the Circumstances Test have looked at some of the external factors. Courts have been hesitant to include these factors since it would require them to accept the fact that not all employment doors are open to all workers, i.e., the American dream is a myth. Let's get real. When was the last time you saw a T.V. announcer who was under 4 feet tall, or with Cerebral Palsy, or with extensive physical deformities? Our society has preferences and discriminates by age, race, ethnicity, religion, gender, sexual orientation, disability, height, weight, general attractiveness, and many more. All these factors impact a debtor's chances for employment.

There are many societal factors that impact particular debtors in their search for work. We present only a few of the major ones below:
- U.S. Economy
- Discrimination Based on Age
- Discrimination Against the Highly Educated
- Discrimination Based on Sexual Orientation
- Discrimination Based on Race, Gender, Ethnicity, Disability, Physical Characteristics, Religion, and others.
- Past Terminations or Whistleblower

We encourage you to look over some of the factors and determine if they apply to you. If so, include a discussion of them in your case. In general, we suggest that you first develop your argument with academic research of the societal problem and then make it specific with examples out of your own life story.

Can you think of other factors that are applicable to your situation?

U.S. Economy

Since the pandemic of 2020, the U.S. economy has lost millions of jobs, which impacts debtors' chances to find work. This is particularly true if the kind of work you are trained for has been subjected to "downsizing" and "outsourcing," or those that work in social settings with groups of people (like restaurant servers, sporting events, musical and art events, teachers), personal care, education, airlines, hotels, schools, and so on, you can make a strong case about the difficulty in finding work in the future. See Appendix F for an article on this topic. Combine the statistics of the article with your personal experiences to build your case.

Discrimination Based on Age

Ageism is such a problem in the United States that federal and state laws have been passed to protect workers based upon age. Every state and most major cities have departments of aging. Bottom line: as you get older it is harder to find employment. After 50-years of age, it is next to impossible to find work.

If this factor applies to you, two articles in Appendix F will help you formulate your writing. Then, make the research real by using examples from your own life. For example, if comments were made to you about your age while applying for a job, cite the details of the interview.

Discrimination Against the Highly Educated

Most educated workers can tell stories of being told he or she was "over-qualified" for a particular position. Appendix F contains an article giving the research on this problem. Personalize the research by telling your own experiences.

Discrimination Based on Sexual Orientation

If you are lesbian, gay, bisexual, transgender (LGBT), surely you have many experiences to call upon to demonstrate discrimination. Appendix F contains an article that gives empirical data proving discrimination. Cite the evidence and give your personal story detailing how sexual orientation discrimination has impacted your ability to gain employment.

Discrimination Based on Race, Gender, Ethnicity, Disability, Physical Characteristics, Religion, and other

The United States is not supportive of many classes of people. If you have direct experience with employment discrimination due to any of these factors, include them in your report to the court.

> ### Strategy Tip
> ### Combine Factors!
>
> One strategy to combat the court's belief your situation will improve in the future is to combine factors that show they will, in fact, make your situation worse in the future. This really is how life is, not how the courts want it to be. Most medical conditions worsen with time, not get better. Dependents may come and go, but all the while you were caring for them, you were getting older, and it becomes more and more difficult to obtain employment when you are old. Many forms of discrimination exist that directly impact your ability to find work. These need to be brought to the attention of the court.

Visit the government website for the Equal Employment Opportunity Commission (EEOC) at www.eeoc.gov. There are many articles and statistics showing rampant discrimination in the United States. Put together the information you need to show the court the extent of the problem, and then personalize the statistics <u>by presenting your own personal experiences</u> of discrimination. Making broad statements about discrimination will not be effective. Your story must include specific examples from your life. Emphasize how this will affect your future. If these problems are not explained to the court, they will not consider them to be important.

Reverse discrimination can also present a problem for certain debtors. See Appendix F for ideas of how to write your own case.

Past Terminations or Whistleblower

Many job applications ask if you have ever been terminated or forced to resign. Of course, this must be answered truthfully. If the later discovers that you were terminated or forced to resign, they may legally terminate you for lying on the application. That poses a problem for those who have been discriminated against. Your termination may not have been ethical or legal but placing it on the application opens you to the prying eyes of interviewers who probably will not believe or accept your answer without prejudice.

In your adversary proceeding, you will need to tell the court about the effect prior terminations or being a whistleblower has had on your job searches. If possible, use statements made by interviewers who mentioned the problem. Being viewed as a "pariah" impacts all future efforts to obtain employment.

In general, tell the court about the factors that impact your ability to obtain employment. You must emphasize how this impacts your future.

Overall, most courts require the debtor to demonstrate "exceptional," "unique," "extraordinary," "extreme," or "rare" circumstances in order to satisfy the second *Brunner* prong,[6] the Ninth Circuit has held that "'undue hardship' does not require an exceptional circumstance beyond the inability to pay now and for a substantial portion of the loan's repayment period."[7]

Characteristic C—Good Faith and Loan Repayment

Congress was most concerned with debtors who seemingly "defrauded" the government by bankrupting their student loans soon after graduation. To reinforce that concern, courts want debtors to demonstrate "good faith" attempts to repay student loans. This is shown by answering a few questions:

- Did the debtor make payments when he or she could? There is an expectation that any time the debtor's net income exceeds the Federal Poverty Guidelines, payments would be made on the student loans. It is suggested that debtors make a table showing their yearly net income and payments, if any, made on the student loans. If payments were not made, an explanation is required. Some debtors have met this expectation even when they never made any payments on the loans.

- If the debtor was in financial trouble, did he or she contact the Department of Education to arrange for restructuring the loan or delaying the payments? Debtors are expected to show diligence in maintaining their loans and keeping them out of default. Whenever there were times of financial difficulty, debtors must show that they worked with the lender to resolve the issue instead of letting loans fall in arrears.

- What is the ratio of the student loan debt to the total debt being bankrupted? If the student loans exceed approximately 50 percent of the debtor's total debt load, courts will be suspicious that the primary purpose of the bankruptcy is to discharge the student loans. In these cases, debtors must give a strong showing regarding the other common characteristics developed above.

- How soon after receiving the last student loan is the debtor trying to bankrupt the debt? Debtors who bankrupted their student loans months or days after finishing college are the ones that alarmed Congress, enough for them to pass the Bankruptcy Reform Act of 1978. Courts are still sensitive to the timing of bankruptcy filings. In general, at least five or more years should have passed since obtaining the last student loan. Otherwise, there is a presumption of fraud, which the debtor must overcome. You can use forbearances, deferments, and consolidations to drag out repaying the loans for almost a decade.

Part of the problem with the "good faith" clause is that it is of little utility in determining true undue hardship. Of course, as a matter of statutory construction, this "prong" of the *Brunner* test lacks any textual basis in the Bankruptcy Code. No place in any other part of the Bankruptcy Code does debtors need to show they made efforts to make payments on their debt. As a practical matter, requiring a debtor to clear this hurdle can condemn the student-borrower to a lifetime of burdensome debt under one or more of the creditors' long-term repayment programs.

Summary

Characteristics Common to Undue Hardship Tests

To discharge student loans, debtors must show:

- Current Living Condition and the Impact of Repaying Loan on "Minimal Living" Standard
    - Debtor's current living condition is not much above the Social Security Federal Poverty Guidelines
    - Repaying the student loan will push debtor into poverty
- Prospects for Repaying the Loans
    - Debtor is already working and/or taking care of dependents full-time
    - Debtor has <u>personal limitations</u> that impact the ability to work in the future. These may include:
        - Medical illness (of self and/or dependents)
        - Taking care of dependents
        - Lack of useable job skills
    - There are societal factors impacting the debtor's chances for future work. These include:
    - U.S. economy and lack of jobs
    - Ageism
    - Discrimination against the highly educated
    - Discrimination based on sexual orientation
    - Discrimination based on race, gender, ethnicity, disability, physical characteristics, religion, and others.
    - Past terminations and whistleblower
    - Other
- Good Faith and Loan Repayment
    - Debtor made loan payments when he or she could
    - When in financial trouble, contacted the Department of Education to arrange for restructuring the loan or delay in payments
    - Ratio of the student loan debt to the total debt being bankrupted is less than 50 percent
    - five years have passed between the time the debtor received his or her last student loan and filing bankruptcy

[1] *Zook*, 2009 WL 512436, at *4. *See also, e.g.*, Educ. Credit Mgmt. Corp. v. Waterhouse, 333 B.R. 103, 111 (W.D.N.C. 2005) ("*Brunner*'s 'minimal standard of living' does not require a debtor to live in squalor."); *McLaney*, 375 B.R. at 674 ("A 'minimal standard of living' is not such that debtors must live a life of abject poverty."); White v. U.S. Dep't of Educ. (*In re* White), 243 B.R. 498, 508 n.8 (Bankr. N.D. Ala. 1999) ("Poverty, of course, is not a prerequisite to . . . dischargeability.").

[2] *Zook*, 2009 WL 512436, at *4; Douglas v. Educ. Credit Mgmt. Corp. (*In re* Douglas), 366 B.R. 241, 252 (Bankr. M.D. Ga. 2007); Ivory v. United States (*In re* Ivory), 269 B.R. 890, 899 (Bankr. N.D. Ala. 2001).

[3] *See, e.g.*, Evans-Lambert v. Sallie Mae Servicing Corp. (*In re* Evans-Lambert), Bankr. No. 07-40014-MGD, Adv. No. 07-5001-MGD, 2008 WL 1734123, at *5 (Bankr. N.D. Ga. Mar. 25, 2008) ("The Court finds Debtor's reported $250-$295 per month expense for phone service to be above a 'minimal' standard of living."); Mandala v. Educ. Credit Mgmt. Corp. (*In re* Mandala), 310 B.R. 213, 218-19, 221-23 (Bankr. D. Kan. 2004) (denying undue hardship discharge where debtors spent "excessive" amounts of money on food, vitamins, and long-distance telephone costs); Pincus v. Graduate Loan Ctr. (*In re* Pincus), 280 B.R. 303, 311, 317-18 (Bankr. S.D.N.Y. 2002) (holding that debtor's monthly telephone, beeper, and cable expenses were "excessive" and denying undue hardship discharge).

[4] *See* Miller v. Sallie Mae (*In re* Miller), 409 B.R. 299, 320-21 (Bankr. E.D. Pa. 2009).

[5] *See* Lozada v. Educ. Credit Mgmt. Corp. (*In re* Lozada), 594 B.R. 212, 225 (Bankr. S.D.N.Y. 2018) ("A debtor is not required to abstain entirely from dining out to satisfy the first prong of the *Brunner* test, but the Plaintiff's practice of frequently dining out is problematic."); Richardson v. Educ. Credit Mgmt. Corp. (*In re* Richardson), No. 16-11197, Adv. No. 17-01014, 2018 WL 4719083, at *5 (Bankr. S.D. Ga. Sept. 28, 2018) ("Debtor's projected budget clearly includes expenses exceeding the 'minimal standard of living' contemplated by the *Brunner* test . . . Debtor's budget . . . reflects he eats out almost every day . . . ."); Gibson v. ECMC (*In re* Gibson), 428 B.R. 385, 390 (Bankr. W.D. Mich. 2010) ("The number and variety of restaurant charges . . . undercuts Ms. Gibson's testimony that she is minimizing unnecessary expenses. Eating out is a luxury, in the court's view.").

[6] *See, e.g.*, Educ. Credit Mgmt. Corp. v. Frushour (*In re* Frushour), 433 F.3d 393, 396, 401, 404 (4th Cir. 2005); *In re* Roberson, 999 F.2d 1132, 1136 (7th Cir. 1993); McLaney v. Ky. Higher Educ. Assistance Auth., 375 B.R. 666, 673 (M.D. Ala. 2007).

[7] Educ. Credit Mgmt. Corp. v. Nys (*In re* Nys), 446 F.3d 938, 941 (9th Cir. 2006). *See also* Douglas v. Educ. Credit Mgmt. Corp. (*In re* Douglas), 366 B.R. 241, 256 (Bankr. M.D. Ga. 2007) ("The debtor is *not* required to prove that her financial situation will persist due only to a serious illness, psychological problem, disability, *or other exceptional circumstance* . . . ." (emphasis added)).

CHAPTER 7
Example Court Cases With Analysis

This chapter presents forty-five examples of court cases where debtors attempted to have their student loans discharged through bankruptcy. In thirty-four of these cases, the debtor **won** a full or partial discharge of his/her student loans. In each case, the details are given, the court ruling, and brief analysis of the tactics of the case. Even if you are not planning a bankruptcy but are pursuing a Compromise or Write-Off, this chapter will help you understand the Department of Education's defense logic.

We suggest you read through each case as each one presents a different resolution. They may give you ideas for your own case. The cases are presented in chronological order to help show how courts have evolved on the topic. Those cases with a small icon of a bean person holding a flame discuss important aspects in bankruptcy law.

1987 Case: In re Courtney
(attorney-assisted and lost the discharge)
Courtney v. Gainer Bank, 79 B.R. 1004, 1010-11 (Bankr. N.D. Ind. 1987)

Details: Thirty-one-year-old male attempted to discharge through bankruptcy $2,500 in student loans which were incurred when taking courses at vocational school. The debtor did not have a high school diploma and failed to complete the vocational training program. The debtor was induced to file for bankruptcy after he received a $300,000 judgment against him attributed to a car accident for which he had no insurance. The debtor supported his wife and three young children on an annual income of $21,000. He worked intermittently, and his income fluctuated accordingly. His incomes for the four years prior to filing for bankruptcy in 1987 were $10,000, $14,600, $14,000, and $21,800, respectively. At the time of the bankruptcy, the debtor stated his monthly take-home pay at $1,200 and claimed monthly expenses of $1,545. In his expense account, he failed to quantify medical bills not covered by insurance for the treatment he received for his eye injury or for the medication his wife took to control epilepsy. He failed to list another student loan of $2,500. Also absent from the family's budget was anything for medical insurance, savings, car insurance, or entertainment. The debtor's assets included two old automobiles valued less than $500 each, a recreational vehicle valued at $3,000, $750 in household goods, and a boat valued at $750. All these assets were exempted under section 522 of the Bankruptcy Code.

Court Decision: Discharge denied. The court purported to use two prongs of the Johnson test— the mechanical and good faith tests— while rejecting the policy test. The court decided the debtor could raise money to pay the student loans if he liquidated his recreational vehicle and boat. Although these items were exempt and, thus, protected from creditors, the court believed these items were not essential and could be sold. Moreover, the court found the debtor's list of expenses not credible since, in a prior court filing, he listed his expenses at $894 a month instead of the $1,545 claimed at trial. The court decided this discrepancy amounted to fraud and that the debtor's income must be higher than listed.

Analysis: <u>This case shows the importance of the facts and figures listed in a bankruptcy matching those listed in the adversary proceeding</u>. The court, in this case, did not believe the debtor's income or expenses; they just did not add up. Furthermore, the debtor failed to include all expenses and missed listing another outstanding student loan debt. The court might not have gone after his RV or boat, but they did, demonstrating the capricious nature of courts in these kinds of legal proceedings. He also needed to make a compelling case for his family's marginal living for many years to come because of having small children and an ill wife.

1988 Case: In re Conner
(attorney-assisted and lost the discharge)
Conner v. Illinois State Scholarship Comm'n, 89 B.R. 744, 744-46 (Bankr. N.D. Ill. 1988)

Details: Ruth Conner was a fifty-one-year-old divorcee with debts of approximately $65,000, including $36,000 in student loan debt. All her debts were past due and in default. She held a managerial position in a small company where she earned $25,000 annually. She supported two children in college and received no child support from her former husband. She lived with her youngest daughter in a one-bedroom apartment and drove an eleven-year-old car. She needed glasses and dental work but delayed both because she could not afford the cost. She had been evicted from several apartments for non-payment of rent.

Court Decision: Discharge denied. Court reasoned that after her children finished college, she would be able to pay her student loans over twenty-five years using a graduated monthly payment schedule. The court ordered a four-year deferment on repayment and ordered the parties to renegotiate the loan for payments over twenty-five years.

Analysis: The court did not have evidence about the debtor's future ability to service her loan. Ms. Conner may have prevailed by showing that her income would most likely drop or be insufficient in the future. At age fifty-one, the debtor could have made a compelling case for age-related restrictions on future employment. A twenty-five-year repayment plan that did not start until her 55th birthday would last until she reached age eighty. She could have argued against any repayment plan past age sixty-five, as the taxes on the discharged portion would have been an undue hardship. See Appendix F for two articles on ageism, and Chapter 7 for discussion on the ICR.

1989 Case: In re Gravante
(represented herself and **won** the discharge)
In re Correll, 105 B.R. 302 (W.D. Bankr. Pa 1989), at 309.

Details: Jimilene Gravante took out student loans to finance training as a medical office assistant. When she enrolled, she was a single mother with two children. She did not finish the training program because one of her children became ill, and later she remarried and had two more children. Her husband was employed as a field engineer and earned a "substantial" income. There was a history of family illness that placed their finances on a tight budget. She claimed she received no benefit from the education.

Court Decision: Discharge granted. The court concluded that if she were required to pay back the student loan, the family's finances would become unstable and place all six family members on the public welfare rolls. As such, the court believed forcing Gravante to repay her student loans would violate the Bankruptcy Code's fresh start policy.

Analysis: Showing that the large family was at risk of being thrown onto the public welfare rolls convinced the court to discharge the loans.

1993 Case: In re Healey
(attorney-assisted and lost the discharge)
Healey v. Massachusetts Higher Education, 161 B.R. 389, 394 (E.D. Mich. 1993)

Details: Ms. Healey graduated in 1990 with a master's degree in education. She was unable to find full-time employment and settled for substitute teaching that paid $35-$50 per day. That summer, she took a job at McDonald's to pay the bills. Later that year, she received a full-time teaching position for the teaching year 1991-1992 that paid $1,000 per month for ten months. Renewal of her teaching contract in 1992 resulted in a $50/month raise. Her net annual income at the time of filing totaled $9,064 a year. She shared an apartment to cut expenses. She estimated her monthly expenses to total $764 for food, rent, clothing, transportation, and medical costs. Her telephone expenses included $35 a month in long-distance charges attributed to phone calls to her family that lived out of state. She claimed it was impossible for her to pay the minimum $219 a month in student loan payments.

Court Decision: Discharge denied. Court used the *Brunner* test. The court was very suspect of her expenses. They believed she was spending a "fairly sizeable amount" for a single person, but, without explanation, agreed that she was minimizing her expenses (contradictory conclusions). However, the court claimed that she failed part two of the first *Brunner* test— that the debtor must maximize his or her personal income. The court asked Ms. Healey why she did not look for work outside the teaching field. She responded that it took considerable time and money to go to college to get a teaching credential and that she really wanted to stay in the field and teach. The court did not approve of her response and concluded that she was not maximizing her personal resources. Further, the court concluded that she failed the second prong of the *Brunner* test for undue hardship. They claimed that to pass this test; the debtor is required to show "additional circumstances" indicating her state of affairs would persist for a significant portion of the repayment period. Ms. Healey failed to do so.

Analysis: Her expenses of $764 a month were not a sizeable amount, as the court claimed. What we don't know from the details of the case is the debtor's age. If she were under fifty-years-of-age, her best bet would have been to delay repaying the loans through the use of deferments or forbearances until her income improved or decreased. If her income improved, she could have serviced her loan. If it decreased, she would have had a stronger case since more time would have passed after college graduation. Finally, perhaps if she had emphatically argued that the value of the education (see Chapter 7 under Judicial Lawmaking— "Discrediting the Value of Education") should have been considered, the court may not have made the outrageous contention that she needed to look for work outside her field.

1993 Case: In re Ford

(attorney-assisted and lost the discharge)
Ford v. Tennessee Student Assistance Corp., 151 B.R. 135, 138-39 (Bankr. M.D. Tenn. 1993)

Details: Ms. Ford was a partially disabled woman in her fifties. She had co-signed on her daughter's educational loan that she (the mother) attempted to bankrupt. Ms. Ford was trained as a nurse's assistant and employed for sixteen years from 1972 until 1988 when she suffered a back injury and had to quit working. She was considered to be fifty percent disabled and received Social Security Disability payments along with food stamps and mortgage assistance from the Department of Housing and Urban Development. Her low income qualified her for free legal services through the local bar association.

Court Decision: Discharge denied. Using the Totality of the Circumstances Test, the court decided that Ms. Ford failed to maximize her income by finding appropriate part-time work. The court believed that if she had done so, she would have been able to make payments on the loans. Also, the state appellate court had previously turned down her request for unemployment compensation because she placed greater restrictions on work than were medically necessary. Finally, the student loans represented the bulk of her total unsecured debt, demonstrating that she filed the case primarily to have the student loans discharged.

Analysis: Ms. Ford could have benefited by finding a physician who would declare her permanently disabled and have the loans discharged that way. Barring that, she could have made major issues about her age and the ability to find work, and the inappropriateness of the ICR. See Appendix F for two articles on age and Chapter 7 for discussion on the ICR.

1993 Case: In re Kraft
(attorney-assisted and lost the discharge)
Kraft v. New York State Higher Educ. Servs. Corp., 161 B.R. 82, 84 (Bankr. W.D.N.Y. 1993)

Details: Kraft, a thirty-eight-year-old divorced female, attempted to have $18,000 in student loans discharged. She currently worked as a school bus driver and earned approximately $800 a month. For the previous sixteen years, she worked for a fast-food restaurant at minimum wage and raised three children. She enrolled in a trade-school program for tourism and travel management. After completing the program, she looked for work in a number of states near her immediate area. She found employment opportunities slim and discovered that she had been trained on an obsolete computer ticketing system that few travel agencies used. After eighteen months of looking for appropriate work, she accepted a job as a school bus driver, although it did not provide year-round work. She lived a frugal life, consuming only the essentials—shelter, food, and transportation. She made no allowances for clothing, health care, or health insurance. She paid $200 a month for a one-room apartment, requiring her children to live with their paternal grandparents.

Court Decision: Discharge denied. The court applied the *Brunner* test and concluded the debtor made a poor educational decision to pursue a course of study that was neither high paying nor opportunity laden. The court decided that she failed the second prong test since she could not prove she was doomed to a life of low-income jobs. Further, she failed the third prong of the test because she filed within eighteen months of accepting the final student loan. Thus, the court found no exceptional circumstances and a lack of good faith.

Analysis: The decision, in this case, shows the absurdity by some courts to punish poor debtors. Regardless, Ms. Kraft could have waited almost five years before filing for bankruptcy and delayed repaying her loans with deferments and forbearances in the meantime. Proving that she was doomed to low-paying jobs for the rest of her life is next-to-impossible at age thirty-eight. She may have been successful by aggressively attacking the legality of the bankruptcy code, as discussed in Chapter 8—Advocacy.

1993 Case: In re Myers
(attorney-assisted and lost the discharge)
Myers v. Pennsylvania Higher Education Assistance Agency, 150 B.R. 139 (Bankr. W.D. Pa. 1993).

Details: A fifty-year-old woman took out student loans to acquire a Bachelor of Science degree in Public Administration from Slippery Rock University. The woman had previously been trained and worked as a nurse. Unfortunately, she was unable to find a job in public administration and returned to nursing. Her monthly expenses included mental health treatment and telephone calls to her daughter.

Court Decision: Discharge denied. The court was not convinced that she had done enough to minimize her expenses. It is in this case where the court stated, undue hardship analysis entailed more than "mere unpleasantness" or "garden variety" hardship.

Analysis: Unfortunately, not much more is known about this case. It is often cited because of its use of the terms "mere unpleasantness" or "garden variety" to indicate the level of prejudice in the court to convince the court.

1993 Case: In re Roberson
(represented themselves and **won/lost** the discharge)
In re Roberson, 999 F.2d 1132, 1135 (7th Cir. 1993)

Details: Mr. Roberson was thirty-five years old and accumulated approximately $10,000 in student loan debt. He obtained a degree in industrial technology in 1986. He was laid off from his job at an automobile assembly plant. At the time of his bankruptcy filing, he was unemployed, occupied a one-room apartment that lacked a toilet or kitchen, and was divorced. He had child support obligations and two drunken-driving convictions.

Court Decision: Discharge granted but reversed by Seventh Circuit that reinstated the debt. The court used the *Brunner* test. According to the Seventh Circuit, Mr. Roberson failed to show a "certainty of hopelessness" in his future employment opportunities as required under the second prong test. The court stated, "Mr. Roberson has not indicated his road to recovery is obstructed by the type of barrier that would lead us to believe he will lack the ability to repay for several years." Further, the court found that it was immaterial whether he received any value from his college education.

Analysis: It is in this case that the term and measure "certainty of hopelessness" came about. It raised the level to which debtors must prove financial adversity. At age thirty-five and with a technical degree, Mr. Roberson's best bet would have been to obtain delays in repaying his loans using deferments and forbearances. After six years of deferments or forbearances, he could have refinanced (consolidated) his loans to restart the clock. Without a medical illness, it would be impossible for him to show a bleak employment future. Another approach would be to aggressively attack the validity of the bankruptcy code (see Chapter 8—Advocacy).

1994 Case: In re Cheesman
(attorney-assisted and **won** the discharge)
Cheesman v. Tennessee Student Assistance Corp., 25 F.3d 356 (6th Cir. 1994)

Details: Dallas and Margaret Cheesman filed a Chapter 7 bankruptcy in 1991. Of their approximately $30,000 in outstanding debt, $14,267 was attributed to student loans guaranteed by the Tennessee Student Assistance Corporation (TSAC). Margaret Cheesman took out approximately $5,000 in student loans and received a Bachelor of Arts in English in 1984. After a six-month grace period and five-month extension, she made two payments toward her student loan debt. She worked as a teacher's aid from 1989 to 1991 with a gross monthly salary of $651. She took maternity leave in 1991, during which her position at the school was eliminated. She began to receive unemployment compensation of $53 a week.

Dallas Cheesman earned a bachelor's degree from Austin Peay State University. He took out $3,500 in student loans in 1985 to study educational psychology. He withdrew from college in 1985 to take a second job. He made two $50 payments on his student loans. From October 1986 through October 1987, he earned a gross salary of $1,538 a month as director of Giles County Alternative School. From 1988 to 1990, he worked as a worker in a family residential treatment program for emotionally disturbed children for a gross salary of $1,632 a month. At the time of the bankruptcy filing, he worked a similar job but at the reduced pay of $1,123 a month.

In 1991, the Cheesman household had a net income of $13,720 a year. They had monthly expenses of $1,594 (or $19,128 a year) that included $100 monthly tuition to send their seven-year-old daughter to private school; they also had a fourteen-month-old son. Cheesmans explained that they sent their daughter to private school because they disapproved of corporal punishment used in public schools. The daughter also had asthma and required medical treatment. The Cheesmans owned a 1988 Chevrolet Nova worth approximately $3,000, which they made monthly payments of $350.

Court Decision: Discharge granted. Appeal court affirmed. The bankruptcy court stated that the Cheesmans were "in a downward spiral and will continue to go deeper in debt." The court recognized that the Cheesmans had a monthly deficit of approximately $400 and that there was no indication that their financial situation would improve in the foreseeable future. The bankruptcy court decided to place the case on its docket to be reviewed in eighteen months to see if the family's financial status had improved before fully discharging the student loan debt. The court held that section 105(a) [bankruptcy equitable powers] authorized the bankruptcy court to impose the eighteen-month stay.

Analysis: Delaying the final decision of this case for eighteen months through the use of equitable powers caused much controversy. The Cheesmans prevailed, but they had to take the case through appeal.

1994 Case: In re Stebbins-Hopf
(attorney-assisted and lost the discharge)
Stebbins-Hopf v. Texas Guaranteed Student Loan Corp., 176 B.R. 784, 785 (Bankr. W.D. Tex. 1994)

Details: Catherine Stebbins-Hopf suffered from arthritis, bronchitis, and nerve damage in her foot. Her daughter was epileptic, and her mother had cancer. A couple of her grandchildren were asthmatic. Debtor used her limited financial resources to help her daughter, mother, and grandchildren.

Court Decision: Discharge denied. "She intentionally chose to help her family financially even though these individuals were not legally her dependents ... Her moral obligation to family members ... does not take priority over her legal obligation to repay her educational loans," concluded the court.

Analysis: Unfortunately, not much is known about this case except that the court denied her request because she spent much of her income to help people the court did not accept as her dependents (mother and grandchildren). The lesson learned here is that debtors need to be clear that "dependents" are legal dependents as courts have difficulty understand non-traditional family arrangements.

1995 Case: In re Walcott
(attorney-assisted and lost the discharge)
Walcott v. U.S.A. Funds, Inc., 185 B.R. 721 (Bankr. E.D.N.C. 1995)

Details: Stephanie Walcott graduated with a Bachelor of Arts degree in English in 1991. She accumulated $14,000 in student loans. Upon graduation, she searched for professional positions but was told that she was under-qualified. Out of desperation, she widened her search to include salesperson, restaurant hostess, secretary, child-care provider, hotel desk clerk, and temporary worker to only be told that she was over-qualified or inexperienced. During the three-year period 1991 to 1994, she worked various minimum wage-paying jobs. These included vacuum cleaner salesperson, soliciting pledges, cleaning condominiums, stockroom clerk at J.C. Penny, distributing flyers at apartment complexes, answering the phone, and aiding a blind man– none of these jobs ever exceeded $5.50 an hour. She also took computer courses to improve her marketability. She continued to search for better jobs. She minimized her expenses by living at home with her parents. While her bankruptcy case was pending, she applied for thirty-eight more jobs and finally acquired one that paid $9.00 per hour teaching literacy classes. This was her highest salary ever.

Court Decision: Discharge denied. *Brunner* test was used. The court recognized that she had made a substantial effort to find work and minimized expenses, thus complying with the first prong of the *Brunner* test. However, the court noticed that she found a new job with an increased monthly income. They concluded that she did not demonstrate that her future prospects for employment and increased income were "hopeless" as required by the second prong of the *Brunner* test.

Analysis: Ms. Walcott made the mistake of trying to bankrupt her student loans too soon. Because only four years had gone by since graduating from college, she really had no track record for the courts to determine if she experienced more than "garden variety" hardship and the predictability of her future employment prospects. She could have used deferments and forbearances to delay the on-set of repayment.

1996 Case: In re Skaggs
(attorney-assisted and **won** the discharge)
Skaggs v. Great Lakes Higher Educ. Corp., 196 B.R. 865, 867-68 (Bankr. W.D. Okla. 1996).

Details: Mr. Skaggs owed approximately $47,000 in student loans originating from a Bachelor of Arts degree in history and a master's degree in education. He made a "vigorous and good faith effort" to find employment but resorted to working as an insurance agent for $20,000 a year. He lived with his wife and three children in a mobile home. They owned three high-mileage automobiles. The family used discount coupons extensively to purchase food, and clothing was acquired at discount stores and garage sales.

Court Decision: Discharge granted. The courts stated, "The common-sense approach to whether or not repayment of a student loan under the facts in a particular case amounts to an undue hardship is, in itself, a sufficient guide to the exercise of judicial discretion under 523(a)(8)." It is from this case we have the quote, "there are as many factors and tests which have been used to determine undue hardship as there are courts to decide the issue."

Analysis: Finally, a court that used common sense reason to treat honest debtors fairly.

1996 Case: In re Wetzel
(attorney-assisted and lost the discharge)
Wetzel v. New York State Higher Educ. Servs. Corp., 213 B.R. 220, 223 (Bankr. N.D.N.Y. 1996)

Details: Genevieve Wetzel was a fifty-four-year-old divorced woman in 1996, suffering from Meniere's disease, degenerative disc disease, and fibrocystic breast disease. She lived with her dependent nineteen-year-old autistic son in a two-bedroom apartment. She owed $17,567 in student loans— a combination of four student loans used to attend business school. After graduation, she was unable to procure employment. She landed one job only to have the position eliminated soon after being hired. Subsequently, she was able to find part-time work for only two days a week at $6.50 an hour. The job did not provide health insurance. She had difficulty finding appropriate work since she needed to stay home to take care of her son. She sought bankruptcy relief from the student loans since she claimed she could not simultaneously repay the student loans and maintain a minimal lifestyle for herself and her son.

Court Decision: Discharge denied. The court decided that she was not entitled to an undue hardship discharge of her entire student loan obligation because she failed to demonstrate "a showing of exigent or exceptional long-term circumstances which [were] beyond [her] control."

Analysis: This case is cited in many academic papers to illustrate the absolute wrong-headedness of courts in their analysis of undue hardship. At age fifty-four, she could have made a compelling case for age impact on her ability to find work. See Appendix F for two articles on age and Chapter 8— Advocacy for discussion on the ICR.

1997 Case: In re Rivers
(represented self and **won** partial discharge)
Rivers v. United Student Aid Funds, 213 B.R. 616, 620 (Bankr. S.D. Ga. 1997).

Details: Ms. Rivers earned a master's degree in social work and held a job typical for someone with her credential in that career. Her $30,000 a year salary supported her and her son in an austere lifestyle. She owed approximately $55,000 in student loans at the time of her bankruptcy filing. If she were to make payments over thirty years, the loan payment would have been $427 a month. She claimed making such payments would have prevented her from maintaining a minimal standard of living.

Court Decision: Partial discharge granted. The court used the *Brunner* test but was critical of the second prong. The court stated, "projecting income over a period of years is a very difficult undertaking for a finder of fact. Such projections rest as much on evidence of future income prospects, which in this case is scant to nonexistent, as on common sense and experience, which are both highly subjective." Further, the court referred to the equitable nature of bankruptcy and stated that a "court should not read and apply a statute in a manner which leads to an 'absurd' result." The court decided that a partial discharge was the most equitable legal path to take.

Analysis: This is an example of a lower-middle-class debtor being successful at having her student loans partially discharged. She could have challenged the court's use of a partial discharge; however, if she challenged the use of partial discharge, she could have run the risk of the court denying the discharge completely.

1997 Case: In re Innes

(attorney-assisted and **won** the discharge) *Innes v. Kansas State Univ.*, 207 B.R. 953, 957 (Bankr. D. Kan. 1997). (This case is given in detail to better understand what the courts review.)

Details: The Innes filed a Chapter 7 bankruptcy petition in 1995 but converted the case to Chapter 13 soon thereafter because they found that they would be unable to retain their two vehicles in a Chapter 7 case. They proposed a Chapter 13 plan under which they would pay $130 per month to the Chapter 13 trustee for fifty-seven months, an amount that would pay debts secured by their vehicles and their washer and dryer, and also pay their attorney's fees and the costs of administering the plan. They continued paying for their home outside the plan.

Over a number of years before the debtors filed for bankruptcy, Mr. Innes borrowed more than $45,000 in student loans towards a bachelor's degree in history. He did not finish his master's degree, thereby failing to qualify to teach history at the secondary school level. By April 2000, interest added another $17,000 to his debt, increasing his total to $61,184.68. Mrs. Innes had no legal liability on the student loans. Other than student loans, the debtors listed almost $30,000 in unsecured debts, most of which was owed on credit cards.

When they initially filed for bankruptcy, the Innes were in their mid-thirties. She worked at Walmart. Mr. Innes was unemployed for eighteen months, then got a job as a locksmith and general maintenance worker with a contractor at Fort Riley military base. Since their income varied during the early years of the Chapter 13 bankruptcy, they supplemented their income with public assistance (when they qualified) in the form of medical cards, food stamps, a school lunch program, and the Women, Infants, and Children program. Their vehicles then had 150,000 and 160,000 miles on them.

By the year 2000, Mrs. Innes had become a department manager for Walmart, earning $13.44 per hour for an annual income of $28,149. Mr. Innes earned $14.74 per hour and grossed an annual income of $30,690.32. Both figures included some overtime. Their combined annual gross income was $58,839.32, yielding a monthly gross of approximately $4,900. The debtors had no reasonable expectations of receiving anything more than cost-of-living wage increases. Both debtors' employment histories indicated they were not likely to move into substantially better-paying jobs in the foreseeable future. Mrs. Innes had a retirement fund at work that was worth about $26,000 in 1995.

The Innes had six children ranging in age from one to seventeen. A four-year-old and a fifteen-month-old were not yet in school, and the other children were in second, sixth, tenth, and eleventh grades. The Innes' combined gross income exceeded the federal Department of Health and Human Services annual income poverty guideline for a family of eight by about 100 percent. [*See Annual Update of the HHS Poverty Guidelines*, 65 Fed. Reg. 7555, 7555 (2000) (poverty level for family of eight is $28,650)]. Eligibility for some public assistance programs, for example, Kansas Legal Services, Inc., is set at 185 percent of the HHS poverty guidelines. The debtors' income was about $5,000 above this threshold. Neither of the debtors had any inheritance expectancy. One of their children worked part-time for Walmart in 1999 and earned $4,951.28 before deductions for taxes and social security. From the net, the child paid some of his expenses for clothing, auto (including gasoline), and school (except lunches). During their Chapter 13 case, the debtors paid off their vehicles, wore them out, and replaced them with used ones. Mr. Innes made a one-hundred-mile round trip to and from work every day in a 1985 Honda with 225,000 miles on it. Mrs. Innes drove a 1995 Ford Windstar that had 60,000 miles on it when they purchased it. She drove about 30,000 miles per year, mostly to and from work. The debtors were making monthly payments on the Windstar.

The Innes lived in the country to have lower house payments than they could have in town. During the Chapter 13 case, they were allowed to use part of a tax refund to help them pay to convert their garage into a third bedroom. They got permission to use a portion of another tax refund to help pay for repairs to their septic tank, which had been draining raw sewage into their yard. Nevertheless, as indicated by the testimony, their home still needed substantial repairs. They set up a method of borrowing small amounts to accomplish some repairs, and it was obvious that it would be a continuing process because they did not have the ability to pay for all the needed repairs at the same time. The debtors used much of their 1999 tax refund for a family vacation to Colorado. According to the testimony, the family rarely ate out during the vacation in order to save money. For their meals, the family economized by eating canned rather than fresh fruit and vegetables; for meat, they ate hamburger.

The family had health insurance through Mrs. Innes's job. The policy had a $1,000 deductible and a 20 percent co-pay requirement for covered services beyond that amount. The co-pay requirement appeared to set a maximum annual obligation of $4,450 with 100 percent coverage over that amount.

Of the family, only Mr. Innes had any ongoing medical problems. He has a below-the-knee amputation of his left leg and usually wore a prosthesis, although he sometimes used a wheelchair; and, a bone spur on the leg-stump that needed to be surgically removed. His prosthesis must be replaced on an irregular basis at the cost of $5,000, and its use required disposable sleeves that cost about $1,500 per year. He had been diagnosed as having bipolar disorder, for which Prozac had been prescribed.

Based on a student loan debt of $61,184.68 and an adjusted gross income of $58,856, three payment plans were considered to be available to Mr. Innes. Under the plans, he would pay: (1) $459.66 per month for thirty years; (2) $514.60 per month for a maximum of twenty-five years, with any remaining balance being discharged and treated as taxable debt forgiveness; or (3) $750.45 per month for ten years. Also possible was the graduated repayment plan for people who expect their income to steadily increase under which payments would increase every two years to a maximum of one-and-one-half times the standard repayment amount. Since Mr. Innes had no reason to expect his income to increase, he chose not to participate in this plan. The debtors' net take-home pay was $3,842.04 per month with monthly expenses totaling $4,327.47, meaning the family faced an almost $500 net underfunding each month.

Court Decision: Discharge granted. The *Brunner* test was used. Creditors took exception to the expenses listed by the debtors. In general, there was the feeling that since the Innes had a net income exceeding the Social Security's Federal Poverty Guidelines, then discretionary income should have been available to pay creditors, including the student loans. The court analyzed item-by-item and determined that the expenses were not excessive but, in fact, actually lower than expected for such a large family. The court stated, "families are not required to live at a poverty level or to obtain public assistance in order to service student loans; a modest budget without frivolous expenditures is sufficient to establish that student loans should be discharged."

The state of Kansas fought the discharge of its student loans to the Innes, claiming that they were not bound by a decision made by a federal bankruptcy court. The district court determined that when a state enters into an agreement with the U.S. Department of Education for lending money for education loans, then all the federal rules and legislation regulating the loans apply. Thus, the federal bankruptcy court had the legal power to discharge the loans even though the loans originated through the state of Kansas.

Analysis: This is an example where student loans were discharged through a Chapter 13 bankruptcy.

1998 Case: In re Lehman
(attorney-assisted and lost the discharge)
Lehman v. New York Higher Educ. Servs. Corp., 226 B.R. 805, 809 (Bankr. D. Vt. 1998).

Details: A thirty-four-year-old single male who attended Oxford University in England applied to have his student loans discharged. He had no dependents nor physical disability or illness. He taught for three years immediately after graduation at an annual income of $28,000. He quit his job to open a pottery studio. Never once did he make a payment toward his student loan debt.

Court Decision: Discharge denied. The court concluded that the debtor's conduct failed to meet the good faith (third prong) requirement of the

Brunner test.

Analysis: This case demonstrates the importance of debtors to stay in the good graces of the lender. Lehman should have made loan payments during the three years his income was $28,000 unless he had significant medical or other qualified expenses that took most of his income. He demonstrated bad faith in repaying the loans. He may have achieved a discharge if he attacked the legitimacy of the bankruptcy code itself. *See* Chapter 8—Advocacy for various arguments.

1998 Case: In re Pena

(represented themselves and **won** the discharge)
Pena v. United Student Aid Funds, 155 F.3d 1108, 1110 (9th Cir.1998).

Details: Ernest and Julie Pena filed for Chapter 7 bankruptcy in 1994. Besides other debts, the Pena's sought relief from federally guaranteed student loans used by Ernest to attend ITT Technical Institute (ITT) in Phoenix, Arizona. The student loans totaled $9,399.60. Ernest discovered the certificate he earned at ITT was useless, not accepted by other colleges, and did not lead to increased employment. He made several payments on the loan before losing his job. He ceased making payments on his student loans. Later, he found employment in the wafer fabrication room of a technology company for which he earned $22,600 per year. Ernest Pena was forty years old. Julie Pena suffered from serious mental disability (bipolar disorder) for most of her life. In 1992, she became psychotic and was hospitalized. She has never been able to hold a job for longer than six months. In August 1995, Julie received a lump-sum payment of approximately $8,000 as an award for past-due disability benefits attributed to her mental condition. The Pena's used the lump sum to buy a twenty-year-old car and to pay other bills. Julie received $378 per month in disability payments. At the time of the bankruptcy filing, the Pena's claimed a monthly income of $1,748 and monthly expenses of $1,803. The Pena's also had a nine-year-old dependent son.

Court Decision: Discharge granted and affirmed by the 9th Circuit Court. The court used the *Brunner* test and found for the Pena's. U.S.A.F. appealed, claiming that, besides other reasons, the bankruptcy court erred by considering evidence regarding the value of the IT education. The district court concluded, "We agree that consideration of educational value as a separate factor in analyzing undue hardship would improperly place too much emphasis on this evidence. However, as part of the second prong analysis, the value of Ernest's education is relevant to this future ability to pay off the student loans. The bankruptcy court did not err in considering that Ernest's income was not likely to increase as a result of his ITT education."

Analysis: The important finding of this case is that undue hardship was determined by taking into consideration Pena's present marketable skills, the extent of his education, and the prospects of increased education or skill training at his age and economic status. The debtor was not required to prove that "exceptional circumstances" existed to block improvements in their future financial status.

2002 Case: In re Goulet

(attorney-assisted and **won** the discharge)
Goulet v. Educational Credit Management Corp., 284 F.3d 773 (7th Cir. 2002).

Details: At the time of his bankruptcy filing, John P. Goulet was fifty-five years old and lived with his mother in Eau Claire, Wisconsin. He worked occasionally and helped his mother around the house. He had an eleven-year-old son for whom he did not have custody and owed $228 per month in child support. His mother did not charge him rent or lodging expenses and paid half of the child support. Goulet did not receive any form of public assistance.

Goulet graduate from high school in 1963. In 1972, he earned a bachelor's degree in history. Between 1972 and 1983, he worked various jobs, including bartending and restaurant management. In 1984, he returned to Eau Claire and worked as a life insurance agent living comfortably on $20,000 to $30,000 a year. In 1989, he was charged with insurance fraud and lost his insurance license. He was also arrested for felony cocaine possession with intent to deliver. From 1988 to 1990, he attended outpatient counseling and worked as a bouncer and bartender. From 1991 to 1995, he returned to school and completed most of the coursework for a master's in psychology. He received twenty-one student loans totaling $76,000. He failed to obtain his degree because he did not complete a statistics course. He also decided against continuing schooling toward a counseling license since it required 3,000 additional hours of post-degree experience, and he was concerned his felony conviction would prevent him from securing a state certificate needed for employment as a counselor. After quitting school, he was not hired for the counseling positions for which he applied and returned to bartending. He attempted to work in real estate but without success. He delayed making payments on his student loans through the use of forbearances. He never made a single payment on his student loans.

Goulet testified that he suffered from alcoholism for thirty-years and attended Alcoholics Anonymous, although witnesses claimed not to see a problem with his drinking. At the time of his bankruptcy filing, he earned $1,490 a year and had yearly expenses of approximately $5,904, without factoring in the student loan payments.

Court Decision: Discharge granted, but the Appeals court reversed the decision affirming that the student loans were not dischargeable. The *Brunner* test was used. The bankruptcy court accepted Goulet's contention that his age, the enormous amount of his debt, his substance and alcohol abuse, and his felony conviction created significant barriers to future, well-paying employment. As such, his ability to repay his loans was impacted. However, the circuit court concluded that Goulet's circumstances failed to rise to the level of "additional, exceptional circumstances" necessary to satisfy *Brunner*'s second prong. Further, the court noted that even if his prospects in the mental health field and insurance industry are closed, he presented no evidence to conclude that he was unemployable in other fields. As such, the court concluded that Goulet's situation did not reach the "certainty of hopelessness" required by the second prong of the *Brunner* test for undue hardship.

Analysis: The bankruptcy court was correct in its handling of this case. There is no way a fifty-five-year-old man with a twenty-year history of earning below the poverty level would be able to make a $600 a month payment on student loans. The appeals court raised the bar so that it was impossible to prevail. In retrospect, Goulet could have made a stronger case about his age impacting future employment. He could have better documented his alcoholism and related it to other medical conditions. Also, he could have argued that being placed on the ICR would create an undue burden. In his case, when the ICR plan finished up after twenty-five years, he would be eighty years old living on social security with no discretionary income. Thus, the tax liability on the loan discharge amount would be a severe burden.

2006 Case: In re Lorna Nys
(attorney-assisted and **won** the discharge)
In re Lorna Nys, 446 F.3d 938 (9th Cir. 2006).

Details: Between 1988 and 1992, Lorna Nys took out thirteen separate student loans to finance an Associate of Arts Degree in Science and Drafting Technology from the College of the Redwoods and a Bachelor of Arts Degree from Humboldt State University. In 1996, Nys began working at Humboldt State University as a drafting technician. She was employed as a Drafter II, the highest drafter position available at Humboldt State. In 2002, Nys's net gross income was about $40,000 a year. The bankruptcy judge found that this income was about as high as she could reasonably expect in Humboldt County, given her profession and educational background. The evidence also showed that Nys lived in a modest home in Fortuna, California, which was in need of extensive repairs. At the time of trial, Nys was fifty-one years old. She planned to retire at age sixty-five, and at that time, her income would drop considerably. She borrowed about $30,000 but by the time of trial, she owed about $85,000 in accumulated principal and interest. She made no payments on her loans for many years and then made payments for about a year. ECMC sued, and her wages were garnished. She tried to negotiate an income-sensitive payment plan, but ECME insisted that she pay the $14,000 initial assessment fee before being allowed on the plan. She claimed "additional circumstances" were that: (1) she was fifty-one years old (fourteen years from legal retirement age), (2) she had "maxed out" in her career, and her income was as high as it was ever going to be, (3) her house was in need of substantial repairs, and (4) she commuted daily at some distance in an old automobile with high mileage that would soon need to be replaced.

Court Decision: The bankruptcy court surprisingly ruled against Nys with convoluted logic, first stating that: "Nys is clearly incapable of repaying more than a portion of her student loans and this situation will almost certainly persist for the foreseeable future," yet it found no undue hardship because she had demonstrated no exceptional circumstances beyond the mere inability to pay." Upon appeal, the Bankruptcy Appellate Panel (BAP) reversed and remanded the bankruptcy court to reevaluate Nys's claim using the correct legal standard. Determining whether the repayment of student loans would impose an "undue hardship" on the debtor or her dependents requires the debtor to show "additional circumstances" (note the difference between the words *exceptional* and *additional*) that prove that her inability to pay in the present will likely persist for a significant portion of the loan's repayment period.

The court developed a non-exhaustive list of "additional circumstances" that would qualify debtors for discharging student loans:

1. Serious mental or physical disability of the debtor or the debtor's dependents which prevents employment or advancement; *Brunner*, 831 F.2d at 396;
2. The debtor's obligations to care for dependents; Id.;
3. Lack of or severely limited education; *Pena*, 155 F.3d at 1114;
4. Poor quality of education; 9 Page 447
5. Lack of usable or marketable job skills; *Birrane*, 287 B.R. at 497;
6. Underemployment;10
7. Maximized income potential in the chosen educational field, and no other more lucrative job skills;
8. A limited number of years remaining in work-life to allow payment of the loan; *Brunner*, 831 F.2d at 396;
9. Age or other factors that prevent retraining or relocation as a means for payment of the loan;
10. Lack of assets, whether or not exempt, which could be used to pay the loan;
11. Potentially increasing expenses that outweigh any potential appreciation in the value of the debtor's assets and/or likely increases in the debtor's income;
12. Lack of better financial options elsewhere.

Analysis: The Nys case is cited in many other bankruptcy proceedings as evidence that many bankruptcy judges are incorrectly applying the *Brunner* test. The BAP Court developed a list of "additional circumstances" under the second prong of the *Brunner* test that would qualify to determine undue hardship and that proving "exceptional circumstances" was unnecessary.

2007 Case: Mendoza v. Educational Credit

(represented self and **won** the discharge)
Christian D. MENDOZA, Chapter 7, Debtor. Christian D. Mendoza, Plaintiff, Educational Credit Management Corporation; Hemar Insurance Corporation of America, Defendants. Case No.-01-53238-MM. Adversary No. 01-5283. United States Bankruptcy Court, N.D. California. June 20, 2007

Details: Christian Mendoza owed approximately $107,000 at the time of filing for bankruptcy and adversary. Mendoza used the loans to fund his education at Tufts University School of Medicine, but it was interrupted when he suffered a severe head injury in a car accident. Although he was able to complete his second year of course work, several attempts to pass a test required to continue with his medical education proved to be unsuccessful. Further, his substantial efforts to gain admission to a different medical school were unsuccessful.

After determining that he would not be able to continue his medical education, Mendoza began to seek out ways to earn enough income to cover his living expenses and to repay his student loans. Mendoza testified that he first tried to enter the lucrative commercial real estate market. When that did not work out, he turned to his former profession as a real estate broker, soliciting and promoting various refinancing options. He had no medical insurance and, during the two previous years, had lived in a variety of rented rooms, with friends, or out of his car. The testimony of an expert witness established that Mendoza suffered from acquired attention deficit disorder (ADD) that inhibited his ability to work.

Court Decision: The court concluded that Mendoza met the first two prongs of the *Brunner* test. He used deferments and forbearances to keep his loans current and made payments as best he could thereby, satisfy the third prong. However, the DOE contested the ruling, and the case worked its way to the Ninth Circuit in 2006. Here, the court affirmed the bankruptcy court finding that Mendoza attempted "good faith" in repaying the student loans, and they were discharged.

Analysis: Mendoza's efforts to maximize his income as best he could and to make payments whenever possible outweigh any shortfall in pursuing further loan consolidation programs. Additionally, the evidence at trial demonstrates that Mendoza lived as inexpensively as possible, at times living out of his car when he could not afford housing.

2007 Case: Carnduff v. DOE
(attorney-assisted and **won** the discharge)
Carnduff v Department of Education BAP No. WW-06-1200-MoSPa (2007) United States Bankruptcy Appellate Panel of the Ninth Circuit

Details: Brett and Janeth Carnduff, both in their mid-thirties, began college in pursuit of a particular degree and later switched to other fields. Ultimately, they racked up over $350,000 in government-backed student loans [they also had almost $300,000 in private student loans that were discharged as part of the bankruptcy since they were private and not protected under §523(a)(8)]. Their combined monthly income was about $5,100; far short of what was needed to make payments of almost $4,000 a month on their student loans besides living expenses. The Government argued that Carnduff's financial difficulty was temporary: they were "fresh out of school," had not "even started repaying the debt," had "25 years of working left, both of them," and, the Government argued, it "should at least be given the benefit of looking at their earning capacity for a few years."

Court Decision: The bankruptcy court found that the Carnduff's would never be able to pay their student loan debt of over $350,000 unless one or both of them "wins the lottery." Nevertheless, without deciding whether they had made good faith efforts to repay their loans, the bankruptcy court held that it could not discharge any of their student loans because their earning capacity should improve in the future. The judgment was appealed to the Ninth Circuit court which reversed the decision and allowed the loans to be discharged through bankruptcy.

Analysis: Comment: A young married couple with over $350,000 in student loans had their debts discharged due to the impossibility of ever servicing such a large debt.

2007 Case: In re Barrett
(attorney-assisted and **won** the discharge)
In re Barrett, 487 F.3d 353 (6th Cir. 2007)

Details: Thomas Barrett filed a voluntary Chapter 7 bankruptcy petition in 2001, seeking the discharge of $302,342 in unsecured nonpriority debt. Among those claims are two student loans totaling $94,751. Barrett took on these loans while pursuing a master's degree in both Health Administration and Business Administration from Saint Louis University in 1999. Barrett had a long history of medical problems, including Hodgkin's disease, and has undergone intravenous chemotherapy treatment for over nine months. He experienced many other severe medical problems and required high doses of OxyContin. As such, he is unable to work full time; and then only on a computer pushing a mouse.

Court Decision: Bankruptcy Court for the Northern District of Ohio ordered Barrett's student loan debt discharged due to "undue hardship." Educational Credit Management Corporation (ECMC) appealed, stating that Barrett did not meet the requirements of the second and third prong of the *Brunner* test. ECMC argued that Barrett was required to provide corroborating evidence in the form of expert medical proof to establish that the circumstances underlying his inability to repay the loans would likely continue for a substantial portion of the repayment period. ECMC also contended that Barrett failed to establish that he had made a good faith effort to repay his loans considering his decision not to participate in the Income-contingent Repayment Plan.

The case was appealed to The Sixth Circuit Court of Appeals. The court was quick to dismiss ECMC's objections to Barrett's claim that his illnesses prevented him from productive work. The more interesting discussion revolved around the third prong of the Brunner test—that Barrett failed to show that he made a good faith effort to repay his student loans— because he did not enroll in the Income-contingent Repayment program (ICR). ECMC claimed, "Barrett's refusal to apply for the ICR payment option was without factual and legal justification," and that this refusal demonstrated a lack of good faith under *Brunner*. The court concluded:

> ECMC argued that Barrett's tax concerns are overblown because Barrett would only be forced to pay those taxes if he became solvent. We disagree. If ECMC's position is accepted, then Barrett is faced with the following choice: resign himself to insolvency for the rest of his life or be forced to repay a student debt that is twice its current size. Moreover, ECMC's argument overlooks the psychological effect of having a significant debt remain, *see Balaski v. Educ. Credit Mgmt. Corp. (In re Balaski)*, 280 B.R. 395, 400(Bankr.N.D. Ohio 2002) ("While defendant may believe holding debtor hostage for twenty-five years to debt and compounding interest is not an undue hardship, the court does not accept this view."); BAP op. 337 B.R. at 904 ("ECMC . . . fails to take account of the additional worry and anxiety that the debtor is likely to suffer if he is compelled to watch his debt steadily increase knowing that he does not have the ability to repay it for reasons beyond his control"), and discards the central aim of the Bankruptcy Code — to provide the debtor a fresh start

Analysis: This is an important case because the court rejected the IDR repayment plan argument of DOE, claiming that the programs inherently make it impossible to bankrupt student loans. No, for debtors in bankruptcy, these programs are not appropriate and do not invalidate the third prong of the *Brunner* test.

2009 Case: In re Scott
(attorney-assisted and **won** the discharge)
In re Scott, 417 B.R. 623 (Bankr. W.D. Wash., 2009).

Details: Robert and Sarah Scott were thirty-three and thirty-years-old, respectively, when they filed for bankruptcy. They were a married couple with two sons, ages five and two. They took out various student loans totaling $322,443 from 1998 to 2005 to pursue study at Bellevue Community College, Central Washington University, and the University of Idaho. Sarah Scott received an Associates of Arts degree from Bellevue Community College in 2002 and a Bachelor of Arts in Elementary Education, with a minor in Spanish Education, and a teaching certificate from Central Washington University in the Spring of 2003. Robert Scott received a Bachelor of Science degree, specializing in Microbiology, from Central Washington University in June 2000. Robert Scott pursued a doctorate at the University of Idaho in 2001 but did not graduate because of health problems that affected his concentration and learning ability. Subsequently, Robert began a master's program at Central Washington University from September 2002 to June 2005 but likewise did not graduate.

Court Decision: The Scotts demonstrated to the satisfaction of the court that they were earning the most that they could consider their educational levels (or lack thereof) and that they minimized household expenses. The court agreed that their inability to pay on loans would likely persist throughout a substantial portion of the loan repayment period. The court stated, "Accordingly, despite the fact that Plaintiffs are relatively young, the court finds that they will not have sufficient income to pay the loans through a substantial portion of the repayment period." Similarly, the court determined that the Scotts made good faith efforts to repay the loans through the concerted use of furloughs, forbearances, and payments. Still, the size of the loan and subsequent payments exceed the capacity of the Scotts to service the loans. After application of the *Brunner* factors, the court concluded that requiring Plaintiffs to pay any portion of the Loans would impose an undue hardship on them and their dependents.

Analysis: The importance of this decision is the court recognizing that the size of the loans and the monthly payment outstripped the ability of the household to service the loans and that the conditions of household income and expenses were not expected to change in the foreseeable future. It did not matter that the debtors were in their early thirties. Typically, young debtors have a more difficult time convincing courts that their future earning ability is compromised.

2011 Case: Johnson et al v. ECMC
(represented self and **won** the discharge)

In re: George A. Johnson and Melanie Raney-Johnson, Debtors. George A. Johnson and Melanie Raney-Johnson, Plaintiffs, v. Sallie Mae, Inc., and Educational Credit Management Corporation, Defendants, Case No. 11-23108, Adv. No. 11-6250, United States Bankruptcy Court for The District of Kansas, 2015, Bankr. LEXIS 525.

Details: George Johnson borrowed $25,000, and Melanie Raney-Johnson borrowed $20,00 in student loans. These were consolidated into one loan and with interests totaled about $83,000 at the time they filed their adversary. They were both in their mid-thirties with three young children. The parents sustained no physical or mental disabilities that prevented them from working. The children also did not suffer from any physical or mental disabilities other than one child with asthma. They owned a home with two mortgages. Melanie almost completed a degree in biology,y and George earned a bachelor's degree in sociology. At the time of filing in 2011, Melanie and George had a net monthly income of approximately $2,900 and $2,010, respectively. George soon lost his job, putting major financial strain on the family. The court calculated that at the time of trial, the family net monthly income was negative $1,797.84. The couple made payments on student loans when they both worked and delayed payment when one of them was out of work. They were very frugal with no frivolous purchases.

Court Decision: The Polleys' court adopted a less restrictive application of the *Brunner* test that did not require the debtor to demonstrate dire circumstances to discharge a student loan. The court stated, "an overly restrictive interpretation of the *Brunner* test fails to further the Bankruptcy Code's goal of providing a 'fresh start' for the honest but unfortunate debtor." The court refrained from adopting wholesale the "totality of the circumstances test" employed by the Eighth Circuit.

Analysis: The court upheld the Tenth Circuit's directive "that debtors who truly cannot afford to repay their loans may have their loans discharged." Further, courts "should base their estimation of debtor's prospects on specific articulable facts, not unfounded optimism."

2012 Case: Shaffer v. U.S. DOE
(attorney-assisted and **won** the discharge)

Shaffer v. U.S. Department of Education, 481 B.R. 15 (8th Cir. BAP 2012)

Details: Susan M. Shaffer was an unmarried woman in her mid-thirties. She had no dependents. Since her mid-teens, Shaffer has suffered from a variety of mental health issues, including eating disorders, depression, self-harm (cutting), and anxiety. These mental health issues adversely affected both her academic endeavors and her ability to maintain employment.

In 1994, debtor enrolled at the University of

Northern Iowa. At the end of the school year, she returned to Iowa City to be closer to her family. In August 1995, she enrolled at the University of Iowa. She attended that school, as either a full-time student or a part-time student, until 2002, when she received a Bachelor of Arts degree in psychology. Schaffer also attended Kirkwood Community College from time to time to obtain pre-pharmacy credits and to maintain her coverage under her parents' health insurance. In March 2007, she enrolled at the Palmer College of Chiropractic Medicine. She attended that school until June 2008. Schaffer left without completing her degree when she realized she would never be able to repay her outstanding student loans. To fund her education at these various institutions, Schaffer obtained educational loans totaling approximately $204,525, which included $57,489 she owed to the United States Department of Education, $47,900 she owed to Educational Credit Management Corporation, and $99,136 she owed to Iowa Student Loan. These figures do not include accruing interest.

After leaving the Palmer College of Chiropractic Medicine, Schaffer again returned to Iowa City to live with her mother. In November 2008, she began working in the Women's Health Clinic at the University of Iowa. In August 2009, she left that job and began working as an account receivable specialist for Precision Revenue Strategies. While there, Schaffer suffered from depression, which caused her to take two medical leaves of absence. In 2010, following her second leave of absence, Schaffer believed she would eventually be fired, so she left that job, too. While she sought another job, Schaffer met her living expenses by taking temporary jobs, cashing in her retirement funds, utilizing her disability insurance payments, and accepting contributions from other members of her family. In July 2011, she began working in the radiation oncology department at the University of Iowa. Schaffer filed a petition for relief under Chapter 7 of the bankruptcy code on April 15, 2010. The bankruptcy court approved the discharge of all loans. Iowa Student Loan appealed the decision. The appeal court sided with Schaffer and affirmed the bankruptcy court and the discharge of Schaffer's loans.

Court Decision: In its memorandum decision, the bankruptcy court carefully considered and addressed each of the foregoing factors. On appeal, Iowa Student Loan raised three issues: (1) whether the bankruptcy court erred in not separately evaluating each of its thirteen loans to determine whether each such loan imposed an undue hardship on Schaffer; (2) whether the bankruptcy court erred in finding Schaffer's income limitations were not self-imposed; and (3) whether the bankruptcy court erred in considering, without the aid of expert testimony, the effect of Schaffer's mental health issues on her ability to obtain and maintain employment. The appeal court rejected these three arguments.

Analysis: <u>The three claims by Iowa Student Loan ring hollow and smacks of harassment against Schaffer. They probably hoped she would drop the case in appeal since it takes resources poor people don't have to continue the battle.</u> Of the three arguments: (1) although the courts are to evaluate each loan separately since the issue was not brought up in the bankruptcy court by the defendant, they obviously didn't think it was important enough at that time, (2) although the Eighth Circuit Court of Appeals has held "[a] debtor is not entitled to an undue hardship discharge of student loan debts when his current income is the result of self-imposed limitations, rather than lack of job skills [.]" what does "self-imposed" mean? This argument fails for several reasons. It presupposes—with no support in the record—had Schaffer not dropped out: (a) she would have graduated; (b) she would have found employment as a chiropractor; and (c) she would have earned enough as a chiropractor to generate sufficient net income to pay off not only her current educational loan debts but also the additional educational loan debts she would have incurred in completing her degree. <u>This is hopeful thinking and wrong.</u> The court quoted Will Rogers, who said, "When you find yourself in a hole, stop digging," and Kenny Rogers, who sang, "You got to ... know when to fold 'em." The appeal court did not accept DOE's position.

2013 Case: In re Roth

(represented self and **won** the discharge)
In re Roth, 490 B.R. 908 (9th Cir. BAP 2013).

Details: Janet Roth took out thirteen federally guaranteed student loans totaling over $33,000 to fund her attendance at Mesa Community College and Arizona State University. Her employment history was checkered between low-paying jobs and unemployment. During this time, she made no voluntary payments on her loans and defaulted on three of them. For a while, DOE administratively garnished her wages. She suffered from several chronic medical conditions, including a thyroid condition, diabetes, macular degeneration, cataracts, high cholesterol, and depression. Some of her medical conditions required surgery. All of her medical ills necessitated many medical appointments, which in some instances precluded eligibility for new employment. Although hampered by her ailments, she felt that she was not totally disabled from working unless her "sight goes and ... can't read." By the time she filed for bankruptcy, she was sixty-four years old, and her student loans totaled "$95,403.

Court Decision: *Brunner's* additional requirement that a debtor show that he or she had made "good faith efforts" to repay a student loan was also of little utility in determining true undue hardship. Of course, as a matter of statutory construction, this "prong" of the test lacked any textual basis in the Bankruptcy Code. As a practical matter, requiring a debtor to clear this hurdle condemns the student-borrower to a lifetime of burdensome debt under one or more of the creditors' long-term repayment programs, some of which may span thirty-to-forty years. This aspect of the *Brunner* test also failed to account for the potentially devastating debt-forgiveness tax consequences to the debtor resulting from the "successful" completion of such a program, which was one reason that the repayment programs were not that popular with borrowers. At the lest, requiring debtors to participate in these creditor programs as a condition to obtaining a bankruptcy discharge simply meant that creditors, not bankruptcy judges, would decide which loans could be repaid and which could properly be forgiven. This was surely not what Congress intended in enacting § 523(a)(8).

Analysis: <u>The Ninth Circuit Court of Appeals concluded that Roth had complied with the *Brunner* test's third prong requiring that debtors show good faith with regard to their student loan repayment obligations, even though Roth had never made a single voluntary payment in over a period of approximately twenty years</u>. The court recommended the Ninth Circuit Court to abandon this prong of the *Brunner* test and challenged DOE reliance on IDR programs to circumvent the third prong of the *Brunner* test.

2013 Case: Krieger v. Educational Credit

(attorney-assisted and **won** the discharge)
Krieger v. Educational Credit Management Corporation, 713 F.3d 882 (6th Cir. 2013).

Details: Fifty-three-year-old Susan Krieger was destitute, and the court determined that she had an "unquestioned" right to a discharge of her $25,000 in student loans through bankruptcy. However, her largest creditor—Educational Credit Management (ECM), which acted on behalf of some federal loan guarantors—objected. The court applied the *Brunner* test and agreed that she could not pay the debt then or in the foreseeable future. She was living with her seventy-five-year-old mother in a rural community with very few job prospects. Krieger and her daughter lived on very little money provided through government programs. Krieger was too poor to search for better employment, and her decades-old car needed repairs. She also lacked internet access.

Although she applied to over two-hundred jobs in the prior decade, ECM claimed she did not try hard enough. The district judge agreed with ECM and reversed the discharge. The judge further agreed with ECM that Krieger failed the "good-faith" standard of the *Brunner* test because "she had not enrolled in a program that would have offered her a 25-year payment schedule." Krieger appealed the decision.

Court Decision: The Seventh Circuit disagreed with the district court, noting that if good faith necessitated a commitment to future efforts to repay, then "no educational loan ever could be discharged, because it is always possible to pay in the future should prospects improve." The appellate court concluded that "it is important not to allow judicial glosses, such as language in Roberson and *Brunner*, to supersede the statute itself."

The Seventh Circuit further stated that even the debtor's creditor agreed that the result of a twenty-five-year payment plan would likely be no payment as the debtor "simply cannot pay."

Analysis: DOE attempted to use the IDR plans as a "logical" attack on the third prong of the *Brunner* test making all such discharges impossible. The court rejected the logic and showed that such an approach would circumscribe any attempt to obtain an "undue hardship" and invalidate Congressional intent.

2013 Case: Hedlund v. The Educ. Res.

(attorney-assisted and **won** partial discharge)
Hedlund v. The Educ. Resources Inst., Inc. & Pa. Higher Educ. Assistance Agency, 718 F.3d 848 (9th Cir. 2013).

Details: Michael Hedlund, thirty-three years old, was a law school graduate who owed $85,000 in student loan debt. After graduating from law school, he failed the Oregon bar examination twice and planned a third attempt but missed the exam when accidentally locking his keys in his car. Making only $10/hour as an intern, he was unable to service his student loan debt. He reached out to his lenders to explore applying for the Income-contingent Repayment plan (ICR) but was unable to negotiate more lenient terms with his creditors.

Hedlund asserted that he could not pay off his student loan and filed for bankruptcy and an adversary proceeding. He sought a discharge of his student loans under 11 U.S.C. § 523(a)(8).

Court Decision: The court applied the three-prong Bruner test and determined that Hedlund met all three prongs. The bankruptcy court granted a partial discharge, but, on appeal, the district court reinstated the student loan debt in full as non-dischargeable. Specifically, the district court ruled that Hedlund did not sufficiently minimize expenses and maximize income; and failed to make an adequate effort to negotiate a repayment plan. As such, the court said he had not acted in "good faith," which is one of three prerequisites for relief under §523(a)(8). The case was appealed to the Ninth Circuit and applied *de novo* review of the bankruptcy court's good faith determination. The Ninth ruled that the original bankruptcy court's good faith finding was correct, and Hedlund received a partial discharge of his debts.

Analysis: This decision is important for a different reason. The appeals court rejected the district court reasoning, thereby reining in its power, and may offer greater freedom to bankruptcy judges to give student loan borrowers and other debtors the benefit of the doubt if they can show that they tried to pay a debt.

2013 Case: In re Wolfe

(represented self and **won** the discharge)
In Re Wolfe Case No. 8:11-BK-10760-MGW. Adv. Pro. No. 8:11-AP-638-KRM, 501 B.R. 426 (2013), Florida.

Details: Terence Wolfe filed a Chapter 7 case in 2011 at age forty-seven. More than twenty years earlier, he earned a bachelor's degree in English, *magna cum laude*, from Northeastern University. Although he attended graduate school in law, he did not finish. In the intervening twenty-one years, he held full-time employment for only thirty-five months and was terminated from all of them. He was under medication treatment for depression, anxiety, and other issues. His medical doctor testified that some of Wolfe's issues would be life-long and likely to interfere with work performance and relationships. Wolfe's mental issues made it impossible for him to hold a job. At the time of filing, Wolfe owed $131,685 in student loans. In July 2012, just months before filing for bankruptcy, the debtor reapplied for Social Security disability and was approved.

Court Decision: The Court evaluated this debtor's "undue hardship" through the *Brunner* framework. Although Wolfe was intelligent and able, from time to time, to perform at a very high level, he had been unable, for more than two decades, to maintain full-time employment for any meaningful length of time. Wolfe was living at a minimal standard of living, and it was unlikely that he will ever be able to repay these loans. Wolfe testified, credibly and in great detail, as to the origins and consequences his personality difficulties have had in his life and, in particular, in the workplace. Wolfe's work history was not contrived to support his claims for this case. Wolfe's testimony was corroborated by Dr. Pruitt and two former employers and established the presence of some combination of personality and mental disorders that were plausibly linked to his inconsistent work history. Because most of Wolfe's working years were behind him, and because Wolfe struggled to maintain a minimal standard of living, the failure to make meaningful payments on his student loans and the failure to participate in an income-contingent repayment plan were not a lack of good faith. Therefore, Wolfe met his burden to prove that excepting the student loans guaranteed by DOE would be an "undue hardship" on him.

Analysis: In the late 1980s, the *Brunner* test performed a gatekeeping function when the statute allowed an automatic discharge after only five years. Relying on comments in the legislative history, courts developed and refined the *Brunner* test to focus more on whether a debtor was gaming the system (by discharging student loan debts while looking to reap the future financial rewards from the financed education) than on the nature or extent of the undue hardship. An "overly restrictive interpretation of the *Brunner* test fails to further the Bankruptcy Code's goal of providing a 'fresh start' for the honest but unfortunate debtor." (Polleys, 356 F.3d at 1308.)

There is merit to the argument that the rigors of the *Brunner* test are no longer appropriate to curb borrower abuse from a premature discharge amidst only temporary financial distress. Further, proving future financial stress is truly impossible. For example, how does a debtor prove that financial circumstances will not improve in the future, a "future" which was five years long when the *Brunner* test was first adopted, but which may now be twenty-five years or longer? How do debtors prove that in the midst of a 'certainty of hopelessness,' they attempted to maximize their income? Lately, there have been calls for rethinking the *Brunner* test.

2014 Case: Conway v. National Collegiate

(attorney-assisted and **won** partial discharge) *Conway v National Collegiate Trust* (2014) 8th Circuit.

Details: Chelsea Conway took out fifteen student loans to earn a B.A. in Media Communications for a total of $118,000. Following a series of jobs and layoffs, she filed for bankruptcy in 2014.

Court Decision: The court determined that Conway could make monthly payments of $170.30 towards four of the loans. The remaining eleven loans were discharged. Ms. Conway's private student loan provider, National Collegiate Trust, contested the discharge and the Missouri bankruptcy court refused to discharge, citing Conway's college degree and "at least thirty years left to navigate the job market" as support for her ability to repay the loans.

On appeal, the Eighth Circuit Bankruptcy Appellate Panel overturned the bankruptcy court's decision applying a test that looked beyond the *Brunner* test to instead review the debtor's past, present, and future financial resources to determine whether the student loans presented an undue hardship (*Conway v. Nat'l Collegiate Trust (In re Conway)*, 495 B.R. 416 (B.A.P. 8th Cir. 2013)). The court found that even with her degree, she did not necessarily have the ability to make enough money to make minimum monthly payments, given that she had been laid off from previous jobs, had applied to hundreds of jobs in the interim, and was currently employed as a waitress. While the court found that Conway's disposable income was insufficient to make the full monthly payments on all fifteen loans, the panel remanded the case to the Bankruptcy Court to determine whether the debtor's disposable income could be sufficient to service the minimum monthly payment on any of the individual loans.

Analysis: While the <u>*Conway* decision may provide a more flexible test for the discharge of student loans</u>, the impact of the decision should not be overstated. The Eighth Circuit merely remanded the matter to the bankruptcy court to evaluate each loan individually, and the Eighth Circuit only includes South Dakota, North Dakota, Minnesota, Nebraska, Iowa, Missouri, and Arkansas.

2014 Case: In re Lamento
(represented self and **won** the discharge)
In re Lamento, 520 B.R. 667 (Bkrtcy. N.D. Ohio 2014).

Details: Alethea Lamento attended Notre Dame College for three years majoring in psychology. She met and married a man. That led to a tumultuous life of abuse, divorce, remarrying the same man, and divorcing him two more times, and more. The man was abusive and controlling and kept her home with the two children, out of school and out of work for extended periods of time. Each time she returned to school, she took out student loans but was never able to complete an educational program. She worked a multitude of low-paying jobs. She sought medical help for depression. By the time she filed for bankruptcy, her student loan debt was about $72,000, and she had been under-employed for three years. She often took the kids and lived with her mother since she was broke. She never made a voluntary payment on the loans and went into default. In 2013, part of her tax refund was used to make payment, and her wages were garnished. She was offered to be placed on two Income-Driven Repayment Program. She rejected the offers since she was unable to meet even her current monthly expenses. She stated in court, "With two children and no support and a part-time job, there is no way to pay the student loans under any program… I have held the same job for five years. I have no degree as I was unable to finish school due to the birth of my children and divorce…If I tried to find a place to rent, I would not be able to buy food and clothing. I am barely surviving and cannot meet even basic monthly expenses without a free roof over my head."

Court Decision: ECMC stated the only way for Alethea to show good faith would be if she agreed to forego her undue hardship lawsuit. That would mean that any debtor who decided not to participate would be subject to a *per se* finding of lack of good faith, contrary to *Barrett. See* 487 F.3d at 364 ("Although ECMC doesn't state so explicitly, its position would create a *per se* rule requiring enrollment in the ICRP to satisfy the third *Brunner* prong and thus would, in effect, eliminate the discharge of student loans for undue hardship from the Bankruptcy Code.")

The court found Alethea's reasons for declining to enter into the agreements to be credible, convincing, and offered in good faith: she could not pay anything now, and she could not pay anything in the foreseeable future, meaning that her participation in the programs would be futile. If she continued to receive raises at her current rate of twenty-five cents every four months, she would have a seventy-five cent an hour raises in the next year and another seventy-five cents in the year after that. There was no evidence that the debtor would ever be able to repay the loans on that income; it is simply conjectured to say that at some point in the future, there is a likelihood that Alethea would be able to stretch her low wage income to both provide for her family and to make payments.

Additionally, there are burdens associated with entering into these agreements. First, ECMC required a debtor to enter into new, nondischargeable loans. Alethea, would, as a result, be "trading one nondischargeable debt for another." (*Barrett,* 487 F.3d at 364.) Second, Alethea would have to supply financial information each year for the next twenty-five years so that the minimum payment could be recalculated. A debtor who is entitled to and receives a hardship discharge does not have that additional burden. And third, as in *Barrett,* "ECMC's argument overlooks the psychological effect of having a significant debt remain[.]" *Id.* at 365 n. 8. Given Alethea's desperate circumstances and her status as the proverbial honest but unfortunate debtor, she was entitled to sleep at night without these unpayable debts continuing to hang over her head for the next twenty-five years. Her debts were discharged.

Analysis: Lamento was only thirty-eight years old when the court discharged her student loans. The court agreed that she met all three-prong of the *Brunner* test even though the defendant, ECMC, argued otherwise. The most essential element to emerge from the case is the DOE argument that IDR plans automatically make student loans non-dischargeable because anyone can make a "zero-dollar" payment. The court rejected the argument. In your own adversary, do not let the DOE get away with this argument. Cite these cases.

2014 Case: Blanchard v. New Hampshire

(attorney-assisted and **won** the discharge)
Blanchard v. New Hampshire Higher Education Assistance Foundation, U. S. Bankruptcy Court District of New Hampshire, Adv. No. 13-1038-JMD, August 14, 2014.

Details: William Blanchard was forty-five years old with five children ages six to sixteen at the time of his filing for bankruptcy. Blanchard borrowed a modest amount of money to pursue a degree in nursing. He obtained a nursing degree and was successfully employed in that field. He was married and struggled to support his family for thirteen years while employed full time as a nurse. During those thirteen years, he paid what he was able on his student loans and received temporary payment relief under applicable law.

Court Decision: At the end of thirteen years of making payments on his loans and minimizing his expenses, his efforts have appeared to accomplish little beyond the passage of time, as the balance of $53,000 due on his student loans did not decrease in any material way. Under the Totality of the Circumstances, the court found that Blanchard did not have the ability to repay the loans while maintaining a minimal standard of living. Accordingly, judgment was entered for the Blanchard discharging his student loans.

Analysis: The court was reasonable to conclude that Blanchard's conditions were not really going to change for the duration of repaying the loans and that no progress would be made reducing the balance of the loans. "None of the testimony or evidence suggests that the debtor has attempted to shirk his obligations to the defendant or that the debtor has sought an easy way out. To the contrary, it appears that the debtor has attempted to repay the loans to the extent he was able, but he has been unsuccessful in substantially reducing the balance due on the loans."

2015 Case: Abney v. U.S. Dept. of Educ.

(represented himself and **won** the discharge)
Abney v. U.S. Dept. of Educ., 540 B.R. 681 (Bankr. W.D. Mo. 2015).

Details: Michael Abney incurred his student loans while attending school at Missouri Southern State University from the spring of 1994 to the fall of 1998. He incurred a total of $25,000 in student loans, which were consolidated. He did not graduate. He testified that the monthly payment at the time he left school was about $210 per month and that he defaulted early in the loan history. However, in about 2001, he brought the loans out of default by paying $1,600 and then began to make the $210 monthly payments. He had at least one deferment after 2001 but made a total of about $11,000 in payments before he defaulted again in January 2008. As of August 2015, Abney owed $37,243.28 in principal and interest on the consolidated student loans.

Court Decision: The court found that Abney proved by a preponderance of the evidence that not discharging his student loans would impose an undue hardship on him and his dependents. He maximized his earnings potential; indeed, the evidence was that he worked as much overtime as regulations permit. The court found that his future financial resources were not likely to improve significantly, and he had essentially no savings for retirement. His expenses were exceptionally modest. The court further found that, despite the fact that the child support payments would end at some point, Abney should be afforded the opportunity to buy a car and save at least something for retirement, something he would not likely be able to do if he were required to make student loan payments. Furthermore, Abney made good faith efforts to defer his obligations and to make payments under deferral agreements. And, based on the amount of other debt being discharged, he had good and sufficient reasons for filing bankruptcy apart from his student loans. In sum, Abney made every humanly possible effort to pay his child support and student loans, to the point of riding a bicycle to work and living out of his employers' trucks and homeless shelters for periods of time. In addition, the mere availability of the IBRP was of no help to Abney's current or future situation but, rather, imposed additional burdens on him. Undue hardship should not be interpreted so harshly as to prevent this debtor — who is acting in good faith to fulfill his obligations — from ever getting the fresh start that the Bankruptcy Code is intended to provide. As a result, Abney met his burden of proving that the repayment of his student loans imposed an undue hardship on him and that they should, therefore, be discharged pursuant to 11 U.S.C. § 523(a)(8).

Analysis: Comment about the IBRP: Discharge of a debt in bankruptcy is not itself a taxable event. However, the forgiveness of a student loan at the end of an Income-Based Repayment Program (IBRP) period is taxable in the same way as forgiveness of any other debt outside bankruptcy. That is, to the extent a debtor's assets exceed liabilities after the forgiveness, the forgiven debt is taxable income. While the mere possibility of tax consequences at the expiration of the twenty-five-year repayment period is not dispositive of the issue of whether the IBRP represents a viable avenue for repayment of the student loan debt, it is a factor that may and should be considered in a determination under 11 U.S.C.S. §523(a)(8) based on the facts of a particular case.

2015 Case: Acosta-Conniff v. ECMC
(represented herself and **won** the discharge)
Acosta-Conniff v. ECMC, Case No. 12-31448-WRS, 2015 Bankr. LEXIS 937 (M.D. Ala. March 25, 2015).

Details: Conniff was a forty-four-year-old single mother with two sons. She earned a Ph.D. from Auburn and taught high school in Eufaula, Alabama. At the time of filing the adversary, she owed $112,000 and had a monthly take-home pay of $2,950. Conniff could not make the $915/month student loan payment that was being demanded by ECMC and support herself and her children with a minimal standard of living. She had worked for the school district for ten years and anticipated to continue working for the same district in the foreseeable future with no significant changes in income.

Court Decision: Based upon her circumstances, Conniff could not maintain even a minimal standard of living if she were required to repay the loan. It was established that her circumstances would persist into the foreseeable future. Moreover, Conniff showed that she had made a good faith effort to repay her loan. Therefore, requiring Conniff to repay the loan would impose an undue hardship on her, and this renders the loan discharged.

Analysis: Importantly, ECMC claimed that Conniff could make such an ICR payment and ultimately satisfy her loan. Arguments such as this have been rejected both by the Eleventh Circuit and by this Court. [*Mosley*, 494 F.3d at 1327; *McLaney*, 375 B.R. at 677; *Al-Riyami v. U.S. Dept. of Educ.* (*In re Al-Riyami*), 2014 WL 2800815, *4 (Bankr. M.D. Ala. Order entered 1/6/2014) (Williams, B.J.); see also, *Bumps v. Wells Fargo Ed. Fin. Svcs.*, (*In re Bumps*), 2014 WL 185336, *3 (Bankr. M.D. Fla. Jan. 15, 2014)] (holding that the failure to enroll in an income-contingent repayment plan does not preclude a finding that the loan imposes an undue hardship). The availability of an ICR plan does not preclude the possibility of a discharge where, as here, the undue hardship requirement is met.

2015 Case: DeLaet v. National Collegiate Trust

(attorney-assisted and **won** the discharge)
DeLaet v, National Collegiate Trust, 2015, WL 850629 (Bank. D. Neb February 15, 2015).

Details: Unmarried twenty-eight-year-old, Noelle DeLaet graduated from Nebraska Wesleyan University with a Bachelor's in English in 2009. She owed $169,711 in student loans. Although employed, she did not make enough to service the student loan payments and maintain a household.

The court applied the "totality-of-the-circumstances" test. The court determined that she had made a good-faith effort over the years to find better-paying employment to no avail and that her living expenses were reasonable. NCT tried to make the argument that DeLaet's financial situation would improve after she married her fiancé, but he did not want to get married while she had this debt. The court rejected NCT's approach and declared that her debts were interfering with her personal life.

Court Decision: Ultimately, this case boiled down to the DOE's argument that, with time and a willingness to relocate, Ms. DeLaet might be able to find a better-paying job. Well, that might be true: given time and a willingness to relocate, she "might" be able to find a better-paying job – that is probably true of any employed person – but that is certainly not a reasonably reliable future financial resource. Also, what about the payments that are coming due in the meantime? The numbers are what they are – at this time, she did not have the net income to pay the loans owed to the defendants. So, the debt just kept getting larger with default interest and capitalization, and the DOE could sue her to try to collect their debts. Accordingly, the judge found that Ms. DeLaet did not have sufficient past, present, or reasonably reliable future financial resources to pay any of the loans owed to NCT or Discover. It would be an undue hardship on Ms. DeLaet to exclude those loans from her bankruptcy discharge.

Analysis: Oftentimes, <u>DOE will claim that a debtor has a future prospect for increased income to service the student loan debt. More and more courts are dismissing this perspective. In DeLaet, it was argued that her future finances would improve through marriage or moving for better job opportunities. Luckily, the court rejected both arguments.</u>

2015 Case: In Re Nightingale

(attorney-assisted and **lost** the discharge)
In Re Nightingale No. 13-10834, Adversary No. 13-02060. United States Bankruptcy Court, M.D. North Carolina, Greensboro Division. April 20, 2015.

Details: Alice Nightingale took out student loans to earn a master's degree at the University of North Carolina. She made minimum payments on the loans while receiving private disability payments. She moved from New Mexico to live with her son in Florida to reduce her expenses. She claimed that most of her food costs went to a specialized nutrition program she must adhere due to numerous physical maladies. She was not clear to the court about her medical conditions, treatment, or medications and offered no corroborating evidence. She had been through multiple cancer treatments. She began to draw on social security since she was sixty-seven years old. As such, her disability payments ceased.

Court Decision: The court applied the three-prong *Brunner* test. Nightingale made a concerted effort to minimize her living expenses. At age sixty-seven with severe medical conditions, there was a "certainty of hopelessness." Despite the unrebutted evidence of illness and disability, it was troubling to the court, and at this point insurmountable, that Nightingale did not attempt to enter into evidence corroborating materials even though at least some such evidence apparently was available to her. Due to the paradox of an impoverished debtor seeking to pay for medical examinations and testimony, the court in *Burton* refused to require expert testimony in every instance. *Id.* at 879 (quoting *Swinney v. Academic Fin. Servs. (In re Swinney),* 266 B.R. 800, 805 (Bankr.N.D.Ohio 2001). *See also Doherty v. United Student Aid Funds. Inc. (In re Doherty),* 219 B.R. 665, 669 (Bankr. W.D.N.Y. 1998) (observing that the price of medical evidence and medical testimony is often a luxury that a debtor seeking undue hardship cannot afford). This court agreed that corroborating evidence necessary to meet the burden of proof under the *Brunner* standard did not necessarily have to consist of extensive expert testimony, but the degree of corroborating evidence that was required depended upon the particular facts of each case.

Analysis: Nightingale satisfied the first and third prong of the *Brunner* test but failed to satisfy the second prong by failing to provide corroborating evidence of her disability. It was absurd for the courts to not recognize that a disabled sixty-seven-year-old woman would never be able to service her student loans. An important conclusion did come from the court. It ruled that a repayment plan of $0.00 does not *ipso facto* cause a debtor to fail to satisfy the requirement that any "repayment" will not prevent the debtor from maintaining a minimal standard of living. *See In re Nightingale,* 529 B.R. 641, 650 (Bankr. M.D.N.C. 2015). The claim by DOE that anyone can afford a zero-dollar payment has been rejected by the court.

2015 Case: Kelly v. ECMC
(attorney-assisted and **won** partial discharge)
Kelly v. ECMC, et al. ("Kelly I"), Adv. No. 2:10-ap-01681, judgment (Bankr. W.D. Wash., Jul. 18, 2011); *ECMC, et al. v. Kelly* ("Kelly II"), No. 2:11-cv-01263, order (W.D. Wash., Apr. 20, 2012); *Kelly v. Sallie Mae, et al.* ("Kelly III"), No. 12-35377, slip op. (9th Cir., Feb. 27, 2015).

Details: Kelly obtained a degree from Seattle University in political science in 1992. By the time she filed for Chapter 13 bankruptcy in March 2008 and the adversary a half year later, her total student loan debt was more than $105,000.

Court Decision: The bankruptcy court found that the debtor had satisfied all three parts of the *Brunner* test. It ruled that all but $21,706.51 of her student loan debt was dischargeable and ordered her to repay the balance in $250 monthly payments over nine years. The creditors appealed, claiming that she failed the third part of the *Brunner* test at a "good faith effort" at repayment because she failed to apply for the Public Service Loan Forgiveness (PSLF) program.

Analysis: Bankruptcy court discharged part of her student loan debt. The bankruptcy court further concluded that to the extent Kelly's expenses were excessive, a partial discharge was justified rather than the complete discharge. A district court rejected this judgment. The 9th Circuit reversed this, thereby allowing the partial discharge to occur.

2016 Case: Fern v. FedLoan
(represented self and **won** the discharge)
Fern v FedLoan Servicing, U.S. Department of Education, et al., U.S. Bankruptcy Court, Northern District of Iowa, June 22, 2016, Adversary No. 14-09027.

Details: Sara Fern obtain a number of student loans toward earning a degree to become an accounting clerk. She did not complete the program and reentered schooling to become an esthetician. After graduating, she rented space at a commercial tanning salon and began working in her field of study. Unfortunately, the business did not grow, and she was unable to support her family. She placed all student loans in deferments and forbearance, never having made a payment. Her loans totaled $27,000 at the time of filing for bankruptcy and adversary.

Court Decision: DOE challenged the bankruptcy court's determination that Fern's student loans were dischargeable based on undue hardship under 11 U.S.C. 523(a)(8). The bankruptcy appellate panel concluded that there was no error in the bankruptcy court's determination where the evidence supported the bankruptcy court's conclusion that the debtor's income had been consistent and is unlikely to improve in the future; Fern's monthly expenses were reasonable, necessary, modest and commensurate with her income; and Fern's emotional burden related to the student loan obligations, the continued accrual of interest on the loans, the negative credit effect of the loans, and the potential tax obligation when the repayment plan expires were in error, also weigh in favor of discharging the student loans for undue hardship. Accordingly, the panel affirmed the bankruptcy court's judgment.

Analysis: Comment: DOE argued that debtor should be on ICR plan and that anyone can afford $0 monthly payments. Court found that placing Plaintiff on ICR would pose an undue burden due to the mounting indebtedness over twenty to twenty-five years and her inability to repay when she reached age fifty-five or sixty (she was thirty-five-years-old at the time of filing).

2016 Case: McDowell v. ECMC

(attorney-assisted and **won** partial discharge)
McDowell v ECMC (May 2016) United States Bankruptcy Court, D. Idaho., Bankruptcy Case No. 10–40845–JDP Adv. Proceeding No. 14–08005–JDP

Details: Elizabeth McDowell obtained student loans in pursuit of degrees in social work from Idaho State University and Walla Walla University in 2005 and 2006, respectively. She borrowed roughly $56,000, but interests and penalties pushed the total to approximately $93,000. She was in dire financial debt and filed for Chapter 7 bankruptcy in 2010. A discharge was entered, and the case closed. McDowell did not attempt to include her student loans.

Three years later, McDowell, now forty-three-year-old single mother of two children, filed a motion to reopen her bankruptcy case to address the student loans. Although she worked full time as a clinical social worker, she did not make enough to support herself and other family members even when she took on additional shifts. She did change jobs and reduced hours due to her health. She often helped her adult children with their own personal expenses and sometimes borrowed money from her mother. In light of her challenging financial circumstances, the court and ECMC concluded that McDowell made some regrettable financial decisions. She was unable to make payments on the loan and negotiated with ECMC a compromise to discharge a portion of the debt. However, they were unable to come to an agreement, and they proceeded to the adversary.

Court Decision: The Code did not define undue hardship. *Educ. Credit Mgmt. Corp. v. Jorgensen (In re Jorgensen)*, 479 B.R. 79, 86 (9th Cir. BAP 2012) (citing *Educ. Credit Mgmt. Corp v. Nys (In re Nys)*, 446 F.3d 938, 944 (9th Cir.2006)). However, McDowell would struggle if a student loan must be repaid is not enough, since "the existence of the adjective 'undue' indicates that Congress viewed garden-variety hardship as an insufficient excuse for a discharge of student loans." *Rifino*, 245 F.3d at 1087.

The *Brunner* test consists of three prongs, requiring a debtor to prove: (1) the debtor cannot maintain, based on current income and expenses, a minimal standard of living if forced to repay the loans; (2) additional circumstances exist indicating that this state of affairs is likely to persist for a significant portion of the repayment period of the student loans; and (3) the debtor has made good faith efforts to repay the loans. *Brunner*, 46 B.R. 752, 756 (S.D.N.Y.1985).

The debtor bears the burden of proving all three prongs by a preponderance of the evidence. *Rifino*, 245 F.3d at 1087-1088; *Bryant v. Wells Fargo Bank (In re Bryant)*, 99.3 IBCR 118, 119 (Bankr.D.Idaho 1999). Because the three prongs are independent requirements, "[failure to prove any one precludes discharge." *Roth*, 490 B.R. at 916 (citing *Carnduff v. U.S. Dep't of Educ. (In re Carnduff)*, 367 B.R. 120, 127 (9th Cir. BAP 2007).

The second prong required the plaintiff to prove that her "present inability to pay will likely persist through a substantial portion of the loan's repayment period." *Nys*, 446 F.3d at 945

"Bankruptcy courts may exercise their equitable authority under § 105(a) to partially discharge student loans." *Jorgensen*, 479 B.R. at 86 (citing *Saxman*, 325 F.3d at 1173) "However, a bankruptcy court's discretion to grant a partial discharge is not unlimited. In each case, the bankruptcy court must find that all three prongs of the *Brunner* test were satisfied as to the portion of debt discharged." *Jorgensen*, 479 B.R. at 86. And, the debtor still bears the burden of establishing undue hardship as to any portion of the debt to be discharged. *Carnduff*, 367 B.R. at 133.

McDowell clearly demonstrated that she could not repay the full balance due on the ECMC student loan debt without an undue hardship. Based upon the facts and equities, the court concluded that a partial discharge of that debt should be entered. Accordingly, as explained above, and based upon the facts and equities, all amounts owed by plaintiff on the ECMC loan in excess of $10,000 will be excepted from discharge.

Analysis: What we get most out of this case is: (a) a previous bankruptcy can be reopened for the purpose of launching an adversary proceeding to discharge student loan debt, (b) the bankruptcy court may order a partial discharge when appropriate.

2016 Case: Murphy v. ECMC
(represented self and <u>won</u> the discharge)
Robert Murphy v ECMC (2016)

Details: Robert Murphy was sixty-three years old when he filed for bankruptcy and an adversary. He was married and lived in good health in Duxbury, Massachusetts. He has been unemployed since 2002. He last worked as president of a corporation, but in 2002, the corporation was sold, its operations were moved overseas, and Murphy's employment was terminated. He looked for work, without success, since then. He attributed his prolonged unemployment to the shrinking American manufacturing base, his age, his overqualification for some non-executive positions, and the stigma of prolonged unemployment itself.

Murphy financed — at least in part — the college education of his three now-grown children. He took out twelve loans between 2001 and 2007 in the total amount of $220,765. The loans had been consolidated and were all held by the defendant Educational Credit Management Corporation (ECMC). The balance at the time of filing was approximately $242,697.90.

Murphy's children were not responsible for repaying the loans.

Court Decision: At the outset, the judge clarified two issues. First, Murphy and ECMC disagreed about the breadth and depth of Murphy's job search. Murphy stated that he "earnestly" looked for work "at all levels from positions of president to accountant," including, unsuccessfully, for a job as a chauffeur. ECMC thought he was too focused on executive positions only.

Second, Murphy failed to participate in the William D. Ford Direct Loan Program's Income-contingent Repayment plan (ICRP) and thereby reduce or eliminate his monthly payments. *See* 34 C.F.R. § 685.209. Murphy contended it would be a "pointless exercise" to "shackle" him to the ICRP because interest would continue to accrue

At the end of the bankruptcy trial, the judge claimed the law did not support a discharge because (1) Murphy was well educated and held high-earning jobs in the past; (2) he was near, but not yet at, the retirement age; and (3) with his children grown, he was unburdened from other debt. A bankruptcy judge and district court judge ruled that Murphy failed to prove repaying the loans was an undue hardship, as required under the bankruptcy law. Murphy appealed both decisions. <u>Before the case was heard by the First Court of Appeals, ECME agreed to a complete discharge.</u>

Analysis: Murphy represented himself pro se at trial. The bankruptcy judge praised his pro se representation as "the best [he'd] seen." Tr. at 64. Four months after the U.S. First Court of Appeals heard oral arguments in the case and urged the parties to try to settle. The company signed an agreement acknowledging that Murphy's debt should be discharged because he has proven that repaying it would pose an undue hardship. As such, the settlement would preempt a decision that could establish a precedent.

<u>Why did ECME settled before the trial when they had won twice before?</u> That is not explored in the court documents, but it is thought that Murphy asked core questions about the legitimacy of the *Brunner* test that the DOE did not want to be brought up. In particular, the second prong of the *Brunner* test requires debtors to show that additional circumstances exist, indicating that this state of affairs is likely to persist for a significant portion of the repayment period of the student loans. DOE has developed a number of IDR plans that they claim, completely override the second *Brunner* prong making it impossible for any debtor to bankrupt student loans. More and more courts have seen through the fallacy. Murphy faced

it head-on. We can only speculate that DOE did not want to lose in court the primary tool they have been using against debtors, and lose in a higher court such that the decision would apply to all courts. We encourage debtors going through the adversary to challenge DOE claims about IDR plans.

2016 Case: Precht v. U.S. DOE
(represented self and **won** the discharge)

Precht v. United States Department of Education, AD PRO 15-01167-RGM (Bankr. E.D. Va. Feb. 11, 2016 (Consent Order).

Details: Richard Precht, sixty-seven years old, unmarried, with no dependent children. He became disabled in 2003 and received Social Security Disability payments. That was converted to standard social security when he reached age sixty-five. His net income of $1205.55 a month included a small federal pension. This income was garnished due to consolidated and defaulted federal student loans. He borrowed approximately $55,000, which ballooned to over $130,000 from interest and fines. He was married, widowed, and divorced a number of times, experienced multiple car accidents (one that put him in a hospital for over a year), held over one-hundred different jobs, lived in over sixty-nine different places in sixty-seven years, been through two previous bankruptcies (mostly caused by horrendous medical bills), and was never able to land a job in the field he obtained a Master's degree in Health Administration. He represented himself in court because he could not afford an attorney.

In 2014, he filed for a cancellation/forgiveness of his student loans with DOE under the Total Disability Provision (TDP). It was denied.

Court Decision: DOE initially denied Precht's filing and filed a motion to strike his complaint. Before the trial, DOE reviewed Precht's voluminous evidence and signed a stipulation agreeing to discharge his student loans.

Analysis: So often, bureaucracies operate on automatic. All complaints are initially denied forcing a formal review. Social Security Administration is notorious for initially denying all claims of disability, forcing the claimant to appeal and hearing. That typically drags out the process over multiple years. Precht was on disability for almost fifteen years before filing the adversary. DOE should have approved his application for loan cancellation/forgiveness under the TDP. Probably some office workers automatically denied his application without even reading his application and supporting evidence. It is unknown why he did not challenge this decision. This oversight spilled over into the adversary. What is learned from this case is that if you are officially permanently disabled (receiving SSDI), apply for DOE's TDP discharge. Suppose they deny your application, appeal. This should be automatic, but you are dealing with expansive bureaucracies. If you are permanently disabled, and your SSDI checks are being garnished by DOE for student loan payments, immediately file for TDP discharge.

2017 Case: In Re Murray
(attorney-assisted and **won** partial discharge)

In re Murray, 563 B.R. 52, 60 (Bankr. D. Kan. 2016), aff'd sub nom. *Educ. Credit Mgmt. Corp. v. Murray*, No. 16-2838, 2017 WL 4222980 (D. Kan. Sept. 22, 2017).

Details: Similar to the Vicki Metz case, Alan and Catherine Murray, a married couple in their late forties, borrowed $77,000 in student loans in the 1990s and made monthly payments totaling seventy percent of what they borrowed. However, many life challenges made it difficult for them to continue making payments, and the student loans exploded from interests and fines to $311,000 by 2016. They could not service the student loan debt besides personal debt. They filed bankruptcy and an adversary to discharge both sources of debt.

Court Decision: Fortunately for the Murray's, the Kansas bankruptcy judge overruled ECMC objections and provided a partial discharge of the student loan debt. ECMC proposed Murray's go onto one of the IDR payment plans. But the judge noticed that the monthly rate would amount to less than half of the monthly accruing interest. The Murray's debt would grow to over a half-million dollars over the twenty-year repayment period. And, at the end of the period, the unpaid loan would be forgiven but liable for an enormous tax bill by the IRS. The judge determined that Murray's could service their $77,000 debt but discharged all the accrued interest and service charges and prevented any more interest from being levied against the outstanding loan.

Analysis: Bankruptcy judges have the authority to issue a partial discharge of student loan debt and are challenging DOE's position on IDR plans. This judge noticed that by participating in an IDR payment plan, no payments would be made on the principal and, thus, there would be no progress made in repaying the loan, just servicing the interest. So, what's the point? The debt needed to be discharged.

2018 Case: In Re Metz

(attorney-assisted and **won** partial discharge)

Metz v. Navient Education Loan Corp and Educational Credit Management Corporation, Case No. 12-13120 Adv. No. 17-5119, 589 B.R. 750 (2018)

Details: Vicki Metz, age fifty-nine at time of trial, borrowed $16,613 in student loans to attend community college between 1989 and 1991. Metz worked as a community health worker for Sunflower Health Services, a subsidiary of Centene Management Corporation. Centene was a contractor for the State of Kansas, providing assorted services to the State concerning aging and disability services. She previously worked for the Kansas Department of Aging and Disability Services as a senior care administrator and, before that, spent nineteen years working at the Kansas Department of Transportation. Her income was never enough to cover living expenses and to service her debt. But with capitalized and accrued interest, she owed over $67,277.88.

Court Decision: Metz argued that not only could she not manage any of the payments posited by ECMC, but also that the payment plans were constantly changing, creating uncertainty about her future payment and tax liabilities. She cautioned that the discharged debt that she might recognize when her loan is eventually forgiven might potentially bury her in another non-dischargeable obligation in the form of unpaid or unpayable income taxes, thwarting whatever fresh start she may gain by completing her Chapter 13 plan.

The judge disagreed with Met'sz arguments about the confusion created by the ever-changing repayment plans as a reason to discharge her loans completely. ECMC claimed that Metz's budget would allow her to pay "something" on her debt. The judge believed that "something" should have a meaningful positive effect on her financial situation. In other words, she should be able to reduce the debt — not simply service it. The court determined that her earning power would likely remain static and, when she reached retirement age, it would diminish. Her payments had mostly come through a succession of three Chapter 13 plans. She did not participate in the income-based payment programs offered by the Department of Education. The court concluded that she could afford to repay the principal balance of the loan within a reasonable time, but she could not hope to repay the capitalized interest and the new interest that would accrue on her student loan debt. Requiring her to remain liable for those consequences would be an undue hardship. Therefore, the principal balance of the claim, $16,613.73, is excepted from discharge, but the remainder of the debt was declared discharged.

Analysis: Again, DOE keeps pushing IDR plans as the panacea to all debtors who cannot service their student loan debt. Luckily, the judge in Metz rejected that idea and required payments made on student loans to have an impact on paying down the principal, not just service an ever-increasing debt. In Metz's case, if she had accepted MCEC's IBRP, she would have paid about $200 a month for twenty-five years. Unfortunately, that was about $300 less than the amount necessary to pay the accruing interest. As such, after making minimal payments for twenty-five years, at age eighty-four, Metz's loan balance would be $152,277.88—nine times more than she borrowed.

2020 Case: Bukovics v. ECMC
(represented self and **won** the discharge)
Bukovics v. Educational Credit Management Corporation, 612 B.R. 174 (Bankr. N.D. 2020).

Details: Laurina Bukovics, forty-eight years old, borrowed $20,000 in the late 1980s to earn her undergraduate degree from the University of Wisconsin. Over the years, she paid back $29,000 toward the student loan balance. DOE gave her ten deferments or forbearances, but of course, the interest continued to accrue until she owed $80,000--four times more than what she initially borrowed. She experienced decades of inconsistent employment and periods of unemployment. Still, she applied for over 200 jobs over a sixteen-month period without success. She defaulted on her loans in 1992.

Court Decision: She filed for Chapter 7 bankruptcy relief in 2015, but she did not receive a discharge because she failed to submit her *Certification About a Financial Management Course*. She did not include her student loans in the initial filing. While she was in bankruptcy, she lost her job and was living at a friend's condominium and receiving food stamps and medical care through Medicaid.

Two years later, she reopened her bankruptcy case pro se and, this time, filed an adversary proceeding to address the student loan debt. Her motion to reopen her bankruptcy case was granted, and subsequently the consumer debt totaling $145,484 was discharged.

The judge applied the *Brunner* test in her adversary proceeding. Initially, the judge determined that she failed the first two prongs of the *Brunner* test, and a Judgement Order was entered in favor of DOE. Bukovics moved to alter and amend the judgment and findings of fact with new evidence. The judgment was reopened. The court still felt that she had not met the second prong. Bukovics provided further evidence concerning her attempts to seek employment. That satisfied the court, and her student loan debt was discharged. Interestingly, the judge cited the *Krieger* decision out of the Seventh Circuit and the recent *Rosenberg* case out of the Southern District of New York.

Analysis: The original *Brunner* test, as adopted by the Seventh Circuit, required applying a "certainty of hopelessness" standard, which has since been heavily applied to the second prong. (*Roberson,* 999 F.2d at 1135.) This strict standard has been heavily criticized by many courts as overtaking the language of the statute itself. [*See e.g. In re Rosenberg,* 610 B.R. 454, 459 (Bankr. S.D.N.Y. 2020) (criticizing the "certainty of hopelessness" standard as dicta that have overtaken the language of the *Brunner* test).] Recently, Seventh Circuit has softened the harsh standard. In *Krieger v. Educ. Credit Mgmt. Corp.,* the Seventh Circuit noted that "[boiling] the three criteria [of the *Brunner* test] down to `certainty of hopelessness' ... sounds more restrictive than the statutory `undue hardship' [requirement]." 713 F.3d 882, 885 (7th Cir. 2013). In that case, the Seventh Circuit clarified that "[i]t is important not to allow judicial glosses, such as the language in *Roberson* and *Brunner,* to supersede the statute itself." *Id.* at 884. Replacing the statutory requirement with a harsher standard would only obstruct the "fresh start" purpose of the discharge provided by the Bankruptcy Code to the honest but unfortunate debtor.

In *Krieger,* the Seventh Circuit affirmed the bankruptcy court's holding that the debtor was eligible for a discharge of her student loans based on the debtor's extensive job search, her difficulty in obtaining employment, and on the fact that "there is no reason to think that a brighter future is in store" in light of her sparse work history.

What we learn with Bukovics is that a bankruptcy may be reopened to add in student loans and file an adversary. That much of the past interpretation of the *Brunner* test has been incorrect and a misinterpretation of "undue hardship."

2020 Case: In Re Rosenberg
(represented self and **won** the discharge)
In re Rosenberg, Case No. 18-35379 (Bankr. S.D.N.Y. Jan. 7, 2020)

Details: Kevin Rosenberg earned an undergraduate degree from the University of Arizona and a Juris Doctor degree from Yeshiva University's Benjamin N. Cardozo School of Law in 2004. He borrowed and consolidated $116,464 in student loans. The debt grew to $221,385 by the time he filed for bankruptcy in 2019. The facts of the case were agreed upon by both Rosenberg and ECMC.

Court Decision: Before considering the merits of the case, U.S. Bankruptcy Chief Judge Cecelia Morris of the Southern District of New York gave an analysis of the *Brunner* test and its misapplication. She claimed that many of the "harsh results" came from the interpretations of *Brunner* rather than by applying *Brunner* itself. She stated, "over the past 32 years, many cases have pinned on *Brunner* punitive standards that are not contained therein."

She cited the "infamous and oft-cited term 'certainty of hopelessness'" in connection with a debtor's ability to repay student loan debt did not originate with the *Brunner* case. Instead, the term came from a case six years earlier (quoting *Briscoe v. Bank of New York (In re Briscoe)*, 16 B.R. 128, 131-32 (Bankr. S.D.N.Y. 1981). Unfortunately, the "certainty of hopelessness" phrase became adopted by other bankruptcy courts as a requirement under the second prong. She stated the phrase has been "applied and reapplied so frequently in the context of *Brunner*" that it has "subsumed the actual language of the *Brunner* test," and "become a quasi-standard of mythic proportions so much so that most people (bankruptcy professionals as well as lay individuals) believe it impossible to discharge student loans."

Similarly, she felt the third prong of *Brunner* had also become warped over time, such that "some courts have even called it 'bad faith' when someone struggling with repaying a student loan attempts to discharge that debt in bankruptcy court."

To right these wrongs, Morris applied her insight to the Rosenberg case.

Rosenberg had negative income at the time of filing. He was also, at the time, in default on his student loans, and the entire $219,000 balance had been accelerated and was currently due and payable in full. Thus, he satisfied the first prong of the *Brunner* test since he had no money available to pay his student loan debt in full and maintain a "minimal" standard of living.

The second prong asks if Rosenberg's current affairs were likely to persist for a significant portion of the repayment period as per contract. In Rosenberg's case, his loans were in default, which automatically changed the conditions of the loan, making the due in full immediately. As such, the repayment period for the loan had ended, and Rosenberg was unable to make payment. Consequently, Rosenberg easily satisfied the second prong.

Reviewing Rosenberg's payment history, he either kept his loans in deferment or forbearance and made about forty percent of the payments due while not being deferred. As such, the court concluded that Rosenberg had made a good faith effort to repay his student loans, thereby satisfying the third prong of the *Brunner* test.

Analysis: This is a very important decision. As of this writing, ECMC has since sought and obtained leave to appeal the interlocutory portion of the order denying its summary judgment motion. In its notice of appeal, ECMC has indicated its election to have the U.S. District Court, rather than the Bankruptcy Appellate Panel, hear the appeal.

No wonder DOE wants this case overturned. The judge attempted to scrape the crud that has built up around the adversary process. At the same time Judge Morris issued the judgment, she issued General Order M-536 adopting the "Student Loan Mediation Before Litigation Program Procedures" (SLM program), a "uniform, comprehensive, court-supervised student loan mediation program" intended to "facilitate consensual resolutions of student loan issues for the benefit of debtors and lenders." While the SLM program is not mandatory, and neither debtors nor lenders can be compelled to participate, the adoption of this new resource suggests that relief for struggling student loan borrowers may become less of an "impossibility."

Finally, the tactic that infuriated ECMC the most was Judge Morris's interpretation of the second prong. It is not known if any other adversary proceeding has ever noticed this approach. Once a loan goes into default, the entire amount becomes due payable immediately. The repayment period is over. Thus, if the loan were to last ten years (like the standard repayment plans) or twenty to twenty-five years (like the income-sensitive repayment plans), the time for repayment under default is eliminated, and the full loan becomes due immediately. The second prong states that "this state of affairs is likely to <u>persist for a significant portion of the repayment period of the student loans." Since filing for bankruptcy indicates that the debtor is in dire financial straits and it has lasted during the repayment period (now over), the second prong is satisfied</u>. This means that anyone filing an adversary who cannot maintain a minimal standard of living **and** has defaulted on his/her student loans will automatically meet the requirements of the second prong. This interpretation will put all student loans that are in default into play for bankruptcy consideration. This is something DOE dreads.

Summary

In each of the cases described above, there are insights to be made.

1987 Case: In re Courtney— (lost) Important that the facts and figures listed in the bankruptcy match those listed in the adversary proceeding.

1988 Case: In re Conner— (lost) The court often makes erroneous assumptions about the debtor's future income prospects for repaying the loan.

1989 Case: In re Gravante— (represented self and **won**) The court concluded that if she were required to pay back the student loan, the family's finances would become unstable and place all six family members on the public welfare rolls

1993 Case: In re Healey— (lost) Court claimed her expenses seemed excessive and that she needed to look harder for work outside her field of study.

1993 Case: In re Ford— (lost) Court did not accept that debtor was partially disabled and did not take her age into consideration. Her student loans accounted for most of the debt she tried to bankrupt.

1993 Case: In re Kraft— (lost) Court blamed the debtor for choosing a course of study that was neither high paying nor opportunity laden; thus doomed to a life of low-paying jobs. Also, she filed too soon—within eighteen months of receiving her last student loan.

1993 Case: In re Myers— (lost) Court was not convinced that she had done enough to minimize her expenses. It is in this case that the court stated, undue hardship analysis entailed more than "mere unpleasantness" or "garden variety" hardship. This demonstrates that courts were going beyond the law and turning the *Brunner* test into a moral crusade.

1993 Case: In re Roberson— (represented self and **won** then lost) The bankruptcy court agreed with the discharge but was overruled by the Seventh Circuit court as DOE pressed for a stricter interpretation of the *Brunner* test. It is from this case the term "certainty of hopelessness" was coined and subsequently influenced future courts, making it nearly impossible to bankrupt student loans.

1994 Case: In re Cheesman— (**won**) Court granted the discharge but wanted to review it eighteen months later to see if their financial situation improved. Delaying the final decision of this case for eighteen months through the use of equitable powers caused much controversy since it violates the bankruptcy process. The Cheesmans prevailed, but they had to take the case through appeal.

1994 Case: In re Stebbins-Hopf— (lost) The court denied her request because they believed she helped people the court did not accept as her dependents (mother and grandchildren). The lesson learned here is that debtors need to be clear that "dependents" are legal dependents as courts have difficulty understanding non-traditional family arrangements.

1995 Case: In re Walcott— (lost) The court concluded that she did not demonstrate that her future prospects for employment and increased income were "hopeless" as they believed the second prong of the *Brunner* test required.

1996 Case: In re Skaggs— (**won**) The court stated: "there are as many factors and tests which have been used to determine undue hardship as there are courts to decide the issue."

1996 Case: In re Wetzel— (lost) This case is cited in many academic papers to illustrate the absolute wrong-headedness of courts in their analysis of undue hardship.

1997 Case: In re Rivers— (represented self and **won** partial discharge) Courts have the right to offer a partial discharge (DOE often claims that bankruptcy courts do not have that right). Also, the court challenged the second prong of the Brunner test: "projecting income over a period of years is a very difficult undertaking for a finder of fact. Such projections rest as much on evidence of future income prospects, which in this case is scant to nonexistent, as on common sense and experience, which are both highly subjective."

1997 Case: In re Innes— (**won**) The court stated: "families are not required to live at a poverty level or to obtain public assistance in order to service student loans; a modest budget without frivolous expenditures is sufficient to establish that student loans should be discharged." This case also established that the federal bankruptcy court had the legal power to discharge the loans even though the loans originated through the state.

1998 Case: In re Lehman— (lost) This case demonstrates the importance of debtors to stay in the good graces of the lender. When a debtor has difficulty making payments, contact the lenders to, at least, establish a paper trail of being diligent. Lehman failed to do so and, as such, failed the third prong of the *Brunner* test by displaying "bad faith."

1998 Case: In re Pena— (represented self and **won**) The debtor was not required to prove that "exceptional circumstances" existed to block improvements in their future financial status.

2002 Case: In re Goulet— (**won** then lost) The Circuit court overturned the bankruptcy discharge claiming that "additional, exceptional circumstances" were necessary to satisfy *Brunner*'s second prong. Interestingly, the word "exceptional" was never in the original *Brunner* case. This is an example of courts making it more and more difficult to discharge student loans through bankruptcy when that was never the intent of Congress.

2006 Case: In re Lorna Nys— (**won**) The Circuit court chastised the bankruptcy court for changing the conditions of the *Brunner* second prong to require "exceptional circumstances beyond the mere inability to pay." To clarify the situation, the Circuit court developed a list of "additional circumstances" (as stated in *Brunner*; note the difference between the words *exceptional* and *additional*) to prove an inability to pay.

2007 Case: Mendoza v. Educational Credit— (represented self and **won**) Efforts to maximize his income as best he could and to make payments whenever possible outweigh any shortfall in pursuing further loan consolidation programs.

2007 Case: Carnduff v. DOE— (**won**) A young married couple with over $350,000 in student loans had their debts discharged due to the impossibility of ever servicing such a large debt.

2007 Case: In re Barrett— (**won**) The court rejected DOE claim that IDR plans automatically disqualifies debtors from mounting a successful adversary proceeding. These plans are not appropriate for debtors in bankruptcy.

2009 Case: In re Scott— (**won**) The court recognized that the size of the loans and the monthly payment outstripped the ability of the household to service the loans regardless that the debtors were young with decades of employment ahead of them.

2011 Case: Johnson et al v. ECMC— (**won**) The court adopted a less restrictive application of the *Brunner* test that did not require debtor to demonstrate dire circumstances to discharge a student loan. The court stated, "an overly restrictive interpretation of the *Brunner* test fails to further the Bankruptcy Code's goal of providing a 'fresh start' for the honest but unfortunate debtor." The court refrained from adopting wholesale the "totality of the circumstances test" employed by the Eighth Circuit. Further, courts "should base their estimation of debtor's prospects on specific articulable facts, not unfounded optimism."

2012 Case: Shaffer v. U.S. DOE— (won) The Circuit court found the bankruptcy court to be engaging in "hopeful" thinking when contesting the second prong of the *Brunner* test, i.e., the ability to predict future earnings.

2013 Case: In re Roth— (won) This important case brought out two issues: (1) the attempt by DOE to push IDR plans as a "cure" to the *Brunner* second prong is misguided and deceptive; (2) the third prong of the *Brunner* test requiring "good faith efforts" to repay a student loan as no textual basis in the Bankruptcy Code and makes no sense for debtors who are struggling to make payments. In the Roth case, he never made a payment over twenty years, yet the court agreed that he satisfied the third prong. The Ninth Circuit court suggested both the second and third prong of the *Brunner* test be eliminated.

2013 Case: Krieger v. Educational Credit— (won) DOE attempted to use the IDR plans as a "logical" attack on the third prong of the *Brunner* test making all such discharges impossible. The court rejected the logic and showed that such an approach would circumscribe any attempt to obtain an "undue hardship" and invalidate Congressional intent.

2013 Case: Hedlund v. The Educ. Res— (won partial discharge) The results affirm that bankruptcy courts may issue partial discharges. Also, the appeals court rejected the district court reasoning, thereby reining in its power; and may offer greater freedom to bankruptcy judges to give student loan borrowers and other debtors the benefit of the doubt if they can show that they tried to pay a debt.

2013 Case: In re Wolfe— (won) An "overly restrictive interpretation of the *Brunner* test fails to further the Bankruptcy Code's goal of providing a 'fresh start' for the honest but unfortunate debtor." There is merit to the argument that the rigors of the *Brunner* test are no longer appropriate to curb borrower abuse from a premature discharge amidst only temporary financial distress. Further, proving future financial stress is truly impossible.

2014 Case: Conway v. National Collegiate— (won partial discharge) The Eighth Circuit Bankruptcy Appellate Panel asked that the bankruptcy court looks beyond the *Brunner* test to instead review the debtor's past, present, and future financials in a more holistic way.

2014 Case: In re Lamento— (won) ECMC stated the only way for the debtor to show good faith would be if she agreed to forego her undue hardship lawsuit. The court rejected that approach saying, "Although ECMC doesn't state so explicitly, its position would create a *per se* rule requiring enrollment in the ICRP to satisfy the third *Brunner* prong and thus would, in effect, eliminate the discharge of student loans for undue hardship from the Bankruptcy Code."

2014 Case: Blanchard v. New Hampshire— (won) The court was reasonable to conclude that Blanchard's conditions were not really going to change for the duration of repaying the loans and that no progress would be made reducing the balance of the loans.

2015 Case: Abney v. U.S. Dept. of Educ— (won) Another successful challenge to the IDR plans. Discharge of a debt in bankruptcy is not itself a taxable event. However, the forgiveness of a student loan at the end of an Income-Based Repayment Program (IBRP) period is taxable in the same way as forgiveness of any other debt outside bankruptcy. That is, to the extent a debtor's assets exceed liabilities after the forgiveness, the forgiven debt is taxable income. While the mere possibility of tax consequences at the expiration of the twenty-five-year repayment period is not dispositive of the issue of whether the IBRP represents a viable avenue for repayment of the student loan debt, it is a factor that may and should be considered in a determination under 11 U.S.C.S. § 523(a)(8) based on the facts of a particular case.

2015 Case: Acosta-Conniff v. ECMC—(won) Importantly, ECMC claimed that Conniff could make such an ICR payment and ultimately satisfy her loan. Arguments such as this have been rejected both by the Eleventh Circuit and by this Court. [*Mosley*, 494 F.3d at 1327; *McLaney*, 375 B.R. at 677; *Al-Riyami v. U.S. Dept. of Educ.* (*In re Al-Riyami*), 2014 WL 2800815, *4 (Bankr. M.D. Ala. Order entered 1/6/2014)(Williams, B.J.); see also, *Bumps v. Wells Fargo Ed. Fin. Svcs.*, (*In re Bumps*), 2014 WL 185336, *3 (Bankr. M.D. Fla. Jan. 15, 2014)] (holding that the failure to enroll in an income-contingent repayment plan does not preclude a finding that the loan imposes an undue hardship). The availability of an ICR plan does not preclude the possibility of a discharge where, as here, the undue hardship requirement is met.

2015 Case: DeLaet v. National Collegiate—(won) Oftentimes, DOE will claim that a debtor has a future prospect for increased income to service the student loan debt. More and more courts are dismissing this perspective.

2015 Case: In Re Nightingale— (lost) Nightingale failed to provide evidence of her medical disabilities. An important conclusion did come from the court. It ruled that a repayment plan of $0.00 does not *ipso facto* cause a debtor to fail to satisfy the requirement that any "repayment" will not prevent the debtor from maintaining a minimal standard of living.

2015 Case: Kelly v. ECMC—(won partial discharge) Bankruptcy court discharged part of her student loan debt.

2016 Case: Fern v. FedLoan—(won) Comment: DOE argued that debtor should be on ICR plan and that anyone can afford $0 monthly payments. Court found that placing plaintiff on ICR would pose an undue burden due to the mounting indebtedness over twenty to twenty-five years and her inability to repay when she reached age fifty-five or sixty (she was thirty-five-years-old at the time of filing).

2016 Case: McDowell v. ECMC—(won partial discharge) Able to reopen previous bankruptcy filing to add in the student loans and file an adversary proceeding. The bankruptcy court can award a partial discharge.

2016 Case: Murphy v. ECMC—(won) Debtor represented himself, and the judge commented that it was the best *pro se* representation that he had seen. Although he was denied the discharge by the bankruptcy court, during the appeal process, ECMC agreed to discharge the entire amount. It is thought that DOE does not want a high court decision to shoot down the IDR plans as they vocally claim such plans negate the second and third prong of the *Brunner* test.

2016 Case: Precht v. U.S. DOE—(won) Debtor was disabled receiving SSDI payments, yet DOE and bankruptcy court first ignore the status. If you are officially permanently disabled (receiving SSDI), apply for DOE's TDP discharge. Suppose they deny your application, appeal. This should be automatic, but you are dealing with expansive bureaucracies. If you are permanently disabled, and your SSDI checks are being garnished by DOE for student loan payments, immediately file for TDP discharge.

2017 Case: In Re Murray—(won partial discharge) ECMC proposed the Murray's go onto one of the IDR plans. But the judge noticed that the monthly rate would amount to less than half of the monthly accruing interest. The Murray's debt would grow to over a half-million dollars over the twenty-year repayment period. And, at the end of the period, the unpaid loan would be forgiven but liable for an enormous tax bill by the IRS.

2018 Case: In Re Metz—(won partial discharge) DOE keeps pushing IDR plans as the panacea to all debtors who cannot service their student loan debt. Luckily, the judge in Metz rejected that idea and required payments made on student loans to have an impact on paying down the principal, not just service an ever-increasing debt.

2020 Case: Bukovics v. ECMC—(won) Reopened bankruptcy and included student loans. Even though she initially failed the first and second prong of the *Brunner* test, the judge allowed her to amend her documents to satisfy the deficit. As such, she was awarded a partial discharge. Further, much of the past interpretation of the *Brunner* test has been incorrect and a misinterpretation of "undue hardship."

2020 Case: In re Rosenberg— (**won** but pending) This is a very important case that could change the entire landscape surrounding student loans and bankruptcy. DOE is so concerned about this case that they have asked that it be transferred from the Bankruptcy appellate panel to the U.S. District Court. Please see the write-up of this case in the previous page.

CHAPTER 8
Advocacy

United States Code Chapter 11, §523(a)(8) as specified in the 1998 Bankruptcy Reform Act is bad law. The language specifying "undue hardship" is vague, misleading, and unworkable. As seen in previous chapters, court interpretations of the Act have led to a virtual block to anyone seeking relief from student loan debt. Congress did not intend that to happen.

The Department of Education has extreme power over debt collection, and its employees and attorneys often abuse this power. The Department may seize or garnish part of a borrower's paycheck, social security benefits, or tax refund without a court order. Only the IRS has as much power to collect on debts; such power is difficult to moderate.

Often the Department of Education threatens borrowers instead of counseling them on their rights to debt reorganizing or having debt discharged. Many consumer credit organizations have tracked and reported such abuses. For example, as stated in an earlier chapter, *persons who are supported through certain government benefit programs (disability, SSI, etc.), cannot be*

Disability Check Garnished to Pay Loans!

When Clay S., thirty-nine years old, returned from the hospital after a lengthy stay to combat a viral infection related to AIDS, he received a distressing phone call from a private collection agency acting on behalf of the U.S. Department of Education. They demanded that he pay $69 a month on a long-forgotten student loan. The bill collector claimed that if he did not make the payment, a larger sum of $189 per month would be taken from his Social Security disability checks.

Mr. S took out $3,700 in student loans twenty years ago to attend community college in Hot Springs, Arkansas. He did not complete school since he had to go to work to support himself. For the next twenty years, he worked many jobs, including as a clerk in a hospital, a toy-store manager, bartender, and blackjack dealer, never earning more than $7 per hour.

He was diagnosed with AIDS about ten years earlier and completely depended upon Social Security disability checks for his income. He is 6 feet 2 inches tall but weighs only 106 pounds. Rubber bands help hold a ring on his finger. He cannot hold a job and takes sixteen pills a day to stay alive. He shares an apartment to help reduce rental costs.

His monthly income from Social Security was $696. His monthly expenses included $225 to pay for an old car he used primarily to drive to a medical clinic located many miles away in the next major city. The bill collector suggested he get rid of the car to make student loan payments!

His loans could be discharged if his doctor declared him permanently disabled. But, for some reason, his doctor would not sign the forms.

Early in 2005, Mr. S's Social Security disability check rose to $785 per month. He immediately received a letter from the Department of Education saying it had directed the Treasury Department to make automatic deductions from his disability checks toward his delinquent loan. The letter said the government was permitted to take up to 15% of his check, providing the monthly benefit did not fall below $750.

Hechinger, J. (January 6, 2005) U.S. Gets Tough on Failure to Repay Student Loans, *Wall Street Journal*, v. CCXLV n.4, p.1

forced to repay government debt (including student loans). Yet, there are continued reports of the Department of Education going after borrowers with such loans. These kinds of debts are legally uncollectible, but have not stopped the Department of Education from making harassing phone calls, sending threatening letters, or attaching disability checks. These are abusive collection methods that need to stop!

Similarly, the Department of Education has been overly aggressive in defending against bankruptcy challenges. The law allows discharge in cases of "undue hardship." Because of aggressive tactics by Department attorneys, the courts have interpreted this to mean "certainty of hopelessness." *This is not what Congress intended.* The Department of Education is to blame for the development of the four major court tests and the resultant harsh court decisions.

Many consumer groups have called upon the Department of Education to stop abusing its power and give accurate information to debtors. Most legal experts and writers on the topic of §523(a)(8) agree that it needs to be rescinded or overturned and replaced with a law that better balances the needs to keep the student loan program viable while at the same time allowing honest debtors a fresh start. You can be part of this process by advocating changes to the law through your own bankruptcy and adversary proceeding.

Rate of Success at Discharging Student Loans Through Bankruptcy

How many people each year are successful at having their student loans discharged under the 1998 Bankruptcy Reform Act? Unfortunately, the Department of Education keeps no statistics on this topic. It is unknown how many people file an adversary proceeding as part of their Chapter 7 Bankruptcy. Nor is it known the outcome of those proceedings. In a 2009 study of 115 bankruptcy filings in the Western District of Washington, 57 percent of those who filed adversary proceedings seeking discharge of their student loans were able to get some or all of their loans discharged.[1]

From informal conversations the author of this book had with attorneys at the Department of Education, they estimated that less than 200 people nationwide file adversary proceedings each year. A handful of debtors, maybe one hundred, are successful at winning their cases and have their student loan debt discharged. This is amazing, considering approximately 1.6 million people filed for bankruptcy each year during the economic downturn of 2008-2009. A similar number is expected for the coming years due to the Covid-19 pandemic, and almost half of them have student loan debts.

Academic researchers Rafael Pardo and Michelle Lacey (2005) found that "More than half (57%) (of student loan debtors who filed an adversary proceeding were). . . granted some form of relief (through bankruptcy)."[2] And this research was done before the advent of this book. Just imagine how many more people are successfully discharging their student loans through bankruptcy!

In a more recent study that covered all bankruptcy districts in the United States, Jason Iuliano, J.D. Harvard Law School and Ph.D. student in Politics, Princeton University, found that 40% of those who sought discharge through the adversary proceeding were successful. Also, he found that there was no greater success in having an attorney

---

Strategy Tip
<u>Mediation is Where You Win</u>

You will learn in the Step-By-Step chapters that mediation and negotiation are where student loans can be rewritten or forgiven. We believe many adversary proceedings are resolved this way. It is unknown how many people succeed at bankrupting their student loans through mediation or negotiation, but it is definitely more than those who go all the way to trial. For example, the author of this book was successful at bankrupting 90% of his student loans during the mediation process.

represent the debtor versus those who represented themselves. Importantly, less than 0.1% of those with student loans who entered into bankruptcy attempted to also bankrupt their student loan, meaning that 99.9% of debtors did not try.[3]

What is missing from all these studies is an analysis of cases that never make it to trial. Chuck Stewart, the author of the book, is such a case. He settled with the Department of Education for 10% of the total—i.e., pay $50/m for ten years. As such, his case is not counted in these studies. It is estimated that half of all adversary proceedings do not enter into trial. The DOE would rather come to some agreement rather than potentially lose a case in court that would affect all future cases. Regardless, if academic research says 60% or 40% of adversary proceedings are successful (and I believe the real number is 80-90% when you take in all cases that are settled out of court), <u>the important thing is to file</u>. It costs nothing to file. I believe if just 10% of those who could file were to do so, the system would collapse. DOE simply does not have enough attorneys to handle that many cases. That would force Congress to take action and alleviate the bad law.

Which brings us to the point of this chapter—we believe that it will strengthen your case to include arguments asking the court to mitigate or overturn 11 U.S.C.A. §523(a)(8). This is a long shot at best. Most judges are cautious and do not want to establish legal precedent. However, if your judge agrees with your arguments and repeals or overturns §523(a)(8), then your student loans will be treated as any other unsecured debt and be discharged as part of your Chapter 7 Bankruptcy. In one fell swoop, the debt will be discharged without having to go through the rigors of the court tests described in previous chapters. And you will be helping thousands more honest debtors who deserve to have their student loans discharged as part of their Chapter 7 Bankruptcy.

The Step-By-Step plan given later in this book asks you not only to advocate overturning §523(a)(8) but also to fully prepare arguments for the various court tests. This way, you will be ready for the intense scrutiny of the court.

Challenges to 11 U.S.C.A. §523(a)(8)

Chapter 11, Section 523(a)(8) of the 1998 U.S.C.A. Bankruptcy Reform Act should be rescinded. Some of the arguments against the law are discussed below.

The Law Is, and Was, Unnecessary

As discussed in earlier chapters, "a few serious abuses of the bankruptcy laws by debtors with large amounts of educational loans, few other debts, and well-paying jobs, who filed bankruptcy shortly after leaving school and before any loans became due, generated the movement for an exception to discharge."[4] Until 1978, student loans were processed through bankruptcy courts the same as any other unsecured debt.

How threatening was student bankruptcy to the educational loan program? In 1976, the General Accounting Office (GAO) was directed to conduct a study to "determine how bad the abuse, if any, there was so that"[5] Congress could consider the facts during a discussion on revising the bankruptcy system. The GAO found the problems with the student loan program stemmed from a high default rate that was <u>not</u> caused by bankruptcy. At that time, approximately 18 percent of all student loans were in default, yet only 3-4 percent of these were through bankruptcy. The study[6] concluded that:

- only half to three-quarters of 1 percent of all matured educational loans [were] discharged in bankruptcy
- only 20 percent of bankruptcy filers had student loan debt exceeding 80 percent of their total debt load
- the average individual earnings for the year prior to filing the bankruptcy were at or below the Federal Poverty Guideline.

Most people filing for bankruptcy were poor, and their educational loans represented a contributing factor to their financial woes. Even still, these debtors represented a minuscule fraction of the borrowers defaulting on student loans. This fact is very different from the hype which surrounded the Congressional discussion to change the bankruptcy laws.

The *House Report on the Bankruptcy Law* was concerned with the overall increase in student loan bankruptcies but realized the "rise appears not to be disproportionate to the rise in the amount of loans becoming due or to the default rate generally on educational loans."[7] This pattern held true in later years. The *National Bankruptcy Review Commission Report of 1997* recognized that bankruptcy rates rise and fall with the economy and other factors "irrespective of [the] dischargeability [of student loans in] bankruptcy."[8]

So, what caused the financial problems with the educational loan programs in the 1970s to 1990s? The default rate peaked in 1990 at 22.4 percent. But by 2001, this rate dropped to 5.4 percent. Was this because it became more difficult to bankrupt student loans? No! *As one bankruptcy judge commented, "it appears to be primarily the program itself and the manner in which it is administered that is causing the difficulty and not that of bankruptcy abuses."*[9]

Loan defaults plummeted and increases in loan repayments came about because of better debt collection techniques by the Department of Education. Restricting student loan bankruptcies with §523(a)(8) played a negligible part in the improvements in overall loan collection.

The Department of Education implemented several programs and initiatives designed to improve the recovery of student loans. These included simple things such as notifying borrowers if they fell behind in payments (which surprisingly was not done in the early years), tracking borrowers after college so as to keep in communication with them, verifying that borrowers who claimed disability discharge or death discharge were really disabled or dead, and more. Once defaulters were identified and located, actions such as a change in the payment plan, intercepting IRS tax refunds, wage garnishing, and other techniques helped reduce the loan losses.

Schools were also scrutinized. Schools would be evaluated annually to determine the number of their students who defaulted on student loans. If the school's Cohort Default Rate was above a certain level, then the school forfeited eligibility to participate in the student loan program. This alone eliminated more than 1,000 schools nationwide (mostly trade proprietary schools), which were often loan mills providing very little real education or training.

The frequency of bankruptcies of student loans, which were done in bad faith, is not known. Richard Fossey reported on research conducted from 1990 to 1993 in which bankruptcy cases were evaluated for bad faith. Of the cases reviewed, he found "little evidence" of bad faith, but rather "most of the cases involved individuals who encountered difficult life circumstances and whose economic situations were made more precarious by the burden created by their educational loans."[10] Indeed, only a handful of published cases involved the kind of abuse Congress was concerned about when it passed §523(a)(8). In most cases, debtors experienced true hardship that made repaying student loans virtually impossible. Most people seeking bankruptcy were unemployed or under-employed, single parents trying to get by on too small an income, and often in poor health. Many debtors received little value for the education they so dearly paid for with debt, time, and effort.

The research indicates that only a handful of debtors used the bankruptcy process to defraud the government out of repaying student loans. Most (and we mean virtually all) debtors using bankruptcy do so in good faith. Making student loans dischargeable in bankruptcy, as they previously were as common unsecured debt, will not result in a massive increase of defaults. *The decrease in default rates is related to better collection methods, not making student loans virtually impossible to discharge through bankruptcy.* There was no actual need for §523(a)(8), and it should be rescinded or overturned.

Law Violates Equal Protection Clause of the U.S. Constitution

The U.S. Constitution requires laws to be fairly applied to all citizens. The question to ask is, "Have the courts applied the undue hardship clause of §523(a)(8) equally to all debtors?" In the only known research on this question, Andrew M. Campbell reported in *American Law Reports* (ALR)

(1998)[11] his findings on how courts have applied undue hardship.

The table below *(Success Rate for "Undue Hardship" Discharges)* shows that low-income debtors with chronic medical conditions and dependents have the highest rate of success at proving undue hardship (77 percent). For these same categories of debtors (low-income and having medical conditions), not having dependents drops the success rate by almost a third (to 55 percent). We see a similar pattern for low-income debtors with no medical condition. Simply not having dependents drops the success rate by almost two-thirds (from 48 percent to 17 percent). Thus, the courts have shown an overwhelming bias towards debtors with dependents over single debtors seeking the same debt relief.

Some could argue that the courts are recognizing the fact that debtors with dependents have greater responsibility and greater need for debt relief. But, the low-income level from which the analysis is made is higher for those with dependents ($10,000 before 1990 and $15,000 in subsequent years) than those without ($7,000 before 1990 and $10,000 in subsequent years). In a sense, these are similar to the Federal Poverty Guidelines, and the differences in income levels for those with dependents versus those without are reflected in the guidelines. Since the Guidelines adjust for the presence of dependents, courts should treat single debtors without dependents exactly the same as those with dependents– taking into account that the income level cut-offs already accommodate for the difference. *Since the courts favor those with dependents, it means that either there is bias in the court toward debtors with dependents or the court, indirectly, does not believe the validity of the Federal Poverty Guidelines. Either way, the court is violating the U.S. Constitution by treating different classes of debtors differently.*

Medical condition also influences court decisions. Low-income debtors with medical conditions and dependents are one and one-half times more likely to achieve success at discharging their debt than similar debtors without medical conditions (77 percent vs. 48 percent). This effect is even more pronounced for low-income debtors without dependents, where having a medical condition results in three times the success rate over similar debtors without a medical condition (55 percent vs. 17 percent). *Courts have shown an overwhelming bias toward debtors with medical conditions over those without.*

It may be argued that having a medical condition is strong evidence that a borrower will have little success with future employment and even less ability to repay student loans. This is often true, but there are many other factors equally important

TABLE—SUCCESS RATE FOR "UNDUE HARDSHIP" DISCHARGES

Rates of success at discharging student loans
through court finding of "undue hardship"

	Dependents	Overall Discharge Rate	Have Medical Condition?		
			Overall	No College Degree	College Degree
Low income[1]	Yes		Yes— 77% No— 48%	Yes— 80% No— 64%	Yes— 78% No— 25%
Low income[2]	No	36%	Yes— 55% No— 17%		
Higher income[3]	No	13%	Yes— 21% No— 7%		

1 Low income with dependents is defined as under $10,000 before 1990 and below $15,000 in subsequent years.
2 Low income without dependents is defined as under $7,000 before 1990 and below $10,000 in subsequent years.
3 Higher income is defined as being above the low-income cut-offs.

as a medical condition related to a person's ability to find work. We live in an ageist society where it is next-to-impossible for older workers to find full employment at good wages. Expecting someone over sixty-five years of age to find a new job is ludicrous. There are many other social factors that impact just as severely the ability of healthy workers to find employment, as does a medical disability. A list of these factors is discussed in the previous chapters and in Appendix F.

Courts seem to ignore factors other than medical conditions that impact debtors in their ability to secure employment. Courts seem to believe that if a debtor is healthy, then he or she should be able to get work and, if he or she doesn't, it is the debtor's fault, and the court denies the student loan discharge. Courts have shown a bias against factors other than medical conditions that present equal challenges to finding employment.

Having earned a college degree also seems to impact court decisions. For low-income debtors with dependents and medical conditions, there is little difference in the success rates for those with or without a college degree. But for similar debtors who do not have a medical condition, lower-educated debtors have two and one-half better successes at discharging student loans than those who have a college degree (64 percent vs. 25 percent).

Courts act as though a college degree guarantees full-time employment at an income sufficient to service even the largest student loan debt. This is not automatically true and was discussed in the previous chapter, and in Appendix F. The value of a college education has fallen, but court decisions have not reflected that change. Courts show bias when they discharge student loans of debtors without college degrees at a rate that is two and one-half times greater than those with a college degree.

Finally, having income above minimal levels has a significant impact on court decisions. For single debtors with no dependents, those with low-income are almost three times more successful at discharging their loans than those with higher income (36 percent vs. 13 percent). Again, we see the influence that medical conditions have on courts where higher income single debtors with medical conditions are three times more likely to succeed at achieving a debt discharge than similar debtors with no medical conditions (21 percent vs. 7 percent).

In reality, this is an issue of courts accepting the Social Security's Federal Poverty Guidelines as the correct criteria to evaluate a debtor's undue hardship. Neither the Bankruptcy Code nor the Department of Education Regulations requires debtors to be evaluated by the Federal Poverty Guidelines. There are other federal measures that are considered more accurate. A complete discussion regarding this topic is included later in this chapter. Courts show bias against those whose incomes may be near but above the income level specified by the Federal Poverty Guidelines.

In conclusion, we see courts have a demonstrable bias in finding undue hardship for debtors who are low-income, with dependents, and who have a medical condition. Debtors who are single or without medical conditions are treated less equitably by the courts. Having a college degree severely impacts the success of debt relief for low-income debtors who do not have a medical condition. Single debtors without medical conditions, particularly those with incomes above the poverty level, are the least successful at obtaining a student loan discharge.

Chapter 11 U.S.C.A. §523(a)(8) of the U.S. Bankruptcy Code is not applied equally to all persons, violates the equal protection clause of the U.S. Constitution, and should be overturned.

Unintended Impact on the Poor and Minorities

The media and Congressional frenzy in the 1970s concerning student loan defaults painted a picture of the typical defaulter as a "middle-class college graduate who obtained good value from [his or her] education then refused to pay for it."[12] This is the debtor to whom Congress aimed §523(a)(8) to impact, and the stereotype that the courts and the Department of Education envisioned in their harsh interpretation of the law. Many studies have shown the reality to be very different.

Logic tells us that students most needing help to finance college or trade school would be poor— minorities, single parents, independent students (those not receiving support from home), and partially disabled. That is, in fact, what the research confirms. The typical student loan borrower is not a middle-class man or woman attending a four-year college. For example, during the 1989-1990 academic year, students coming from families with less than $10,000 annual income represented 32 percent of all student loan borrowers, whereas students coming from families with $100,000 annual income represented only 3.1 percent of all student loan borrowers.[13] In the same timeframe, African American students accounted for 29 percent of all borrowers compared to 17.7 percent of the white population. Also, short-term programs (primarily operated by proprietary schools) offered specific job training that attracted poor workers as a path to more lucrative job placement. Approximately 46.5 percent of students attending short-term programs borrowed government money to finance their education, whereas only 25 percent of students attending a four-year college incurred similar debt.

Again, logic would suggest that the class of debtors most likely to <u>default</u> on student loans would be the poor— minorities, single parents, independent students, and those partially disabled. Again, the facts[14] affirm this position. Students who attended short-term programs are three times more likely to default on student loans than those who attended four-year institutions. The poorer or more marginalized the family, the greater the likelihood of default. The GAO summarized in their 1988 report, "Many defaulters are poor, attended proprietary school, dropped out of their course of instruction, and have little or no means to repay."[15]

Probably the two most disturbing findings from the 1988 GAO report were:
- recognizing that African Americans and American Indians who came from families with very little education had default rates from 30 percent to 60 percent[16]— higher than any other category of borrowers.
- many of the proprietary students who defaulted on their educational loans, "were 'pressured' to enroll by unscrupulous recruiters. Moreover, many of these students received poor-quality education that resulted in 'dismal employment prospects'."[17]

Hearings were conducted by the Senate Permanent Subcommittee on Investigations in 1993 and confirmed many of the GAO's observations. Proprietary schools often existed for the sole purpose of collecting student aid money. Representative Maxine Waters[18] of California said that these kinds of scams are common when the poor are victimized by trade schools that take their student loan money while offering worthless courses, producing no job leads, and leaving them with the repayment of loans they cannot afford.

One court, in particular, voiced its belief that the majority of courts err by applying rules (such as the *Brunner* or Johnston Tests) to low-income wage earners but which were designed for well-educated, upper-income professions:

> It is apparent that judicially developed rules defining circumstances, which indicate "abuse" of the bankruptcy system, were developed to apply to high-income professionals, but have come in recent years to be applied to poverty line wage earners. We conclude that the key word in the legislative history is "abuse" and that [it] is inappropriate to apply the same standards to poverty line wage earners as is applied to high income professionals and other college graduates.[19]

Our culture promotes education as the key to a better future. Mostly the poor (minority, single parents, partially disabled, and others) have heeded the call and taken out student loans, often with disastrous results. The passage of §523(a)(8) was aimed at college-educated middle-class debtors but had the unintended impact of blocking large numbers of poor debtors from obtaining a fresh start through bankruptcy. Debtors faced with bankruptcy should encourage courts to rescind or overturn §523(a)(8) because it has a disproportionate impact on poor, mostly minority, debtors.

Violates Bankruptcy's "Fresh Start" Concept

As described in Chapter 4, the bankruptcy of debts serves important social and economic purposes. It frees hopeless debtors to become responsible and productive members of society[20]. The Bankruptcy Act of 1898 stated two major goals: (1) to provide honest, hard-working debtors with a "fresh start" in which they are free of oppressive debt, and (2) to obtain fair and equitable treatment for debtors and creditors alike.[21]

Forty years of litigation surrounding §523(a)(8) reveals that the Department of Education and bankruptcy courts distinctly favor the repayment of student loans over providing a fresh start for debtors.

The goal of the fresh start policy is to help debtors restore financial health through bankruptcy. Without bankruptcy, citizens could be saddled with a lifetime of debts that depresses their participation in society. When creditors are calling, wages garnished, and more, debtors are likely to stop working and become public charges. Unmanageable debt impacts families increases divorce, and, in extreme cases, leads to crime and suicide. All these conditions have significant costs for society. The fresh start policy helps to minimize these costs and bring the debtor back to economic productivity.[22]

Although §523(a)(8) renders student loans presumptively non-dischargeable, a review of the entire Bankruptcy Code reveals that the fresh start provision takes precedent over §523(a)(8).

Here are the reasons:

- Congress stated in Section 507 of the Code which debts are given priority during liquidation or reorganization. Included are tax liabilities, debts owed to employees of bankrupt businesses, and others.[23] Congress perceived these debts to be more important than other kinds of debt and gave them priority status. Student loan claims are absent from Section 507, indicating Congress did not consider student loans to be among the most important kinds of debts considered during bankruptcy proceedings. The Bankruptcy Court in *Fox v. Pennsylvania Higher Education Assistance Agency* came to this same conclusion when it attempted to assess the priority repayment of student loans.[24]
- The structure of §523(a)(8) shows <u>that student loans are not required to be repaid, but rather, are prohibited from discharge</u>. This is a significant distinction because if Congress desired repayment of student loans over all other bankruptcy objectives, it would have done so by enacting specific legislation to that effect. It did not.
- The inclusion of the undue hardship exception to §523(a)(8) indicates, by definition, that the repayment policy is limited in scope and superseded by other objectives deemed by Congress to be more important.
- The undue hardship exception is included in §523(a)(8) to protect debtors, not creditors. As such, it functions to *preserve the fresh start policy* of the Bankruptcy Code.[25]

The Bankruptcy Code gives priority to the repayment of student loans up to the point of impinging upon a debtor's fresh start. At that point, the fresh start policy predominates in the undue hardship analysis and allows for the discharge of student loans.

Now we must consider what constitutes a *fresh start*.

The purpose of a fresh start policy is to allow debtors to afford the necessities of life at a quality and quantity expected within the mainstream American culture. It is consistent within the Bankruptcy Code and the fresh start policy for all debtors, including debtors with student loans, to have lifestyles approximating the middle class. The Bankruptcy Code legislative history supports this position. This is obvious if you review the impact bankruptcy has on debtors. *Neither Chapter 13 nor Chapter 7 debtors are forced into poverty to achieve discharge of their loans.*

But the history of debtors with student loans is different. With very few exceptions, debtors with student loans are unable to discharge their student loan debt unless they are at or below the Poverty Guidelines. The Bankruptcy Commission suggested that the undue hardship criterion meant debtors must observe a "minimal standard of living" during repayment.[26] This does not require poverty levels of living! *Poverty*[27] denotes "subminimal." When Congress and the Bankruptcy Commission spoke of a minimal standard of living, they meant a level of living that brings debtors back into society at the lower ends of the middle class.

> It is far preferable to free debtors from coercive collection techniques, so they have incentive to become employed, and consequently pay taxes, rather than be a drain on society's resources. Society will gain more in the long run by releasing low-income debtors from liability on student loans they are unlikely to repay. This reasoning reflects the essence of the fresh start policy.[28]

The undue hardship analysis must include the fresh start policy, and that is to be evaluated at a middle-class lifestyle, not at a subminimal poverty level. <u>Debtors filing an adversary proceeding should not allow courts to evaluate their financial and living conditions against the Federal Poverty Guidelines (see full discussion below). When courts do this, they are violating the fresh start policy of the Bankruptcy Code. Debtors need to challenge courts that violate the fresh start policy during undue hardship analysis.</u>

Congress Failed to Clearly Define the Law

Congress failed to define "undue hardship" in §523(a)(8). The aggressive defense mounted by the Department of Education in adversary proceedings has led to a severe interpretation of the law. Courts, in desperation to deal with the oversight, have engaged in judicial lawmaking to clear up the meaning of undue hardship. Both of these court actions violate Congress' intent for the law.

Certainty of Hopelessness

Courts universally recognize that the repayment of debt, any debt, represents a certain degree of hardship.[29] Many courts have evaluated undue hardship to mean more than temporary financial adversity[30] and something more than "garden variety"[31] hardship.

A large number of courts have viewed very negatively those debtors attempting to discharge their student loans. They have taken a moralistic stand against debtors trying to discharge student loans through bankruptcy. As one court stated to justify its harsh ruling, "[o]f all the many supplicants for financial relief who come before this and other bankruptcy courts, few, as a class, inspire less sympathy than the well-educated beneficiaries of student loans seeking to avoid those debts on the ground of undue hardship."[32] These courts have ruled that the discharge of student loans requires debtors to be living in dire conditions; that the undue hardship analysis requires "unique and extraordinary circumstances" or "a certainty of hopelessness."[33]

However, courts diverge greatly as to the <u>degree of hardship</u> necessary to meet undue hardship. A minority of courts has ruled less harshly. For example, in *Correll v. Union National Bank of Pittsburgh* (1989), the court stated:

> We do not believe, however, that Congress intended a fresh start under the Bankruptcy Code to mean that families must live at poverty level in order to repay educational loans. Where a family earns a modest income and the family budget, which shows no unnecessary or frivolous expenditures, is still unbalanced, a hardship exists from which a debtor may be discharged of his student loan obligations. Use by the Bankruptcy Court of poverty level or minimal standard of living guidelines are not necessary to meet the congressional purpose of correcting [the abuse Congress perceived].[34]

The Bankruptcy Commission (1978) suggested debtors observe a "minimal standard of living" to meet the undue hardship rule. The Johnson court substituted the phrase "subsistence or poverty level"[35] for "minimal standard of living." No explanation was given for this substitution, but it helped establish the undue hardship analysis at the poverty level. Later, the Bryant court would formalize the adoption of the Federal Poverty Guidelines into the undue hardship analysis.

In the previous section analyzing the *fresh start* concept of bankruptcy, we discovered that *undue hardship* should be evaluated within the bounds of middle-class income and lifestyle. *Poverty is a subminimal level of living rejected by the bankruptcy courts. Yet, during adversary proceedings, a majority of courts have adopted the*

Poverty Guidelines as the level of analysis for debtors with student loans.

So, at what level is *undue hardship* evaluated? Is it at the *middle class*, *modest income*, *poverty*, *minimal standard of living*, *subsistence*, or *poverty level*, with *unique and extraordinary circumstances*, with *a certainty of hopelessness*, or what? That is the entire point of this section. Congress failed to clearly define *undue hardship*. Aggressive defense by the Department of Education has influenced many bankruptcy courts to take a very narrow, harsh reading for the term requiring debtors to live hopelessly at, or below, the poverty level. Yet other courts have seen through this and understood the intent of Congress and blended it with the core concept of bankruptcy for a fresh start, allowing debtors to live above the poverty level and still discharge student loans. This wide reading of *undue hardship* is evidence §523(a)(8) is bad law and should be rejected by courts. Debtors engaged in an adversary proceeding need to help courts understand how the undue hardship analysis is unworkable and encourage rejection of the law.

Judicial Lawmaking

Only the legislative branch of the government has the power to make laws. Courts interpret law and discuss and settle discrepancies between laws but are not authorized to make law. Judges that make law engage in what is known as *judicial lawmaking*.

Laws enacted by Congress take on meaning when they are tested in court. When laws are vague, courts look to the recorded Congressional discussions to help find meaning for the law. *When there is a wide variance in the application of a law, courts are considered to have engaged in judicial lawmaking— something they are professedly prohibited from doing.*

In review of court interpretations of the undue hardship provision, it is apparent that courts have overstepped their bounds in constructing meaning for the phrase. The evidence supporting the contention that courts have engaged in judicial lawmaking includes partial discharges and modified repayment plans, wide variance in hardship tests, arbitrary use of Federal Poverty Guidelines, and discrediting the value of the education.

A. Partial Discharges and Modified Repayment Plans

Because so many courts have ruled harshly against debtors with student loans as a result of the undue hardship test, some courts have modified repayment plans and/or allowed a partial discharge of the student loans in order to "promote fairness by affording some relief to the debtor, while ensuring that the government is not unjustly deprived by a complete discharge of student loans that could be repaid in part without imposing 'undue hardship'."[36]

The concept of partial discharges originates from *Littell v. State of Oregon Board of Higher Education (In re Littell)*, 6 B.R. 85, 89 (Bankr. D. Or. 1980). Here, the court ruled (without giving legal justification), "[I]nstead of the all-or-nothing approach [prevailing in nearly every case to date], the courts should consider whether only part of the debt should be dischargeable and what monthly payment the debtor could afford." As a result of this case, the number of courts granting partial discharges or other equitable relief under section 523(a)(8) increased considerably.

Courts that favor partial discharges infer their authority from the equitable powers as codified in section 105(a) of the Bankruptcy Code. It states:

> (a) The court may issue any order, process, or judgment that is necessary or appropriate to carry out the provisions of this title. No provision of this title providing for the raising of an issue by a party in interest shall be construed to preclude the court from, *sua sponte*, taking any action or making any determination necessary or appropriate to enforce or implement court orders or rules, or to prevent an abuse of process. [37]

The equitable powers allow bankruptcy courts to fashion solutions to problem cases "as are necessary to further the purposes of the substantive provisions of the Bankruptcy Code."[38] But the defects in §523(a)(8) are so great, as evidenced by the wide range of rulings, that courts are necessarily engaging in judicial lawmaking. *"The courts are not granted power to remedy perceived defects in legislation by the failure of Congress to legislate precisely or equitably.*"[39] The language of §523(a)(8) is clear and unambiguous concerning the discharge of the entire loan. *Only Congress has the power to modify the law to allow for partial discharges.*

For similar reasons discussed above, some courts have <u>modified student loan repayment plans</u> to lessen the harsh outcomes of the undue hardship analysis and/or obtain greater repayment than would otherwise be realized if the loans were completely discharged. <u>These legal approaches are controversial</u>. For example, in *Hawkins v. Buena Vista College* (*In re Hawkins*), 187 B.R. 294, 300-01 (Bankr. N.D. Iowa 1995), the court noted that it only had the authority under §523(a)(8) to determine dischargeability of student loans. "Congress has not given bankruptcy courts the authority to rewrite student loans," noted the court. "Congress could have provided that student loans will be dischargeable 'to the extent' excepting such debt will impose undue hardship upon a debtor and her dependents" but did not explicitly state that. Further, the Hawkins court observed, "the bankruptcy court's power under section 105 is not a limitless authorization to do whatever seems equitable."

The Bankruptcy Code provides for the discharge of student loans but grants no authority to modify student loan repayment. <u>Putting debtors on a court-imposed payment schedule resembles a mandatory Chapter 13 proceeding, which is rejected by the Bankruptcy Code.</u>[40]

Conclusion: Courts do not have the power to <u>partially</u> discharge student loans or <u>modify</u> the payment schedules of student loans during bankruptcy proceedings. Either the loans are discharged in total or not. Any other decision represents judicial lawmaking, which is prohibited by law.

B. Wide Variance in Hardship Tests

In order for the undue hardship test to be valid, there needs to be consistency in the application and outcome of the test. Research indicates the contrary. Courts and judges have differed dramatically in the application of the undue hardship analysis. Besides the four major tests previously detailed in this book, there have been many other tests developed and used. Even courts using one of the standard tests often give vastly different interpretations of the law and modify the tests at will. As a result, similarly situated debtors often receive wildly different results.

There is strong disagreement, if not animosity, between courts in interpreting the law. For example, a Georgia bankruptcy court allowed a partial discharge when applying the *Brunner* test even though the debtor did not satisfy all prongs of the test. The court believed the *Brunner* test was "inequitable"[41] and chose to give a partial discharge.

Lack of Congressional guidance has led to this appalling situation of courts applying many different tests in determining undue hardship, restructuring loans, and allowing partial discharges. Judges have been given unbridled discretion to use their own personal values, biases, and sensitivities to determine the meaning of "undue hardship." As the Johnson court so succinctly stated, "there are as many factors and tests which have been used to determine undue hardship as there are courts to decide the issue."[42]

The lack of uniformity by the courts in the interpretation of undue hardship tests has resulted in several cases of *forum shopping* by debtors attempting to get the best deal for their situation. Forum shopping adds to the public's perception that the bankruptcy system is unfairly administered and leaves debtors confused. The *principle of uniformity* within the legal system requires debtors to be treated consistently under the Bankruptcy Code. Debtors with similar situations should be treated similarly. By making student loans dischargeable like other forms of unsecured debt, courts would no longer have to conduct adversary proceedings to evaluate debtors under the undue hardship exception. <u>Debtors filing an adversary proceeding should encourage courts to reject all undue hardship analysis, rescind or overturn §523(a)(8), and ask to have their student loan debts treated like other forms of unsecured debt.</u>

C. Arbitrary use of Federal Poverty Guidelines

Undue hardship needs to be measured against some financial and lifestyle guidelines. Aggressive tactics by attorneys from the Department of Education early on influenced courts to use the Social Security's Federal Poverty Guidelines (hereinafter, referred to as Poverty Guidelines) as their unit of measure. As you will read, this was unfortunate since no other poverty measures produce such low cut-off points.

The Poverty Guidelines was used in many of the early court cases and formally adopted in *Bryant v. Pennsylvania Higher Education Assistance Agency* (otherwise known as the Bryant Poverty Test). Subsequent tests, such as *Brunner*, also included the use of the Poverty Guidelines. It was often claimed, as it was in Bryant, that using the Poverty Guidelines brought "objectivity" to the test.[43] But, the Poverty Guidelines are anything but objective. The Social Security Administration developed the guidelines in 1964 by guessing[44] the average family's total expenditure for food and multiplying it by a factor of three. This number is updated yearly, but the basic definition has never been changed. The Social Security Administration's determination for a food budget was based on the **temporary or emergency** dietary needs of a family, and not the cost for an adequate, sustainable diet.[45] Further, food no longer represents one-third of the average American household budget, but closer to one-fourth[46], meaning that the food budget should be multiplied by four instead of three to estimate poverty. Polls conducted of American consumers reveal they believe the Poverty Guidelines for a family of four is set about $6,000 too low.[47]

It is also very indicative of how inappropriate the Poverty Guidelines are when you consider that many other agencies of the U.S. Government reject the scale and use other government guidelines. For example, until 1985, the Bureau of Labor Statistics (BLS) calculated its own measure of poverty. The scale was designed to estimate a budget of minimum adequacy. Living below that level was considered to be subminimal existence. The BLS guideline was substantially higher than the Poverty Guidelines.[48] Even though the BLS no longer produces these figures, the Department of Labor (DOL) updates the figures annually since they are used to measure eligibility for certain job training programs.[49]

Significantly, many federal and state need-based assistance programs do not use the Poverty Guidelines.[50] The Department of Housing and Urban Development (HUD) links eligibility with the median income, not the Poverty Guidelines. For example, HUD classifies families earning between 50-80 percent of the median income as "Lower-Income Families." Those earning less than 50 percent of the median income are "Very Low-Income Families." The HUD guidelines for low-income levels are higher than those of the Poverty Guidelines. The Legal Service Corporation (LSC) determined that people whose incomes do not exceed 125 percent of the Poverty Guidelines are poor enough to receive free legal services. In certain circumstances, this may extend up to 150 percent of the Poverty Guidelines. For tax determination, the Earned Income Tax Credits (EICs) are granted to families far above the Poverty Guidelines. EIC are characterized as a welfare payment made through the tax system to low-income families. In developing the EIC program, Congress believed that families with incomes well above the Poverty Guidelines were entitled to the tax break to help lift them out of "poverty."[51] The Department of Education defines low-income as borrowers with incomes not exceeding 125 percent of the Poverty Guidelines. Such a designation qualifies them for extended repayment periods on direct education loans.[52] Finally, Aid to Families with Dependent Children (AFDC) does not set an income eligibility criteria at all but rather leaves it up to each individual state to establish.

Even sociologists, who strive to define social yardsticks, do not agree on the correct measure of poverty. There are three major schools of sociological thought viewing poverty — absolute definitions, relativistic definitions, and sociocultural definitions. Moreover, within these schools are subgroups of thought. Overall, there is no consensus as to how to define "poverty" and when it is used. Poverty is a social construct molded by nature for how it will be used.

Linking the Federal Poverty Guidelines to undue hardship is, and has been, arbitrary. Neither Congress, the Bankruptcy Code, nor the Department of Education regulations requires student debtors, who are subjected to an undue hardship analysis, to be evaluated against the Poverty Guidelines. The Poverty Guidelines is not an accurate measure of poverty and bear "no relationship at all to bankruptcy law or the fresh start policy."[53] Debtors need to challenge the use of the Federal Poverty Guidelines during their undue hardship analysis.

D. Discrediting the Value of the Education

Initially, when courts evaluated undue hardship cases, they questioned whether or not the debtor benefited financially from the education the loan helped to finance (otherwise known as "educational value" of the loan). This was formalized in the third prong (*policy* test) of the Johnson Test. Under the policy test, if a debtor did not benefit from the education, e.g., obtain employment in the field of his or her degree or certificate, then the student loan debt was open to being discharged.

This position was rejected by the *Brunner* court. The court believed that since student loans were made without consideration of creditworthiness to the student, there was an expectation of payment from future income as a financial quid pro quo; additionally, students accepted the responsibility to repay the loans regardless of the benefit they received from their education.[54] The court further stated that it was improper to consider educational benefit because it placed the government in the role of insurer of educational value.[55] Since the *Brunner* test has become the primary test in bankruptcy courts throughout the United States, this position prevails.

We believe the *Brunner* court was wrong. The relevance of educational value was expressly noted by the 1978 Congressional Bankruptcy Commission. The Commission recommended making student loans nondischargeable because they believed obtaining an education leads people to earn greater income.[56] The converse of this statement is true. If borrowers do not earn greater income from employment related to their educational degree or certificate, then the loans used to obtain this education should be dischargeable. Contrary to the *Brunner* court, it would seem that attention to educational value is mandated in undue hardship cases.

Although the *Brunner* court was concerned about the government becoming an insurer of educational value, this is unfounded. The insurance analogy is not appropriate. True schooling insurance would provide income supplement to graduates who are unable to use their education to enhance their financial status. Simply allowing for the discharge of student loans is not income supplementation. Instead, allowing for the discharge of student loans if the debtor is unable to obtain appropriate employment is better seen as a form of credit insurance, i.e., insurance to reduce the impact of financial failure. Viewed this way, a student loan discharge based on lack of educational value is consistent with the fresh start policy and the role of bankruptcy to the economy and society. Debtors should insist that bankruptcy courts include a review of the educational value of their loans during the undue hardship analysis.

As we saw *In re Pena* (1998), DOE appeal claimed that, besides other reasons, the bankruptcy court erred by considering evidence regarding the value of the IT education. However, the district court concluded, "We agree that consideration of educational value as a separate factor in analyzing undue hardship would improperly place too much emphasis on this evidence. However, as part of the second prong analysis (of the *Brunner* test), the value of Ernest's education is relevant to this future ability to pay off the student loans. The bankruptcy court did not err in considering that Ernest's income was not likely to increase as a result of his ITT education."

Summary concerning the definition of "undue hardship:"

- The Department of Education and courts have misinterpreted the undue hardship clause of §523(a)(8) to mean "certainty of hopelessness." This is not what Congress intended and violates the fresh start policy (see the previous section analyzing *fresh start*). The wide interpretation of the phrase indicates the law is inequitably

applied and should be sent back to Congress for clarification.
- Courts have engaged in judicial lawmaking as evidenced by:
  - Granting partial discharges and modifying repayment plans—neither of which are authorized by law.
  - Wide variance in undue hardship tests; wide variance in court decisions
  - Inclusion of the Federal Poverty Guidelines for which there is no Congressional authorization to do so.
  - Discrediting the Value of the Education ignores the recommendations of the Bankruptcy Commission and other court decisions

The undue hardship clause of §523(a)(8) is extremely vague. The courts need to reject §523(a)(8) for its vagueness and send it back to Congress for clarification. Until that time, student loans should be handled by the bankruptcy courts as common unsecured loans and discharged accordingly.

Challenges to *Brunner* Test

The *Brunner* test has been discussed in other sections of this book. Here, we take an advocacy position as to why it should no longer be used by courts for determining "undue hardship."

The *Brunner* test originated out of a 1985 appeal to a bankruptcy case by Marie Brunner. At that time, student loans could be included and discharged in a standard bankruptcy without the need for an adversary proceeding if more than five years had passed since the last loan was issued. Only if the debtor was trying to discharge the debt before five years had passed was an adversary proceeding needed to prove "undue hardship." Since then, the five-year criteria was extended to seven-years and eventually eliminated. Student loans can no longer be discharged in a standard bankruptcy unless an adversary proceeding is conducted to determine if repaying the loans created an "undue hardship."

Now the *Brunner* test is being applied to cases where the debtor has been out of school for a decade or longer, and the repayment plans can last another twenty to twenty-five years. This is a very different situation than waiting five years before automatically discharging student loans through bankruptcy without having to prove "undue hardship." That alone should disqualify the *Brunner* test for meeting the criteria of §523(a)(8).

The first prong of the *Brunner* test has dissolved into a battle over proving how poor the debtor is living. The DOE pushed the courts to evaluate debtor income against the extreme Social Security Federal Poverty Guidelines. This guideline is just one of many possible measures of poverty used by the federal government. Some courts have recognized the arbitrariness of these guidelines and have made decisions based on a middle-class living standard. The use of the Social Security Federal Poverty Guidelines should be challenged.

The *Brunner* second prong requires debtors to prove that their current dire living conditions will continue for the duration of the loan. This is impossible for a number of reasons:

- No one can predict the future. <u>Even the Brunner court stated that it was "problematic" to try to determine the ability of a debtor to make payments in the future,</u> yet the court blithely proceeded to attempt to devise a method for doing exactly that (which failed).
- Many other courts have also struggled with the second prong precisely because the future is unknowable. <u>Some courts have advocated eliminating this part of the *Brunner* test.</u> Yet, DOE continues to press the false narrative that the economic status of the debtor "should" get better, and the courts should reject the debtor's claim.
- What seems to be missing from court cases is the science behind making predictions. We can take a data set and fit a regression line (equation) that best fits the data. We can extend this line into the future to predict outcomes. This is called *statistical inference*. Predictability comes from past data. From this data, we can predict future events within some level of probability. In our application, if a debtor has a decade or more of economic struggle due to lack of employment, disability, poor choices,

cultural forces, illness, marriage, children, and so on, we can only predict the same conditions will continue into the future—regardless how much we think it "should" change. Courts trying to predict the ability of debtors to make future payments is magical thinking and not based on science. Predicting future earnings should be based on past earnings; nothing more.

- In a surprising change, only recently have some courts come to a new understanding considering loan default and the *Brunner* second prong. In the past, debtors who defaulted on their loans were viewed negatively, and courts did not want to grant a discharge of their student loans. It was advised that debtors clear up the default before attempting an adversary proceeding. This is often impossible since DOE may demand tens of thousands of dollars to bring the loan out of default. Yet, some recent court cases have come to realize that if someone is in a bad enough life situation that he/she is filing for bankruptcy, then he/she is most likely to have defaulted on their student loan. It is reasonable for debtors in dire financial straits to have defaulted on their loans. Further, one court recognized that by defaulting on their student loans, the clock on the repayment period is technically stopped, and the loan becomes immediately due. Since the second *Brunner* prong looks at a debtor's ability to repay the loan over its lifetime and that loan is now due, the debtor has demonstrated his/her inability to make payments on the loan for its lifetime—thereby automatically meeting the requirements of the *Brunner* second prong. This approach suggests that debtors filing an adversary proceeding should default on their loans at the same time. This legal approach is currently being tested in court.

Challenges to Income-Driven Repayment ("IDR" plans)

Department of Education has developed a few income-driven repayment plans (as discussed in Chapter 2). These include Income-Based Repayment (IBR); Pay As You Earn (PAYE); Revised Pay As You Earn (REPAYE); Income-contingent Repayment (ICR); and, Income-sensitive Repayment Plan. This discussion will lump them together under the nomenclature *income-driven repayment* plans ("IDR" plans).

Almost six million people are currently enrolled in one IDR or another, and most are not making payments sufficiently large enough to cover accruing interest. As such, their debts are growing in size. Making payments are not reducing the size of the loans, rather they are just being "serviced." Although IDR enrollees are not technically in default, few will ever pay back their loans.

A complicated formula is used to calculate how much the DOE believes a debtor should be able to afford to make toward loan repayments (*see* Appendix A). If a debtor experiences hard times, and his or her income drops, payments drop accordingly— sometimes to zero. Each year the repayment schedule is recalculated to reflect the financial condition of the debtor. The plan lasts for twenty to twenty-five years, and any outstanding debt remaining at the end of the plan is forgiven (remember that *forgiven* means that the IRS considers the amount as a gift to the debtor and therefore taxable as ordinary income; debt that is *discharged* through bankruptcy is not considered income and is not taxable).

DOE Claims IDR Plans Make it Impossible to Satisfy the Brunner First and Third Prong

It is often stated by the Department of Education attorneys that IDR plans make it impossible for debtors to discharge their student loans in bankruptcy. They contend that anyone can make "zero dollar" payments, thus negating the undue hardship exception of §523(a)(8) and fail to satisfy the *Brunner* first and third prong.

On a personal note. When I (the author of this book) filed my adversary, the attorney for the

DOE laughed to my face and said that "anyone can make zero-dollar payments," and it was "impossible for me to bankrupt my loans." The attorney sneered at me like I was a sub-human idiot. This is a tactic they will take—intimidation. Please try not to be intimidated by them. They take the position that the IDR plans make it impossible to bankrupt student loans. They are wrong, and many courts uphold this perspective!

Many courts have challenged the DOE position on IDR plans. Here are some of the arguments:

Trading One Nondischargeable Loan for Another

The court rejected the use of IDR plans because the debtor would be "trading one nondischargeable debt for another" (*Barrett* 487 F.3d at 364); which is not the point of bankruptcy or adversary proceeding.

Emotional Hardship Having Loan for Twenty-Five Years

Although the payment may be lower or zero on an IDR plan, the emotional consequences of having to report to DOE financial and other personal information every year are, in themselves, a hardship. A debtor who is entitled to and receives a hardship discharge does not have that additional burden. The DOE's "argument overlooks the psychological effect of having a significant debt remain[.]" [*In re Barrett.* at 365 n. 8; *see Balaski v. Educ. Credit Mgmt. Corp,* 280 B.R. 395, 400 Bankr. N.D. Ohio 2002)] ("While defendant may believe holding debtor hostage for twenty-five years to debt and compounding interest is not an undue hardship, the court does not accept this view.") BAP op. 337 B.R. at 904. DOE ". . . fails to take account of the additional worry and anxiety that the debtor is likely to suffer if he is compelled to watch his debt steadily increase knowing that he does not have the ability to repay it for reasons beyond his control," and discards the central aim of the Bankruptcy Code — to provide the debtor a fresh start.

Not Participating in IDR Plan is Tantamount to Violating "Good Faith Effort"

DOE has claimed that debtors who do not enroll in an IDR plan are, by default, violating the "good faith effort" to repay students loans as required under the third prong of *Brunner*. Its position would create a *per se* rule requiring enrollment in the IDR program to satisfy the third *Brunner* prong and thus would, in effect, eliminate the discharge of student loans for undue hardship from the Bankruptcy Code. The court rejected this approach. (*In re Lamento* 2014)

Tax Consequences to Forgiven Loan Are a Hardship

It is true that the unpaid portion of loans will be forgiven for people who successfully complete IDR plans, but the amount of the forgiven debt is considered income by the IRS. Under current IRS regulations, the only people who can escape that tax bill are people who are insolvent at the time the debt is forgiven. DOE has argued that debtors' tax concerns at the end of the twenty to twenty-five-year repayment period on an IDR were "overblown." They claimed the debtor would only be forced to pay those taxes if he/she became solvent. The court disagreed. If DOE's position was accepted, then debtor would be faced with the following choice: resign to insolvency for the rest of his/her life or be forced to repay a student debt that is much much larger than its current size.

Courts Have Recommended Abolishing Brunner Third Prong

DOE has attempted to tie-in IDR plans with the concept of debtors making a "good faith effort" to repay student loans. *In re Roth* (2013), the Ninth Circuit Court recommended abolition of the *Brunner* third prong requirement because it is of little utility in determining true undue hardship. Of course, as a matter of statutory construction, this "prong" of the test lacks any textual basis in the Bankruptcy Code. As a practical matter, requiring a debtor to clear this hurdle can condemn the student-borrower to a lifetime of burdensome debt under one or more of the creditors' long-term repayment programs, some of which may span thirty-to-forty years.

Paying "Something" on the Loans Should Reduce the Debt

Another argument DOE has made requiring IDR plans is that they wanted the debtor to pay "something" toward the debt. But *In re Metz* (2018), the court believed that "something" should have a meaningful positive effect on the financial situation. In other words, the payment should be able to reduce the debt — not simply service it.

"Good Faith" Argument to Repay Loan Makes Bankruptcy Impossible

In *Krieger v. Educational Credit* (2013), the Seventh Circuit disagreed with the district court, noting that if "good faith" necessitated a commitment to future efforts to repay, then "no educational loan ever could be discharged, because it is always possible to pay in the future should prospects improve." The appellate court concluded that "it is important not to allow judicial glosses, such as language in *Roberson* and *Brunner*, to supersede the statute itself."

The Repayment Period is Over Once a Loan is in Default

And finally, one of the more interesting interpretation occurred *In re Rosenberg* (2020). Judge Morris noted that once a loan goes into default, the entire amount becomes due payable immediately. The repayment period is over. Thus, if the loan were to last ten years (like the standard repayment plans) or twenty to twenty-five years (like the income-sensitive repayment plans), the time for repayment under default is eliminated, and the full loan becomes due immediately. The second prong states that "this state of affairs is likely to persist for a significant portion of the repayment period of the student loans." Since filing for bankruptcy indicates that the debtor is in dire financial straits and it has lasted during the repayment period (now over), the second prong is satisfied. This means that anyone filing an adversary who cannot maintain a minimal standard of living **and** has defaulted on his/her student loans will automatically meet the requirements of the second prong.

2005 Changes to Bankruptcy Code

In April 2005, Congress passed a major revision to the Bankruptcy Code. Primarily, debtors now must pass a means test to determine if they qualify for a Chapter 7 bankruptcy or are forced into Chapter 13 reorganization. Also, persons filing for bankruptcy must take an approved Credit Counseling Course within six months of filing. During the process, an approved Financial Management Course must be taken and completed.

The Bankruptcy Institute of American estimates approximately 5 percent of those currently filing a Chapter 7 bankruptcy will not qualify and, instead, be redirected into a Chapter 13 bankruptcy. Thus, the changes in bankruptcy law affect relatively few of those who commonly use Chapter 7 bankruptcy.

Chapter 13 Bankruptcies

For those debtors forced into a Chapter 13 bankruptcy by the new means test, the process of discharging student loans has become legally confused. What has happened is that some debtors have listed their student loans in their Chapter 13 plan without filing an adversary proceeding, and judges have approved their plan. Creditors (including educational loan agencies) have been duly informed, the plan executed, and judges have discharged the student loans once the plan was completed. The educational creditors have come back to say that the discharges were improper because there was no adversary proceeding. Ultimately, the Supreme Court ruled that if the lender was duly notified of the Chapter 13 plan, which included discharging the student loans, then the bankruptcy judge has the authority to discharge the student loans. The lender would have to object to including the student loans in the discharge plan forcing the debtor to file an adversary proceeding. The case, *Espinosa v. United Student Aid Funds*

(Ninth Circuit Court of Appeals No. 06-16421, 2008).

It is best if debtors file an adversary proceeding in conjunction with a Chapter 13 plan. We advocate that judges should have the right to include student loans in Chapter 13 plans without the need of an adversary proceeding.

Student loan payments may be reduced during the five years of Chapter 13 court oversight. However, when the entire loan balance comes due, the interest accrued during the time at the end of the process is included. If this happens to you, your only recourse is to negotiate with your student loan agency for a new repayment plan. Debtors faced with this situation may want to argue any of the challenges given previously to have the court rule 11 U.S.C.A. §523(a)(8) invalid. Then the debt can be discharged similarly to any other unsecured debt.

Summary

- Chapter 11, §523(a)(8) is bad law
- Chapter 11, §523(a)(8) passage was unnecessary
    - Only half to three-quarters of 1 percent of all matured education loans were discharged in bankruptcy in the 1970s.
    - High loan default rate is not related to the ability to bankrupt student loans.
    - Better debt collection techniques by the Department of Education drove down the default rate, not the enforcement of Section 523(a)(8) in bankruptcy court.
- Chapter 11, §523(a)(8) violates the Equal Protection Clause
    - Different debtors are treated differently.
    - Single debtors without medical conditions are treated most stringently by the court.
    - Debtors with dependents and medical condition fair the best in court.
- Chapter 11, §523(a)(8) has a disproportionate impact on debtors who are poor and/or member of a minority
    - Mostly poor default on student loans.
    - Mostly minorities default on student loans.
    - Mostly those attending proprietary schools default on student loans.
    - Section 523(a)(8) was targeted at the upwardly mobile professional who wanted to skip repaying their student loans. In actuality, mostly the poor and minorities have been subjected to section 523(a)(8).
- Chapter 11, §523(a)(8) violates bankruptcy's *fresh start* policy
    - The goal of fresh start policy is to help honest debtors restore financial health through bankruptcy.
    - Fresh start policy takes precedence over section 523(a)(8).
    - Fresh start is evaluated within the parameters of the middle-class standard of living.
- Congress failed to define *undue hardship* in §523(a)(8)
    - Most courts have interpreted this harshly to mean *certainty of hopelessness*.
    - Should be evaluated at the middle-class standard of living.
- Courts have engaged in judicial lawmaking
    - Granting partial discharges and modifying repayment plans—neither of which courts are authorized to do by law.
    - Wide variance in undue hardship tests; wide variance in court decisions.
    - Inclusion of the Federal Poverty Guidelines for which there is no Congressional authorization to do so.
    - Discrediting the Value of the Education ignores the recommendations of the Bankruptcy Commission.
- Income-Driven Repayment (IDR)
    - Most flexible repayment plan offered by the Department of Education.
    - Debt remaining after twenty-five years is forgiven.
    - The debtor is liable for the income taxes due on the forgiven amount. If the debt was actually "discharged" (through bankruptcy), then there would be no tax liability.
    - IDR plans are trading one nondischargeable debt for another and should not be allowed.
    - IDR plans place debtors under decades of emotional hardship.
    - Being on IDR plans are not necessary to prove "good faith effort" to repay student loans as required under the third *Brunner* prong.

- o DOE position that the tax liability on forgiven debt is "overblown" has been rejected by the courts.
- o There is no textual basis in the bankruptcy code for proving "good faith effort" to repay loans.
- o It has been suggested by courts to abolish the second and third prong of the Brunner test.
- o A student loan that enters default and who has filed an adversary proceeding has automatically meet the requirements of the Brunner second prong.
- o IDR plans violate the fresh start policy of the Bankruptcy Code.
- o IDR plans violate the undue hardship exception for debtors on a restricted or fixed income.
- 2005 Changes to the Bankruptcy Code
  - o Established means test to qualify for Chapter 7.
  - o Can be forced into Chapter 13 reorganization if debtor fails means test.
  - o Chapter 13 reduces loan payments over five years, the balance plus interest becomes due.
  - o Only recourse is to renegotiate the loan with the agency that granted the student loan.
  - o Should file adversary proceeding during Chapter 13 plan.
  - o OK to contest Chapter 11, §523(a)(8) as invalid.

[1] Freeman, Ryan. (2013). "Student-Loan Discharge: An Empirical Study of the Undue Hardship Provision of §523(a)8) Under Appellate Review. *Emory Bankruptcy Developments Journal,* v.30, p. 147-205.

[2] Pardo, Rafael, and Michelle Lacey. (20 Apr 2005). "Undue Hardship in the bankruptcy Courts: An Empirical Assessment of the Discharge of Educational Debt." *University of Cincinnati Law Review*, v. 74, n. 2, Winter 2005.

[3] Iuliano, Jason, An Empirical Assessment of Student Loan Discharges and the Undue Hardship Standard (July 24, 2011). 86 American Bankruptcy Law Journal 495 (2012), Available at SSRN: https://ssrn.com/abstract=1894445 or http://dx.doi.org/10.2139/ssrn.1894445
https://papers.ssrn.com/sol3/papers.cfm?abstract_id=1894445

[4] H.R. Rep. No. 95-595, at 133 (1978), reprinted in 1978 U.S.C.C.A.N. 5963, 6094.

[5] A&P 123 Cong. Rec. H11690, H11705 (Oct. 27, 1977) (statement of Rep. Volkmer).

[6] See H.R. Rep. No. 95-595, at 133 (1977), reprinted in 1978 U.S.C.C.A.N 5963, 6094.

[7] See also A&P 124 Cong. Rec. 1794 (daily ed. Feb. 1, 1978) (statement of Rep. Dodd) ("The GAO report also recites the number of bankruptcies or the increase in the student loan bankruptcies in comparison to the overall increase in bankruptcies across the country and shows that they have been relatively stable, and I am quoting relatively stable.").

[8] *National Bankruptcy Review Commission Report.* (Oct. 20, 1997). Pub. L. No. 103-394, at 179.

[9] A&P 124 Cong. Rec. 1796 (daily ed. Feb. 1, 1978); see also supra notes 44-45.

[10] Fossey, Richard. (1997). The certainty of hopelessness: Are courts to harsh toward bankrupt student loan debtors? *J. L. & Educ., (26),* 29.

[11] Andrew M. Campbell, Annotation, *Bankruptcy Discharge of Student Loan on Ground of Undue Hardship Under § 523(a)(8)(B) of Bankruptcy Code of 1978,* 144 A.L.R. Fed. 1 (1998).

[12] See Fossey, Richard (1997). The certainty of hopelessness: Are courts too harsh toward bankrupt student loan debtors? *Journal of Law and Education, (26),* 29, 30 (supra note 251).

[13] National Center for Education Statistics. (May 1993). *Financing Undergraduate Education, (1990),* at 27.

[14] U.S. Gen. Acct. office Defaulted Student Loans: Preliminary Analysis of Student Loan Borrowers and Defaulters. (June 1998). GAO HRD 88-1128. [Herein noted as 1988 GAO Report.]

[15] 1988 GAO REPORT, Supra Note 43

[16] Volkwein, James F. & Cabrera, Alberto F.\ (1998). Factors associated with student loan default in borrowing against America's future. Richard Fossey & Mark Bateman (Eds.), *Student loans, higher education and public policy.*

[17] 1988 GAO REPORT, Supra Note 43.

[18] Winerip, Martin, et al. (Feb. 4, 1994). Overhauling school grants: Much debate but little gain. *N.Y. Times.*

[19] Correll v. Union Nat'l Bank of Pittsburgh (*In re Correll*), 105 B.R. 302, 304-07 (Bankr. W.D. Pa. 1989) at 304.

[20] Jackson, Thomas H. (1985). The fresh start policy in bankruptcy law. *Harvard Law Rev., (98)*, 1393, 1420.

[21] King, Lawrence & Cook, Michael. (1996). *Creditors' rights, debtors' protection, and bankruptcy* (3rd Edition). New York, NY: Matthew Bender and Col., Inc.

[22] See Howard, Margaret. (1987). A Theory of Discharge in Consumer Bankruptcy, *Ohio St. L.J., (48),* 1047, 1085-87 supra note 23, at 1085 ("The availability of a debtor's earning capacity as an asset free from the reach of creditors is what gives the debtor a new start.").

[23] Other priority claims include: rental security deposits, contributions to employee benefit plans, and claims for alimony and support. See id. s 507(a)(4), (a)(6) & (a)(7).

[24] Fox v. Pennsylvania Higher Educ. Assistance Agency (*In re Fox*), 163 B.R. 975, 978 (Bankr. M.D. Pa. 1993).

[25] See, e.g., Baker v. University of Tenn. at Chattanooga (*In re Baker*), 10 B.R. 870, 872 (Bankr. E.D. Tenn. 1981) (stating that Congress did not intend make student loans generally nondischargeable to those who fell on hard times); Clay v. Westmar College (*In re Clay*), 12 B.R. 251, 255 (Bankr. N.D. Iowa 1981) (stating that the fresh start policy would be defeated if continuing liability on a loan would impose an undue hardship on debtor). The court in Lohman v. Connecticut Student Loan Foundation (*In re Lohman*), 79 B.R. 576 (Bankr. D. Vt. 1987) actually stated that undue hardship requires courts to consider the "premise for discharge." Id. at 580.

[26] Comm'n Report, supra note 40, pt. II, at 141.

[27] One dictionary defines "Poverty" as, "1. the condition or quality of being poor; indigence; need 2. deficiency in necessary properties or desirable qualities, or in a specific quality, etc.; inadequacy ... 3. smallness in amount; scarcity; paucity." Webster's New World Dictionary of the American Language 1116 (David B. Guralnik ed., 2d ed. 1970).

[28] Salvin, Robert F. (1996). Student loans, bankruptcy, and the fresh start policy: Must debtors be impoverished

to discharge educational loans? Tul. L. Rev. (71), Supra note 178.

[29] See Healey v. Massachusetts Higher Educ. (*In re Healey*), 161 B.R. 389, 392 (E.D. Mich. 1993); Law v. Educational Resources Inst., Inc. (*In re Law*), 159 B.R. 287, 291 (Bankr. D.S.D. 1993); Bakkum v. Great Lakes Higher Educ. Corp. (*In re Bakkum*), 139 B.R. 680, 682 (Bankr. N.D. Ohio 1992); Evans v. Higher Educ. Assistance Found. (*In re Evans*), 131 B.R. 372, 374-75 (Bankr. S.D. Ohio 1991); Johnson v. U.S.A. Funds, Inc. (*In re Johnson*), 121 B.R. 91, 93 (Bankr. N.D. Okla. 1990); Burton v. Pennsylvania Higher Educ. Assistance Agency (*In re Burton*), 117 B.R. 167, 169 (Bankr. W.D. Pa. 1990); D'Ettore v. Devry Inst. of Tech. (*In re D'Ettore*), 106 B.R. 715, 718 (Bankr. M.D. Fla. 1989); Coleman v. Higher Educ. Assistance Found. (*In re Coleman*), 98 B.R. 443, 447 (Bankr. S.D. Ind. 1989); Bey v. Dollar Sav. Bank (*In re Bey*), 95 B.R. 376, 377 (Bankr. W.D. Pa. 1989); Conner v. Illinois State Scholarship Comm'n (*In re Conner*), 89 B.R. 744, 747 (Bankr. N.D. Ill. 1988); United States v. Brown (*In re Brown*), 18 B.R. 219, 222 (Bankr. D. Kan. 1982); Briscoe v. Bank of N.Y. (*In re Briscoe*), 16 B.R. 128, 130-31 (Bankr. S.D.N.Y. 1981); see also Smith v. Pittsburgh Nat'l Bank (*In re Smith*), Adv. No. 87-0399, 1988 WL 59209, at *3 (Bankr. W.D. Pa. June 7, 1988) ("[A]ll those petitioning for relief under the bankruptcy laws are presumed to be suffering severe financial difficulties.").

[30] See Law, 159 B.R. at 291; Evans, 131 B.R. at 374-75; Johnson, 121 B.R. at 93; Burton, 117 B.R. at 169; D'Ettore, 106 B.R. at 718; Coleman, 98 B.R. at 448; Bey, 95 B.R. at 377; Pendergrast v. Student Loan Servicing Ctr. (*In re Pendergrast*), 90 B.R. 92, 94 (Bankr. M.D. Pa. 1988) ("[L]iving on a tight budget is a common rather than an undue hardship."); Childs v. Higher Educ. Assistance Found. (*In re Childs*), 89 B.R. 819, 820 (Bankr. D. Neb. 1988); Courtney v. Gainer Bank (*In re Courtney*), 79 B.R. 1004, 1010-11 (Bankr. N.D. Ind. 1987); North Dakota State Bd. of Higher Educ. v. Frech (*In re Frech*), 62 B.R. 235, 243 (Bankr. D. Minn. 1986); Brunner v. New York State Higher Educ. Servs. Corp. (*In re Brunner*), 46 B.R. 752, 755 (Bankr. S.D.N.Y. 1985), aff'd, 831 F.2d 395 (2d Cir. 1987); Panteli v. New York State Higher Educ. Servs. Corp., 41 B.R. 856, 858 (Bankr. S.D.N.Y. 1984) (requiring a certainty of hopelessness to discharge student loan); Shoberg v. Minnesota Higher Educ. Coordinating Council, 41 B.R. 684, 687 (Bankr. D. Minn. 1984) (stating that student loans are discharged only under exceptional circumstances); Brown, 18 B.R. at 222; Briscoe, 16 B.R. 130-31; Virginia Educ. Loan Auth. v. Archie (*In re Archie*), 7 B.R. 715, 718 (Bankr. E.D. Va. 1980).

[31] See Healey, 161 B.R. at 393; Law, 159 B.R. at 291; Evans, 131 B.R. at 374-75; D'Ettore, 106 B.R. at 718; Coleman, 98 B.R. at 448; Courtney, 79 B.R. at 1010-11; Frech, 62 B.R. at 243; *Brunner*, 46 B.R. at 753; see also Love v. United States, (*In re Love*), 33 B.R. 753, 755 (Bankr. E.D. Va. 1983) (stating that undue hardship is more than the "unpleasantness" associated with the repayment of an educational debt).

[32] Financial Collection Agencies v. Norman (*In re Norman*), 25 B.R. 545, 549 (Bankr. S.D. Cal. 1982) (quoting Fischer v. State Univ. (*In re Fischer*), 23 B.R. 432, 433 (Bankr. W.D. Ky. 1982)).

[33] *In re Roberson*, 999 F.2d 1132, 1136 (7th Cir. 1993); Barrows v. Illinois Student Assistance Comm'n (*In re Barrows*), 182 B.R. 640, 648 (Bankr. D.N.H. 1994); Healey, 161 B.R. at 392-93; Ford v. Tennessee Student Assistance Corp. (*In re Ford*), 151 B.R. 135, 138-39 (Bankr. M.D. Tenn. 1993); Kraft v. New York State Higher Educ. Servs. Corp. (*In re Kraft*), 161 B.R. 82, 84 (Bankr. W.D.N.Y. 1993); Phillips v. Great Lakes Higher Educ. Corp. (*In re Phillips*), 161 B.R. 945, 947-48 (Bankr. N.D. Ohio 1993); Reyes v. Oklahoma State Regents For Higher Educ. (*In re Reyes*), 154 B.R. 320, 322-23 (Bankr. E.D. Okla. 1993); Woodcock v. Chemical Bank (*In re Woodcock*), 149 B.R. 957, 961-63 (Bankr. D. Colo. 1993), aff'd, 45 F.3d 363 (10th Cir. 1995); Cadle Co. v. Webb (*In re Webb*), 132 B.R. 199, 201-02 (Bankr. M.D. Fla. 1991); Garneau v. New York State Higher Educ. Servs. Corp. (*In re Garneau*), 122 B.R. 178, 180 (Bankr. W.D.N.Y. 1990); D'Ettore, 106 B.R. at 718; Coleman, 98 B.R. at 454; Taylor v. Tennessee Student Assistance Corp. (*In re Taylor*), 95 B.R. 550, 552 (Bankr. E.D. Tenn. 1989); Gearhart v. Clearfield Bank & Trust Co. (*In re Gearhart*), 94 B.R. 392, 393 (Bankr. W.D. Pa. 1989); Strauss v. United States Dep't of Educ. (*In re Strauss*), 91 B.R. 872, 874 (Bankr. E.D. Mo. 1988); Childs, 89 B.R. at 820-21; Courtney, 79 B.R. at 1010-11; Craig v. Pennsylvania Higher Educ. Assistance Agency (*In re Craig*), 64 B.R. 854, 857 (Bankr. W.D. Pa. 1986); *Brunner*, 46 B.R. at 754- 55; Holzer v. Wachovia Servs., Inc. (*In re Holzer*), 33 B.R. 627, 631 (Bankr. S.D.N.Y. 1983); Lezer v. New York State Higher Educ. Servs. Corp. (*In re Lezer*), 21 B.R. 783, 787-88 (Bankr. N.D.N.Y. 1982); Brown, 18 B.R. at 222; Briscoe, 16 B.R. at 129-30; Rappaport v. Orange Sav. Bank (*In re Rappaport*), 16 B.R. 615, 616-17 (Bankr. D.N.J. 1981); Virginia Educ. Loan Auth. v. Archie (*In re Archie*), 7 B.R. 715, 717-18 (Bankr. E.D. Va. 1980); New York State Higher Educ. Servs. Corp. v. Kohn (*In re Kohn*), 5 Bankr. Ct. Dec. (CRR) 419, 424 (Bankr. S.D.N.Y. 1979); see also Myers v. Pennsylvania

Higher Educ. Assistance Agency (*In re Myers*), 150 B.R. 139, 142 (Bankr. W.D. Pa. 1993); Harris v. Pennsylvania Higher Educ. Assistance Agency (*In re Harris*), 103 B.R. 79, 82 (Bankr. W.D.N.Y. 1989); Medeiros v. Florida Dep't of Educ. (*In re Medeiros*), 86 B.R. 284, 286 (Bankr. M.D. Fla. 1988) ("To prove undue hardship, the Debtor must show that his financial resources will allow him to live only at a poverty level standard for the foreseeable future ..."); Preisser v. University of Maine (*In re Preisser*), 33 B.R. 63, 65 (Bankr. D. Me. 1983) ("[D]ebtor must demonstrate that it would be impossible 'in the foreseeable future' for him to generate enough income to pay off the loan and maintain himself and his dependents above the poverty level.")

[34] Correll v. Union Nat'l Bank of Pittsburgh (*In re Correll*), 105 B.R. 302, 304-07 (Bankr. W.D. Pa. 1989); Dyer, 40 B.R. at 874

[35] See Johnson, 5 Bankr. Ct. Dec. (CRR) at 544.

[36] See Pashman, Scott. (2001). Note, Discharge of student loan debt under 11 U.S.C.A. § 523(A)(8): Reassessing "undue hardship" after the elimination of the seven-year exception N.*Y.L. Sch. L. Rev., (44)*. 605, 617-18, at 618.

[37] 11 U.S.C.A. § 105(a) (2000).

[38] United States v. Sutton, 786 F.2d 1305, 1307 (5th Cir. 1986).

[39] Skaggs v. Great Lakes Higher Educ. Corp. (*In re Skaggs*), 196 B.R. 865, 867 (Bankr. W.D. Okla. 1996).

[40] Chapter 13 proceedings must be voluntary. See 11 U.S.C.A. s 303(a) (stating that involuntary cases may be filed only under Chapters 7 and 11); id. s 706(c) (indicating that a case may be converted to Chapter 13 only on request of debtor); see also Gross, supra note 229, at 119- 20 (observing that the purpose of Chapter 13 is to give debtors the voluntary choice of repaying creditors).

[41] *In re Heckathorn*, 199 B.R. at 194.

[42] Johnson v. U.S.A. Funds, Inc. (*In re Johnson*), 121 B.R. 91, 93 (Bankr. N.D. Okla. 1990).

[43] See Bryant, 72 B.R. at 915.

[44] Even the federal government admits the official poverty level is subjective. See Bureau of the Census, U.S. Department of Commerce, Series P-60, No. 178, Workers With Low Earnings: 1964-1990, at B-3 (1992) (hereinafter Census II) ("The choice of a threshold for determining whether annual earnings are low or not low is necessarily subjective.") Cf. Teresa A. Sullivan et al., Forklore and Facts: A Preliminary Report from the Consumer Bankruptcy Project, 60 Am. Bankr. L.J. 293, 294, 312, 314 (1986) ("[A]ny inference from the data will still require a normative view about when repayment appears so onerous that the debtor 'can't pay'.")

[45] See Census II, supra note 241, at 9 ("[T]he USDA food budget that underlies the SSA index is at best a measure of temporary/emergency food needs and thus not appropriate as a long-run market basked.")

[46] Winnick, Andrew J. (1989). *Toward two societies: The changing distributions of income and wealth in the U.S. since 1960* (p. 10-11). New York: Praeger.

[47] See Ross, Sonya. (December 8, 1994). Americans think welfare benefits are higher than they are. *Phila. Inquirer*, at A30; Rainwater, Lee. (1974). What money buys. *Tul. L. Rev.. (31)*, supra note 233, at 132-33.

[48] Winnick, Andrew J. (1989). *Toward two societies: The changing distributions of income and wealth in the U.S. since 1960* (p. 24-25). New York: Praeger.

[49] *See* Notice of Determination of Lower Living Standard Income Level, 59 Fed. Reg. 19241-46 (1994).

[9] Salvin, Robert F. (1996). Student loans, bankruptcy, and the fresh start policy: Must debtors be impoverished to discharge educational loans? Tul. L. Rev. (71), 139, at 10.

[51] McGinley, Laurie. (March 31, 1993). Outline is given for expansion of a tax credit (supra note 298). *Wall St. Journal*.

[52] See 34 C.F.R. s 674.33(c)(2).

[53] Salvin, Robert F. (1996). Student loans, bankruptcy, and the fresh start policy: Must debtors be impoverished to discharge educational loans? Tul. L. Rev. (71), 139 at 11.

[54] See *Brunner*, 46 B.R. at 756

[55] See *Brunner*, 46 B.R. at 755 n.3 & 756.

[56] The 1978 Bankruptcy Commission described the reasons for limiting the dischargeability of student loans in the following terms: A separate clause to provide for a limited nondischargeability of educational loan debts is desirable for two kinds of reasons. First, a loan or other credit extended to finance higher education that enables a person to earn substantially greater income over his working life should not as a matter of policy be dischargeable before he has demonstrated that for any reason he is unable to earn sufficient income to maintain himself and his dependents and to repay the educational debt. Second, such a policy cannot be appropriately carried out under any other nondischargeability provision. Comm'n Report, supra note 40, pt. II, at 140 (emphasis added).

Whew!

Take a deep breath.

You can do it.

It takes planning and determination.

CHAPTER 9
Preparing for the Adversary Proceeding

This chapter helps you gather all the data and documents you will need to prove your claim that having to repay your federally guaranteed student loan(s) will cause you an "undue hardship" and, therefore, should be discharged.

It does not matter if you are filing an adversary proceeding as part of a Chapter 7 or Chapter 13 bankruptcy or attempting to have your loans discharged through Compromise or Write-Off (*see* Chapter 2); the preparation is similar. This chapter discusses only the adversary proceeding. See Chapter 11 for details for preparing a Compromise or Write-Off.

Some courts have developed forms to gather the data needed to establish undue hardship. For example, see Appendix B to view a sample of the Interrogatories used by the United States Bankruptcy Court for the Western District of Kentucky. Most courts use the *Brunner* test to determine undue hardship, whereas a few courts use the other tests detailed in Chapter 5. Regardless of which test is used by the court or forms used to gather information, the categories of information are very much the same as described in Chapter 6.

Many of the steps below refer to forms or worksheets located in Appendix C, D, and E. **The Chapter 7 bankruptcy forms in Appendix C are for the Central District of California. They are there for illustrative purposes only. You will need to locate the corresponding forms used in your bankruptcy court.**

Items that are bulleted and bolded are the data or documents you need to collect or create.

If you are filing an *adversary proceeding*, read this chapter. If you are attempting to discharge your student loans through a *Compromise* or *Write-Off*, see Chapters 11 and 12.

The Adversary Proceeding

An adversary proceeding is filed in conjunction with a bankruptcy filing. The steps below assume you have already filed, or are planning to file, or are reopening, a bankruptcy. You will need copies of some of the forms used in your bankruptcy filing.

PRE-INFO—
Undue Hardship Test and Student Loan History

Before you file the bankruptcy, it is important for you to be up-to-date about all your student loans. Thus, you need to contact each lender and get a copy of your student loans and their payment histories. It is most important to know payment, forbearance, and deferment dates.

> **Step 1 • Obtain** a printout from your lenders of the history of your student loans. It is important to know the payment amounts, forbearances, and deferment dates for each loan. **Transfer** this information on the Student Loan History worksheet found in Appendix D. If you do not know who has your loans, please see the document in Appendix E for help.

Comments about what constitutes a "student loan"— One of the major questions asked of the author of this book is whether or not particular student loans are federally guaranteed or not. This used to be an important question as private loans were not protected under the code. Changes in the Education code extended the protection to all loans. In reality, virtually all loans made for educational purposes are federally guaranteed. Further, the Bankruptcy Abuse Prevention and Consumer

Protection Act of 2005 amended the U.S. Bankruptcy Code to include "qualified education loans" within the scope of the exception for discharging student loans. Private loans that are not "school certified" generally do not meet the definition of qualified education loans. "School certified" means the school complies with restrictions imposed by 26 USC 221(d)(l), which enforces limits on the amount of debt and other qualifications. Why would a school give private loans that are not "qualified education loans?" Easy, the school can lend more money than they otherwise would be permitted on a school-certified loan. Thus, if you received private loans, you need to determine if the school is "certified" as described above. [See Kantrowitz, Mark (August 19, 2007). *Limitations on Exception to Discharge of Private Student Loans*, FinAid.org.]

Step 2 • **Ask** the court which undue hardship test they use **and/or obtain** Interrogatories Form. Ask for a sample from the court. Often, they are available online for download. You will use this information later to tailor the data to meet the needs of the hardship test.

Chapter 6 detailed the kinds of information you must provide in order to achieve the claim of undue hardship. These were identified as *Characteristics*:

- **Characteristic A**—Current Living Condition and the Impact of Repaying Loan on "Minimal Living" Standard
- **Characteristic B**—Prospects for Repaying the Loans
- **Characteristic C**—Good Faith and Loan Repayment

Each *Characteristic* will be discussed below in detail, along with the sequential steps used to produce the appropriate documents. The problem of the *Income-Driven Repayment (IDR) plan* also is addressed.

CHARACTERISTIC A—
Current Living Condition and the Impact of Repaying Loan on "Minimal Living" Standard

First, you need to establish your current financial and living conditions. When you filed a bankruptcy, you gave information concerning your family and you and your spouse's income, net pay, and total monthly income. Forms for a Chapter 7 bankruptcy will be used to illustrate the following steps.

Step 3 • From your Chapter 7 bankruptcy filing; **make a copy** of your *Form 106I-Current Income of Individual Debtor* (this is a California Central District form, use your state's equivalent Chapter 7 bankruptcy form). If you have business income/expenses, make a copy of that form also (sample in Appendix C). A sample is included in Appendix C if you need a blank form. If you have multiple employers,

---

—WARNING—
A Word of Caution about Income Statements

The income you list on Form 106I of your Chapter 7 bankruptcy should match the income you claim during the adversary proceeding—which should match the income you claim with the IRS. *If these are not similar, the court will view you with suspicion.*

---

you may need to make additional copies of Form 106I.

The time span from when you first file your bankruptcy and then enter into mediation or trial for the adversary proceeding may be six months or longer. As such, your income and living conditions may have changed since the bankruptcy filing and needs to be updated.

Step 4 • **Update** your income and living conditions by **making a copy** of the worksheet *Current Income Status* (in Appendix D), **fill in** old information using your Form 106I, and **write** in any new changes.

As you will learn later, part of the strategy of proving undue hardship or negotiating a

Compromise or Write-off is for you to present yourself as a hopeless and helpless debtor who is representing him or herself. As such, it is **best not to let the defendant or court know that you are using this book**. Instead of handing them the *Current Income Status* worksheet, we suggest that you write, in your own words and on a blank piece of paper, the changes in your financial and living status. The *Current Income Status* worksheet will help guide you in your writing in that process.

> **Step 5 •** **On** a blank piece of paper, **write** your name, adversary case number, and date. Title the page "Current Income and Family Status" (or similar words). Below this, write a few short paragraphs telling how your income or family has changed, if at all, since filing your Chapter 7 bankruptcy. *See* a sample in Appendix D— Current Income and Family Status.

It is recommended that you write all these documents on a computer and save the files. Later, you will be asked to blend all the documents together into one master document. If you write them on a computer, all you will have to do is cut and paste the sections, thereby eliminating the need to retype everything.

Now we evaluate your expenditures.

> **Step 6 •** From your Chapter 7 bankruptcy filing, **make a copy** of your *Form 106J—Current Expenditures of Individual Debtor* (again, this is a California Central District form, use your equivalent Chapter 7 bankruptcy form). A sample is included in Appendix C if you need a blank form.

As with the income statement being updated as necessary, you need to update your expenses if they have changed between the time of filing the bankruptcy to the time of the adversary proceeding mediation or trial.

> **Step 7 •** **Update** your expense conditions by **making a copy** of the worksheet *Current Expenditure Status* (in Appendix D), **fill in** old information (column 1) using your Form 106J, and **write in** any new changes (column 2).

Also, you need to demonstrate that your expenses are comparable to a similarly situated debtor. This is achieved by showing: (a) that your income is within range of the Federal Poverty Guidelines for a family your size, and (b) your expenses are similar to other families of your size and circumstances.

> **Step 8 •** **Go to** the website of the United States Department of Health and Human Services (https://aspe.hhs.gov/poverty-guidelines) and **download a copy** of the current Federal Poverty Guidelines (a copy of this homepage and document are in Appendix B). If you do not have access to the web, your local library should have a copy of this government publication. Be sure it is the current year. **Write** your information on the *Current Expenditure Status* worksheet.

> **Step 9 •** Go **to the website** of the IRS to gather data on Collection Financial Standards https://www.irs.gov/businesses/small-businesses-self-employed/collection-financial-standards. The IRS has established standards used to determine the ability of taxpayers to make delinquent payments. Use the data found here to **fill-in** the National Norms (column 3) on the *Current Expenditure Status* worksheet.

> **Step 10 •** For those cases where there are significant differences between your expenditures and the national norms, **write** an explanation for each on the *Current Expenditure Status* worksheet (column 4).

—WARNING—
A Word of Caution about Expense Statements

The expenses you list on Form 106J of your Chapter 7 bankruptcy should match the expense you claim during the adversary proceeding— which should match the expenses you claim with the IRS. *If these are not similar, the court will view you with suspicion.*

You need to explain that you have minimized your living expenses and are not living extravagantly and that there is no extra income available to pay on your student loans.

Step 11 • On a blank piece of paper, write your name, adversary case number, and date. Title the page "Current Expenditures and Minimalized Living" (or similar words). Below this, write a few short paragraphs telling how your expenditures have changed (if it has changed since filing your bankruptcy), how you live frugally, and that it would be impossible to make payments on your student loans. *See* a sample and instructions in Appendix D— Current Expenditure and Minimalized Living.

CHARACTERISTIC B—
Prospects for Repaying the Loans

In so many cases, debtors make a strong showing for their situation only to have the court reject the claim and tell the debtor to get a part-time, minimum-wage job and use that money to make loan payments. Regardless of how laughable or tragic this may seem, it happens all the time. Thus, the debtor needs to account for his or her time working or providing dependent care, or both. Debtors need to clearly point out to the court that asking the debtor to take on any more work would push him or her over a standard workweek, and that would be an undue hardship.

Step 12 • Make a copy of the worksheet *Work Time Accounting Table* (Appendix D) and complete it as instructed. **Write** on a blank piece of paper your name, date, and adversary number and entitle it *Work Time Accounting* (or similar words). In your own words (using the *Work Time Accounting Table*), explain why all your available time is committed, making it impossible for you to take on another job. *See* a sample document in the Samples section of Appendix D, under *Work Time Accounting Statement*.

The debtor needs to address in detail any personal limitations that may impact the ability to obtain appropriate employment. This includes personal medical limitations, support of dependents (and their medical conditions, if applicable), and lack of useable job skills. These need to be described in detail, with supporting documents (like medical records), etc.

Step 13 • On a blank piece of paper, **write** your name, date, and adversary number and entitle it *Personal Limitations* (or similar words). Here you explain why medical problems for you and/or your dependents, the lack of usable job skills, and/or the existence of a large number of dependents impact your future ability to work at a job that will provide sufficient income to service your student loan debt. *See* a sample document in the Samples section of Appendix D under *Personal Limitations Statement*. **In general, you must show there are "unique" or "exceptional" circumstances that impact future employment and earnings.**

The last step to this Characteristic is to discuss the impact of external factors on your future employment. Courts have been hesitant to include these factors since it would require them to accept the fact that not all employment doors are open to all workers, i.e., the American dream is not really attainable by all.

External factors that affect future employment opportunities include:
- U.S. Economy
- Discrimination based on age, race, ethnicity, gender, sexual orientation, and others.
- Reverse Discrimination
- Past Terminations
- Whistleblower
- And others

Chapter 6 explains in greater detail about these issues. In many cases, academic papers on these topics are included in Appendix F.

Step 14 • On a blank piece of paper, **write** your name, date, and adversary number and entitle it *External Factors* (or similar words). In general, it is suggested that you first develop your argument through academic research of the societal problem that impacts future employment, and then make it specific with examples from your own life story. You need to tell the court about the factors that impact your ability to secure employment. It is important to emphasize how this impacts your future earnings. No sample is provided in the Appendix because each case is very specific to the debtor, and no generalization is possible.

The process described above explains for the court the reasons why you can't take on any more work and why your future employment is not going to improve. As such, you will not be able to service your student loans and request they be discharged as an undue hardship.

CHARACTERISTIC C—
Good Faith and Loan Repayment

Debtors are required to demonstrate "good faith" attempts to repay student loans. There is an expectation that any time the debtor's net income exceeded the Federal Poverty Guidelines, payments were made on the student loans. During times of financial difficulty, debtors must show that they worked with the lender to resolve the issue instead of letting loans fall into arrears. When contemplating filing bankruptcy, keep in mind that student loans should not exceed about 50 percent of the debtor's total debt load; otherwise the court will be suspicious that the primary purpose of the bankruptcy is to discharge the student loans. Additionally, at least seven or more years should have passed since obtaining the last student loan before filing an adversary proceeding, otherwise, the courts have a presumption of fraud the debtor must overcome.

Step 15 • **Make copies** of your IRS Income Tax filings for each year since receiving your last student loan. **Fill out** the worksheet *Income and Student Loan Payment* (Appendix D). Instructions are on the worksheet form. This form tracks your income for the years since obtaining your most recent student loans and the status of student loan repayments.

You now have everything needed to write a history of your employment, attempts to find work, family income, and servicing your student loans. The purpose of the narrative is to show that you have been diligent in trying to make income sufficient to repay your student loans.

Step 16 • On a blank piece of paper, **write** your name, date, and adversary number, and entitle it *Good Faith and Loan Repayment* (or similar words). Here, you write a history of your employment, family income, and student loan repayment. Be sure to indicate when your family income dropped below the Federal Poverty Guidelines, that you received deferments or forbearances whenever you were unable to make payments, and more. You want to show you have been diligent in servicing your student loans and that there is no fraud in seeking their discharge. Review the sample provided in Appendix D entitled *Good Faith and Loan Repayment Statement*.

INCOME-DRIVEN REPAYMENT (IDR) PLANS

Finally, the last problem that must be addressed are the *Income-Driven Repayment (IDR)* plans. As described at length in Chapter 7, the IDR plans allow debtors to make loan payments when they can and sometimes pay nothing at all if their income drops below a particular level. The plan lasts for twenty-five years, and any outstanding student loan debt remaining at the end of the plan is forgiven. However, and this is a big however, debtors are liable for the income taxes on the forgiven amount. That could be tens of thousands of dollars in tax liability.

It is often stated by the Department of Education attorneys that IDR plans make it impossible for debtors to discharge their student loans in bankruptcy or otherwise. They contend that anyone can make "zero dollar" payments, thus negating the undue hardship exception of §523(a)(8).

In many cases, this is true. But we argue in Chapter 8 that, for most debtors, the IDR plans are inappropriate. Perhaps you are one of the debtors who would benefit from arguing that the IDR plans cause you an undue hardship?

Step 17 • On a blank piece of paper, **write** your name, date, and adversary number, and entitle it *Income-Driven Repayment* (or similar words). Tell why, in your case, the IDR plans are not appropriate and cause an undue hardship. See *Income-Driven Repayment* statement in Appendix D for a sample.

Review

If you have completed all seventeen steps listed above, you have all the necessary documents and arguments to file an adversary proceeding. There will be no surprises, and you will have all the facts and documents needed to defend your position.

To review; you have completed the following forms and worksheets:

Step 1 — Contacted your student loan lenders and obtained a complete history of their payment and status. Completed the Student Loan History worksheet (Appendix D).

Step 2 — Contacted your local bankruptcy court and determined which undue hardship test will be used in your jurisdiction and/or obtained a copy of interrogatories if used.

Step 3 — Made a copy of your bankruptcy Schedule I—Current Income of Individual Debtor (Appendix C) (or similar form used in your bankruptcy court) and business income/expense) (if needed).

Step 4 — Completed the Current Income Status worksheet (Appendix D).

Step 5 — Wrote a **Current Income and Family Status*** statement on a blank piece of paper (Appendix D).

Step 6 — Made a copy of your bankruptcy Form 106J—Current Expenditures of Individual Debtor (Appendix C) (or similar form used in your bankruptcy court).

Step 7 — Completed most of the Current Expenditure Status worksheet (Appendix D).

Step 8 — Downloaded a copy of the U.S. Department of Health and Human Services Federal Poverty Guidelines and completed more of the Current Expenditure Status worksheet.

Step 9 — Went to IRS website, obtained Collection Financial Standards, and used the data to fill in the Current Expenditure Status worksheet.

Step 10 — Compared your family expenditures against the national norms and completed the Current Expenditure Status worksheet.

Step 11 — Wrote a **Current Expenditures and Minimalized Living***. (Appendix D) statement on a blank piece of paper

Step 12 — Completed the Work Time Accounting Table worksheet (Appendix D). Wrote a **Work Time Accounting Statement*** (Appendix D) on a blank piece of paper.

Step 13 — Wrote a **Personal Limitations*** (Appendix D) statement on a blank piece of paper.

Step 14 — Wrote an **External Factors*** (Appendix D) statement on a blank piece of paper.

Step 15 — Made copies of your IRS Income Tax forms. Completed the Income and Student Loan Payment worksheet.

Step 16 — Wrote a **Good Faith and Loan Repayment*** (Appendix D) statement on a blank piece of paper.

Step 17 — Wrote an **Income-Driven Repayment*** (Appendix D) statement on a blank piece of paper.

(Each underlined item is either a worksheet from the Appendix, letter you wrote, or document you downloaded. **Each bolded and asterisked item are documents you wrote on a blank piece of paper that will be used in the adversary proceeding**. We suggest that you do not submit or show the attorneys for the Department of Education any of the worksheets you used. You do not want to tip them off that you are using this book.) The next chapter will give step-by-step guidance on filing an adversary proceeding and strategies for forcibly making the case to have your student loans discharged. If you are not filing an adversary proceeding but trying to negotiate a discharge of your debt through Compromise or Write-off, see Chapter 11.

CHAPTER 10
Step-By-Step Procedures for The Adversary Proceeding

This chapter presents the steps required to file and argue an adversary proceeding as part of a bankruptcy. The steps here are based on the personal experience of the author and are not legal advice.

The previous chapter helped you to bring together all the documents and data needed to present your case. Hopefully, you have read the rest of this book to familiarize yourself with the legal concepts, language, and court cases that are used to prove cases of "undue hardship." Remember, the strength of your case will ultimately rest on your shoulders, and the better prepared you are, the greater the chance of prevailing and having your student loans discharged or severely reduced.

A check-off box is placed in front of each step. Once you have completed a step, check-off the box so as to keep track of where you are in the process.

The Adversary Proceeding

Chapter 11, §523(a)(8) of the 1998 U.S.C.A. Bankruptcy Reform Act declares that government-backed student loans are not dischargeable unless there is evidence showing that repaying the loans would cause an "undue hardship." To prove this point, the debtor must file a formal complaint with the bankruptcy court. This is legally termed an "adversary proceeding."

An adversary proceeding is the bankruptcy court's execution of a civil complaint. It is governed by Federal Rules of Bankruptcy Procedure (FRBP) Rule 7001 and is used to determine the dischargeability of a debt, as well as other purposes. Since student loans backed by the government are considered not dischargeable, *an adversary proceeding asks the court to determine if they are dischargeable.*

An adversary proceeding is just like any other formal court action and consists of the following steps:

- Filing the Complaint with Proof of Service
- Status Hearing
- Mediation
- Pretrial Hearing
- Trial

Some of these steps may be combined or skipped at the discretion of the court. For example, the court where the person who won a discharge of $225,000 of student loans did not hold a status hearing or send the parties to mediation but rather used interrogatories to gather the information for the judge to make a determination. Still, being prepared for each of these steps helps prepare you for any variation in the process since the same basic questions will be asked.

Before Filing the Complaint

Before filing the adversary complaint, you must clarify some of the legal details for your specific bankruptcy court. Then, you will prepare your documents for filing.

Bankruptcy Filing

Remember to list ALL outstanding student loans in your bankruptcy (one of the cases listed in Chapter 7 illustrates how courts become confused by debtors who fail to list all student loans and conclude there is something wrong with, or being hidden, by the debtor). Chapter 7 forms will be used here to illustrate the process. Student loans are listed on Form 106E/F - *Creditors Holding Unsecured Nonpriority Claims*. A sample and blank form are provided in Appendix C.

Court Details

Although federal law dictates bankruptcy law, each district court, and in fact some judges, have very specific rules related to how to file the case, the layout of the documents, court procedures, costs, and more. Further, you need the specific forms for the court. Most bankruptcy courts make all these documents available online for free download.

Local Bankruptcy Rules and Forms

❑ **Step 1:**
Contact or go online to your bankruptcy district court and obtain a copy of:
(1) *Local Bankruptcy Rules*
(2) *Adversary Proceeding Sheet (Cover)*
(3) *Summons*
(4) *Proof of Service*
(5) *Joint Status Report*

The samples given in this book are for the Central District of California. The *Local Bankruptcy Rules* gives many details, such as the size of the paper, blue back, hole spacing, number of lines maximum per document, and much more. Review these, and if necessary, modify the samples in this book to comply with your local rules.

Timeframe for Filing and Federal Addresses

In general, you need to file the adversary proceeding within 60 days of the meeting of the creditors for Chapter 7 cases. [Bankruptcy Rules 4007 (c)]

For Chapter 13 cases, the time for notifying the creditors is 30 days. [Bankruptcy Rules 4007 (d)] As discussed in Chapter 8, it is unclear when, or if, a debtor files an adversary proceeding as part of a Chapter 13 bankruptcy. Please check our website—

www.HowToBankruptYourStudentLoans.com—for an update on this issue.

❑ **Step 2**:
Although the *Local Bankruptcy Rules* should list the timeframe for filing an adversary proceeding, it may be difficult to locate. Thus, we suggest you contact your local United States Attorney. This is the office that will be defending the United States Department of Education against your adversary proceeding. In this initial phone call, you want to find out:

(a) Ask for the timeframe for filing the adversary proceeding

Write the timeframe here:_____

(b) Ask for the correct mailing address for the defendant (the Department of Education)

Write the name and address here:

_____

_____

_____

_____

(c) Ask for the proper person and address for hand delivery of the complaint.

Write the name and address here:

_____

_____

_____

_____

Do not be alarmed that they will keep a record of when you call them. They may be very "helpful," so much so they may try to engage you in a lengthy conversation and try to convince you not to file the adversary proceeding. They may lie to you, saying that you cannot bankrupt the loans. They will probably tell you that the Income-Driven Repayment (IDR) plans guarantee that you will lose the case. If you have come this far in the book, you have already developed your arguments to satisfy this condition. It is probably best that you do not engage them in a lengthy discussion. Just find out the three items listed above in Step 2.

If you have missed the time for filing the adversary proceeding, you may still be able to file. Some courts have allowed filings years later, whereas other courts insist upon the stated timeframe. It costs you nothing to file, so you might as well try. Another approach is to reopen your bankruptcy for the purpose of filing an adversary proceeding. See Chapter 1 for details on reopening a bankruptcy.

Fees and Verify Bankruptcy Addresses

There should be no fee for filing an adversary proceeding if it is filed within the stipulated timeframe and by the debtor. However, in some bankruptcy districts, the fee may be as high as $150.

❑ **Step 3**:

Contact your bankruptcy district court:

(a) Ask what the fee is for filing a Complaint to Determine Dischargeability. You may need to remind them that you are filing within the timeframe specified for an adversary proceeding as part of a bankruptcy and that you are the debtor. In fact, the instructions given on the back of the *Adversary Proceeding Sheet (Cover)* states, "The fee is not required if the Plaintiff is the United States government or the debtor." Thus, there should be no fee in your case. (In the author's experience, the clerks at the California Central Distinct Court thought there was a fee. A supervisor had to be called over, who then verified that the fee was zero.)

Write the fee here: _____

(b) Ask for the mailing address of the trustee in your Chapter 7 case. You should already know this from your Chapter 7 bankruptcy filing. But ask anyway just to verify.

Write the address here:

_____

_____

_____

(c) Ask for the mailing address of the U.S. trustee, i.e., the U.S. trustee who oversees all bankruptcies in your district.

Write the address here:

_____

_____

_____

(d) Ask the timeframe for filing an adversary proceeding.

Write the timeframe here: _____
Review

In preparation for filing a complaint, you have:
1. Listed all your student loans in your Chapter 7 bankruptcy.
2. Obtained a copy of rules and forms you will need to file—(1) *Local Bankruptcy Rules*, (2) *Adversary Proceeding Sheet* (Cover), (3) *Summons*, (4) *Proof of Service*, and (5) *Joint Status Report*.
3. Used your *Local Bankruptcy Rules* to adjust forms, and more, to conform to the rules.
4. Contacted the local United States Attorney and verified: (a) the timeframe for filing an adversary proceeding, (b) the mailing address for the defendant, and (c) the address for hand delivery (serving) of the complaint.
5. Contacted the bankruptcy district court and verified: (a) the filing fee, (b) address of

your Chapter 7 trustee, (c) address of the U.S. trustee, and (d) the timeframe for filing an adversary proceeding.

You may have noticed that we have had you ask similar questions of the United States Attorney and the bankruptcy district court. Their responses should be the same. <u>If there are differences between the two, you need to contact both and resolve the differences</u>. This way you avoid having your case delayed or thrown out for simple mistakes such as serving the wrong people or missing deadlines.

Let's summarize the final data you will need for the filing. Fill out the table (*Adversary Proceeding Data Summary*) with the data you clarified in Steps 1-3. You will use this table to complete your adversary proceeding.

Filing and Serving the Complaint

In this section, we will first have you prepare your documents for filing, and then show you how to file them with the court and serve them to the defendants.

There are two separate document packages that need to be prepared— the <u>Complaint package</u> and the <u>Proof of Service package</u>.

Appendix E contains instructions, samples, and blanks of these forms in these packets. Remember, the forms in the Appendix are for the U.S. Bankruptcy Court for the Central District of California. You should have obtained blanks of these forms in Step 1 (above) for your specific bankruptcy court district.

Preparing the Complaint Package

The Adversary Complaint package is made up of three documents and a backing:
- A. Summons
- B. *Adversary Proceeding Sheet* (otherwise known as the *Cover* form)
- C. Adversary Complaint
- D. Blue Back

❑ **Step 4:**
Obtain a few sheets of legal (pleading) paper. A blank is provided in Appendix E if you want to make photocopies.

Obtain a few sheets of blue back. See Appendix E for details on how to prepare the backing and how court documents are assembled.

❑ **Step 5**:
Prepare the *Summons*. See Appendix E for instructions, samples, and blank form. Sometimes the *Summons* form can only be obtained at the clerk's window. In this case, we suggest that you complete the form in this book and take it with you as a sample.

❑ **Step 6:**
Prepare the *Adversary Proceeding Sheet (Cover)*. See Appendix E for instructions, samples, and blank form.

❑ **Step 7:**
Prepare the *Adversary Complaint*. See Appendix E for instructions and sample form.

❑ **Step 8**:
<u>Make eight copies each of the *Adversary Proceeding Sheet (Cover)* and Adversary Complaint</u>. These spare copies will be used to serve all parties during the Proof of Service step.

Assemble one Adversary Complaint package as follows (top to bottom) using one of each document:
- A. *Adversary Proceeding Sheet (Cover)*
- B. *Adversary Complaint*

The documents are stapled to the Blue Back with just one staple in the left corner.

Assemble the 7 remaining copies into similar sets.

The *Summons* is not stapled into this package since the clerk has to handle it separately to assign a court date. Place the *Summons* loosely on top of the Complaint package.

Preparing the Proof of Service

The *Summons* and Adversary Complaint package must be served upon the defendant and other parties. You, the Plaintiff, are not allowed to serve these documents. Instead, most states allow you to use a friend or other non-relative for this purpose. Some states restrict "service of process" (serving the documents) to law enforcement officers (sheriff, marshal, or constable) or a licensed private process server. Some states allow all the documents to be served by mail, whereas most states require the defendant to be served personally and all others served by mail. Check with the Local Rules or directly with the bankruptcy court to clarify who can serve the documents and how they are served.

The example in this section assumes you will have a friend personally serve the defendant and mail copies to all others.

The Proof of Service package is made up of 3 documents and a backing:
   A. *Proof of Service Cover*
   B. *Proof of Service*
   C. *Mail Matrix*
   D. Blue Back

❏ **Step 9:**
Prepare the *Proof of Service Cover*, *Proof of Service* with *Mail Matrix*. The names and addresses used on the *Proof of Service* and *Mail Matrix* come from the summary of Step 3 (above). The person who will be performing the "service of process" for you completes and signs the *Proof of Service*. See Appendix E for instructions, samples, and blank forms.

Filing the Complaint and Serving/Filing the Proof of Service

You are now ready to file your complaint and serve the documents.

❏ **Step 10:**
Take your Adversary Complaint package to the bankruptcy court. Bring along your checkbook in case there are any fees. Be sure you are filing before the deadline.

ADVERSARY PROCEEDING DATA SUMMARY

Write the timeframe for filing an adversary proceeding (e.g., within 60 days of meeting with the creditors): _____

Write the filing fee (if any) here:

_____

Names and addresses of people and agencies you need to serve:
- Civil process clerk at the office of the United States attorney for the district in which the action is brought (local U.S. Attorney used to defend the case). This is who you hand-deliver the complaint and summons. Everyone else you mail a copy. Write the Name and Address here:
-

   _____

- Office of the U.S. Trustee in your bankruptcy district. Write the Name and Address here:
-

   _____

- The Attorney General in Washington, D.C. Write the Name and Address here:
-

   _____

- Particular agency named in or affected by the lawsuit (in other words, the agency you are suing—most likely the Dept. of Education). Write the Name and Address here:
-

   _____

-

   Your Chapter 7 bankruptcy trustee. Write the Name and Address here:
-

   _____

When you get to the clerk, hand him or her your *Summons*. If you did not fill one out in advance, ask for a blank *Summons* form.

If you are handed a blank *Summons* form, get out of line, and fill it out on the spot. You may use a pen (it does not have to be typed).

Get back in line with the completed *Summons* and give it to the clerk along with the Adversary Complaint package (the one you have bound in a Blue Back) plus one more copy. The clerk will stamp everything. The court will keep the original complaint (the one that is Blue Back) plus the one copy. If needed, you will pay fees at this time.

Then give the clerk the other copies of the *Adversary Proceeding Sheet (Cover)* and *Adversary Complaint* to stamp (i.e., be "conformed"). These will be handed back to you.

❑ **Step 11:**
You will now receive a date for the "status conference" hearing.

Some bankruptcy clerk offices will issue the status conference date at the same time you file the *Adversary Complaint*. If so, usually they make a copy of the *Summons* and write the court date and address information on it, or they may give you a separate piece of paper with this information (known as the *Order*). In either case, you need to leave with a copy of the *Summons* (and *Order* if given) that contains the status conference date and details.

Some bankruptcy clerk offices will mail the *Summons/Order* to you.

Make nine copies of the final *Summons* and any *Order* giving the details of the "status conference."

❑ **Step 12:**
Finally, the documents must be served.

Most courts require the *Adversary Complaint* and *Summons* with any *Order* to be served within ten days of the filing. Check with your bankruptcy court or local rules to be sure.

❑ Preparing the Envelopes

Obtain a quantity of 9" x 12" (or larger) envelopes equal to the number of addresses on the Mail Matrix plus one. (In the sample given in Appendix E, there are four names/addresses on the Mail Matrix. Thus, five envelopes would be needed).

In each envelope, place a copy of:
A. *Adversary Proceeding Sheet (Cover)*
B. *Adversary Complaint*
C. *Summons/Order*

❑ Serving the Documents

The defendant listed on the *Proof of Service* must be hand-delivered a set of documents. Take one of the envelopes prepared above and have your friend (or whoever agreed to deliver the *Summons* and who signed the *Proof of Service*) go to the address and deliver the envelope. Usually, a secretary will accept the envelope, not the person listed. Ask the name of the person receiving the envelope and write it on the *Proof of Service* next to the address.

Make copies of this *Proof of Service* (the one that has written on it the name of the person who accepted it) and *Mail Matrix* equal to the number names/address on the *Mail Matrix* plus three more. (In the sample in Appendix E, this would be four plus three for a total of seven).

❑ Mailing the Documents

Take the remaining envelopes and prepare each one for mailing by writing a name/address from the *Mail Matrix*. Place a copy of the notated Proof *of Service* with *Mail Matrix* inside along with the other documents. Use enough postage and mail the envelopes.

❏ Filing the Documents

Now you are ready to file with the court your *Proof of Service*.

Assemble one *Proof of Service* package as follows (top to bottom) using one of each document:
- A. *Proof of Service Cover*
- B. *Proof of Service* (the one that contains your notation of who accepted it)
- C. *Mail Matrix*
- D. *Adversary Proceeding Sheet (Cover)* (conformed copy)
- E. *Adversary Complaint* (conformed copy)
- F. *Summons/Order*

The documents are stapled to the Blue Back with just one staple in the left corner.

Assemble the two remaining copies into similar sets (without the Blue Back).

Return to the bankruptcy court clerk. Hand him or her the Proof of Service package (with Blue Back) plus one copy. They will stamp these and accept them. Hand them the one last copy to have them stamp; it will be handed back to you as your conformed copy.

Congratulations! You have finished filing your adversary complaint. Each court is different, and the procedure outlined above could be different. You need to learn to adapt to the situation. Sometimes clerks tell you something different than what you know or ask a question you are not sure how to answer. Often, courts have a help desk to clarify these steps. They cannot offer legal advice, but they can guide you in which documents are needed and how they are filed.

The important thing to remember is the process. You are asking the court to appoint a date to hear your complaint. Obviously, you must let the defendant and related people know that you are taking these legal actions and where and when the court action will take place. The court needs to know that you have properly notified all interested parties with enough time to respond.

It must be emphasized that you are now entering into a formal legal process that is much different from the simple bankruptcy procedures. It is highly recommended that you get a copy of Bergman and Berman-Barrett, *Represent Yourself in Court* (NOLO Press) or a similar type of book. Although this book will discuss ways to avoid pitfalls of a typical lawsuit, you should be prepared for anything.

Status Hearing

Typically, the defendant (probably the Department of Education) has 60-days in which to file a response to your complaint. Of course, they will deny your complaint.

You may, if you wish, respond to the defendant's response. See the Bergman and Berman-Barrett book for details on filing a response. It is probably better not to respond at this point and let the negotiations occur during mediation.

The *Summons* and *Order* you received were for a Status Hearing. The court does not make a decision at a Status Hearing, and it is not a trial. It simply is a step where the court wants to know if the two parties are talking and trying to resolve the problem.

❏ **Step 13:**

Approximately two weeks before the Status Hearing, a report must be filed with the court. The court wants to know if the two parties have come to some kind of agreement, and if not, do they want to enter into mediation. Typically, the defendant's attorney (local U.S. Attorney) will offer to prepare a *Joint Status Report*. They will fill out their part, send you a copy, you fill out your part and mail it back. They will file it with the court. The form asks if you want to go into mediation. You want to check off "yes." It is mediation where you will win your case. If you check off "no," the case will end, and you will still owe on your student loans. A sample and blank form of a *Joint Status Report* is provided in Appendix E. Be sure to file your own status report if a joint one is not filed by the defendant.

❑ **Step 14:**

Attend your Status Hearing. This is probably the first time you'll meet the U.S. attorney who is representing the defendant (U.S. Department of Education). Be calm. The judge will ask you to come forward and identify yourself. He or she will ask if you agree to mediation. By responding, "yes," the judge will direct the case to mediation.

Mediation

You will receive notice in the mail about the mediation. Sometimes you are given the opportunity to select the mediator. Most often, you do not know who the mediators are. Probably it is best to just go with whomever the court assigns, particularly if the mediation site is nearby.

MEDIATION AND NEGOTIATION ARE WHERE YOU WIN YOUR CASE!

You really don't want to go to trial. Review the cases presented in Chapter 7, and you will notice how the courts often rule against the debtor. There is an unreasonable bias against debtors that the courts reinforce.

The Department of Education also does not want to go to trial. It costs them a lot of money to defend against adversary proceedings. Before the trial, they will have to put you through deposition and other steps that all cost them money. Further, they want to avoid having a court make an adverse decision against them that may affect their future ability to defend against similar adversary proceedings.

I've noticed over the years that some debtors become very angry going through this process and want to go to trial to "teach" the DOE a lesson. That is a very different mindset than focusing on having your loans discharged. You need to be clear about your goals. I recommend that debtors take care of themselves. Isn't it better to have 90 percent of your loan discharged than lose in court and have the debt hang over your head for the rest of your life? It is your decision.

Strategies

Going into mediation and negotiating with the attorneys for the Department of Education requires some strategy. In general, they believe the Income-Driven Repayment (IDR) plans precludes anyone from discharging his or her student loans regardless of meeting the "undue hardship" court requirement. They will be aggressive and intimidating. They may, in fact, lie to you. Thus, you need to prepare for the negotiations.

There are three levels of strategy to mediation the author found effective. They are identified as:

- **Playing the Game**

- **Resisting Their Arguments**

- **Attacking the Agency and Law**

The strategies represent increasing levels of resistance to the psychological and legal intimidation they will use on you.

Playing the Game

Section 523(a)(8) of the bankruptcy laws require you to show that it would cause an undue hardship to you and your dependents if you were required to repay your student loans. Thirty years of litigation on this issue has resulted in the courts developing a number of tests. Most courts use the *Brunner* test, as discussed in Chapters 5 and 6. In Chapter 9, we had you verify with your court which test they use.

In Chapter 6, we developed a set of guidelines needed to prove undue hardship. In Chapter 9, we had you complete a number of worksheets that helped you develop and compose written responses to prove these guidelines.

Your first step is to comply with proving the "undue hardship" test used by your court. We call this "playing the game" because the court expects you to make this proof, whereas the Department of Education believes that the Income-Driven Repayment (IDR) plans negates any "undue hardship" test.

- First— you need to show that your current family income does not allow you to make repayments on your student loans. To that end, you composed in Chapter 9 the letter *Current Income and Family Status*.

- Second— you need to show that your family expenditures are minimized and equal to other similarly situated families. To that end, you composed in Chapter 9 the letter *Current Expenditures and Minimalized Living*.

- Third— you need to show that there are personal limitations and external factors that impact your ability to find better-paying work. To that end, you composed in Chapter 9 the letters *Personal Limitations* and *External Factors*.

- Fourth— you need to show that you have been diligent in making student loan payments when you were financially able and received deferments or forbearances whenever you were unable to make payments. To that end, you composed in Chapter 9 the letter *Good Faith and Loan Repayment*.

We want to blend these five documents into one letter and deliver it to the defendant a few weeks before the Mediation. By doing so, you are showing the court that you are trying to work with the defendant by honestly presenting your case. Hopefully, you wrote all these documents on a computer, so you only have to cut and paste the sections into one master document. If you did not, or could not, use a computer, you will have to retype all the letters.

❏ **Step 15:**
A few weeks before your Mediation, write one letter that contains all five documents—
Current Income and Family Status
Current Expenditures and Minimalized Living
Personal Limitations
External Factors
Good Faith and Loan Repayment

Address the letter to the attorney representing the defendant. On the first lines of the letter state that, "repaying my student loans represents an undue hardship because . . . "(now copy each of your letters, one-by-one, in the order above). Mail the letter to the attorney. Be sure to keep a copy of the master letter for yourself (or, if on a computer, save the file). A few days after you mail the letter, call the attorney to see that he or she received it.

A word about grammar and wording: If you have a high college degree such as Doctorate or Master's, take time to use proper wording and grammar. If you have a technical degree, no degree or limited education, or are mentally disabled, do not worry that your letter is not perfect; they expect you to make mistakes. If your letter is too good, they may suspect you had professional help.

You should not expect to hear from the attorney for the defendant before the Mediation. The attorney should forward the letter to the defendant.

A word about the attorney for the defendant: Usually, this person is not a direct employee of the Department of Education. Instead, he or she is an attorney for the U.S. Attorney's office and is retained to negotiate for the Department. Ultimately, a decision to accept an out-of-court settlement comes from the Department itself, not from the attorney. The attorney is just a conduit to the Department, although the attorney will fully represent the Department if your case goes all the way to trial.

You should feel proud that you have made the effort to present your position. Many, if not most, people filing an adversary proceeding do not make their position clear. They leave it up to the attorney for the defendant and court to pull this information out of the debtor. As such, they control how they present your information; and you can be sure it is not in your best interest. By clearly stating your position, you have taken control of the process.

It is now time for the Mediation.

Before going to the Mediation, we want you to be prepared for a number of contingencies:

- Although the attorney probably will be very pleasant at the beginning of the Mediation, he or she may try to unnerve you soon into the Mediation by pointing out "problems" in your master letter. These may or may not be true. You may answer the best you can, but <u>it would be better to write down the supposed problem for you to work on after the Mediation</u>.

- If your "undue hardship" arguments are strong, the attorney will most likely ignore your master letter and attack other "problems." <u>Write these down for you to research after the Mediation</u>.

- Regardless if the discussion begins with reference to your letter or not, eventually, the <u>attorney is going to claim that you should agree to an Income-Driven Repayment (IDR) plan</u>. You must have a strong answer to this. You prepared a letter in Chapter 9 to address this issue. Thus, a day before going to the Mediation, review your letter *Income-contingent Repayment*. Don't bring this with you; just know the contents so you can <u>recite the reasons IDR is inappropriate for you</u>.

- Similarly, the <u>attorney is going to claim that you can work more to make more income that can be used toward student loan payments</u>. In Chapter 9, you prepared a letter to address this issue. The day before the Mediation, review your letter *Work Time Accounting Statement*. Don't bring this letter with you but know the contents so you can <u>recite why you are not able to take on more work</u>.

- The attorney will most likely tell a story about some other debtor he or she is currently negotiating who is in much "worse" financial stress than you and that the Department of Education is not accepting his or her claim of "undue hardship." This is meant to unnerve you and make you feel that the process is hopeless. <u>Don't give up</u>.

- <u>Give some thought to a "fair" settlement for your particular situation</u>. Maybe your situation is so dire that complete discharge of the loans is necessary. However, maybe you could pay a <u>portion</u> of the loans. In the banking industry, bad debts are often settled at 10 cents on the dollar. Ask yourself if you could pay 10 percent of your loan (or 5 percent or 2 percent). The Department of Education will not accept payments less than $50 a month because of bookkeeping expenses. For example, let's say you owe $60,000; maybe you could pay $50 a month for ten years. That works out to a total of $6,000 repayment saving you $54,000. If you owe a smaller amount, maybe you could pay $50 a month for five years, or whatever. <u>Don't have the loan last more than ten years</u>. Also, consider the issue of furlough. Obviously, you would like the ability to have a number of furloughs available just in case something terrible goes wrong, and you do not have money for a brief time. The problem with including furloughs in your settlement is that then your repayment program begins to look too much like the IDR plan. Congress set the terms for the IDR, and the Department of Education does not have the authority to amend them. We suggest that if you seek a reduced loan settlement, ask for furloughs knowing that you are using them as bargaining chips. Be sure to have any <u>discharged</u> loan amount passed through your <u>bankruptcy</u> (see the *Stipulation* sample in Appendix E). The keywords here are "discharge" and "bankruptcy." If they use the words "forgiven," then you will owe taxes. "Discharged through the bankruptcy" means you *will not owe any income tax on the discharged amount*.

❑ **Step 16:**
The day before the Mediation, review the letters you wrote in Chapter 8 —
Income-contingent Repayment
Work Time Accounting Statement
Be prepared to cite the reasons listed in these letters.

❑ **Step 17:**
Attend your Mediation. Be early. Be rested. Take a copy of your master letter with you to make notes on. Remember, they already have this letter. *Do not take any other letters or worksheets*. Take a pen and pencil and writing paper.

The first thing that is going to happen at the Mediation is that they are going to have you sign a non-disclosure form. It means that you cannot call the mediator or attorney to court to testify that various statements or promises were made. In a way, this allows the attorney to make any statement (including lying to you) without future legal consequences. Personally, we don't think this should be allowed since a trial is a public event, and mediation should be treated the same. Regardless, the mediation will not happen unless you agree to the NDA.

The purpose of the mediator is to help both sides discuss the issues and hopefully find a mutually agreed resolution. The mediator is not to take anyone's side. About three-fourths the way into the time allotted for the mediation, the mediator most likely will try to get you and the attorney to come to some settlement. Here is where you "hold tough," keeping in mind what you consider a "fair" settlement (as discussed above).

Negotiate strongly. Here is a hierarchy of possible proposals from the greatest discharge to the least.

Be aware of where your lowest "fair" settlement is:

- The entire loan is discharged through the bankruptcy.

- A monthly payment of $50 for so many years with five furloughs. The remaining portion of the loan to be discharged through the bankruptcy.

- A monthly payment of $50 for so many years with no furloughs. The remaining portion of the loan to be discharged through the bankruptcy.

- A modified Income-Driven Repayment (IDR) plan for so many years. The remaining portion of the loan to be discharged through the bankruptcy. (We've included this idea because, in reality, the Department of Education could conceivably obtain the most money through such a program but they are not allowed to offer such a plan because Congress specified 25-year terms and no opportunity to discharge the remaining portion through a bankruptcy. However, bringing up this idea makes you look fair and not greedy.)

Perhaps you can think of other settlement plans. Remember that whatever amount is discharged, be sure it is "discharged through the bankruptcy" so as to avoid owing income taxes on the amount discharged.

If you are seeking a portion settlement (like $50 a month for so many years), they will write into the settlement that you have the right to prepay the loan. This means that if you have a lump sum available to pay on the loan, you could negotiate to pay only this sum immediately, and the rest is discharged through the bankruptcy.

If you and the attorney come to an impasse, the mediator will move you into separate rooms. Typically, the mediator will meet with you first to clarify what you are trying to offer. Then, the mediator will go to the attorney to see if he or she will accept the terms. The mediator may go back and forth a few times to each of you. Eventually, the mediator will bring the two of you back together where, hopefully, you have made clear your offer. The attorney may not agree with you but has an obligation to take your offer to the Department of Education for their approval. Remember, the attorney cannot make a binding offer. That must come from the Department of Education.

One more thing about Mediation: Most likely, the attorney representing the Department of Education will speak down to you and treat you with contempt. He or she may even laugh at you by making snide remarks about your "feeble attempt" to have the loans discharged. Don't get mad. Stay focused. Realize it is a psychological tactic to make you feel inadequate and give up. Listen to what the attorney has to say. In his or her arrogance, he or she may give leads to how to succeed later in the negotiation process. Remember, the attorney does not make the final decision about a negotiated settlement; the Department of Education does.

Congratulations, you have gotten through the Mediation.

A few weeks may go by before the attorney gets back to you with the Department of Education's response. Hopefully, they will have accepted your offer. If so, the attorney will write up a stipulation detailing the settlement. Appendix E contains a sample stipulation. A stipulation is a document that tells the court what you and the defendant have agreed to. This is presented to the judge, who almost always approves the stipulation whereupon it is recorded making it legally binding. A trial or judgment is no longer needed.

Let's take some time to review the *Stipulation (Sample)* in Appendix E. It is important for you to know the elements of the stipulation so that you can be assured the discharged portion of your student loans is discharged through the bankruptcy. Otherwise, you will owe income tax on the discharged amount.

On page 2 of *Stipulation (Sample),* Item 1 gives the repayment terms— so much per month for so many years, when due each month, when the plan begins, and how payment is made (check, electronic transfer, etc.). Page 3, Item 2 is the most important item. It states that the "remaining amount of the Debt will be considered by Education as discharged through Plaintiff's bankruptcy." This eliminates income taxes on the discharged amount. Think about it. **The stipulation means you were successful at bankrupting your student loans**; maybe not the entire debt, but some of it. Take pride in the fact that you succeeded at something most lawyers claim is impossible, and you did it yourself. Item 3 allows you to prepay the debt. Item 4 spells out the consequences of not making the payments specified in Item 1. The other items are important legal clarifications. If you and the Department of Education enter into a stipulation, be sure it is similar to this sample.

If the Department of Education rejects your offer, we go to the next step of the process— "Resisting Their Arguments." When the attorney calls you to inform you of the rejection, he or she should give you some idea why it was rejected. Also, during the Mediation, you should have been aware of concerns expressed by the attorney.

You still have time before going to trial to try and seek a settlement, and it often happens.

Resisting Their Arguments

❑ **Step 18:**
Write another letter to the Department of Education. In this letter, you need to address any issues that came up in the Mediation.

Further, cut and paste from the Chapter 9 letters— *Income-contingent Repayment* and *Work Time Accounting Statement.* You need to be clear about why the IDR is not appropriate for you and why you cannot take on any more work. The IDR is the major sword used by the Department of Education to convince the court that you cannot meet the provisions of the undue hardship tests. Reiterate your points in the letter and restate your offer, emphasis that it is fair. Mail the letter to the attorney.

If the Department of Education accepts your offer, a stipulation will be written, and the case will be over (see discussion above on stipulation).

But, if the Department of Education rejects your offer, the author found it effective to make a very aggressive attack on the Department of Education and the bankruptcy law. Most people who read the early cases presented in Chapter 7 shake their heads in disbelief over the injustice perpetrated on so many honest poor debtors. Basically, 11 U.S.C.A. §523(a)(8) is bad law that has been distorted through aggressive enforcement by the Department of Education.

The DOE rejected the initial offer proposed by the author of this book. As a result, he took a 3-fold strategy before the trial:

First—request lots and lots of documents from the Department of Education to prove the concerns discussed in Chapter 7.

Second–let the Department of Education know that you expect to bring up during the trial many of the concerns discussed in Chapter 8. In general, the Department does not want a court ruling on many of these issues as they may lose— resulting in 11 U.S.C.A. §523(a)(8) being overturned.

Third—be such an annoyance that they will be encouraged to settle in your favor before the trial.

Attacking the Agency and Law

❏ **Step 19:**

Immediately write a new letter to the Department of Education. At the top of the letter, express your dissatisfaction with their rejection of your fair offer. Then continue writing the letter similar to that presented in *Request for Documents from Department of Education (Sample)* found in Appendix E. Mail the letter to the attorney.

Hopefully, the attorney will call to say that the Department of Education has accepted your offer, a stipulation will be written, most if not all of your debt discharged, and the case closed.

The author of this book was contacted just three days before the trial by DOE and offered the stipulation discussed in the mediation. He was to pay 10 percent of the total owed over ten years. He accepted the offer, and the court case was ended without trial.

If they do not accept your offer, you have no choice but to continue to the trial.

Pretrial Hearing and Trial

It is impossible to write in detail about what could happen between now and the pretrial hearing or at the trial. So much depends on the state the court is located, the court itself, and the particular judge. Writing generalized instructions is impossible.

The defendant may subpoena you to take your deposition. Or you may be given interrogatories to fill out. Don't panic. They will be asking for information that you have already prepared in Chapter 9. If you are being deposed, request a copy of the questions they intend to ask before you go. They legally must provide you these questions if you ask.

The Department of Education probably will not provide you with the documents you requested in your previous letter. You can demand this information through what is termed discovery. Be sure to let the court know that the Department failed to provide you with the information you requested. You want the court to see how difficult and uncooperative the Department of Education is toward resolving this issue.

If your case has not been settled and you have gotten this far, we really recommend you obtain the Berman & Berman-Barrett book *Represent Yourself in Court* (NOLO) or a similar book. Or, you may want to bring in an attorney.

In many states, the next step will be the *Pretrial Hearing*. By law, this hearing is to occur as close to the trial time as reasonable under the circumstances. Here, you, the defendant, and the judge develop a plan for the trial. The judge will want you and the defendant's attorney to agree to the legal issues to be decided, documents to be submitted, and more. Once this has been resolved, the judge will issue a *Pretrial Order*. In many ways, this is the most important document for the trial. It supplants the original pleading and establishes the legal theories that will be presented during the trial. Thus, it is important that you have included in the Pretrial Order any of the arguments you want to be brought to the court's attention, including the "undue hardship" tests, but also the advocacy issues described in Chapter 8 if you want to pursue them.

In some bankruptcy courts, the judge will provide you with guidelines for preparing for the trial since you are representing yourself.

❑ **Step 20:**
Read, understand, and respond to any document sent to you by the defendant's attorney or the court. Do so in a timely manner.

Attend the *Pretrial Hearing*. You may want to try to negotiate one more time with the defense attorney before going to trial. Remember, it has been shown time and again that leaving it up to judges to decide the merits of an "undue hardship" case usually goes poorly for the debtor.

Prepare a Statement. Oftentimes court can be so emotionally daunting for those who are not attorneys that you may want to prepare and read a statement to the court. The court should allow you to read your statement. We suggest that it not exceed 3-4 pages and emphasize your financial hardship explaining why it will not improve in the future. Make it larger type size and double-spaced. This will make it easier to read under stress.

Attend the *Trial*.
We hope the best for you.

*

The author of this book would like to hear the results of your adversary proceeding or Compromise or Write-Off. Although the author cannot provide legal advice, he would like to hear how your case developed and was resolved. Also, any comments, corrections, or insight concerning the content of this book would be appreciated. Contact information is given in "About the Author."

CHAPTER 11
Preparing Your Case for _Compromise_ or _Write-Off_

This chapter helps you prepare documents for arguing for a *Compromise* or *Write-Off* directly to the Department of Education. This section helps you pull together all the documents and data necessary to prove repaying your student loans would cause an "undue hardship."

We suggest you complete the Chapter 7 bankruptcy forms located in Appendix C. These forms— Schedule I, Schedule J, and Business Income and Expense— form the basis of your financial arguments and are familiar to the Department of Education.

PRE-INFO—
   Student Loan History

Before you even attempt to have your student loans discharged through *Compromise* or *Write-Off*, it is important for you to be up-to-date about all your student loans. Thus, you need to contact each lender and get a copy of your student loans and their payment histories. It is most important to know payment, forbearance, and deferment dates.

> **Step 1 • Obtain** a printout from your lenders of the history of your student loans. It is important to know the payment amounts, forbearances, and deferment dates for each loan. **Transfer** this information on the Student Loan History worksheet found in Appendix D.

Chapter 6 detailed the kinds of information you must provide in order to achieve the claim of undue hardship.

These were identified as *Characteristics*:

- **Characteristic A**—Current Living Condition and the Impact of Repaying Loan on "Minimal Living" Standard
- **Characteristic B**—Prospects for Repaying the Loans
- **Characteristic C**—Good Faith and Loan Repayment

Each *Characteristic* will be discussed below in detail along with the sequential steps used to produce the appropriate documents. The problem of the *Income-Driven Repayment (IDR)* plan also is addressed.

CHARACTERISTIC A—
   Current Living Condition and the Impact of Repaying Loan on "Minimal Living" Standard

First, you need to establish your current financial and living conditions.

> **Step 2 • Make a copy and complete** Schedule I-Current Income of Individual Debtor.). If you have business income/expenses, make a copy of that form also. Samples and blank forms are included in Appendix C. If you have multiple employers, you may need to make additional copies of Form 106I.

As you will learn later, part of the strategy of proving undue hardship or negotiating a Compromise or Write-Off is for you to present yourself as a hopeless and helpless debtor who is representing him or herself. As such, it is **best not to let the Department of Education know that you are using this book**. Instead of handing them *Schedule 106I*, we suggest that you write, in your own words and on a blank piece of paper, your financial and living status.

> **Step 3 •** On a blank piece of paper, **write** your name and date. Title the page "Current Income and Family Status" (or similar words). Below this, in your own words, write a few short paragraphs telling how your family and income. Use *Schedule 106I* as a basis for discussion. *See* a sample in Appendix D— Current Income and Family Status.

It is recommended that you write all these documents on a computer and save the files. Later, you will be asked to blend all the documents together into one master document. If you write them on a computer, all you will have to do is cut and paste the sections, thereby eliminating the need to retype everything.

Now we evaluate your expenditures.

—WARNING—
A Word of Caution about Income and Expense Statements

The income you list during the *Compromise* or *Write-Off* should match the income you claim with the IRS. If these are not similar, you will be viewed with suspicion.

The expenses you list during the *Compromise* or *Write-Off* should match the expenses you claim with the IRS. If these are not similar, you will be viewed with suspicion.

Step 4 • Make a copy and complete *Schedule 106J-Current Expenditures of Individual Debtor.* This form is found in Appendix C under Chapter 7 Bankruptcy Forms.

Step 5 • Transfer your expense data from *Schedule 106J-Current Expenditures of Individual Debtor* to column 2 of the *Current Expenditure Status* worksheet.

You need to demonstrate that your expenses are comparable to a similarly situated debtor. This is achieved by showing: (a) that your income is within range of the Federal Poverty Guidelines for a family your size, and (b) your expenses are similar to other families of your size and circumstances.

> **Step 6 • Go to** the website of the United States Department of Health and Human Services (https://aspe.hhs.gov/poverty-guidelines) and **download a copy** of the current Federal Poverty Guidelines (a copy of this homepage and document are in Appendix B). If you do not have access to the web, your local library should have a copy of this government publication. Be sure it the current year. **Write** your information on the *Current Expenditure Status* worksheet.

Step 7 • Go to the website of the IRS to gather data on Collection Financial Standards (https://www.irs.gov/businesses/small-businesses-self-employed/collection-financial-standards). The IRS has established standards used to determine the ability of taxpayers to make delinquent payments. Use the data found here to **fill-in** the National Norms (column 3) on the *Current Expenditure Status* worksheet.

> **Step 8 •** For those cases where there are significant differences between your expenditures and the national norms, **write** an explanation for each on the *Current Expenditure Status* worksheet (column 4).

You need to explain that you have minimized your living expenses and are not living extravagantly and that there is no extra income available to pay on your student loans.

> **Step 9** • On a blank piece of paper, write your name and date. Title the page "Current Expenditures and Minimalized Living" (or similar words). Below this, write a few short paragraphs telling how you live frugally and that it would be impossible to make payments on your student loans. *See* a sample and instructions in Appendix D— Current Expenditure and Minimalized Living.

CHARACTERISTIC B—
Prospects for Repaying the Loans

In so many cases, debtors make a strong showing for their situation, only to have the Department of Education reject the claim and tell the debtor to get a part-time minimum-wage job and use that money to make loan payments. Regardless of how laughable or tragic this may seem, it happens all the time. Thus, the debtor needs to account for his or her time working or providing dependent care, or both. Debtors need to clearly point out to the court that asking the debtor to take on any more work would push him or her over a standard workweek, and that would be an undue hardship.

> **Step 10** • **Make a copy** of the worksheet *Work Time Accounting Table* (Appendix D) and complete it as instructed. **Write** on a blank piece of paper your name and date and entitle it *Work Time Accounting* (or similar words). In your own words (using the *Work Time Accounting Table*), explain why all your available time is committed, making it impossible for you to take on another job. *See* a sample document in the Samples section of Appendix D, under *Work Time Accounting Statement*.

The debtor needs to address in detail any personal limitations that may impact the ability to obtain appropriate employment. This includes personal medical limitations, support of dependents (and their medical conditions, if applicable), and lack of useable job skills. These need to be described in detail, with supporting documents (like medical records), etc.

> **Step 11** • On a blank piece of paper, **write** your name and date and entitle it— *Personal Limitations* (or similar words). Here you explain why medical problems for you and/or your dependents, the lack of usable job skills, and/or the existence of a large number of dependents impact your future ability to work at a job that will provide sufficient income to service your student loan debt. *See* a sample document in the Samples section of Appendix D, under *Personal Limitations Statement*. **In general, you must show there are "unique" or "exceptional" circumstances that impact future employment and earnings.**

The final step to this Characteristic is to discuss the impact of external factors on your future employment. Courts and the Department of Education have been hesitant to include these factors since it would require them to accept the fact that not all employment doors are open to all workers, i.e., the American dream is not really attainable by all.

External factors that affect future employment opportunities include:
- U.S. Economy
- Discrimination based on age, race, ethnicity, gender, sexual orientation, and others.
- Reverse Discrimination
- Past Terminations
- Whistleblower
- And others

Chapters 5 and 6 explained in greater detail these issues. In many cases, academic papers on these topics are included in Appendix F.

> **Step 12** • On a blank piece of paper, **write** your name and date and entitle it— *External Factors* (or similar words). In general, it is suggested that you first develop your argument with academic research of the

societal problem that impacts future employment, and then make it specific with examples from your own life story. You need to tell the Department of Education about the factors that impact your ability to secure employment. It is important to emphasize how this impacts your future earnings. No sample is provided in the Appendix because each case is very specific to the debtor, and no generalization is possible.

The process described above documents for the Department of Education the reasons why you can't take on any more work and why your future employment is not going to improve. As such, you will not be able to service your student loans and request they be discharged as an undue hardship.

CHARACTERISTIC C— Good Faith and Loan Repayment

Debtors are required to demonstrate "good faith" attempts to repay student loans. There is an expectation that any time the debtor's net income exceeded the Federal Poverty Guidelines, payments were made on the student loans. Whenever there were times of financial difficulty, debtors must show that they worked with the lender to resolve the issue instead of letting loans fall into arrears. Additionally, at least seven or more years should have passed since obtaining the last student loan, otherwise, there is a presumption of fraud, which the debtor must overcome.

> **Step 13** • **Make copies** of your IRS Income Tax filings for each year since receiving your last student loan. **Fill out** the worksheet *Income and Student Loan Payment* (Appendix D). Instructions are on the worksheet form. This form tracks your income for the years since obtaining your most recent student loans and the status of student loan repayment.

You now have everything needed to write a history of your employment, attempts to find work, family income, and servicing your student loans. The purpose of the narrative is to show that you have been diligent in trying to make income sufficient to service your student loans.

> **Step 14** • On a blank piece of paper, **write** your name and date and entitle it *Good Faith and Loan Repayment* (or similar words). Here, you write a history of your employment, family income, and student loan repayment. Be sure to indicate when your family income dropped below the Federal Poverty Guideline, that you received deferments or forbearances whenever you were unable to make payments, and more. You want to show you have been diligent in servicing your student loans and that there is no fraud in seeking their discharge. Review the sample provided in Appendix D entitled *Good Faith and Loan Repayment Statement*.

INCOME DRIVEN REPAYMENT (IDR) PLAN

Finally, the last problem that must be addressed are the *Income-Driven Repayment (IDR)* plans. As described at length in Chapter 8, the IDR allows debtors to make loan payments when they can and sometimes pay nothing at all if their income drops below a particular level. The plan lasts for twenty-five years, and any outstanding student loan debt remaining at the end of the plan is "forgiven." <u>However, and this is a big however, debtors are liable for the income taxes on the discharged amount</u>.

It is often stated by the Department of Education attorneys that IDR makes it impossible for debtors to discharge their student loans in bankruptcy or otherwise. They contend that anyone can make "zero dollar" payments, thus negating the undue hardship exception of §523(a)(8).

In many cases, this may be true. But, as argued in Chapter 8, for some debtors, the IDR is inappropriate. Perhaps you are one of the debtors who would benefit from arguing that the IDR causes you an undue hardship.

Step 15 • On a blank piece of paper, **write** your name and date and write the title *Income-Driven Repayment* (or similar words). Tell why, in your case, the ICR is not appropriate and causes an undue hardship. See *Income-Driven Repayment* statement in Appendix D for a sample.

Review

If you have completed all 15 steps listed above, you are ready to file a *Compromise* or *Write-Off*. There will be no surprises, and you will have all the facts and documents needed to defend your position.

To review, you have taken these actions and completed the following forms and worksheets:

Step 1 — Contacted your student loan lenders and obtained a complete history of their payment and status. Completed the Student Loan History worksheet (Appendix D).

Step 2 — Made a copy of and completed Schedule 106I—Current Income of Individual Debtor (Appendix C) and business income/expense (if needed).

Step 3 — Wrote a **Current Income and Family Status*** (Appendix D) statement on a blank piece of paper.

Step 4 — Made a copy and completed Schedule 106J—Current Expenditures of Individual Debtor (Appendix C).

Step 5 — Completed most of the Current Expenditure Status worksheet (Appendix D).

Step 6 — Downloaded a copy of the U.S. Department of Health and Human Services Federal Poverty Guidelines and completed more of the Current Expenditure Status worksheet.

Step 7 — Went to IRS website, obtained Collection Financial Standards, and used the data to fill in the Current Expenditure Status worksheet.

Step 8 — Compared your family expenditures against the national norms and completed the Current Expenditure Status worksheet.

Step 9 — Wrote a **Current Expenditures and Minimalized Living*** statement (Appendix D) on a blank piece of paper.

Step 10 — Completed the Work Time Accounting Table worksheet (Appendix D). Wrote a **Work Time Accounting Statement*** (Appendix D) on a blank piece of paper.

Step 11 — Wrote a **Personal Limitations*** statement (Appendix D) on a blank piece of paper.

Step 12 — Wrote an **External Factors*** statement (Appendix D) on a blank piece of paper.

Step 13 — Made copies of your IRS Income Tax forms. Completed the Income and Student Loan Payment worksheet (Appendix D).

Step 14 — Wrote a **Good Faith and Loan Repayment*** statement (Appendix D) on a blank piece of paper.

Step 15 — Wrote an **Income-Driven Repayment*** statement (Appendix D) on a blank piece of paper.

(Each underlined item is either a worksheet from the Appendix, letter you wrote, or a document you downloaded. **Each bolded and asterisked item are documents you wrote on a blank piece of paper that will be used in the** *Compromise* **or** *Write-Off.* We suggest that you do not submit or show the attorneys for the Department of Education any of the worksheets you used. You do not want to tip them off that you are using this book.)

The next chapter will give step-by-step guidance on how to negotiate directly with the Department of Education through the use of a *Compromise* or *Write-Off* to have your student loans discharged.

CHAPTER 12
Step-By-Step Negotiations for _Compromise_ or _Write-Off_

This section discusses negotiation strategies to improve your chances at having all, or part, of your student loans discharged.

Chapter 2 discussed the conditions under which the Department of Education may Compromise or Write-Off student loans. The details are summarized here. Please see the three documents in Appendix B: "Standardized Compromise and Write-Off Procedures" (2019); "Notice to All Guaranty Agencies" (1994); and "FFEL Compromise and Write-Off Procedures for Guaranty Agencies" (1993). These documents give the authorization and clarification on the ability of DOE to engage in Compromise and Write-Off. Many employees of DOE do not know these programs exist. You may need to send them copies of the documents.

Compromise

Under the **Compromise** plan, the Department is allowed to accept less than the total amount due to fully satisfy the conditions of the loan (and end a default status). This policy was specified in a regulation the Director of the U.S. Department of Education, Policy Development Division approved on 12/23/93.

The collections supervisor at a guarantee agency may reduce ("compromise") your loan under the following conditions:

- If you agree to pay the full amount of the loan— principal and interests owed on defaulted loans— then all collection costs, including the standard 25 percent collection fee may be waived.

- If you agree to pay the remaining principal and interest owed on a defaulted loan, then up to 30 percent of the principal and interest may be waived.

- If you are in dire financial straits and it looks like you won't be able to service your loans in the future, the agency's director has the authority to waive even more than 30 percent of the principal and interest of your defaulted loans.

- If you agree to pay off the entire principal of your defaulted loans within 30 days of negotiating the compromise (and paid with a certified check), then all interest charges may be waived.

The agency determines if the Compromise represents the best interest of the _government_. Obviously, this is very subjective and open to the judgment of the agency director. If you can show that you have very limited income and that it will not change in the future, they may accept your request since the alternative is to sue, which is a fairly expensive process for the government.

As a strategy, Compromise works best for old loans where most of the principal has been paid and has been in default for a while. If you can afford to pay the remaining principal in one lump sum, they are most likely to cancel the interest and collection fees.

Write-Off

An even more radical idea is to ask the guarantee agency of the Department of Education to **Write-**

Off your loans. This works only if you are in dire financial straits, do not believe you will ever be able to repay your loans, and you don't qualify for other forms of discharge or Compromise. The three conditions most likely to be written-off include:

- The balance on your principal is $100 or less.

- The total balance of your loans does not exceed $1000.

- The balance of your loans is for interest, court fees, collection costs, and costs other than the principal, regardless of the total loan amount.

If you can convince the Department of Education that your situation is financially hopeless, <u>it can write-off much larger loans and end collection efforts.</u>

Contacting the Agency

❑ **Step 1**:
Review the conditions for <u>Compromise</u> and <u>Write-Off</u> described above and determine which plan best meets your situation. Write that information here:

I will be seeking a: ❑ Compromise ❑ Write-Off
I will be asking to have $_____ discharged.
This amount represents:
Principal: $ _____
Interest: $ _____
Court Fees: $ _____
Collection Costs: $ _____
Other: $ _____
The loans are currently in default:
❑ Yes ❑ No
Other Conditions: _____
_____
_____

(Note: you should have the specifics about your loans since you were asked to gather that information in the last chapter.)

Now you need to know whom to contact at the Department of Education and learn if any forms or guidelines have been developed concerning Compromise or Write-Off.

❑ **Step 2**:
Contact the Department of Education and find out who has the authority to approve a Compromise or Write-Off (we will refer to this person as a Supervisor). The phone operator may have no idea what you are asking. Be patient and persistent. If need be, offer to fax or send them the three documents from the Appendix that clearly state the programs and their guidelines.

Contact the Supervisor and explain that you have severe financial problems that will make it impossible to repay your student loans. Ask how to file for a Compromise or Write-Off. *We advise you not to talk too long with this person; just find out if they have developed some procedures or forms for these kinds of discharges.* The Supervisor will probably ask if you have spoken with a counselor at the Department of Education about changing your repayment plan, furloughs, the Income-Driven Repayment (IDR) Plan, and more. Be courteous, but be firm explaining that none of these options work for you and that you really need to apply for a Compromised or Write-Off.

They may have developed some guidelines for filing such claims. If they have forms or guidelines, ask to have them mailed to you.

Write the Supervisor's contact information here:
Name: _____

Title: _____

Agency: _____

Department: _____

Mailing Address: _____

_____

_____

Telephone: _____

Fax: _____

E-mail: _____

Are there forms or guidelines? ❏ Yes ❏ No

If they are sending you some guidelines, wait, and see what they state. More than likely, there are no guidelines or forms. Regardless, if they are sending you forms and/or guidelines, the basic problem you have is to convince the Department of Education that your financial situation is hopeless and that it would cost them more to sue you than what they would recover. This is similar to proving "undue hardship" under the bankruptcy laws, and we will proceed as such.

Section 523(a)(8) of the bankruptcy laws require you to show that it would cause an undue hardship to you and your dependents if you were required to repay your student loans. Thirty years of litigation on this issue has resulted in the courts developing a number of tests. Most courts use the *Brunner* test, as discussed in Chapters 4, 5, and 6.

In Chapter 6, a set of guidelines was developed and used to prove undue hardship. In the last chapter, you completed a number of worksheets that helped you develop and compose written responses to prove these guidelines. They are:

- First— you need to show that your current family income does not allow you to make repayments on your student loans. To that end, you composed the letter *Current Income and Family Status*.

- Second— you need to show that your family expenditures are minimized and equal to other similarly situated families. To that end, you composed the letter *Current Expenditures and Minimalized Living*.

- Third— you need to show that there are personal limitations and external factors that impact your ability to find better-paying work. To that end, you composed the letters *Personal Limitations* and *External Factors*.

- Fourth— you need to show that you have been diligent in making student loan payments when you were financially able and received deferments or forbearances whenever you were unable to make payments. To that end, you composed the letter *Good Faith and Loan Repayment*.

We want to blend these five documents into one letter and deliver it to the Supervisor. Hopefully, you wrote all these documents on a computer, so you only have to cut and paste the sections into one master document. If you did not, or could not, use a computer, you will have to retype all the letters.

Writing the Agency

❏ **Step 3:**
Write one letter merging all five documents—
Current Income and Family Status
Current Expenditures and Minimalized Living
Personal Limitations
External Factors
Good Faith and Loan Repayment
Address the letter to the Supervisor. On the first lines of the letter state that, "repaying my student loans represents an undue hardship because . . ." (now copy each of your letters, one-by-one, in the order above). <u>At the end of the letter, state that you want your entire student loan debt to be discharged</u>. Mail the letter to the Supervisor. Be sure to keep a copy of the master letter for yourself (or, if on a computer, save the file). A few days after you mail the letter, call the Supervisor to see that he or she received it.

A word about grammar and wording: If you have a graduate college degree such as Doctorate or Master's, take time to use proper wording and grammar. If you have a technical degree, no degree or limited education, a high school diploma, or are mentally disabled, do not worry if your letter is not perfect. They expect you to make mistakes. If your letter is too good, they may suspect you had professional help.

Notice that we have purposely left out discussion about the Income-Driven Repayment (IDR) plans or your time commitment. The strategy is to see if what you have submitted is sufficient. If not, then you have more to send. This gives a little backup to the negotiation process.

Expect it to take a few weeks for the Supervisor to get back to you. Hopefully, they accept your arguments and discharge your entire loan. *If they "forgive" your loans, you will be responsible for the income tax on that amount*. Only through bankruptcy can the discharge be tax-free.

The supervisor most likely will tell a story of some other debtor he or she is currently negotiating who is in much worse financial stress than you and that the Department of Education is not accepting his or her claim of "undue hardship." *This is meant to unnerve you and make you feel that the process is hopeless*. Your situation is unique. Don't give up.

They most likely will not accept your request the first time asked.

Stronger Negotiations

❑ **Step 4:**

If your request is rejected, ask for specific details as to why it was rejected. Now compose a letter back to the Supervisor that addresses the specific reasons for the rejection and include the arguments you developed in the *Income-Driven Repayment* and *Work Time Accounting Statement*. You need to be clear as to why the IDR is not appropriate for you and why you cannot take on any more work. The IDR is the major sword used by the Department of Education to convince the court that you cannot meet the provisions of the undue hardship tests. Again, they may or may not accept your arguments and discharge your entire loan. You still have one more negotiation attempt.

Give some thought to a "fair" settlement for your particular situation. Maybe your situation is so dire that a complete discharge of the loans is the only solution. However, maybe you could pay a portion of the loans. In the banking industry, bad debts are often settled for 10 (or 5 or 2) cents on the dollar. Ask yourself if you could pay 10 (or 5 or 2) percent of your loan. The Department of Education will not accept payments less than $50 a month because of bookkeeping expenses. For example, let's say you owe $60,000; maybe you could pay $50 a month for ten years. That works out to a total of $6,000 repayment saving you $54,000. If you owe a smaller amount, maybe you could pay $50 a month for five years, or whatever. Try not to have the loan last more than ten years. Also, consider the issue of furlough. Obviously, you would like the ability to have a number of furloughs available just in case something terrible goes wrong, and you do not have money for a short time. The problem with including furloughs in your negotiated repayment plan is that your repayment program then begins to look too much like the ICR plan. Congress set the terms for the ICR, and the Department of Education does not have the authority to amend them. We suggest that if you seek a reduced loan settlement, ask for furloughs, knowing that you are using them as bargaining chips.

Negotiate strongly. Here is a discharge hierarchy of possible proposals from the greatest discharge to the least. Be aware of where your lowest "fair" settlement is:

DISCHARGE HIERARCHY

- The entire loan is discharged.

- Only a portion of the loan is paid right now, and the rest is discharged.

- A monthly payment of $50 for so many years with five furloughs.

- A monthly payment of $50 for so many years with no furloughs.

- A modified Income-Driven Repayment (IDR) Plan for so many years; the remaining portion of the loan to be discharged. (We've included this idea because, in reality, the Department of Education could conceivably obtain the most money through such a program, but they are not allowed to offer such a plan because Congress specified 25-year terms and no opportunity to discharge the remaining portion through a bankruptcy. However, bringing this idea up makes you look fair and not greedy.)

Perhaps you can think of other settlement plans?

If you are seeking to negotiate a new repayment plan (like $50 a month for so many years), it should include wording that you have the right to prepay the loan. This means that if you have a lump sum available to pay on the loan, you could negotiate to pay only this sum immediately, and the rest is forgiven.

Proposing a Settlement

❏ **Step 5:**
   If your request is rejected, again ask for the reasons it was rejected. <u>If you seem to be at an impasse, now is the time to consider proposing a new repayment plan or settlement plan for some percentage of your loan (as described above) instead of the entire amount.</u> Compose a letter back to the Supervisor where you propose a "fair" repayment or settlement plan. Mail it to the Supervisor.

<u>If the Department of Education rejects your offer after all these efforts, it may be necessary to file for bankruptcy, in which you also file an adversary proceeding.</u> See Chapters 9 and 10 for details for this process. Decide if it is worth it to you to go through the challenge of bankruptcy while attempting to have your student loans discharged.

We wish you the best.

Just Who Does the Negotiations at DOE?

Since the release of the first edition of this book, many people have asked how realistic is the Compromise or Write-Off strategy. There are many debtors who only have large student loan burdens that are causing hardship. They don't want to file bankruptcy since the rest of their financial situation is livable. So, let's look at who it is that you will be negotiating with at the Department of Education.

Yes, the DOE is a large bureaucratic institution, but there are real people that you must negotiate with. How are these people rated on job performance? Will forgiving your loan look bad on their job performance? Like with a bank or other financial institution, loan managers handle a caseload of loans. Because few workers stay on the exact same job for more than a few short years, loan managers are not evaluated on how much money they bring in over the long-run but rather on how many loans are classified as "current," "late," "troubled," or in "default." The goal of any loan manager is to have all loans "current." In the case of student loans that means payments are up to date or the loans are in forbearance or deferment. Obviously, DOE employees don't care how much money is actually coming in, just that the loans are "current." Thus, you can see their motivation with severe hardship cases to shift the debtor to an Income-Driven Repayment plan. It doesn't matter that they may not get any money for twenty-five years, but that the loan is technically "current." Although DOE claims a default rate of a few percentage points, other research indicates as much as two-thirds of all education loan will ultimately end up in default. This is something DOE, and Congress does not want to publicly acknowledge.

From this perspective, when negotiating with DOE, think about how you can make your loan "current" or that you bring up issues so threatening to their house of cards that they would be hesitant to go to court. For example, the author of this book settled for paying $50 a month for ten years for a total of $6,000 while discharging $54,000 (adjusted to $72,000 in today's dollars) through the bankruptcy. Since the monthly payments are on time, the loan is considered "current," which makes the loan officer look good. It doesn't matter that 90 percent of the loan was discharged.

If your situation is dire, but you are not in the position to file bankruptcy at this time, maybe an IDR plan would be an acceptable option. This can always be changed due to future circumstances. Perhaps your financial situation deteriorates, then you could file for bankruptcy. If you become disabled, then file for a disability discharge. Of course, if you live to a ripe old age, the loans should be able to be discharged with a disability discharge. The worst thing to do is become delinquent with the loans since, if you need to file for bankruptcy, this will make you look bad and negatively impact your success with the adversary proceeding.

We hope this book was helpful.

*

The author of this book would like to hear the results of your adversary proceeding or Compromise or Write-Off. Although the author cannot provide legal advice, he would like to hear how your case developed and was resolved. Also, any comments, corrections, or insight concerning the content of this book would be appreciated. Contact information is given in "About the Author."

APPENDIX

APPENDIX A — Department of Education Repayment Plans and Discharge Optons

APPENDIX B — Laws and Legal Guidelines

APPENDIX C — Chapter 7 Bankruptcy Forms

APPENDIX D — Worksheets

APPENDIX E — Forms

APPENDIX F — Academic Articles

APPENDIX G — Resources

APPENDIX A
Department of Education Repayment Plans and Discharge Options

Repay Your Direct Loans and Federal Family Education Loan (FFEL) Program Loans

Summary Table

https://studentaid.gov/manage-loans/repayment/plans

Overview of Direct Loan and FFEL Program Repayment Plans

Repayment Plan	Eligible Loans	Monthly Payment and Timeframe	Eligibility and Other Information
Standard Repayment Plan	Direct Subsidized and Unsubsidized Loans Subsidized and Unsubsidized Federal Stafford Loans all PLUS loans all Consolidation Loans (Direct or FFEL)	Payments are a fixed amount that ensures your loans are paid off within 10 years (within 10 to 30 years for Consolidation Loans).	All borrowers are eligible for this plan. You'll usually pay less over time than under other plans. Standard Repayment Plan with a 10-year repayment period is not a good option for those seeking Public Service Loan Forgiveness (PSLF). Standard Repayment Plan for Consolidation Loans is not a qualifying repayment plan for PSLF.
Graduated Repayment Plan	Direct Subsidized and Unsubsidized Loans Subsidized and Unsubsidized Federal Stafford Loans all PLUS loans all Consolidation Loans (Direct or FFEL)	Payments are lower at first and then increase, usually every two years, and are for an amount that will ensure your loans are paid off within 10 years (within 10 to 30 years for Consolidation Loans).	All borrowers are eligible for this plan. You'll pay more over time than under the 10-year Standard Plan. Generally not a qualifying repayment plan for PSLF.

Overview of Direct Loan and FFEL Program Repayment Plans

Repayment Plan	Eligible Loans	Monthly Payment and Timeframe	Eligibility and Other Information
<u>Extended Repayment Plan</u>	Direct Subsidized and Unsubsidized Loans Subsidized and Unsubsidized Federal Stafford Loans all PLUS loans all Consolidation Loans (Direct or FFEL)	Payments may be fixed or graduated, and will ensure that your loans are paid off within 25 years.	If you're a Direct Loan borrower, you must have more than $30,000 in outstanding Direct Loans. If you're a FFEL borrower, you must have more than $30,000 in outstanding FFEL Program loans. Your monthly payments will be lower than under the 10-year Standard Plan or the Graduated Repayment Plan. You'll pay more over time than under the 10-year Standard Plan. Not a qualifying repayment plan for PSLF.
<u>Revised Pay As You Earn Repayment Plan (REPAYE)</u>	Direct Subsidized and Unsubsidized Loans Direct PLUS loans made to students Direct Consolidation Loans that do not include PLUS loans (Direct or FFEL) made to parents	Your monthly payments will be 10 percent of <u>discretionary income</u>. Payments are recalculated each year and are based on your updated income and family size. You must update your income and family size each year, even if they haven't changed. If you're married, both your and your spouse's income or loan debt will be considered, whether taxes are filed jointly or separately (with limited exceptions). Any outstanding balance on your loan will be forgiven if you haven't repaid your loan in full after 20 years (if all loans were taken out for undergraduate study) or 25 years (if any loans were taken out for graduate or professional study).	Any Direct Loan borrower with an eligible loan type may choose this plan. You'll usually pay more over time than under the 10-year Standard Plan. **You may have to pay income tax on any amount that is forgiven.** Good option for those seeking PSLF.
<u>Pay As You Earn Repayment Plan (PAYE)</u>	Direct Subsidized and Unsubsidized Loans Direct PLUS loans made to students Direct Consolidation Loans that do not	Your monthly payments will be 10 percent of discretionary income, but never more than you would have paid under the 10-year Standard Repayment Plan.	You must be a <u>new borrower</u> on or after October 1, 2007, and must have received a <u>disbursement</u> of a

Overview of Direct Loan and FFEL Program Repayment Plans

Repayment Plan	Eligible Loans	Monthly Payment and Timeframe	Eligibility and Other Information
	include (Direct or FFEL) PLUS loans made to parents	Payments are recalculated each year and are based on your updated income and family size. You must update your income and family size each year, even if they haven't changed. If you're married, your spouse's income or loan debt will be considered only if you file a joint tax return. Any outstanding balance on your loan will be forgiven if you haven't repaid your loan in full after 20 years.	Direct Loan on or after October 1, 2011. You must have a high debt relative to your income. Your monthly payment will never be more than the 10-year Standard Plan amount. You'll usually pay more over time than under the 10-year Standard Plan. **You may have to pay income tax on any amount that is forgiven.** Good option for those seeking PSLF.
<u>Income-Based Repayment Plan (IBR)</u>	Direct Subsidized and Unsubsidized Loans Subsidized and Unsubsidized Federal Stafford Loans all PLUS loans made to students Consolidation Loans (Direct or FFEL) that do not include Direct or FFEL PLUS loans made to parents	Your monthly payments will be either 10 or 15 percent of discretionary income (depending on when you received your first loans), but never more than you would have paid under the 10-year Standard Repayment Plan. Payments are recalculated each year and are based on your updated income and family size. You must update your income and family size each year, even if they haven't changed. If you're married, your spouse's income or loan debt will be considered only if you file a joint tax return. Any outstanding balance on your loan will be forgiven if you haven't repaid your loan in full after 20 years or 25 years, depending on when you received your first loans. You may have to pay income tax on any amount that is forgiven.	You must have a high debt relative to your income. Your monthly payment will never be more than the 10-year Standard Plan amount. You'll usually pay more over time than under the 10-year Standard Plan. **You may have to pay income tax on any amount that is forgiven.** Good option for those seeking PSLF.
<u>Income-contingent Repayment Plan (ICR)</u>	Direct Subsidized and Unsubsidized Loans Direct PLUS Loans made to students	Your monthly payment will be the lesser of 20 percent of discretionary income, or	Any Direct Loan borrower with an eligible loan type may choose this plan.

Overview of Direct Loan and FFEL Program Repayment Plans

Repayment Plan	Eligible Loans	Monthly Payment and Timeframe	Eligibility and Other Information
	Direct Consolidation Loans	the amount you would pay on a repayment plan with a fixed payment over 12 years, adjusted according to your income. Payments are recalculated each year and are based on your updated income, family size, and the total amount of your Direct Loans. You must update your income and family size each year, even if they haven't changed. If you're married, your spouse's income or loan debt will be considered only if you file a joint tax return or you choose to repay your Direct Loans jointly with your spouse. Any outstanding balance will be forgiven if you haven't repaid your loan in full after 25 years.	You'll usually pay more over time than under the 10-year Standard Plan. **You may have to pay income tax on any amount that is forgiven.** Good option for those seeking PSLF. Parent borrowers can access this plan by consolidating their Parent PLUS Loans into a Direct Consolidation Loan.
Income-sensitive Repayment Plan	Subsidized and Unsubsidized Federal Stafford Loans FFEL PLUS Loans FFEL Consolidation Loans	Your monthly payment is based on annual income, but your loan will be paid in full within 15 years.	You'll pay more over time than under the 10-year Standard Plan. The formula for determining the monthly payment amount can vary from lender to lender. Available only for FFEL Program loans, which are not eligible for PSLF.

Postponing Repayments

Deferments
Information found at:
https://studentaid.gov/manage-loans/lower-payments/get-temporary-relief/deferment#eligibility

There are a variety of circumstances that may qualify you for a deferment on your federal student loan.
- Cancer Treatment Deferment
- Economic Hardship Deferment
- Graduate Fellowship Deferment
- In-School Deferment
- Military Service and Post-Active Duty Student Deferment
- Parent PLUS Borrower Deferment
- Rehabilitation Training Deferment
- Unemployment Deferment

Cancer Treatment Deferment
You may qualify for this deferment while you are undergoing cancer treatment and for the six-month period after your treatment ends.
Complete the *Cancer Treatment Deferment Request*.

Economic Hardship Deferment
You may qualify for this deferment if you
- are receiving a means-tested benefit, like welfare (e.g., Temporary Assistance for Needy Families (TANF));
- work full-time but have earnings that are below 150% of the poverty guideline for your family size and state of residence; or
- are serving in the Peace Corps.
  You can only receive this deferment for up to three years.
  Complete the *Economic Hardship Deferment Request*.

Graduate Fellowship Deferment
You may qualify for this deferment if you are enrolled in an approved graduate fellowship program. A graduate fellowship program is generally a program that provides financial support to graduate students to pursue graduate studies and research. Most graduate fellowship programs are for doctoral students, but some are available to master's degree students.
Complete the *Graduate Fellowship Deferment Request*.

In-School Deferment
You are eligible for this deferment if you are enrolled at least half-time at an eligible college or career school. If you are a graduate or professional student who received a Direct PLUS Loan, you qualify for an additional six months of deferment after you cease to be enrolled at least half-time.
Important! If you are enrolled in an eligible college or career school at least half-time, in most cases, your loan will be placed into a deferment automatically based on enrollment information reported by your school, and your loan servicer will notify you that the deferment has been granted. If you enroll at least half-time but do not automatically receive a deferment, you should contact the school where you are

enrolled. Your school will then report information about your enrollment status so that your loan can be placed into deferment.
Complete the *In-School Deferment Request*.
> Note: In-school deferment is generally automatic, so in most cases, it isn't necessary to complete the In-School Deferment Request. However, if you are enrolled at least half-time but do not automatically receive a deferment, you can either ask your school to report your enrollment information, as explained above, or complete the In-School Deferment Request.

Military Service and Post-Active Duty Student Deferment
You may be eligible for this deferment if
- you are on active duty military service in connection with a war, military operation, or national emergency; or
- you've completed qualifying active duty service and any applicable grace period. This deferment ends when you resume enrollment in an eligible college or career school on at least a half-time basis or 13 months following the completion date of active duty service and any applicable grace period, whichever is earlier.

Complete the *Military Service and Post-Active Duty Student Deferment Request*.

Parent PLUS Borrower Deferment
You may qualify for this deferment if you are a parent who received a Direct PLUS Loan to help pay for your child's education, and the student you took the loan out for is enrolled at least half-time at an eligible college or career school. You can also receive a deferment for an additional six months after the student ceases to be enrolled at least half-time.
> Complete the *Parent PLUS Borrower Deferment Request*.
> Note: As an alternative to completing the *Parent PLUS Borrower Deferment Request*, if the school your child is attending requires you to complete a Direct PLUS Loan Request, you can request this deferment when you submit the Direct PLUS Loan Request. Check with your child's school.

Rehabilitation Training Deferment
You may qualify for this deferment if you are enrolled in an approved rehabilitation training program that is designed to provide vocational, drug abuse, mental health, or alcohol abuse rehabilitation treatment.
> Complete the *Rehabilitation Training Deferment Request*.

Unemployment Deferment
You may be eligible for this deferment if you receive unemployment benefits or you are seeking and unable to find full-time employment. You can receive this deferment for up to three years.
Complete the Unemployment Deferment Request.
> If you received federal student loans before July 1, 1993, you might be eligible for additional deferments. For more information about these deferments, contact your loan servicer.

Loan Types Eligible for Deferment
> All the deferments are available to Direct Loan, FFEL Program loan, and Perkins Loan borrowers. If you received a Perkins Loan, you may also be eligible for a deferment while you are working toward cancellation on your Perkins Loan. Get contact information regarding your Perkins Loan.
> In most cases, Perkins Loan recipients who receive a deferment will receive a six-month post-deferment grace period that begins on the date they no longer meet the deferment eligibility requirements. No payments are required during the post-deferment grace period. You MUST continue making payments on your student loan(s) until you have been notified that your request for deferment has been granted. If you

stop paying and your deferment is not approved, your loan(s) will become delinquent, and you may go into default.

Forbearances

Information found at:
https://studentaid.gov/manage-loans/lower-payments/get-temporary-relief/forbearance

If you are granted a forbearance, you are still responsible for paying the interest that accrues during the forbearance period.

How It Works
During a forbearance, you can either pay the interest as it accrues, or you can allow it to accrue and be capitalized (added to your loan principal balance) at the end of the forbearance period. If you don't pay the interest on your loan and allow it to be capitalized, the total amount you repay over the life of your loan may be higher. Unpaid interest is capitalized only on Direct Loans and Federal Family Education Loan FFEL Program loans. Unpaid interest is never capitalized on Federal Perkins Loans.

Request a Forbearance
Most types of forbearance are not automatic—you need to submit a request to your student loan servicer, often using a form. Also, for some types of forbearance, you must provide your student loan servicer with documentation to show that you meet the eligibility requirements for the forbearance you are requesting. Learn more about requirements and how to access request forms.

Understand Eligibility for a Forbearance
There are two main types of forbearance: general and mandatory.

   General Forbearance
Your loan servicer decides whether to grant a request for a general forbearance. For this reason, a general forbearance is sometimes called a "discretionary forbearance."
You can request a general forbearance if you are temporarily unable to make your scheduled monthly loan payments for the following reasons:
- Financial difficulties
- Medical expenses
- Change in employment
- Other reasons acceptable to your loan servicer

   Loan Programs Eligible for General Forbearance
General forbearances are available for Direct Loans, Federal Family Education (FFEL) Program loans, and Perkins Loans.

   Duration of a General Forbearance
For loans made under all three programs, a general forbearance may be granted for no more than 12 months at a time. If you are still experiencing a hardship when your current forbearance expires, you may request another general forbearance. However, there is a cumulative limit on general forbearances of three years.
   For more information, review the *General Forbearance Request*.

   Mandatory Forbearance

If you meet the eligibility requirements for a mandatory forbearance, your loan servicer is required to grant the forbearance. You may be eligible for a mandatory forbearance in the following circumstances.

Note: The mandatory forbearances discussed below apply only to Direct Loans and FFEL Program loans unless otherwise noted.

AmeriCorps

You are serving in an AmeriCorps position for which you received a national service award.

Request an AmeriCorps forbearance.

Department of Defense Student Loan Repayment Program

You qualify for partial repayment of your loans under the U.S. Department of Defense Student Loan Repayment Program.

Complete the *Mandatory Forbearance Request: Medical or Dental Internship/Residency, National Guard Duty, or Department of Defense Student Loan Repayment Program.*

Medical or Dental Internship or Residency

You are serving in a medical or dental internship or residency program, and you meet specific requirements.

Complete the *Mandatory Forbearance Request: Medical or Dental Internship/Residency, National Guard Duty, or Department of Defense Student Loan Repayment Program.*

National Guard Duty

You are a member of the National Guard and have been activated by a governor, but you are not eligible for a military deferment.

Complete the Mandatory Forbearance Request: Medical or Dental Internship/Residency, National Guard Duty, or Department of Defense Student Loan Repayment Program.

Student Loan Debt Burden

The total amount you owe each month for all the federal student loans you received is 20 percent or more of your total monthly gross income, for up to three years.

Complete the Mandatory Forbearance Request: Student Loan Debt Burden.

Note: This mandatory forbearance type applies to Direct Loans, FFEL Program loans, and Perkins Loans.

Teacher Loan Forgiveness

You are performing teaching service that would qualify you for teacher loan forgiveness.
Apply using this form: Teacher Loan Forgiveness Forbearance Request.

Duration of Mandatory Forbearances

Mandatory forbearances may be granted for no more than 12 months at a time. If you continue to meet the eligibility requirements for the forbearance when your current forbearance period expires, you may request another mandatory forbearance.

You MUST continue making payments on your student loan(s) until you have been notified that your request for forbearance has been granted. If you stop paying and your forbearance is not approved, your loan(s) will become delinquent and you may go into default.

Forbearances Request Form—General 2021

GENERAL FORBEARANCE REQUEST

William D. Ford Federal Direct Loan (Direct Loan) Program / Federal Family Education Loan (FFEL) Program / Federal Perkins Loan (Perkins Loan) Program

OMB No. 1845-0031
Form Approved
Exp. Date 02/28/2022

WARNING: Any person who knowingly makes a false statement or misrepresentation on this form or on any accompanying document is subject to penalties that may include fines, imprisonment, or both, under the U.S. Criminal Code and 20 U.S.C. 1097.

SECTION 1: BORROWER INFORMATION

Please enter or correct the following information.

☐ Check this box if any of your information has changed.

- SSN
- Name
- Address
- City ____ State ____ Zip Code
- Telephone - Primary
- Telephone - Alternate
- Email (Optional)

SECTION 2: FORBEARANCE REQUEST

Carefully read the entire form before completing it. Answer all questions in Section 2. Your loan holder has sole discretion in whether to grant your general forbearance request, and, if granted, for what period your forbearance will be applied. Instead of forbearance, consider requesting a deferment (which has an interest benefit for some loan types) or changing to a repayment plan that determines your monthly payment amount based on your income. Visit StudentAid.gov/IDR for more information.

1. I am requesting a forbearance because I am experiencing a temporary hardship related to one of the following situations (check one):

   ☐ Financial difficulties
   ☐ Change in employment
   ☐ Medical expenses
   ☐ Other (explain the situation below)

2. If approved for a forbearance, I would like to:

   ☐ Temporarily stop making payments.
   ☐ Temporarily make smaller payments of _____ per month.

3. I would like my forbearance to begin with the monthly payment that is due in the month and year below:

   _____

4. If approved for forbearance, I would like my forbearance to end in the month and year below, and begin making payments the following month:

   _____

Page 1 of 4

Borrower Name _____   Borrower SSN _____

SECTION 3: BORROWER/ENDORSER UNDERSTANDINGS, CERTIFICATIONS, AND AUTHORIZATION

I understand that:

- I am not required to make payments of loan principal or interest during my forbearance, but interest will continue to be charged on all my loans.
- Interest may capitalize on my loans during or at the expiration of my forbearance, but interest never capitalizes on Perkins Loans. Interest capitalization usually increases the amount of interest I will pay, and may increase my monthly payment.
- My loan holder has sole discretion in whether to grant my general forbearance request and for what dates it will be granted.
- For Perkins Loans, there is a cumulative limit on general forbearance of 3 years. For Direct Loans and FFEL Program loans, my loan holder may set a limit on general forbearance.
- My forbearance will end on the earlier of the end date that I requested, 12 months from the date my forbearance begins, or when I exhaust any limit that my loan holder has on forbearance.
- I can request another forbearance after my forbearance ends if I am still experiencing financial hardship.
- Any payment I make during forbearance will not count towards forgiveness under income-driven repayment plans or Public Service Loan Forgiveness.

I certify that:

- The information I have provided on this form is true and correct.
- I will provide additional documentation to my loan holder, if requested, to support my general forbearance request.
- I will repay my loans according to the terms of my promissory note, even if my request is not granted.

I authorize the entity to which I submit this request and its agents to contact me regarding my request or my loans at any cellular telephone number that I provide now or in the future using automated telephone dialing equipment or artificial or prerecorded voice or text messages.

Borrower's/Endorser's Signature _____   Date _____

SECTION 4: INSTRUCTIONS FOR COMPLETING THE FORBEARANCE REQUEST

Type or print using dark ink. Enter dates as month-day-year (mm-dd-yyyy) or (mm-yyyy) as appropriate. Example: March 14, 2019 = 03-14-2019. Include your name and account number on any documentation that you may be requested to submit with this form. If you want to apply for a forbearance on loans that are held by different loan holders, you must submit a separate forbearance request to each loan holder. **Return the completed form and any requested documentation to the address shown in Section 6.**

If you are an endorser, you may request forbearance only when you are required to repay the loan because the borrower is not making payments. If you have a loan made jointly with another borrower (as co-makers), you must both individually meet the requirements for a forbearance and each of you must request forbearance.

SECTION 5: DEFINITIONS

Capitalization is the addition of unpaid interest to the principal balance of your loan. Capitalization causes more interest to accrue over the life of your loan and may cause your monthly payment amount to increase. Interest never capitalizes on Perkins Loans. Table 1 (below) provides an example of the monthly payments and the total amount repaid for a $30,000 unsubsidized loan. The example loan has a 6% interest rate and the example deferment or forbearance lasts for 12 months and begins when the loan entered repayment. The example compares the effects of paying the interest as it accrues or allowing it to be capitalized.

A **co-maker** is one of the two individuals who are joint borrowers on a Direct or Federal Consolidation Loan or a Federal PLUS Loan. Both co-makers are equally responsible for repaying the full amount of the loan.

A **deferment** is a period during which you are entitled to postpone repayment of your loans. Interest is not generally charged to you during a deferment on your subsidized loans. Interest is always charged to you during a deferment on your unsubsidized loans. On loans made under the Perkins Loan Program, all deferments are followed by a post-deferment grace period of 6 months, during which time you are not required to make payments.

An **endorser** is an individual who signs a promissory note and agrees to pay the loan if the borrower does not.

The **Federal Family Education Loan (FFEL) Program** includes Federal Stafford Loans, Federal PLUS Loans, Federal Consolidation Loans, and Federal Supplemental Loans for Students (SLS).

The **Federal Perkins Loan (Perkins Loan) Program** includes Federal Perkins Loans, National Direct Student Loans (NDSL), and National Defense Student Loans (Defense Loans).

A **forbearance** is a period during which you are allowed to postpone making payments temporarily, allowed an extension of time for making payments, or temporarily allowed to make smaller payments than scheduled. A forbearance can be a mandatory forbearance, meaning that your loan holder must grant the forbearance if you qualify for the forbearance and supply all supporting documentation. A forbearance can also be a discretionary forbearance, meaning that your loan holder may grant the forbearance, but is not required to do so.

The **holder** of your Direct Loans is the Department. The holder of your FFEL Program loans may be a lender, guaranty agency, secondary market, or the Department. The holder of your Perkins Loans is an institution of higher education or the Department. Your loan holder may use a servicer to handle billing and other communications related to your loans. References to "your loan holder" on this form mean either your loan holder or your servicer.

A **subsidized loan** is a Direct Subsidized Loan, a Direct Subsidized Consolidation Loan, a Federal Subsidized Stafford Loan, portions of some Federal Consolidation Loans, Federal Perkins Loans, NDSL, and Defense Loans.

An **unsubsidized loan** is a Direct Unsubsidized Loan, a Direct Unsubsidized Consolidation Loan, a Direct PLUS Loan, a Federal Unsubsidized Stafford Loan, a Federal PLUS Loan, a Federal SLS, and portions of some Federal Consolidation Loans.

The **William D. Ford Federal Direct Loan (Direct Loan) Program** includes Federal Direct Stafford/Ford (Direct Subsidized) Loans, Federal Direct Unsubsidized Stafford/Ford (Direct Unsubsidized) Loans, Federal Direct PLUS (Direct PLUS) Loans, and Federal Direct Consolidation (Direct Consolidation) Loans.

Table 1. Capitalization Chart

Treatment of Interest with Deferment/Forbearance	Loan Amount	Capitalized Interest	Outstanding Principal	Monthly Payment	Number of Payments	Total Repaid
Interest is paid	$30,000	$0	$30,000	$333	120	$41,767
Interest is capitalized at the end	$30,000	$1,800	$31,800	$353	120	$42,365
Interest is capitalized quarterly and at the end	$30,000	$1,841	$31,841	$354	120	$42,420

SECTION 6: WHERE TO SEND THE COMPLETED FORBEARANCE REQUEST

Return the completed form and any documentation to:
(If no address is shown, return to your loan holder.)

If you need help completing this form, call:
(If no telephone number is shown, call your loan holder.)

SECTION 7: IMPORTANT NOTICES

Privacy Act Notice. The Privacy Act of 1974 (5 U.S.C. 552a) requires that the following notice be provided to you:

The authorities for collecting the requested information from and about you are §421 et seq., §451 et seq., or §461 of the Higher Education Act of 1965, as amended (20 U.S.C. 1071 et seq., 20 U.S.C. 1087a et seq., or 20 U.S.C. 1087aa et seq.) and the authorities for collecting and using your Social Security Number (SSN) are §§428B(f) and 484(a)(4) of the HEA (20 U.S.C. 1078-2(f) and 1091(a)(4)) and 31 U.S.C. 7701(b). Participating in the William D. Ford Federal Direct Loan (Direct Loan) Program, Federal Family Education Loan (FFEL) Program, or Federal Perkins Loan (Perkins Loan) Program and giving us your SSN are voluntary, but you must provide the requested information, including your SSN, to participate.

The principal purposes for collecting the information on this form, including your SSN, are to verify your identity, to determine your eligibility to receive a loan or a benefit on a loan (such as a deferment, forbearance, discharge, or forgiveness) under the Direct Loan, FFEL, or Federal Perkins Loan Programs, to permit the servicing of your loans, and, if it becomes necessary, to locate you and to collect and report on your loans if your loans become delinquent or default. We also use your SSN as an account identifier and to permit you to access your account information electronically.

The information in your file may be disclosed, on a case-by-case basis or under a computer matching program, to third parties as authorized under routine uses in the appropriate systems of records notices. The routine uses of this information include, but are not limited to, its disclosure to federal, state, or local agencies, to private parties such as relatives, present and former employers, business and personal associates, to consumer reporting agencies, to financial and educational institutions, and to guaranty agencies in order to verify your identity, to determine your eligibility to receive a loan or a benefit on a loan, to permit the servicing or collection of your loans, to enforce the terms of the loans, to investigate possible fraud and to verify compliance with federal student financial aid program regulations, or to locate you if you become delinquent in your loan payments or if you default. To provide default rate calculations, disclosures may be made to guaranty agencies, to financial and educational institutions, or to state agencies. To provide financial aid history information, disclosures may be made to educational institutions.

To assist program administrators with tracking refunds and cancellations, disclosures may be made to guaranty agencies, to financial and educational institutions, or to federal or state agencies. To provide a standardized method for educational institutions to efficiently submit student enrollment statuses, disclosures may be made to guaranty agencies or to financial and educational institutions. To counsel you in repayment efforts, disclosures may be made to guaranty agencies, to financial and educational institutions, or to federal, state, or local agencies.

In the event of litigation, we may send records to the Department of Justice, a court, adjudicative body, counsel, party, or witness if the disclosure is relevant and necessary to the litigation. If this information, either alone or with other information, indicates a potential violation of law, we may send it to the appropriate authority for action. We may send information to members of Congress if you ask them to help you with federal student aid questions. In circumstances involving employment complaints, grievances, or disciplinary actions, we may disclose relevant records to adjudicate or investigate the issues. If provided for by a collective bargaining agreement, we may disclose records to a labor organization recognized under 5 U.S.C. Chapter 71. Disclosures may be made to our contractors for the purpose of performing any programmatic function that requires disclosure of records. Before making any such disclosure, we will require the contractor to maintain Privacy Act safeguards. Disclosures may also be made to qualified researchers under Privacy Act safeguards.

Paperwork Reduction Notice. According to the Paperwork Reduction Act of 1995, no persons are required to respond to a collection of information unless such collection displays a valid OMB control number. The valid OMB control number for this information collection is 1845-0031. Public reporting burden for this collection of information is estimated to average 5 minutes per response, including time for reviewing instructions, searching existing data sources, gathering and maintaining the data needed, and completing and reviewing the collection of information. The obligation to respond to this collection is required to obtain a benefit in accordance with 34 CFR 674.33, 682.211, and 685.205. If you have comments or concerns regarding the status of your individual submission of this form, please contact your loan holder directly (see Section 6).

Forbearances Request Form—Mandatory 2021

MANDATORY FORBEARANCE REQUEST
Medical or Dental Internship/Residency, National Guard Duty, or Department of Defense Student Loan Repayment Program Forbearance
William D. Ford Federal Direct Loan (Direct Loan Program) / Federal Family Education Loan (FFEL) Program

OMB No. 1845-0018
Form Approved
Exp. Date 8/31/2021

SERV

WARNING: Any person who knowingly makes a false statement or misrepresentation on this form or on any accompanying document is subject to penalties that may include fines, imprisonment, or both, under the U.S. Criminal Code and 20 U.S.C. 1097.

SECTION 1: BORROWER INFORMATION

Please enter or correct the following information.
☐ Check this box if any of your information has changed.

SSN _____
Name _____
Address _____
City _____ State _____ Zip Code _____
Telephone - Primary _____
Telephone - Alternate _____
Email (Optional) _____

SECTION 2: BORROWER DETERMINATION OF FORBEARANCE ELIGIBILITY

Carefully read the entire form before completing it. Complete the applicable part of Section 2 in its entirety. This form covers three different types of forbearance. Review the information for each forbearance type to determine whether you qualify for that forbearance.

PART A. MEDICAL OR DENTAL INTERNSHIP/RESIDENCY

You only qualify for this forbearance if you do not qualify for a medical or dental internship/residency deferment.

1. Have you been accepted into an internship/residency?
   - ☐ Yes - Continue to Item 2.
   - ☐ No - You are not eligible for this forbearance.

2. Did your program require for admission that you have a bachelor's degree?
   - ☐ Yes - Continue to Item 3.
   - ☐ No - You are not eligible for this forbearance.

3. Will you receive supervised training in your internship/residency program?
   - ☐ Yes - Continue to Item 4.
   - ☐ No - You are not eligible for this forbearance.

4. Will completion of your program lead to a degree or certificate awarded by an institution of higher education, a hospital, or a health care facility that offers postgraduate training?
   - ☐ Yes - Complete Section 3 and have an authorized official complete Section 4.
   - ☐ No - Continue to Item 5.

5. Is completion of all or a portion of the program required before you can begin professional practice or service?
   - ☐ Yes - Complete Section 3 and have an authorized official complete Section 4. In addition, you must attach a separate statement from the appropriate state licensing agency certifying this requirement.
   - ☐ No - You are not eligible for this forbearance.

PART B. NATIONAL GUARD DUTY

You only qualify for this forbearance if you do not qualify for a military service deferment.

6. Are you a member of the National Guard?
   - ☐ Yes - Continue to Item 7.
   - ☐ No - You are not eligible for this forbearance.

7. Are you engaged in active state duty for a period of more than 30 consecutive days because a governor activated you based on state statute or policy?
   - ☐ Yes - Continue to Item 8.
   - ☐ No - Skip to Item 9.

8. Is your service being paid for with state funds?
   - ☐ Yes - Skip to Item 11.
   - ☐ No - Continue to Item 9.

Borrower Name _____ Borrower SSN _____

SECTION 2: BORROWER DETERMINATION OF FORBEARANCE ELIGIBILITY (CONTINUED)

9. Are you engaged in active state duty for a period of more than 30 consecutive days under which a governor activated you with the approval of the President or the U.S. Secretary of Defense?
   - ☐ Yes - Continue to Item 10.
   - ☐ No - You are not eligible for this forbearance.

10. Is your service being paid for with federal funds?
    - ☐ Yes - Continue to Item 11.
    - ☐ No - You are not eligible for this forbearance.

11. Were you activated no more than 6 months after the last date on which you were enrolled in school at least half-time?
    - ☐ Yes - Complete Section 3 and have an authorized official (a commanding or personnel officer) complete Section 4.
    - ☐ No - You are not eligible for this forbearance.

PART C. DEPARTMENT OF DEFENSE STUDENT LOAN REPAYMENT PROGRAM

12. Are you performing service that qualifies you for a partial repayment of your loans under any Department of Defense Student Loan Repayment Program?
    - ☐ Yes - Complete Section 3 and have an authorized official from the Department of Defense complete Section 4.
    - ☐ No - You are not eligible for this forbearance.

SECTION 3: BORROWER REQUESTS, UNDERSTANDINGS, CERTIFICATIONS, AND AUTHORIZATION

I request:

- My loan holder grant forbearance for the period during which I meet the qualifications for the forbearance. If approved for a forbearance, I would like to:
  - ☐ Temporarily stop making payments; or
  - ☐ Make smaller payments in the amount of _____ per month.
- My loan holder grant my forbearance for up to 12 months unless I specify an earlier end date: _____ .
  - ☐ If checked, to make interest payments on my loans during forbearance.

I understand:

- I am not required to make payments of loan principal or interest during forbearance.
- My forbearance will begin on the date the program or service that qualifies me for forbearance began, as certified by the authorized official.
- My loan holder may grant me an additional forbearance while processing my form or to cover any period of delinquency that exists when I submit my form.
- My forbearance will end on the earlier of the date I am no longer eligible for the forbearance, 12 months from the start date of the forbearance, or the end date I requested.
- My forbearance will only be granted in increments of up to 12 months, and I must reapply for the forbearance if I continue to meet the eligibility requirements and want to extend my forbearance.
- Interest may capitalize on my loans during or at the expiration of my forbearance.

Borrower Name _____   Borrower SSN _____

SECTION 3: BORROWER REQUESTS, UNDERSTANDINGS, CERTIFICATIONS, AND AUTHORIZATION (CONTINUED)

I certify that:

- The information I have provided on this form is true and correct.
- I will provide additional documentation to my loan holder, as required, to support my forbearance eligibility.
- I will notify my loan holder immediately when my eligibility for the forbearance ends.
- I have read, understand, and meet the eligibility requirements in Section 2.

I authorize the entity to which I submit this request and its agents to contact me regarding my request or my loans at any cellular telephone number that I provide now or in the future using automated telephone dialing equipment or artificial prerecorded voice or text messages.

Borrower's Signature _____   **Date** _____

SECTION 4: AUTHORIZED OFFICIAL'S CERTIFICATION

Do not complete this section unless the borrower has completed the applicable part of Section 2 in its entirety. Note: Instead of having an **authorized** official complete this section, you may attach separate **documentation** from an **authorized** official that includes all of the information requested below and a certification that you and the program meet all conditions indicated by your responses in Section 2. For the National Guard Duty forbearance, you may attach a copy of your orders.

- The program/service begins/began on:
  _____

- The program/service is expected to end/ended on:
  _____

I certify, to the best of my knowledge and belief, that:

- The borrower named above is/was engaged in the program/service indicated in Section 2;
- The borrower and program/service meet all conditions indicated by the borrower's responses in Section 2; and
- The information that I have provided in this section is accurate.

Name of Institution/Organization _____

Address _____ City _____ State _____ Zip Code _____

Official's Name/Title _____ Telephone _____

Official's Signature _____   **Date** _____

SECTION 5: INSTRUCTIONS FOR COMPLETING THE FORM

Type or print using dark ink. Enter dates as month-day-year (mm-dd-yyyy). Example: March 14, 2019 = 03-14-2019. Include your name and account number on any documentation that you submit with this form. If you want to apply for a forbearance on loans that are held by different loan holders, you must submit a separate forbearance request to each loan holder. **Return the completed form and any required documentation to the address shown in Section 7.**

Endorsers may request forbearance only when you are required to repay the loan because the borrower is not making payments. For those who have loans made jointly (as co-makers), both borrowers must individually meet the requirements for a forbearance and each of you must submit a separate forbearance request.

SECTION 6: DEFINITIONS

The **William D. Ford Federal Direct Loan (Direct Loan) Program** includes Federal Direct Stafford/Ford (Direct Subsidized) Loans, Federal Direct Unsubsidized Stafford/Ford (Direct Unsubsidized) Loans, Federal Direct PLUS (Direct PLUS) Loans, and Federal Direct Consolidation (Direct Consolidation) Loans.

The **Federal Family Education Loan (FFEL) Program** includes Federal Stafford Loans, Federal PLUS Loans, Federal Consolidation Loans, and Federal Supplemental Loans for Students (SLS).

An **authorized official** for the medical or dental internship/residency forbearance is an official from your internship/residency program. An authorized official for the National Guard State Duty forbearance is your commanding or personnel officer. An authorized official for the Department of Defense Student Loan Repayment Program forbearance is an official from the Department of Defense.

Capitalization is the addition of unpaid interest to the principal balance of your loan. Capitalization causes more interest to accrue over the life of the loan and may cause your monthly payment amount to increase. Table 1 (below) provides an example of the monthly payments and the total amount repaid for a $30,000 unsubsidized loan. The example loan has a 6% interest rate and the example deferment or forbearance lasts for 12 months and begins when the loan entered repayment. The example compares the effects of paying the interest as it accrues or allowing it to capitalize.

A **co-maker** is one of the two individual who are joint borrowers on a Direct or Federal Consolidation Loan or a Federal PLUS Loan. Both co-makers are equally responsible for repaying the full amount of the loan.

An **endorser** is an individual who sings a promissory note and agrees to pay the loan if teh borrower sdoes not.

A **deferment** is a period during which you are entitled to postpone repayment of your loans. Interest is not generally charged to you during a deferment on your subsidized loans. Interest is always charged to you during a deferment on your unsubsidized loans.

A **forbearance** is a period during which you are allowed to postpone making payments temporarily, allowed an extension of time for making payments, or temporarily allowed to make smaller payments than scheduled. A forbearance can be a mandatory forbearance, meaning that your loan holder must grant the forbearance if you qualify for the forbearance and supply all supporting documentation. A forbearance can also be a discretionary forbearance, meaning that your loan holder may grant the forbearance, but is not required to do so.

The **holder** of your Direct Loan Program loans is the Department. The holder of your FFEL Program loans may be a lender, guaranty agency, secondary market, or the Department. Your loan holder may use a servicer to handle billing and other communications related to your loans. References to "your loan holder" on this form mean either your loan holder or your servicer.

A **subsidized loan** is a Direct Subsidized Loan, a Direct Subsidized Consolidation Loan, a Federal Subsidized Stafford Loan, and portions of some Federal Consolidation Loans.

An **unsubsidized loan** is a Direct Unsubsidized Loan, a Direct Unsubsidized Consolidation Loan, a Direct PLUS Loan, a Federal Unsubsidized Stafford Loan, a Federal PLUS Loan, a Federal SLS, and portions of some Federal Consolidation Loans.

Table 1. Capitalization Chart

Treatment of Interest with Deferment/Forbearance	Loan Amount	Capitalized Interest	Outstanding Principal	Monthly Payment	Number of Payments	Total Repaid
Interest is paid	$30,000	$0	$30,000	$333	120	$41,767
Interest is capitalized at the end	$30,000	$1,800	$31,800	$353	120	$42,365
Interest is capitalized quarterly and at the end	$30,000	$1,841	$31,841	$354	120	$42,420

SECTION 7: WHERE TO SEND THE COMPLETED FORBEARANCE REQUEST

Return the completed form and any documentation to:
(If no address is shown, return to your loan holder.)

If you need help completing this form, call:
(If no phone number is shown, call your loan holder.)

SECTION 8: IMPORTANT NOTICES

Privacy Act Notice. The Privacy Act of 1974 (5 U.S.C. 552a) requires that the following notice be provided to you:

The authorities for collecting the requested information from and about you are §421 et seq. or §451 et seq. of the Higher Education Act of 1965, as amended (20 U.S.C. 1071 et seq. or 20 U.S.C. 1087a et seq.) and the authorities for collecting and using your Social Security Number (SSN) are §§428B(f) and 484(a)(4) of the HEA (20 U.S.C. 1078-2(f) and 1091(a)(4)) and 31 U.S.C. 7701(b). Participating in the William D. Ford Federal Direct Loan (Direct Loan) Program or Federal Family Education Loan (FFEL) Program and giving us your SSN are voluntary, but you must provide the requested information, including your SSN, to participate.

The principal purposes for collecting the information on this form, including your SSN, are to verify your identity, to determine your eligibility to receive a loan or a benefit on a loan (such as a deferment, forbearance, discharge, or forgiveness) under the Direct Loan or FFEL Programs, to permit the servicing of your loans, and, if it becomes necessary, to locate you and to collect and report on your loans if your loans become delinquent or default. We also use your SSN as an account identifier and to permit you to access your account information electronically.

The information in your file may be disclosed, on a case-by-case basis or under a computer matching program, to third parties as authorized under routine uses in the appropriate systems of records notices. The routine uses of this information include, but are not limited to, its disclosure to federal, state, or local agencies, to private parties such as relatives, present and former employers, business and personal associates, to consumer reporting agencies, to financial and educational institutions, and to guaranty agencies in order to verify your identity, to determine your eligibility to receive a loan or a benefit on a loan, to permit the servicing or collection of your loans, to enforce the terms of the loans, to investigate possible fraud and to verify compliance with federal student financial aid program regulations, or to locate you if you become delinquent in your loan payments or if you default. To provide default rate calculations, disclosures may be made to guaranty agencies, to financial and educational institutions, or to state agencies. To provide financial aid history information, disclosures may be made to educational institutions.

To assist program administrators with tracking refunds and cancellations, disclosures may be made to guaranty agencies, to financial and educational institutions, or to federal or state agencies. To provide a standardized method for educational institutions to efficiently submit student enrollment statuses, disclosures may be made to guaranty agencies or to financial and educational institutions. To counsel you in repayment efforts, disclosures may be made to guaranty agencies, to financial and educational institutions, or to federal, state, or local agencies.

In the event of litigation, we may send records to the Department of Justice, a court, adjudicative body, counsel, party, or witness if the disclosure is relevant and necessary to the litigation. If this information, either alone or with other information, indicates a potential violation of law, we may send it to the appropriate authority for action. We may send information to members of Congress if you ask them to help you with federal student aid questions. In circumstances involving employment complaints, grievances, or disciplinary actions, we may disclose relevant records to adjudicate or investigate the issues. If provided for by a collective bargaining agreement, we may disclose records to a labor organization recognized under 5 U.S.C. Chapter 71. Disclosures may be made to our contractors for the purpose of performing any programmatic function that requires disclosure of records. Before making any such disclosure, we will require the contractor to maintain Privacy Act safeguards. Disclosures may also be made to qualified researchers under Privacy Act safeguards.

Paperwork Reduction Notice. According to the Paperwork Reduction Act of 1995, no persons are required to respond to a collection of information unless such collection displays a valid OMB control number. The valid OMB control number for this information collection is 1845-0018. Public reporting burden for this collection of information is estimated to average 15 minutes per response, including time for reviewing instructions, searching existing data sources, gathering and maintaining the data needed, and completing and reviewing the collection of information. The obligation to respond to this collection is required to obtain a benefit in accordance with 34 CFR 682.211 or 685.205.

If you have comments or concerns regarding the status of your individual submission of this form, please contact your loan holder directly (see Section 7).

Loan Delinquency and Default

[U.S. Department of Education webpage located at:
https://studentaid.gov/manage-loans/default]

Delinquency and Default

Understanding Delinquency

It's important to pay the amount shown on your bill—and to pay by the due date.

The **first day** after you miss a student loan payment, your loan becomes past due, or delinquent. Your loan account remains delinquent until you repay the past due amount or make other arrangements, such as deferment or forbearance, or changing repayment plans.

If you are delinquent on your student loan payment for 90 days or more, your loan servicer will report the delinquency to the three major national credit bureaus. If you continue to be delinquent, your loan can risk going into default. Don't ignore your student loan payments—defaulting on your loan can have serious consequences. Learn more on how to avoid default.

Note: Credit bureaus may be called "consumer reporting agencies" on the promissory note you signed before receiving your loan.

If you have a poor credit rating, it can be difficult for you to obtain
- credit cards,
- home or car loans, or
- other forms of consumer credit.

Note: You may also be charged a higher interest rate than someone with a good credit rating.

You also may have trouble
- signing up for utilities,
- getting homeowner's insurance,
- getting a cell phone plan, or
- getting approval to rent an apartment (credit checks usually are required for renters).

Understanding Default

If your loan continues to be delinquent, the loan may go into default. The point when a loan is considered to be in default varies depending on the type of loan you received.

For a loan made under the William D. Ford Federal Direct Loan Program or the Federal Family Education Loan Program, you are considered to be in default if you don't make your scheduled student loan payments for at least 270 days.

For a loan made under the Federal Perkins Loan Program, the holder of the loan may declare the loan to be in default if you don't make your scheduled payment by the due date. Find out where to go for information about your Perkins Loan.

If you defaulted on any of your federal student loans, contact the organization that notified you of the default as soon as possible so you can explain your situation fully and discuss your options. If you make repayment arrangements soon enough after your loan has gone into default, you may be able to resolve the default quickly. Learn more about getting out of default.

Consequences of Default

The consequences of defaulting can not only impact your ability to borrow but can impact your finances as well. Consequences include the following:
- The entire unpaid balance of your loan and any interest you owe becomes immediately due (this is called "acceleration").

- You can no longer receive deferment or forbearance, and you lose eligibility for other benefits, such as the ability to choose a repayment plan.
- You lose eligibility for additional federal student aid.
- The default is reported to credit bureaus, damaging your credit rating and affecting your ability to buy a car or house or to get a credit card.
- It may take years to reestablish a good credit record.
- You may not be able to purchase or sell assets such as real estate.
- Your tax refunds and federal benefit payments may be withheld and applied toward repayment of your defaulted loan (this is called "Treasury offset").
- Your wages may be garnished. This means your employer may be required to withhold a portion of your pay and send it to your loan holder to repay your defaulted loan.
- Your loan holder can take you to court.
- You may be charged court costs, collection fees, attorney's fees, and other costs associated with the collection process.
- Your school may withhold your academic transcript until your defaulted student loan is satisfied. The academic transcript is the property of the school, and it is the school's decision—not the U.S. Department of Education's or your loan holder's—whether to release the transcript to you.
-

If You Are Delinquent or In Default, Your Loan Servicer Can Help

If you're having trouble making payments or are concerned about the status of your federal student loan(s), you have options available to you.

Contact your loan servicer to discuss how to get back on track with payments. There are several affordable repayment options that you may be able to take advantage of to continue making loan payments even when times are tough.

My Loan Was Mistakenly Put in Default

If you believe your loan has been placed in default by mistake, here's what you can do to correct the error.

Situation	Solution
I'm in school at least half-time and should have received an in-school deferment.	Contact your school's registrar to get a record of all your dates of at least half-time attendance. Contact each school you have attended since you received your loan, so your documentation is complete. Ask your loan servicer for the last date of attendance they have on file for you. If they have the incorrect date for your last date of attendance, provide them with a copy of your documentation showing the correct date.
I was approved for deferment or forbearance.	Ask your loan servicer to confirm the start and end dates of any deferments and forbearances that were applied to your loan account. If the loan servicer has incorrect information, provide documentation with the correct information.

Situation	Solution
I've made my payments on time.	Ask your loan servicer for a statement that shows all the payments made on your student loan account. If payments you made are not listed, provide proof of payment to your loan servicer and request that the information in your account be corrected.

Defaulted Federal Loan Servicer

MAXIMUS Federal Services, Inc., is the loan servicer for defaulted federal student loans over 360 days delinquent.

APPENDIX B
Laws and Legal Guidelines

Rules and Regulations

31 U.S.C.A. §3716 — Administrative Offset of Federal Benefits

(a) After trying to collect a claim from a person under section 3711(a) of this title, the head of an executive, judicial, or legislative agency may collect the claim by administrative offset. The head of the agency may collect by administrative offset only after giving the debtor -
    (1) written notice of the type and amount of the claim, the intention of the head of the agency to collect the claim by administrative offset, and an explanation of the rights of the debtor under this section;
    (2) an opportunity to inspect and copy the records of the agency related to the claim;
    (3) an opportunity for a review within the agency of the decision of the agency related to the claim; and
    (4) an opportunity to make a written agreement with the head of the agency to repay the amount of the claim.
(b) Before collecting a claim by administrative offset, the head of an executive, judicial, or legislative agency must either -
    (1) adopt, without change, regulations on collecting by administrative offset promulgated by the Department of Justice, the General Accounting Office, or the Department of the Treasury; or
    (2) prescribe regulations on collecting by administrative offset consistent with the regulations referred to in paragraph (1).
(c) (1) (A) Except as otherwise provided in this subsection, a disbursing official of the Department of the Treasury, the Department of Defense, the United States Postal Service, or any other government corporation, or any disbursing official of the United States designated by the Secretary of the Treasury, shall offset at least annually the amount of a payment which a payment certifying agency has certified to the disbursing official for disbursement, by an amount equal to the amount of a claim which a creditor agency has certified to the Secretary of the Treasury pursuant to this subsection.
    (B) An agency that designates disbursing officials pursuant to section 3321(c) of this title is not required to certify claims arising out of its operations to the Secretary of the Treasury before such agency's disbursing officials offset such claims.
    (C) Payments certified by the Department of Education under a program administered by the Secretary of Education under title IV of the Higher Education Act of 1965 shall not be subject to administrative offset under this subsection.
    (2) Neither the disbursing official nor the payment certifying agency shall be liable -
    (A) for the amount of the administrative offset on the basis that the underlying obligation, represented by the payment before the administrative offset was taken, was not satisfied; or
    (B) for failure to provide timely notice under paragraph (8).
    (3) (A) (i) Notwithstanding any other provision of law (including sections 207 and 1631(d)(1) of the Social Security Act (42 U.S.C. 407 and 1383(d)(1)), section 413 (b) of Public Law 91-173 (30 U.S.C. 923(b)), and section 14 of the Act of August 29, 1935 (45 U.S.C. 231m)), except as provided in clause (ii), all payments due to an individual under -
        (I) the Social Security Act,
        (II) part B of the Black Lung Benefits Act, or
        (III) any law administered by the Railroad Retirement Board (other than payments that such Board determines to be tier 2 benefits), shall be subject to offset under this section.
    (ii) An amount of $9,000 which a debtor may receive under Federal benefit programs cited under clause (i) within a 12-month period shall be exempt from offset under this subsection. In applying the $9,000 exemption, the disbursing official shall -
        (I) reduce the $9,000 exemption amount for the 12-month period by the amount of all Federal benefit payments made during such 12-month period which are not subject to offset under this subsection; and

(II) apply a prorated amount of the exemption to each periodic benefit payment to be made to the debtor during the applicable 12-month period. For purposes of the preceding sentence, the amount of a periodic benefit payment shall be the amount after any reduction or deduction required under the laws authorizing the program under which such payment is authorized to be made (including any reduction or deduction to recover any overpayment under such program).

(B) The Secretary of the Treasury shall exempt from administrative offset under this subsection payments under means-tested programs when requested by the head of the respective agency. The Secretary may exempt other payments from administrative offset under this subsection upon the written request of the head of a payment certifying agency. A written request for exemption of other payments must provide justification for the exemption under standards prescribed by the Secretary. Such standards shall give due consideration to whether administrative offset would tend to interfere substantially with or defeat the purposes of the payment certifying agency's program. The Secretary shall report to the Congress annually on exemptions granted under this section.

(C) The provisions of sections 205 (b)(1) and 1631(c) (1) of the Social Security Act shall not apply to any administrative offset executed pursuant to this section against benefits authorized by either title II or title XVI of the Social Security Act, respectively.

(4) The Secretary of the Treasury may charge a fee sufficient to cover the full cost of implementing this subsection. The fee may be collected either by the retention of a portion of amounts collected pursuant to this subsection, or by billing the agency referring or transferring a claim for those amounts. Fees charged to the agencies shall be based on actual administrative offsets completed. Amounts received by the United States as fees under this subsection shall be deposited into the account of the Department of the Treasury under section 3711 (g) (7) of this title, and shall be collected and accounted for in accordance with the provisions of that section.

(5) The Secretary of the Treasury in consultation with the Commissioner of Social Security and the Director of the Office of Management and Budget, may prescribe such rules, regulations, and procedures as the Secretary of the Treasury considers necessary to carry out this subsection. The Secretary shall consult with the heads of affected agencies in the development of such rules, regulations, and procedures.

(6) Any Federal agency that is owed by a person a past due, legally enforceable nontax debt that is over 180 days delinquent, including nontax debt administered by a third party acting as an agent for the Federal Government, shall notify the Secretary of the Treasury of all such nontax debts for purposes of administrative offset under this subsection.

(7) (A) The disbursing official conducting an administrative offset with respect to a payment to a payee shall notify the payee in writing of -

(i) the occurrence of the administrative offset to satisfy a past due legally enforceable debt, including a description of the type and amount of the payment otherwise payable to the payee against which the offset was executed;

(ii) the identity of the creditor agency requesting the offset; and

(iii) a contact point within the creditor agency that will handle concerns regarding the offset.

(B) If the payment to be offset is a periodic benefit payment, the disbursing official shall take reasonable steps, as determined by the Secretary of the Treasury, to provide the notice to the payee not later than the date on which the payee is otherwise scheduled to receive the payment, or as soon as practical thereafter, but no later than the date of the administrative offset. Notwithstanding the preceding sentence, the failure of the debtor to receive such notice shall not impair the legality of such administrative offset.

(8) A levy pursuant to the Internal Revenue Code of 1986 shall take precedence over requests for administrative offset pursuant to other laws.

(d) Nothing in this section is intended to prohibit the use of any other administrative offset authority existing under statute or common law.

(e) This section does not apply -

(1) ~~to a claim under this subchapter that has been outstanding for more than 10 years~~; [NO LONGER TRUE SINCE U.S. SUPREME COURT DECISION IN DECEMBER 2005, *LOCKHART V. U.S., 04-881*] or

(2) when a statute explicitly prohibits using administrative offset or setoff to collect the claim or type of claim involved.

(f) The Secretary may waive the requirements of sections 552a(o) and (p) of title 5 for administrative offset or claims collection upon written certification by the head of a State or an executive, judicial, or legislative agency seeking to collect the claim that the requirements of subsection (a) of this section have been met.

(g) The Data Integrity Board of the Department of the Treasury established under 552a(u) of Title 5 shall review and include in reports under paragraph (3)(D) of that section a description of any matching activities conducted under this section. If the Secretary has granted a waiver under subsection (f) of this section, no other Data Integrity Board is required to take any action under section 552a (u) of title 5.

(h) (1) The Secretary may, in the discretion of the Secretary, apply subsection (a) with respect to any past-due, legally-enforceable debt owed to a State if -
    (A) the appropriate State disbursing official requests that an offset be performed; and
    (B) a reciprocal agreement with the State is in effect which contains, at a minimum -
        (i) requirements substantially equivalent to subsection (b) of this section; and
        (ii) any other requirements which the Secretary considers appropriate to facilitate the offset and prevent duplicative efforts.
(2) This subsection does not apply to -
    (A) the collection of a debt or claim on which the administrative costs associated with the collection of the debt or claim exceed the amount of the debt or claim;
    (B) any collection of any other type, class, or amount of claim, as the Secretary considers necessary to protect the interest of the United States; or
    (C) the disbursement of any class or type of payment exempted by the Secretary of the Treasury at the request of a Federal agency.
(3) In applying this section with respect to any debt owed to a State, subsection (c)(3)(A) shall not apply.
Source (Added Pub. L. 97-452, Sec. 1(16)(A), Jan. 12, 1983, 96 Stat. 2471; amended Pub. L. 104-134, title III, Sec. 31001(c)(1), (d)(2), (e), (f), Apr. 26, 1996, 110 Stat. 1321-359, 1321-362.)

Standardized Compromise and Write-Off Procedures

April 28, 2019

https://powerreport.debtcollective.org/2019/04/28/legalmemo/

Re: Student Loan Cancellation

From: Laura Hanna and Ann Larson, Co-directors and Co-founders

We believe it is time that the Department of Education use its authority to stop collections on federal student loans. Nothing in the law prevents the Secretary of Education from doing so.

When it was first given the power to issue and collect student loans in 1958, the U.S. Department of Education also received the power to "compromise, waive, or release any right" to collect on them. This power is called "Compromise and Settlement" authority. When the Higher Education Act of 1965 made student loan authorities permanent, it solidified their power to compromise. Just as the Securities and Exchange Commission can cut low-dollar deals with banks that break the law, for example, the Secretary can settle with debtors for a fraction of what they owe or suspend the collection of student debt altogether.

Below you will find a detailed memo about this legal authority developed by the Debt Collective in collaboration with attorneys at the Project on Predatory Student Lending at the Legal Services Center at Harvard Law School.

Compromise and Settlement of Student Loans
This memo addresses (I) the sources of authority for the federal government to cancel existing student loan debts; (II) identifies useful interpretive materials; (III) provides examples of student debt cancellation; and (IV) identifies possible arguments against the cancellation of student loans.

I. Sources of Law
Two separate statutes—each with implementing regulations—set out the obligation of the federal government to collect debt owed to the United States, and specify the circumstances in which collection may be suspended and/or the debt cancelled. First, the Federal Claims Collection Act establishes general standards applicable across the government and confers responsibility on Treasury and the Department of Justice for overseeing the process. Second, the Higher Education imposes duties on the Secretary of Education with respect to the collection and compromise of federal student loans. The relevant sections of these statutes and regulations are excerpted below, with annotations in italics.

a. Federal Claims Collection Act of 1966, as amended by the Debt Collection Improvement Act, 31 U.S.C. 3701 et seq.

§ 3701 Definitions: *
"claim" or "debt" means any amount of funds or property that has been determined by an appropriate official of the Federal Government to be owed to the United States by a person, organization, or entity other than another Federal agency. A claim includes, without limitation, funds owed on account of loans made, insured, or guaranteed by the Government[.] *Federal student loan = claim of the United States.*

§ 3711 Collection and Compromise: *
The head of an executive, judicial, or legislative agency may compromise a claim of the Government of not more than $100,000 (excluding interest) or such higher amount as the Attorney General may from time to

time prescribe that has not been referred to another executive or legislative agency for further collection action.(2)

Each agency has complete authority to cancel a claim if it is under $100,000. But the agency can't cancel a debt if it has been referred to another part of the government (like DOJ for litigation, or Treasury for offset) for collection.

may suspend or end collection action on a claim referred to in clause (2) of this subsection when it appears that no person liable on the claim has the present or prospective ability to pay a significant amount of the claim or the cost of collecting the claim is likely to be more than the amount recovered. (a)(3)

Suspending/ending collection on a claim is distinct from compromise of a claim. An agency can make a decision that collection is a waste of resources, regardless of merits of the debt.

acts under (1) regulations prescribed by the head of the agency; and (2) standards that the Attorney General, the Secretary of the Treasury, may prescribe. (d)

Agencies have to take into account both its own regulations and the regs of DOJ and Treasury regarding debt collection.

A compromise under this section is final and conclusive unless gotten by fraud, misrepresentation, presenting a false claim, or mutual mistake of fact. An accountable official is not liable for an amount paid or for the value of property lost or damaged if the amount or value is not recovered because of a compromise under this section. (c)

Compromise is final but can be undone. Agency decision makers are not liable for their decisions to compromise debts.

b. Federal Claims Collection Standards (FCCS) (regulations of Department of Treasury & Department of Justice/Attorney General issued pursuant to 31 U.S.C. § 3711(d)(2)) §900.1 Prescription of Standards:
Regulations prescribe standards for Federal agency use in the administrative collection, offset, compromise, and the suspension or termination of collection activity for civil claims...unless specific Federal agency statutes or regulations apply to such activities.

If there is a more specific agency statute or regulation on point, it controls the actions of that agency. ** § 900.4 Compromise, waiver, or disposition under other statutes not precluded:**

Nothing precludes agency disposition of any claim under statutes and implementing regulations. The laws and regulations that are specifically applicable to claims collection activities of a particular agency generally take precedence over the FCCS.   Same.

§ 900.6 Subdivision of claims not authorized:
Debts may not be subdivided to avoid the monetary ceiling. A debtor's liability arising from a particular transaction or contract shall be considered a single debt in determining whether the debt is one of less than $100,000 (excluding interest, penalties, and administrative costs). Multiple loans made under the same master promissory note would be treated as a single debt.

§ 900.8 No private rights created:
The FCCS do not create any right or benefit, substantive or procedural, enforceable at law or in equity by a party against the United States, its agencies, its officers, or any other person. Failure of agency to comply with FCCS is not a defense to a debt. Private citizens can't sue the government for not following these regulations.

§ 902.1 Scope and Application (Standards for the Compromise of Claims):
Any agency may exercise such compromise authority for debts arising out of activities of, or referred or transferred for collection services to, that agency when the amount of the debt then due, exclusive of

interest, penalties, and administrative costs, does not exceed $100,000 or any higher amount authorized by the Attorney General. Treasury and DOJ can compromise federal student loan debts if the Department has referred the account for collection/litigation, up to $100,000.

§ 902.2 Bases for compromise:
Agencies may compromise a debt if the Government cannot collect the full amount because…the debtor is unable to pay the full amount in a reasonable time, as verified through credit reports or other financial information (a)(1)…the cost of collecting the debt does not justify the enforced collection of the full amount (a)(3), or there is significant doubt concerning the Government's ability to prove its case in court (a)(4).

If there is significant doubt concerning the Government's ability to prove its case in court for the full amount claimed, either because of the legal issues involved or because of a bona fide dispute as to the facts, then the amount accepted in compromise of such cases should fairly reflect the probabilities of successful prosecution to judgment, with due regard given to the availability of witnesses and other evidentiary support for the Government's claim. In determining the litigative risks involved, agencies should consider the probable amount of court costs and attorneys fees pursuant to the Equal Access to Justice Act, that may be imposed against the Government if it is unsuccessful in litigation. (d).

The "significant doubt" basis is the closest fit to borrower defense, although the language of (d) implies that compromise occurs in a litigation context.

§ 902.3 Enforcement policy:
Agencies may compromise statutory penalties, forfeitures, or claims established as an aid to enforcement and to compel compliance, if the agency's enforcement policy in terms of deterrence and securing compliance, present and future, will be adequately served by the agency's acceptance of the sum to be agreed upon.

An empirical study of agency behavior in compromising/not pursuing statutory penalties it obtained in its enforcement activities shows that agencies do not collect these penalties. In the higher education context, the Department is authorized to levy fines and penalties on participating institutions for violating Department regulations (e.g., Corinthian was fined $15 million for misrepresentation). It's interesting to put fines and penalties on the same plane as student loans and compare the Department's actions.

** § 903.2 Suspension of Collection activity:**
Agencies may suspend collection activity on a debt when…the debtor has requested a waiver or review of the debt. (a)(3)

Agencies shall suspend collection activity during the time required for consideration of the debtor's request for waiver or administrative review of the debt if the statute under which the request is sought prohibits the agency from collecting the debt during that time. (c)(1)

The Department argues that no statute precludes it from collecting student loans while a borrower defense application is pending.

If the statute does not prohibit collection activity pending consideration of the request, agencies may use discretion, on a case-by-case basis, to suspend collection. Further, an agency ordinarily should suspend collection action upon a request for waiver or review if the agency is prohibited by statute or regulation from issuing a refund of amounts collected prior to agency consideration of the debtor's request. However, an agency should not suspend collection when the agency determines that the request for waiver or review is frivolous or was made primarily to delay collection. (c)(2).

The Department claims discretion to suspend collection while a borrower defense claim is pending. However, its imposition of a statute of limitations on refunds of amounts paid by a borrower who later establishes a borrower defense, means that it should not collect while a borrower defense application is pending. The Department's continued collection implicitly suggests that it views borrower defense applications as frivolous.

§ 903.3 Termination of collection activity:
Agencies may terminate collection activity when the costs of collection are anticipated to exceed the amount recoverable (a)(3), the debt is legally without merit or enforcement of the debt is barred by any applicable statute of limitations (a)(4), or the debt cannot be substantiated (a)(5).

Substantiation does not include resolution of affirmative defenses.

§ 3711 requires agencies to sell a delinquent nontax debt upon termination of collection if such a sale is in the best interests of the United States.

§ 904.1 Prompt referral:
Agencies shall promptly refer to the Department of Justice for litigation debts on which aggressive collection activity has been taken and that cannot be compromised, or on which collection activity cannot be suspended or terminated. Preferably within one year. (a)
DOJ has exclusive jurisdiction over the debts referred to it. The referring agency shall immediately terminate the use of any administrative collection activities. The referring agency shall refrain from having any contact with the debtor and shall direct all debtor inquiries concerning the debt to the Department of Justice. (b)
The Department's PCA manuals address its parameters for referring student loan debts to DOJ for litigation, but it is only available in redacted form. However, publicly available information shows that less than 1000 student loan collection actions are initiated every year. A recent review of such complaints shows that they largely seek to collect defaulted FFEL consolidation loans. I have no idea what this means, but one way of reading it is as an acknowledgment that student loan debts can be compromised.

c. Higher Education Act
§ 1082 Legal powers and responsibilities:
The Secretary may enforce, pay compromise, waive, or release any right, title, claim, lien, or demand, however acquired, including any equity or any right of redemption. (a)(6) (Part B, FFEL)

This provision was added by the 1986 amendments to the HEA and was inserted in the FFEL section of the statute, but is read to apply to Direct Loans as well, as reflected in Department regulations.

d. Department of Education regulations
34 C.F.R. § 30.70 How Does the Secretary exercise discretion to compromise a debt or to suspend or terminate collection of a debt?
The Secretary may compromise a debt in any amount, or suspend or terminate collection of a debt in any amount, if the debt arises under the FFEL, Direct, or Perkins Loan program. (e)(1)

The Secretary refers a proposed compromise, suspension, or termination of collection of a debt exceeding $1,000,000 arising under the FFEL, Direct, or Perkins Loan program to DOJ for review. (e)(2)

For non-student loan debts, the Secretary uses the standards of the FCCS. (a)-(c)
The Department's compromise authority is not cabined to claims/debts under a certain amount, although the Department would ask DOJ's view of a compromise/suspension/termination of a claim over $1,000,000. The Department does not look to FCCS for standards when it comes to student loan debts. Those are just entirely within its discretion (except if it has referred the debt to a different agency for litigation/collection).
*e. Common law * Even absent the statutory and regulatory authority identified above, the government has (and has always had) the authority to settle and compromise claims and debts. Intuitively, the power to create debt includes the power to cancel it. However, there has been some question over the years as to which part of the government is authorized to exercise this power. On some theories, the Constitution gives

to Congress the power to dispose of the property of the United States. Article IV, section 3 provides that Congress "shall have power to dispose of and make all needful rules and regulations respecting the territory or other property belonging to the United States[.]" This provision means that "[p]ower to release or otherwise dispose of the rights and property of the United States is lodged in Congress," and thus "[s]ubordinate officers of the United States are without that power, save only as it has been conferred upon them by an Act of Congress or is to be implied from other powers." Royal Indemnity Co. v. United States, 313 U.S. 289, 294 (1941). The creation of the Attorney General by act of Congress has long been read to encompass the power to compromise claims of the United States, so much so that

"argument would seem to be unnecessary to prove his authority to dispose of…cases[.]" Confiscation Cases, 74 U.S. 454, 458 (1868); id. at 457 ("Under the rules of the common law it must be conceded that the prosecuting party may relinquish his suit at any stage of it….").

Within the administrative state, agencies considered themselves powerless to compromise claims of the United States absent a specific congressional directive authorizing them to do so. Prior to the enactment of the Federal Claims Collections Act in 1966:

[E]xisting law, with a few exceptions, restrict[ed] the authority of the agencies to deal adequately and realistically with claims of the United States arising out of their respective activities. If the agency c[ould] not collect the amount it believe[d] due the Government, it c[ould] do little more than refer it to the General Account Office which in turn must attempt collection on the same basis. Very few of the agencies c[ould] compromise such claims; that is, accept a lesser amount in full settlement even if such a settlement would be in the interest of the Government and justified by normal practice in business in the light of the debtor's ability to pay and the risks and costs inherent in litigation. Similarly the agencies c[ould] not terminate or suspend efforts to collect a claim even when the very futility of these efforts serve to add to the cost of government and therefore compound the loss to the United States. It [wa]s not until the matter is finally referred to the Department of Justice that it [wa]s possible to make compromise settlement. The committee notes that it is the present inflexibility in the law which has resulted in recurrent appeals to the Congress for relief. Many of the cases which ultimately became the subjects of private relief bills could have been resolved promptly and equitably on the agency level if the provisions of this bill were a part of the law.

1966 U.S.C.C.A.N. 2532, 2533

II. Interpretive Materials **

a. United States Department of Justice, Justice Manual**

Read in conjunction with 28 C.F.R. §§ 0.160-0.17, Authority to Compromise and Close Civil Claims and Responsibility for Judgments, Fines, Penalties, and Forfeitures, which delimit the authority of Assistant Attorneys General to accept settlement offers. Per these regs and the Justice Manual, 4-3.110, AAgs can accept compromises in civil cases where the difference between the gross amount of the original claim and the proposed settlement does not exceed $10 million or 15% of the original claim, whichever is greater.

b. PCA Manual i. Relevant parts redacted c. OMB Circular A-129

Revised January 2013

Applies to all credit programs of the Federal Government, including Direct loan programs and loan guarantee programs and loan insurance programs in which the Federal Government bears a legal liability to pay for all or part of the principal or interest in the event of borrower default.

OMB is responsible for monitoring agency conformance with FCRA; reviewing agency credit reporting standards; formulating and reviewing agency implementation of credit management and debt collection policy.

Departments and agencies shall manage credit programs and all non-tax receivables in accordance with their statutory authorities and the provisions of this Circular to protect the Government's assets and to minimize losses in relation to social benefits provided.

d. Other Secondary Sources

Colin S. Diver, The Assessment and Mitigation of Civil Money Penalties by Federal Administrative Agencies, 79 Colum. L. Rev. 1435, 1443–44 (1979)

Mitigation clauses are found in conjunction with all types of statutes. The function served by, and indeed the need for, an express mitigation authority depends on the precise context. A mitigation power, in the classical sense, is most obviously useful in the enforcement of statutorily fixed penalties. The mitigation authority makes it clear that the decisionmaker need not be bound to impose the fixed penalty amount where it would be unjust to do so. In fact, Congress has delegated an express mitigation power in 178 of the 197 fixed-penalty statutes. A second function apparently served by mitigation clauses in court-assessment statutes is to delineate the *1444 allocation of settlement authority among the regulatory agency, the Justice Department, and the courts. A clause expressly authorizing the agency to mitigate a court-assessable penalty removes any doubts that the agency may accept payment in compromise of a prospective prosecution without approval by the Justice Department or a court.

Even in the absence of an express mitigation power, agencies have a general authority to compromise civil money penalty claims under the Federal Claims Collection Act of 1966,51 which authorizes the "head of an agency" to "compromise ... claims of the United States for money or property arising out of the activities of, or referred to, his agency."52 This authority is more limited, however, than that arising from an express mitigation clause. First, there are several exclusions from the Act.53 Moreover, an express mitigation clause appears to confer a broader range of discretion to settle cases; the grounds upon which an agency may compromise a claim under the Claims Collection Act are implicitly limited to issues relating to the collectibility of the claim.54 A mitigation authority, by contrast, *1445 permits the agency to reduce the penalty for other reasons, such as the gravity of the offense or the culpability of the violator.

III. Examples

a. Borrower Defense memos (redacted) i. Line from ITT memo makes it seem as though Department may be viewing borrower defense discharge as an exercise of its compromise and settlement authority in that it weighs the likely outcome of litigation:

January 10, 2017 Memo from BDU to Ted Mitchell re: Recommendation for ITT Borrowers Alleging That They Were Guaranteed Employment—California Students

"Given this extensively well-documented, pervasive, and highly publicized misconduct, the Department has determined that the value of an ITT education—like Corinthian—is likely either negligible or non-existent. In a court proceeding, ITT would very likely be unable to produce any persuasive evidence showing why the amount of recovery should be offset by value received by the borrowers from ITT education so as to preclude full recovery. Accordingly, it is appropriate for the Department to award eligible borrowers full relief."

b. IRS Rev Procs on 1099 issue around 1) Corinthian and 2) ACI might contain information about the legal basis of the debt cancellation

c. Is Public Service Loan Forgiveness an exercise of compromise, a specific authorization to Secretary of Education for compromise, or an allocation of funding by Congress? Same question regarding income-driven repayment plans, Elizabeth Warren's proposal.

d. DMS (Treasury) annual report to congress on debt collection activities of agencies FY 17 https://www.fiscal.treasury.gov/files/dms/debt17.pdf i. Department of Education had $1,183.3 (billion) out of $1,519.6 (billion) total government outstanding non-tax receivables (highest) ii. Department of Education collected $102.3 (billion) out of $337.4 (billion) total receivables iii. Department of Education had 81.3% of delinquent debt owed to U.S. (non-tax) ($150.4 (billion) out of $185.0 (billion) total) iv. Department of Education collected $14.2 billion in delinquent non-tax debt (out of $30.7 billion total collected by government) 1. The entire government only collected $1.1 billion in delinquent debt through AWG 2. DOJ collected $14.3 billion in delinquent debt (owed to entire government) v. Department of Education wrote off and "closed out" (meaning all debt collection activity has terminated and write off may be required to be reported to IRS as potential income to the debtor) $6.6 billion (out of $8.8 billion across entire government) 1. See OMB Circular A-129 for write-off requirements vi. Department of Education only referred 44.2% of delinquent "eligible" accounts to Treasury for TOP (11,137,699 out of 25,171,655) 1. This compliance reporting is required by the Digital Accountability and Transparency Act of 2014

IV. Anticipated Arguments
a. Antideficiency Act

The Antideficiency Act prohibits federal employees and agencies from obligating or expending federal funds in advance or in excess of an appropriation.

31 U.S.C. § 3711 states that "an accountable official not liable for an amount paid or for the value of property lost or damaged if the amount or value is not recovered because of a compromise under this section." 31 U.S.C. § 3527 and § 3528 authorize the Comptroller General to relieve accountable officials and agents from liability for the physical loss or deficiency of public money in certain circumstances, which do not seem applicable to a deliberate act of compromise. 31 U.S.C. § 3529 allows the head of an agency to request a decision from the Comptroller General on a question involving a "payment" or "voucher," and it is not clear whether this would apply to a decision to compromise.

Standardized Compromise and Write-Off Authorization Letter 1994

UNITED STATES DEPARTMENT OF EDUCATION
WASHINGTON, D.C. 20202

JAN 21 1994

NOTICE TO ALL GUARANTY AGENCIES

Dear Agency Director:

The enclosed compromise and write-off procedures have been approved for use by all guaranty agencies. These procedures supersede all existing compromise and write-off procedures previously approved by the U.S. Department of Education, and must be used for any compromise or write-off authorized on or after March 1, 1994.

In developing these procedures, the National Council of Higher Education Loan Programs (NCHELP) and the Department worked with a variety of program participants, including lenders, servicers, and student advocate groups. Our goal was to develop *standardized* procedures that could be used by all guaranty agencies.

Two of the major objectives in developing standardized compromise and write-off procedures were to protect the federal taxpayer's interests and ensure equitable treatment of borrowers throughout the country. In keeping with those objectives, we will not permit an agency to alter these procedures unless the proposed change is a truly minor one that is justified because of a unique administrative requirement of the agency. Any proposed change must be submitted for the Department's review and approval.

Sincerely yours,

Robert W. Evans
Director, Division of Policy Development
and Member, Direct Student Loan Task Force

Enclosure

STANDARDIZED COMPROMISE AND WRITE-OFF PROCEDURES

The following guidelines are established to allow a guaranty agency to compromise amounts owing on a defaulted reinsured student loan and to write-off accounts where the loan(s) is determined to be uncollectible and the agency seeks to discontinue its semi-annual reviews as required under the due diligence requirements. Write off in this context does not relate to "writing the loan off the books" but only relates to the cessation of collection activity. In all cases, the reasons for the agency's decision and actions will be documented in the borrower's file.

COMPROMISE AUTHORITY

Compromise refers to a negotiated agreement between the debtor and the guaranty agency to accept a payment of a lesser portion of the total debt as full liquidation of the entire indebtedness. A guaranty agency will be permitted in certain cases to accept a compromise amount from a debtor as full satisfaction of the debt to all parties, including the U.S. Department of Education. The authority to accept a compromise as full satisfaction of the debt is intended to maximize collections on defaulted loans. The guaranty agency may compromise a loan at any time after it pays a default claim on that loan.

A guaranty agency will be permitted to compromise under the following circumstances and in the following amounts:

1. An agency can compromise an amount up to an amount equal to all collection costs in order to obtain payment in full of all principal and interest owing on a defaulted loan(s). The agency shall consider the litigative risk of seeking a judgment on a reinsured loan, the likelihood and timing of the collection of the loan, and the borrower's current and expected financial condition.

2. An agency can compromise an amount up to 30% of all principal and interest owing in order to obtain a payment in full of the reinsured portion of a loan(s). The agency shall consider the litigative risk of seeking a judgment on a reinsured loan, the likelihood and timing of the collection of the loan, and the borrower's current and expected financial condition.

3. An agency can compromise in situations that do not meet the criteria in #1 and #2 above, provided the agency can demonstrate and document the reasons for doing so and the compromise is approved by the agency director. Compromises approved by the agency director allow the guaranty agency to waive the Secretary's right to collect the remaining balance due.

Approval authority for the write-off of a loan(s) will be individualized within each agency. However, the following minimum guidelines will apply:

1. Balances up to $5,000 can be approved by the supervisor responsible for collection of the loan(s).

2. Balances up to $20,000 can be approved by the next level of management within the guaranty agency if the documents authorizing a write-off contain the signatures of each agency official participating or concurring in the write-off decision.

3. Balances exceeding $20,000 can be approved by the division/agency director if the documents authorizing a write-off contain the signatures of each agency official participating or concurring in the write-off decision.

In each case, upon approval of the write-off, the account will be scheduled for permanent assignment to the U.S. Department of Education under the provisions in 34 CFR 682.409, et seq. (except those previously noted.)

A debtor who benefits from a write-off must reaffirm the amount written off if he or she later wants to receive an FFEL Program loan.

Standardized Compromise and Write-Off Guidelines 1993

https://www.studentloanborrowerassistance.org/wp-content/uploads/2013/05/ex_6.pdf

Student Assistance Forms

FFEL Compromise and Write-Off Procedures for Guaranty Agencies

NCHELP

National Council of Higher Education Loan Programs, Inc.

801 Pennsylvania Avenue, S.E., Suite 375
Washington, DC 20003 • (202)547-1571
FAX (202)546-8745

Clearinghouse No. 49,168
Accession No. 1095310

DEC -8 1993

November 7, 1993

Mr. Robert W. Evans
Director of Policy and Program Development
U.S. Department of Education
Office of Student Financial Assistance
Room 4310, ROB #3
7th & D Streets, S.W.
Washington, D.C. 20202

RE: Compromise and Write-Off Procedures

Dear Bob:

Thank you for reviewing the recommendations for standardized write-off and compromise procedures submitted by the Ad Hoc Standardization Group. NCHELP has made all of the clarifications and amendments you requested.

If you have any questions regarding these revised procedures, please let me know. Your prompt approval of these revised procedures will be appreciated by the community.

Sincerely yours,

Jean S. Frohlicher
President

I hereby approve the attached Standardized Compromise and Write-Off Procedures for use by guaranty agencies in the Federal Family Education Loan Program. Agencies may use these procedures without further approval from the Department of Education. Any changes a guaranty agency wishes to make in these approved procedures must be submitted to the Department for specific approval.

Robert W. Evans 11/24/93

Robert W. Evans, Director, Division of Policy Development

cc: Woody Farber
    Art Bilski
    Fred Hasselback
    Dallas Martin

STANDARDIZED COMPROMISE AND WRITE-OFF PROCEDURES

The following guidelines are established to allow a guaranty agency to compromise amounts owing on a defaulted reinsured student loan and to write off accounts where the loan(s) is determined to be uncollectible and the agency seeks to discontinue its semi-annual reviews as required under the due diligence requirements. Write off in this context does not relate to "writing the loan off the books" but only relates to the cessation of collection activity. In all cases, the reasons for the agency's decision and actions will be documented in the borrower's file.

COMPROMISE AUTHORITY

Compromise refers to a negotiated agreement between the debtor and the guaranty agency to accept a payment of a lesser portion of the total debt as full liquidation of the entire indebtedness. A guaranty agency will be permitted in certain cases to accept a compromise amount from a debtor as full satisfaction of the debt to all parties, including the U.S. Department of Education. The authority to accept a compromise as full satisfaction of the debt is intended to maximize collections on defaulted loans. The guaranty agency may compromise a loan at any time after it pays a default claim on that loan.

A guaranty agency will be permitted to compromise under the following circumstances and in the following amounts:

1. An agency can compromise an amount up to an amount equal to all collection costs in order to obtain payment in full of all principal and interest owing on a defaulted loan(s). The agency shall consider the litigative risk of seeking a judgment on a reinsured loan, the likelihood and timing of the collection of the loan, and the borrower's current and expected financial condition.
2. An agency can compromise an amount up to 30% of all principal and interest owing in order to obtain a payment in full of the reinsured portion of a loan(s). The agency shall consider the litigative risk of seeking a judgment on a reinsured loan, the likelihood and timing of the collection of the loan, and the borrower's current and expected financial condition. Compromises of less than 70% of the total indebtedness of principal and interest do not allow the guaranty agency to waive the Secretary's right to collect the remaining balance due.
3. An agency can compromise in situations that do not meet the criteria in #1 and #2 above, provided the agency can demonstrate and document the reasons for doing so and the compromise is approved by the division/agency director.

Approval authority for compromise settlements will be determined within each guaranty agency. However, the following minimum approval authorities will exist:

1. The supervisor directly charged with collections will have the authority to compromise all collection costs and the accrued interest on the loan(s), not to exceed 30% of the principal and interest owing.
2. The next level of management will have the authority to accept compromises in #1 above and any compromise of any principal amounts, not to exceed 30% of the principal and interest owing.
3. The agency director can approve compromises described in #1 and #2 above as well as compromises which exceed the 30% threshold.

DISCRETIONARY WRITE-OFF

Write-off of a reinsured loan(s) is intended only for the purpose of the guaranty agency's ceasing required collection activity as described in 34 C.F.R. 682.410(b)(6) and (7). The write-off of the loan does not relieve the debtor of the debt. Once an agency has "written off" a loan(s), it will insure that the account is permanently assigned to the U.S. Department of Education under 34 C.F.R. 682.409 *et seq.*

Exception to the above policy will be that guaranty agencies will have the authority t off loan(s) with principal balances of less than $100 and a total balance less than $1,000, and any loan(s) where the remaining balance represents only interest, attorney fees, court costs, or collection costs without requiring the permanent assignment of the loan(s) to the U.S. Department of Education.

In making its determination to write off a loan and to cease collection activity, an agency will consider the debtor's and, if applicable, an endorser's current and expected inability to repay the debt. Examples of this condition are:
    a. Borrowers who are repeatedly unemployed and have no prospects for future employment;
    b. Borrowers who are repeatedly public assistance recipients;
    c. Borrowers who are chronically ill, partially disabled, or of an age that results in their inability to work;
    d. Borrowers whose potential for future earnings is limited or non-existent;
    e. Borrowers who have no other funds available to them from other sources, such as an inheritance.

Approval authority for the write-off of a loan(s) will be individualized within each agency. However, the following minimum guidelines will apply:
    1. Balances up to $5,000 can be approved by the supervisor responsible for collection of the loan(s).
    2. Balances up to $20,000 can be approved by the next level of management within the guaranty agency if the documents authorizing a write-off contain the signatures of each agency official participating or concurring in the write-off decision.
    3. Balances exceeding $20,000 can be approved by the division/agency director if the documents authorizing a write-off contain the signatures of each agency official participating or concurring in the write-off decision.

In each case, upon approval of the write-off, the account will be scheduled for permanent assignment to the U.S. Department of Education under the provisions in 34 C.F.R. 682.409, *et seq.* (except those previously noted).

A debtor who benefits from a compromise or write-off must reaffirm the amount compromised or written off if he or she later wants to receive an FFEL Program

Interrogatories— Kentucky

This document is for illustration only. Your own Circuit Court will provide its own Interrogatories if needed.

UNITED STATES BANKRUPTCY COURT
FOR THE WESTERN DISTRICT OF KENTUCKY

IN RE:

                                                CASE #

Debtor

Plaintiff

vs.   ADV. #

KENTUCKY HIGHER EDUCATION
ASSISTANCE AUTHORITY
    Defendant(s)

* * * * * *

INTERROGATORIES

    Pursuant to Rule 33 of the Federal Rules of Bankruptcy Procedure and the Rules of the United States District Court for the Western District of Kentucky, Defendant serves the following written interrogatories upon Plaintiff, XXXXXXXX XXXXX, which shall be answered separately and fully in writing under oath and served upon Defendant within thirty (30) days from service hereof.

    Pursuant to FRCP Rule 26(e), XXXXXX-XXXXX, is under a duty to seasonably supplement his/her responses with respect to any question directly addressed to the identity and location of persons having knowledge of discoverable matters, and to amend a prior response if he/she obtains information upon the basis of which he/she knows that the response was incorrect when made, or the response is no longer true.

    The answers of XXXXXX-XXXXX to the interrogatories should include all information which is in his/her possession or control, or within the possession or control of his/her attorneys, investigators, agents, employees or other representatives of XXXXXX-XXXXX.

                                              Melissa F. Justice
                                              Attorney for Defendant
                                              KHEAA
                                              1050 U.S. 127 South
                                              Frankfort, Kentucky 40601
                                              (502) 696-7309

    <u>Interrogatory No. 1</u>: State your full name, address, telephone number, date of birth, date of marriage(s), date of divorce(s).
        ANSWER:

    <u>Interrogatory No. 2</u>: State whether you and/or your spouse/and or any family member who resides with you and/or any person dependent on you for support are employed, the names and addresses of all employers, dates of employment with each employer, position held with each employer, respective duties of each position held, and the amount of income received from employment for each of the years from December 1, 1997, through the present (including salary, commission, tips, bonuses, profit sharing, and overtime pay).
        ANSWER:

Interrogatory No. 3: For each person referred to in Interrogatory No. 2, state the present amount of take home income (income after deductions) received each pay period; whether this income is received monthly, twice per month, bi-weekly (every 2 weeks), weekly, or otherwise; and state the amounts and respective types of deductions taken from each paycheck each pay period.
ANSWER:

Interrogatory No. 4: State in detail all facts and information you have to support your allegation that your debt to Defendant will impose an undue hardship on you and your dependents.
ANSWER:

Interrogatory No. 5: State your current monthly budget of expenses and your monthly budget of expenses for the last three years, for you, your spouse, and your dependents, including rent, utilities, telephone, gasoline, food, clothes, insurance and any other expenses. If you rent your place of residence, please state the name, business address and telephone number of your landlord.
ANSWER:

Interrogatory No. 6: Do you have any roommates and/or any family members (either immediate or non-immediate) who reside with you? If so, state the amount of money each roommate and/or family member contributes toward each expense listed in your answer for Interrogatory No. 5.
ANSWER:

Interrogatory No. 7: State the respective dates, names and locations of schools attended, major areas of study, and degrees and/or certificates obtained as a result of all postsecondary education and/or training you, your spouse, and any other person dependent on you for support have received, including participation in college (other than Sullivan College), vocational schools, correspondence courses, and technical or union training programs.
ANSWER:

Interrogatory No. 8: State the dates, locations, and results of any and all efforts by you to locate employment or better paying employment since December 1, 1997, including the name and address of each potential employer with whom you have actually applied for work.
ANSWER:

Interrogatory No. 9: State what specific action you have taken to attempt to maximize your income and minimize your expenses in order to make some payment towards your student loan.
ANSWER:

Interrogatory No. 10: Do you and/or your spouse, and/or your dependents presently suffer any permanent injury, persistent infirmity, chronic illness or disability? If so, state the person afflicted, the nature of the condition and:
(a) Whether you and/or your dependents undergo any recurring examination, treatment, counseling, or nursing care for this condition.
(b) The names, addresses, and phone numbers of all treating physicians, other persons, or entities which provide care and/or services for this condition.
(c) The particular way in which the injury or disability incapacitates the person afflicted.
(d) Whether any physician, or other medical personnel, has since December 1, 1997, assigned a disability rating for it, and, if so, the name of such physician and the percentage of the disability rating.
(e) The amount of recurring expenses (including doctors, hospitalization, rehabilitation, prescriptions, nursing care, etc.) not reimbursed through health insurance, disability income, or government assistance.
ANSWER:

Interrogatory No. 11: State the name, address and telephone number of each person whom you intend to call as a witness at the trial of this action, and provide a summary of the testimony of each witness.
ANSWER:

Interrogatory No. 12: If you own your place of residence, state whether you own it jointly or in common with any other person or persons, the nature and extent of their interest in the property, the approximate date(s) whereupon the person or persons acquired the interest in the property, whether the interest of the person or persons was acquired by gift, bequest, or purchase?

ANSWER:

Interrogatory No. 13: Do you have any boarders, tenants, and/or subtenants at your place of residence? If so, give their name(s), the amount of rent payable to you, when and how often rent is to be paid to you, and whether it is paid in cash, by check, or otherwise.
ANSWER:

Interrogatory No. 14: Do you own or hold any interest in any real estate other than your place of residence? If so, identify the property, state the nature and extent of your interest in the property, state whether you obtained the interest and how much money or property was given in exchange for the interest.
ANSWER:

Interrogatory No. 15: Are you a proprietor, part-owner, stockholder, officer, and/or director of any business organization(s)? If so, state the name and location of such organization(s) and your relationship to the organization(s).
ANSWER:

Interrogatory No. 16: Do you have, in your own name or jointly with any other person or organization, a bank, credit union, and/or savings and loan account, either commercial or personal, either savings, checking or otherwise, any shares of stock, bonds, mutual fund shares, certificates of deposit, money market certificates, bills, notes, or other instruments representing money or other property owned by or payable to you? If so, state where and the balance of the account(s).
ANSWER:

Interrogatory No. 17: Do you and/or your spouse and/or any other person dependent on you for support own or use or have you and/or your spouse and/or any other person dependent on you for support owned and used, within the last 6 months, any credit cards. If so, state the company or companies which issued the cards and state the balance owed for any credit card owned.
ANSWER:

Interrogatory No. 18: Does any person or organization owe you money or other property and/or do you anticipate that any person or organization will or may owe you money or other property as the result of a loan, contract, judgment, insurance settlement, accident settlement, conditional transfer, bequest or devise, as payment for services rendered, or otherwise? If so, give full details as to the debtor's identity and location, the amount and type of debt, the date upon which payment or conveyance of property is due, and any encumbrances on such money or other property.
ANSWER:

Interrogatory No. 19: State the amount of income which you and/or your spouse and/or any other person dependent on you for support and/or any family member who resides with you receives from any of the following sources and state whether this income is received weekly, bi-weekly (every two weeks), twice per month, once per month, or otherwise:

(a) Disability or severance pay:

(b) Unemployment compensation:

(c) Workman's compensation:

(d) Social Security:

(e) Veteran's benefits:

(f) Aid to Families with Dependent Children:

(g) Food stamps:

(h) Alimony:

(i)   Child support:

(j)   Interest and/or dividends:

(k)   Inheritance or trust income:

(l)   Income received from parents, in-laws, or other relatives:

(m)   Farm income (including subsidy payments):

(n)   Federal income tax refund for the most recent previous four years:

(o)   State income tax refund for the most recent previous four years:

ANSWER:

Interrogatory No. 20: State the names and respective dates of birth, social security numbers, and relationships to you, of all persons dependent on you for support (including your spouse, children, other relatives, etc.).
ANSWER:

Interrogatory No. 21: State the respective names, addresses and phone numbers of all other persons who have a legal obligation to provide support to any of the dependents identified in Interrogatory No. 21 and identify the dependent(s) to whom such legal obligation relates. If you are owed child support based on a legal obligation, describe what efforts you have made to enforce such obligation.
ANSWER:

Interrogatory No. 22: If you are currently unemployed, state the information requested as follows:
(a)   When and in which position you were last employed?
(b)   Were you laid off or did your voluntarily leave your last job?
ANSWER:

Interrogatory No. 23: State the information requested as follows:
(a)   The number of years and type of occupations, trades, or professions in which you have work experience:

(b)   Have you sought employment in fields other than those in which you have work experience or educational training?

(c)   Have you registered for work with private or governmental employment agencies or services?

(d)   Have you sought retraining through any educational institution or governmental program for occupations in which employment opportunities are available in your community?

ANSWER:

Interrogatory No. 24: Other than the student loans which are the subject of this action, identify the creditor, outstanding balance, and the nature of all debts that you have reaffirmed or that are exempt from discharge so that such debts will not be discharged in this bankruptcy (include student loans which are the subject of other actions not joined with this case).
ANSWER:

Interrogatory No. 25: State the reason and date you ceased enrollment at Sullivan University, and what program(s) of study did you major in while you were enrolled?
ANSWER:

****

The signatory hereof certifies under oath that the foregoing responses to interrogatories are true, complete, and accurate to the best of my knowledge.

DATE   PLAINTIFF(S)

Subscribed and Sworn to before me by XXXXXX-XXXXX on this __ day of _____, 2000.

NOTARY PUBLIC   MY COMMISSION EXPIRES

****

CERTIFICATE OF SERVICE

The undersigned hereby certifies that a true copy of the foregoing Interrogatories were mailed to Plaintiff's Attorney, Nick Thompson, 12404 Aquarius Road, Louisville, Kentucky 40243-1508, on this day by regular mail.

Date
                                                      Melissa F. Justice
                                                     Attorney for Defendant
                                                     Kentucky Higher Education Assistance Authority
                                                     1050 U.S. 127 South
                                                     Frankfort, Kentucky 40601
                                                     (502) 696-7309

Interrogatories Kentucky—Request for Documents

UNITED STATES BANKRUPTCY COURT
FOR THE WESTERN DISTRICT OF KENTUCKY

IN RE:

CASE #

Plaintiff/Debtor

vs.

**REQUEST FOR PRODUCTION
OF DOCUMENTS**

ADV. #

KENTUCKY HIGHER EDUCATION
ASSISTANCE AUTHORITY
    Defendant(s)

****

Pursuant to Rule 7034 of the Rules of Bankruptcy Procedure and Rule 34 of the Federal Rules of Civil Procedure, Defendant, Kentucky Higher Education Assistance Authority, requests Plaintiff to respond within 30 days to the following requests:

1. That Plaintiff submit to the Defendant or produce and permit Defendant to inspect and to copy each of the following documents:

(a) Copies of Plaintiff's state and federal tax returns (form 1040 or its equivalent and attached schedules) and W-2 forms for the three most recent tax years and those of each family member residing in the household.

(b) Copies of all of Plaintiff's cancelled checks for the six most recent preceding months and those of each family member residing in the household.

(c) Current pay stubs for the six most recent preceding months (showing total year-to-date earnings, including wages, commissions, tips and deductions) for each family member (including Plaintiff) residing in the household.

(d) Copies of all of Plaintiff's credit card statements for the six most recent preceding months, and those of each family member residing in the household.

(e) Copies of Medical Records of each family member (including Plaintiff) with an illness or disability which Plaintiff may allege as contributing to an undue hardship in repayment of this debt.

(f) A current rent or mortgage receipt.

(g) A current utilities bill for water, gas and electricity usage.

(h) A current phone bill.

(i) Current receipts for childcare and tuition.

(j) Payment receipts for the six most recent preceding months which show amounts paid or received for child support.

(k) A copy of Plaintiff's(s) bankruptcy petition and schedules.

(I) Copies of Plaintiff's college and/or vocational school transcripts.

(1) Copies of any and all correspondence which relate to requests by the Plaintiff(s) for employment, requests for job interviews, rejection letters, or any other correspondence to or from the Plaintiff(s) relating to job searches by the Plaintiff(s).

(2) Said documents are to be produced at the office of Kentucky Higher Education Assistance Authority, 1050 U.S. 127 South, Suite 102, Frankfort, Kentucky 40601 between 8 a.m. and 4 p.m.

(3) In lieu of said production at the place previously designated, Plaintiff may, at its discretion, mail copies of said documents to the undersigned at Kentucky Higher Education Assistance Authority, 1050 U.S. 127 South, Suite 102, Frankfort, Kentucky 40601; provided that Plaintiff understands that use of this alternative procedure constitutes an admission that each of the documents so mailed is an authentic and genuine copy of the original document.

                Diana L. Barber
                Attorney for Defendant
                KHEAA
                1050 U.S. 127 South
                Frankfort, Kentucky 40601
                (502) 696-7298

CERTIFICATE OF SERVICE

I hereby certify that the foregoing Request for Production of Documents was served upon Plaintiff by mailing a true and accurate copy of same to Plaintiff's attorney: Nick C. Thompson, 12404 Aquarius, Louisville, Kentucky 40243, this the ____ day of January, 1999

                Diana L. Barber

IRS Collection Financial Standards

The IRS has established standards used to determine the ability of taxpayers to make delinquent payments. The main webpage links to other pages that give standards for food, clothing, housing, utilities, transportation, and other expenses. You will use these numbers to show your family expenses are comparable to other similarly situated families.

Collection Financial Standards

https://www.irs.gov/businesses/small-businesses-self-employed/collection-financial-standards

Disclaimer: IRS Collection Financial Standards are intended for use in calculating repayment of delinquent taxes. These Standards are effective on March 30, 2023 for purposes of federal tax administration only. Expense information for use in bankruptcy calculations can be found on the website for the U.S. Trustee Program.

Please note that the standards change, so if you elect to print them, check back periodically to assure you have the latest version.

General

Collection Financial Standards are used to help determine a taxpayer's ability to pay a delinquent tax liability. Allowable living expenses include those expenses that meet the necessary expense test. The necessary expense test is defined as expenses that are necessary to provide for a taxpayer's (and his or her family's) health and welfare and/or production of income.

National Standards for food, clothing and other items apply nationwide. Taxpayers are allowed the total National Standards amount monthly for their family size, without questioning the amount actually spent.

National Standards have also been established for minimum allowances for out-of-pocket health care expenses. Taxpayers and their dependents are allowed the standard amount monthly on a per person basis, without questioning the amount actually spent.

Maximum allowances for monthly housing and utilities and transportation, known as the Local Standards, vary by location. In most cases, the taxpayer is allowed the amount actually spent, or the local standard, whichever is less.

Generally, the total number of persons allowed for necessary living expenses should be the same as those allowed as dependents on the taxpayer's most recent year income tax return.

If the IRS determines that the facts and circumstances of a taxpayer's situation indicate that using the standards is inadequate to provide for basic living expenses, we may allow for actual expenses. However, taxpayers must provide documentation that supports a determination that using national and local expense standards leaves them an inadequate means of providing for basic living expenses.

National Standards: Food, Clothing and Other Items
National Standards have been established for five necessary expenses: food, housekeeping supplies, apparel and services, personal care products and services, and miscellaneous.

The National Standard for Food, Clothing and Other Items includes an amount for miscellaneous expenses. This miscellaneous allowance is for expenses taxpayers may incur that are not included in any other allowable living expense items, or for any portion of expenses that exceed the Collection Financial Standards and are not allowed under a deviation.

The standards are derived from the Bureau of Labor Statistics Consumer Expenditure Survey. The survey collects information from the Nation's households and families on their buying habits (expenditures), income and household characteristics.

Additional information and the standard amounts are available on our National Standards for Food, Clothing and Other Items web page. You may also download the standards (PDF) in PDF format for printing.

National Standards: Out-of-Pocket Health Care Expenses

Out-of-Pocket Health Care standards have been established for out-of-pocket health care expenses including medical services, prescription drugs, and medical supplies (e.g. eyeglasses, contact lenses, etc.).

The table for health care allowances is based on Medical Expenditure Panel Survey data and uses an average amount per person for taxpayers and their dependents under 65 and those individuals that are 65 and older.

The out-of-pocket health care standard amount is allowed in addition to the amount taxpayers pay for health insurance.

You may also download the standards (PDF) in PDF format for printing. Additional information and the standard amounts are available on our Out-of-Pocket Health Care Standards web page.

Local Standards: Housing and Utilities

The housing and utilities standards are derived from U.S. Census Bureau, American Community Survey and BLS data, and are provided by state down to the county level. The standard for a particular county and family size includes both housing and utilities allowed for a taxpayer's primary place of residence. Housing and utilities standards are also provided for Puerto Rico.

Housing and Utilities standards include mortgage or rent, property taxes, interest, insurance, maintenance, repairs, gas, electric, water, heating oil, garbage collection, residential telephone service, cell phone service, cable television, and Internet service. The tables include five categories for one, two, three, four, and five or more persons in a household.

Additional information and the standard amounts are available by state or territory on our Housing and Utilities Standards web page. You may also download the standards (PDF) in PDF format for printing. Please be advised that the housing and utilities document is 108 printed pages.

Local Standards: Transportation

The transportation standards for taxpayers with a vehicle consist of two parts: nationwide figures for monthly loan or lease payments referred to as ownership costs, and additional amounts for monthly operating costs broken down by Census Region and Metropolitan Statistical Area (MSA). A conversion chart has been provided with the standards that lists the states that comprise each Census Region, as well as the counties and cities included in each MSA. The ownership cost portion of the transportation standard, although it applies nationwide, is still considered part of the Local Standards.

The ownership costs provide maximum allowances for the lease or purchase of up to two automobiles if allowed as a necessary expense. A single taxpayer is normally allowed one automobile.

The operating costs include maintenance, repairs, insurance, fuel, registrations, licenses, inspections, parking and tolls.

If a taxpayer has a car payment, the allowable ownership cost added to the allowable operating cost equals the allowable transportation expense. If a taxpayer has a car, but no car payment, only the operating costs portion of the transportation standard is used to figure the allowable transportation expense. In both of these cases, the taxpayer is allowed the amount actually spent, or the standard, whichever is less.

There is a single nationwide allowance for public transportation based on BLS expenditure data for mass transit fares for a train, bus, taxi, ferry, etc. Taxpayers with no vehicle are allowed the standard, per household, without questioning the amount actually spent.

If a taxpayer owns a vehicle and uses public transportation, expenses may be allowed for both, provided they are needed for the health, and welfare of the taxpayer or family, or for the production of income. However, the expenses allowed would be actual expenses incurred for ownership costs, operating costs and public transportation, or the standard amounts, whichever is less.

Additional information and the standard amounts are available on our Transportation Standards web page. You may also download the standards (PDF) in PDF format for printing.

Six Year Rule for Repayment of Tax Liability
The Collection Financial Standards are used in cases requiring financial analysis to determine a taxpayer's ability to pay. The vast majority of installment agreements secured by Collection employees are streamlined agreements, which require little or no financial analysis and no substantiation of expenses.

In cases where taxpayers cannot full pay and do not meet the criteria for a streamlined agreement, they may still qualify for the six-year rule. The timeframe for this rule was increased in 2012 from five years to six years.

The six-year rule allows for payment of living expenses that exceed the Collection Financial Standards, and allows for other expenses, such as minimum payments on student loans or credit cards, as long as the tax liability, including penalty and interest, can be full paid in six years.

Taxpayers are required to provide financial information in these cases, but do not have to provide substantiation of reasonable expenses.

Recent Revisions
March 30, 2023
There were no changes to the methodology for calculating the Collection Financial Standards for 2023. The data for the Operating Costs section of the Transportation Standards are provided by Census Region and Metropolitan Statistical Area (MSA) on the Transportation Standards web page. In 2023, the MSAs did not change.

The revised standards are effective for financial analysis conducted on or after March 30, 2023.
Related Topics

IRS—National Standard: Food, Clothing, and Other Items (2023)

The link on the IRS Collection Financial Standards main webpage will take you to the standards for Allowable Living Expenses. You need to visit the website to gather current data.
https://www.irs.gov/businesses/small-businesses-self-employed/national-standards-food-clothing-and-other-items

Disclaimer: *IRS Collection Financial Standards are intended for use in calculating repayment of delinquent taxes. These Standards are effective on March 30, 2023 for purposes of federal tax administration only. Expense information for use in bankruptcy calculations can be found on the website for the U.S. Trustee Program.*

Download the national standards for food, clothing and other items (PDF) in PDF format for printing. Please note that the standard amounts change, so if you elect to print them, check back periodically to assure you have the latest version.

National Standards have been established for five necessary expenses: food, housekeeping supplies, apparel and services, personal care products and services, and miscellaneous.

The standards are derived from the Bureau of Labor Statistics (BLS) Consumer Expenditure Survey (CES) and defined as follows:

Food includes food at home and food away from home. Food at home refers to the total expenditures for food from grocery stores or other food stores. It excludes the purchase of nonfood items. Food away from home includes all meals and snacks, including tips, at fast-food, take-out, delivery and full-service restaurants, etc.

Housekeeping supplies includes laundry and cleaning supplies, stationery supplies, postage, delivery services, miscellaneous household products, and lawn and garden supplies.

Apparel and services includes clothing, footwear, material, patterns and notions for making clothes, alterations and repairs, clothing rental, clothing storage, dry cleaning and sent-out laundry, watches, jewelry and repairs to watches and jewelry.

Personal care products and services includes products for the hair, oral hygiene products, shaving needs, cosmetics and bath products, electric personal care appliances, and other personal care products.

The miscellaneous allowance is for expenses taxpayers may incur that are not included in any other allowable living expense items, or for any portion of expenses that exceed the Collection Financial Standards and are not allowed under a deviation. Taxpayers can use the miscellaneous allowance to pay for expenses that exceed the standards, or for other expenses such as credit card payments, bank fees and charges, reading material and school supplies.

Taxpayers are allowed the total National Standards amount monthly for their family size, without questioning the amounts they actually spend. If the amount claimed is more than the total allowed by the National Standards for food, housekeeping supplies, apparel and services, and personal care products and services, the taxpayer must provide documentation to substantiate those expenses are necessary living expenses. Deviations from the standard amount are not allowed for miscellaneous expenses. Generally, the total number of persons allowed for National Standards should be the same as those allowed as dependents on the taxpayer's most recent year income tax return.

Expense	One Person	Two Persons	Three Persons	Four Persons
Food	$385	$715	$779	$947
Housekeeping supplies	$45	$67	$73	$71
Apparel & services	$85	$158	$192	$251
Personal care products & services	$43	$73	$74	$88
Miscellaneous	$157	$285	$315	$383
Total	**$715**	**$1,298**	**$1,433**	**1,740**

More than four persons	Additional Persons Amount
For each additional person, add to four-person total allowance:	$378

IRS—Housing and Utilities (2023)

The link on the IRS Collection Financial Standards main webpage will take you to the standards for Housing and Utilities Allowable Living Expenses. These are specific for each state. Click on your state and see the standard. The California Standard is given below. Visit the website to gather current data for your state. https://www.irs.gov/businesses/small-businesses-self-employed/local-standards-housing-and-utilities

Disclaimer: *IRS Collection Financial Standards are intended for use in calculating repayment of delinquent taxes. These Standards are effective on March 30, 2023 for purposes of federal tax administration only. Expense information for use in bankruptcy calculations can be found on the website for the U.S. Trustee Program.*

Download the housing and utilities standards (PDF) in PDF format for printing. Please note that the standard amounts change, so if you elect to print them, check back periodically to assure you have the latest version.

California 2023 standard is provided as an example.

California - Local Standards: Housing and Utilities (2023)

https://www.irs.gov/businesses/small-businesses-self-employed/california-local-standards-housing-and-utilities

The housing and utilities standards are derived from U.S. Census Bureau, American Community Survey and Bureau of Labor Statistics data, and are provided by state down to the county level. The standard for a particular county and family size includes both housing and utilities allowed for a taxpayer's primary place of residence. Generally, the total number of persons allowed for determining family size should be the same as those allowed as exemptions on the taxpayer's most recent year income tax return.Housing and utilities standards include mortgage or rent, property taxes, interest, insurance, maintenance, repairs, gas, electric, water, heating oil, garbage collection, residential telephone service, cell phone service, cable television, and Internet service. The tables include five categories for one, two, three, four, and five or more persons in a household.

The taxpayer is allowed the standard amount, or the amount actually spent on housing and utilities, whichever is less. If the amount claimed is more than the total allowed by the housing and utilities standards, the taxpayer must provide documentation to substantiate those expenses are necessary living expenses.

Maximum Monthly Allowance

County	2023 Published Housing and Utilities for a Family of 1	2023 Published Housing and Utilities for a Family of 2	2023 Published Housing and Utilities for a Family of 3	2023 Published Housing and Utilities for a Family of 4	2023 Published Housing and Utilities for a Family of 5
Alameda County	2,672	3,138	3,307	3,687	3,747
Alpine County	1,799	2,113	2,227	2,483	2,523
Amador County	1,764	2,072	2,183	2,434	2,473
Butte County	1,606	1,887	1,988	2,217	2,252
Calaveras County	1,841	2,162	2,278	2,540	2,581
Colusa County	1,607	1,888	1,989	2,218	2,254
Contra Costa County	2,531	2,972	3,132	3,492	3,549
Del Norte County	1,447	1,700	1,791	1,997	2,029
El Dorado County	2,183	2,564	2,702	3,013	3,061
Fresno County	1,614	1,895	1,997	2,227	2,263
Glenn County	1,486	1,745	1,839	2,050	2,084
Humboldt County	1,702	1,999	2,106	2,348	2,386
Imperial County	1,481	1,740	1,833	2,044	2,077
Inyo County	1,845	2,167	2,283	2,546	2,587

Maximum Monthly Allowance					
County	2023 Published Housing and Utilities for a Family of 1	2023 Published Housing and Utilities for a Family of 2	2023 Published Housing and Utilities for a Family of 3	2023 Published Housing and Utilities for a Family of 4	2023 Published Housing and Utilities for a Family of 5
Kern County	1,538	1,807	1,904	2,123	2,157
Kings County	1,479	1,738	1,831	2,042	2,075
Lake County	1,567	1,840	1,939	2,162	2,197
Lassen County	1,484	1,743	1,837	2,048	2,081
Los Angeles County	2,335	2,743	2,890	3,222	3,274
Madera County	1,540	1,809	1,906	2,125	2,159
Marin County	3,265	3,835	4,041	4,506	4,578
Mariposa County	1,655	1,944	2,048	2,284	2,320
Mendocino County	1,845	2,167	2,283	2,546	2,587
Merced County	1,496	1,758	1,852	2,065	2,098
Modoc County	1,178	1,384	1,458	1,626	1,652
Mono County	1,909	2,242	2,363	2,635	2,677
Monterey County	2,129	2,501	2,635	2,938	2,985
Napa County	2,418	2,840	2,993	3,337	3,391

Maximum Monthly Allowance

County	2023 Published Housing and Utilities for a Family of 1	2023 Published Housing and Utilities for a Family of 2	2023 Published Housing and Utilities for a Family of 3	2023 Published Housing and Utilities for a Family of 4	2023 Published Housing and Utilities for a Family of 5
Nevada County	1,999	2,348	2,474	2,759	2,803
Orange County	2,578	3,028	3,191	3,558	3,615
Placer County	2,225	2,614	2,754	3,071	3,120
Plumas County	1,572	1,846	1,945	2,169	2,204
Riverside County	1,913	2,247	2,368	2,640	2,683
Sacramento County	1,856	2,180	2,297	2,561	2,603
San Benito County	2,293	2,693	2,838	3,164	3,215
San Bernardino County	1,742	2,046	2,156	2,404	2,443
San Diego County	2,371	2,784	2,934	3,271	3,324
San Francisco County	3,243	3,808	4,013	4,474	4,547
San Joaquin County	1,834	2,154	2,270	2,531	2,572
San Luis Obispo County	2,195	2,577	2,716	3,028	3,077
San Mateo County	3,146	3,694	3,893	4,341	4,411

Maximum Monthly Allowance County	2023 Published Housing and Utilities for a Family of 1	2023 Published Housing and Utilities for a Family of 2	2023 Published Housing and Utilities for a Family of 3	2023 Published Housing and Utilities for a Family of 4	2023 Published Housing and Utilities for a Family of 5
Santa Barbara County	2,229	2,618	2,759	3,076	3,126
Santa Clara County	3,016	3,543	3,733	4,162	4,229
Santa Cruz County	2,605	3,060	3,224	3,595	3,653
Shasta County	1,594	1,872	1,973	2,200	2,235
Sierra County	1,433	1,684	1,774	1,978	2,010
Siskiyou County	1,390	1,632	1,720	1,918	1,949
Solano County	2,033	2,388	2,516	2,805	2,851
Sonoma County	2,255	2,649	2,791	3,112	3,162
Stanislaus County	1,668	1,959	2,064	2,301	2,339
Sutter County	1,677	1,970	2,076	2,315	2,352
Tehama County	1,398	1,642	1,730	1,929	1,960
Trinity County	1,450	1,703	1,794	2,000	2,033
Tulare County	1,441	1,693	1,784	1,989	2,021

Maximum Monthly Allowance

County	2023 Published Housing and Utilities for a Family of 1	2023 Published Housing and Utilities for a Family of 2	2023 Published Housing and Utilities for a Family of 3	2023 Published Housing and Utilities for a Family of 4	2023 Published Housing and Utilities for a Family of 5
Tuolumne County	1,702	2,000	2,107	2,349	2,387
Ventura County	2,394	2,812	2,963	3,304	3,357
Yolo County	2,103	2,470	2,603	2,902	2,949
Yuba County	1,646	1,933	2,037	2,271	2,308

IRS—Transportation Standards (2023)

The link on the IRS Collection Financial Standards main webpage will take you to the standards for Transportation. Visit the website to gather current data for your state.
https://www.irs.gov/businesses/small-businesses-self-employed/local-standards-transportation

Disclaimer: *IRS Collection Financial Standards are intended for use in calculating repayment of delinquent taxes. These Standards are effective on March 30, 2023 for purposes of federal tax administration only. Expense information for use in bankruptcy calculations can be found on the website for the U.S. Trustee Program.*

Download the transportation standards (PDF) in PDF format for printing. Please note that the standard amounts change, so if you elect to print them, check back periodically to assure you have the latest version.
    The transportation standards for taxpayers with a vehicle consist of two parts: nationwide figures for monthly loan or lease payments referred to as ownership costs, and additional amounts for monthly operating costs. The operating costs include maintenance, repairs, insurance, fuel, registrations, licenses, inspections, parking, and tolls (These standard amounts do not include personal property taxes).

Ownership Costs

The ownership costs, shown in the table below, provide the monthly allowances for the lease or purchase of up to two automobiles. A single taxpayer is normally allowed one automobile. For each automobile, taxpayers will be allowed the lesser of:
- the monthly payment on the lease or car loan, or
- the ownership costs shown in the table below.

If a taxpayer has no lease or car loan payment, the amount allowed for Ownership Costs will be $0.

Operating Costs

In addition to Ownership Costs, a taxpayer is allowed Operating Costs, by regional and metropolitan area, as shown in the table below. For each automobile, taxpayers will be allowed the lesser of:
- the amount actually spent monthly for operating costs, or
- the operating costs shown in the table below.

Public Transportation

There is a single nationwide allowance for public transportation based on Bureau of Labor Statistics expenditure data for mass transit fares for a train, bus, taxi, ferry, etc. Taxpayers with no vehicle are allowed the standard amount monthly, per household, without questioning the amount actually spent.
    If a taxpayer owns a vehicle and uses public transportation, expenses may be allowed for both, provided they are needed for the health and welfare of the taxpayer or family, or for the production of income. However, the expenses allowed would be actual expenses incurred for ownership costs, operating costs and public transportation, or the standard amounts, whichever is less.
    If the amount claimed for Ownership Costs, Operating Costs or Public Transportation is more than the total allowed by the transportation standards, the taxpayer must provide documentation to substantiate those expenses are necessary living expenses.

Public Transportation

National	$224

Ownership Costs

	One Car	Two Cars
National	**$521**	**$1,042**

Operating Costs

	One Car	Two Cars
Northeast Region	$242	$484
Boston	$221	$442
New York	$319	$638
Philadelphia	$282	$564
Midwest Region	$188	$376
Chicago	$188	$376
Cleveland	$188	$376
Detroit	$314	$628
Minneapolis-St. Paul	$178	$356
St. Louis	$174	$348
South Region	$193	$386
Atlanta	$231	$462
Baltimore	$233	$466
Dallas-Ft. Worth	$289	$578
Houston	$259	$518
Miami	$286	$572
Tampa	$213	$426
Washington, D.C.	$232	$464
West Region	$209	$418
Anchorage	$162	$324
Denver	$217	$434
Honolulu	$178	$356
Los Angeles	$254	$508
Phoenix	$225	$450
San Diego	$230	$460
San Francisco	$231	$462
Seattle	$250	$500

For Use with 2023 Allowable Transportation Table

The data for the Operating Costs section of the Transportation Standards are provided by Census Region and Metropolitan Statistical Area (MSA). The following table lists the states that comprise each Census Region. Once the taxpayer's Census Region has been ascertained, to determine if an MSA standard is applicable, use the definitions below to see if the taxpayer lives within an MSA (MSAs are defined by county and city, where applicable). If the taxpayer does not reside in an MSA, use the regional standard.

MSA Definitions by Census Region

Northeast Census Region: Maine, New Hampshire, Vermont, Massachusetts, Rhode Island, Connecticut, Pennsylvania, New York, New Jersey

MSA	Counties
Boston	*in* MA: Essex, Middlesex, Norfolk, Plymouth, Suffolk
	in NH: Rockingham, Strafford
New York	*in* NY: Bronx, Dutchess, Kings, Nassau, New York, Orange, Putnam, Queens, Richmond, Rockland, Suffolk, Westchester
	in NJ: Bergen, Essex, Hudson, Hunterdon, Middlesex, Monmouth, Morris, Ocean, Passaic, Somerset, Sussex, Union
	in PA: Pike
Philadelphia	*in* PA: Bucks, Chester, Delaware, Montgomery, Philadelphia
	in NJ: Burlington, Camden, Gloucester, Salem
	in DE: New Castle
	in MD: Cecil

Midwest Census Region: North Dakota, South Dakota, Nebraska, Kansas, Missouri, Illinois, Indiana, Ohio, Michigan, Wisconsin, Minnesota, Iowa

MSA	Counties (unless otherwise specified)
Chicago	*in* IL: Cook, DeKalb, DuPage, Grundy, Kane, Kendall, Lake, McHenry, Will
	in IN: Jasper, Lake, Newton, Porter
	in WI: Kenosha
Cleveland	*in* OH: Ashtabula, Cuyahoga, Geauga, Lake, Lorain, Medina, Portage, Summit
Detroit	*in* MI: Lapeer, Livingston, Macomb, Oakland, St. Clair, Wayne
Minneapolis-St. Paul	*in* MN: Anoka, Carver, Chisago, Dakota, Hennepin, Isanti, Le Sueur, Mille Lacs, Ramsey, Scott, Sherburne, Sibley, Washington, Wright
	in WI: Pierce, St. Croix
St. Louis	*in* MO: Franklin, Jefferson, Lincoln, St. Charles, St. Louis county, Warren, St. Louis city
	in IL: Bond, Calhoun, Clinton, Jersey, Macoupin, Madison, Monroe, St. Clair

South Census Region: Texas, Oklahoma, Arkansas, Louisiana, Mississippi, Tennessee, Kentucky, West Virginia, Virginia, Maryland, District of Columbia, Delaware, North Carolina, South Carolina, Georgia, Florida, Alabama

MSA	Counties (unless otherwise specified)
Atlanta	*in* GA: Barrow, Bartow, Butts, Carroll, Cherokee, Clayton, Cobb, Coweta, Dawson, DeKalb, Douglas, Fayette, Forsyth, Fulton, Gwinnett, Haralson, Heard, Henry, Jasper, Lamar, Meriwether, Morgan, Newton, Paulding, Pickens, Pike, Rockdale, Spalding, Walton
Baltimore	*in* MD: Anne Arundel, Baltimore county, Carroll, Harford, Howard, Queen Anne's, Baltimore city
Dallas-Ft. Worth	*in* TX: Collin, Dallas, Denton, Ellis, Hood, Hunt, Johnson, Kaufman, Parker, Rockwall, Somervell, Tarrant, Wise

Houston	*in* TX: Austin, Brazoria, Chambers, Fort Bend, Galveston, Harris, Liberty, Montgomery, Waller	
Miami	*in* FL: Broward, Miami-Dade, Palm Beach	
Tampa	*in* FL: Hernando, Hillsborough, Pasco, Pinellas	
Washington, D.C.	*in* DC: District of Columbia	
	in MD: Calvert, Charles, Frederick, Montgomery, Prince George	
	in VA: Arlington, Clarke, Culpeper, Fairfax county, Fauquier, Loudoun, Prince William, Rappahannock, Spotsylvania, Stafford, Warren, Alexandria city, Fairfax city, Falls Church city, Fredericksburg city, Manassas city, Manassas Park city	
	in WV: Jefferson	

West Census Region: New Mexico, Arizona, Colorado, Wyoming, Montana, Nevada, Utah, Washington, Oregon, Idaho, California, Alaska, Hawaii

MSA	Counties (unless otherwise specified)
Anchorage	*in* AK: Anchorage, Matanuska-Susitna
Denver	*in* CO: Adams, Arapahoe, Broomfield, Clear Creek, Denver, Douglas, Elbert, Gilpin, Jefferson, Park
Honolulu	*in* HI: Honolulu
Los Angeles	*in* CA: Los Angeles, Orange, Riverside, San Bernardino
Phoenix	*in* AZ: Maricopa, Pinal
San Diego	*in* CA: San Diego
San Francisco	*in* CA: Alameda, Contra Costa, Marin, San Francisco, San Mateo
Seattle	*in* WA: King, Pierce, Snohomish

IRS—Out-of-Pocket Healthcare Standards (2023)

The link on the IRS Collection Financial Standards main webpage will take you to the standards for Out-of-Pocket Healthcare Standards.
https://www.irs.gov/businesses/small-businesses-self-employed/national-standards-out-of-pocket-health-care

Disclaimer: *IRS Collection Financial Standards are intended for use in calculating repayment of delinquent taxes. These Standards are effective on March 30 2023 for purposes of federal tax administration only. Expense information for use in bankruptcy calculations can be found on the website for the U.S. Trustee Program.*

Download the out-of-pocket health care standards (PDF) in PDF format for printing. Please note that the standard amounts change, so if you elect to print them, check back periodically to assure you have the latest version.

The table for health care expenses, based on Medical Expenditure Panel Survey data, has been established for minimum allowances for out-of-pocket health care expenses.
Out-of-pocket health care expenses include medical services, prescription drugs, and medical supplies (e.g. eyeglasses, contact lenses, etc.). Elective procedures such as plastic surgery or elective dental work are generally not allowed.

Taxpayers and their dependents are allowed the standard amount monthly on a per person basis, without questioning the amounts they actually spend. If the amount claimed is more than the total allowed by the health care standards, the taxpayer must provide documentation to substantiate those expenses are necessary living expenses. Generally, the number of persons allowed should be the same as those allowed as dependents on the taxpayer's most recent year income tax return.

The out-of-pocket health care standard amount is allowed in addition to the amount taxpayers pay for health insurance.

	Out of Pocket Costs
Under 65	$56
65 and Older	$125

Federal Poverty Guideline

The United States Department of Health and Human Services publishes the Federal Poverty Guideline. Current versions can be found at their website at: https://aspe.hhs.gov/poverty-guidelines

HHS Poverty Guidelines for 2023

U.S. Federal Poverty Guidelines Used to Determine Financial Eligibility for Certain Federal Programs

The 2023 poverty guidelines are in effect as of January 15, 2023
The Federal Register notice for the 2023 Poverty Guidelines was published January 17, 2023.

2023 POVERTY GUIDELINES FOR THE 48 CONTIGUOUS STATES AND THE DISTRICT OF COLUMBIA	
PERSONS IN FAMILY/HOUSEHOLD	POVERTY GUIDELINE
For families/households with more than 8 persons, add $4,480 for each additional person.	
1	$12,760
2	$17,240
3	$21,720
4	$26,200
5	$30,680
6	$35,160
7	$39,640
8	$44,120
2023 POVERTY GUIDELINES FOR ALASKA	
PERSONS IN FAMILY/HOUSEHOLD	POVERTY GUIDELINE
For families/households with more than 8 persons, add $5,600 for each additional person.	
1	$15,950
2	$21,550
3	$27,150
4	$32,750
5	$38,350
6	$43,950
7	$49,550
8	$55,150
2023 POVERTY GUIDELINES FOR HAWAII	
PERSONS IN FAMILY/HOUSEHOLD	POVERTY GUIDELINE
For families/households with more than 8 persons, add $5,150 for each additional person.	
1	$14,680
2	$19,830
3	$24,980
4	$30,130
5	$35,280
6	$40,430

2023 POVERTY GUIDELINES FOR HAWAII

PERSONS IN FAMILY/HOUSEHOLD	POVERTY GUIDELINE
7	$45,580
8	$50,730

The separate poverty guidelines for Alaska and Hawaii reflect Office of Economic Opportunity administrative practice beginning in the 1966-1970 period. Note that the poverty thresholds — the original version of the poverty measure — have never had separate figures for Alaska and Hawaii. The poverty guidelines are not defined for Puerto Rico, the U.S. Virgin Islands, American Samoa, Guam, the Republic of the Marshall Islands, the Federated States of Micronesia, the Commonwealth of the Northern Mariana Islands, and Palau. In cases in which a Federal program using the poverty guidelines serves any of those jurisdictions, the Federal office which administers the program is responsible for deciding whether to use the contiguous-states-and-D.C. guidelines for those jurisdictions or to follow some other procedure.

The poverty guidelines apply to both aged and non-aged units. The guidelines have never had an aged/non-aged distinction; only the Census Bureau (statistical) poverty thresholds have separate figures for aged and non-aged one-person and two-person units.

Programs using the guidelines (or percentage multiples of the guidelines — for instance, 125 percent or 185 percent of the guidelines) in determining eligibility include Head Start, the Supplemental Nutition Assistance Program (SNAP), the National School Lunch Program, the Low-Income Home Energy Assistance Program, and the Children's Health Insurance Program. Note that in general, cash public assistance programs (Temporary Assistance for Needy Families and Supplemental Security Income) do NOT use the poverty guidelines in determining eligibility. The Earned Income Tax Credit program also does NOT use the poverty guidelines to determine eligibility. For a more detailed list of programs that do and don't use the guidelines, see the Frequently Asked Questions (FAQs).

The poverty guidelines (unlike the poverty thresholds) are designated by the year in which they are issued. For instance, the guidelines issued in January 2023 are designated the 2023 poverty guidelines. However, the 2023 HHS poverty guidelines only reflect price changes through calendar year 2019; accordingly, they are approximately equal to the Census Bureau poverty thresholds for calendar year 2019. (The 2019 thresholds are expected to be issued in final form in September 2023; a preliminary version of the 2019 thresholds is now available from the Census Bureau.)

The poverty guidelines may be formally referenced as "the poverty guidelines updated periodically in the Federal Register by the U.S. Department of Health and Human Services under the authority of 42 U.S.C. 9902(2)."

There are two slightly different versions of the federal poverty measure: poverty thresholds and poverty guidelines.

The **poverty thresholds** are the original version of the federal poverty measure. They are updated each year by the **Census Bureau**. The thresholds are used mainly for **statistical** purposes — for instance, preparing estimates of the number of Americans in poverty each year. (In other words, all official poverty population figures are calculated using the poverty thresholds, not the guidelines). Poverty thresholds since 1973 (and for selected earlier years) and weighted average poverty thresholds since 1959 are available on the Census Bureau's Web site. For an example of how the Census Bureau applies the thresholds to a family's income to determine its poverty status, see "How the Census Bureau Measures Poverty" on the Census Bureau's web site.

The **poverty guidelines** are the other version of the federal poverty measure. They are issued each year in the Federal Register by the **Department of Health and Human Services** (HHS). The guidelines are a simplification of the poverty thresholds for use for **administrative** purposes — for instance, determining financial eligibility for certain federal programs.

The poverty guidelines are sometimes loosely referred to as the "federal poverty level" (FPL), but that phrase is ambiguous and should be avoided, especially in situations (e.g., legislative or administrative) where precision is important.

Key differences between poverty thresholds and poverty guidelines are outlined in a table under Frequently Asked Questions (FAQs). See also the discussion of this topic on the Institute for Research on Poverty's web site.

The January 2023 poverty guidelines are calculated by taking the 2018 Census Bureau's poverty thresholds and adjusting them for price changes between 2018 and 2019 using the Consumer Price Index (CPI-U). The poverty thresholds used by the Census Bureau for statistical purposes are complex and are not composed of standardized increments between family sizes. Since many program officials prefer to use guidelines with uniform increments across family sizes, the poverty guidelines include rounding and standardizing adjustments.

Federal Department of Education Poverty Guidelines (2023)
https://www2.ed.gov/about/offices/list/ope/trio/incomelevels.html

Federal TRIO Programs: Current-Year Low-Income Levels 2023

(Effective **January 15, 2023** until further notice)

Size of Family Unit	48 Contiguous States, D.C., and Outlying Jurisdictions	Alaska	Hawaii
1	$19,140	$23,925	$22,020
2	$25,860	$32,325	$29,745
3	$32,580	$40,725	$37,470
4	$39,300	$49,125	$45,195
5	$46,020	$57,525	$52,920
6	$52,740	$65,925	$60,645
7	$59,460	$74,325	$68,370
8	$66,180	$82,725	$76,095

For family units with more than eight members, add the following amount for each additional family member: $6,720 for the 48 contiguous states, the District of Columbia, and outlying jurisdictions; $8,400 for Alaska; and $7,725 for Hawaii.

The term "low-income individual" means an individual whose family's taxable income for the preceding year did not exceed 150 percent of the poverty level amount.

The figures shown under family income represent amounts equal to 150 percent of the family income levels established by the Census Bureau for determining poverty status. The 2023 poverty guidelines are in effect as of January 15, 2023. Federal Register notice was published January 17, 2023

11 U.S.C.A. § 523 (a) (8)

TITLE 11. BANKRUPTCY UNITED STATES CODE
Chapter 5. Creditors, the Debtor, and the Estate
Subchapter II. Debtor's Duties and Benefits
11 USC § 523. Exceptions to discharge

(a) A discharge under section 727, 1141, 1228(a), 1228(b), or 1328(b) of this title does not discharge an individual debtor from any debt--

    (1) for a tax or a customs duty--

        (A) of the kind and for the periods specified in section 507(a)(3) or 507(a)(8) of this title, whether or not a claim for such tax was filed or allowed;

        (B) with respect to which a return, or equivalent report or notice, if required--

            (i) was not filed or given; or

            (ii) was filed or given after the date on which such return, report, or notice was last due, under applicable law or under any extension, and after two years before the date of the filing of the petition; or

        (C) with respect to which the debtor made a fraudulent return or willfully attempted in any manner to evade or defeat such tax;

    (2) for money, property, services, or an extension, renewal, or refinancing of credit, to the extent obtained by--

        (A) false pretenses, a false representation, or actual fraud, other than a statement respecting the debtor's or an insider's financial condition;

        (B) use of a statement in writing--

            (i) that is materially false;

            (ii) respecting the debtor's or an insider's financial condition;

            (iii) on which the creditor to whom the debtor is liable for such money, property, services, or credit reasonably relied; and

            (iv) that the debtor caused to be made or published with intent to deceive; or

        (C)

            (i) for purposes of subparagraph (A)--

                (I) consumer debts owed to a single creditor and aggregating more than $500 [$550] for luxury goods or services incurred by an individual debtor on or within 90 days before the order for relief under this title are presumed to be nondischargeable; and

                (II) cash advances aggregating more than $750 [$825] that are extensions of consumer credit under an open end credit plan obtained by an individual debtor on or within 70 days before the order for relief under this title, are presumed to be nondischargeable; and

[Dollar amounts in subsections 523(a)(2)(C)(i) and (ii) are adjusted on April 1 every 3 years by section 104. Adjusted amounts effective 4-1-07 are in brackets.]

            (ii) for purposes of this subparagraph--

                (I) the terms "consumer", "credit", and "open end credit plan" have the same meanings as in section 103 of the Truth in Lending Act; and

                (II) the term "luxury goods or services" does not include goods or services reasonably necessary for the support or maintenance of the debtor or a dependent of the debtor.

    (3) neither listed nor scheduled under section 521(1) of this title, with the name, if known to the

debtor, of the creditor to whom such debt is owed, in time to permit--
- (A) if such debt is not of a kind specified in paragraph (2), (4), or (6) of this subsection, timely filing of a proof of claim, unless such creditor had notice or actual knowledge of the case in time for such timely filing; or
- (B) if such debt is of a kind specified in paragraph (2), (4), or (6) of this subsection, timely filing of a proof of claim and timely request for a determination of dischargeability of such debt under one of such paragraphs, unless such creditor had notice or actual knowledge of the case in time for such timely filing and request;

(4) for fraud or defalcation while acting in a fiduciary capacity, embezzlement, or larceny;

(5) for a domestic support obligation;

(6) for willful and malicious injury by the debtor to another entity or to the property of another entity;

(7) to the extent such debt is for a fine, penalty, or forfeiture payable to and for the benefit of a governmental unit, and is not compensation for actual pecuniary loss, other than a tax penalty--
- (A) relating to a tax of a kind not specified in paragraph (1) of this subsection; or
- (B) imposed with respect to a transaction or event that occurred before three years before the date of the filing of the petition;

(8) unless excepting such debt from discharge under this paragraph would impose an undue hardship on the debtor and the debtor's dependents, for--
- **(A)**
  - **(i) an educational benefit overpayment or loan made, insured, or guaranteed by a governmental unit, or made under any program funded in whole or in part by a governmental unit or nonprofit institution; or**
  - **(ii) an obligation to repay funds received as an educational benefit, scholarship, or stipend; or**
- **(B) any other educational loan that is a qualified education loan, as defined in section 221(d)(1) of the Internal Revenue Code of 1986, incurred by a debtor who is an individual;**

(9) for death or personal injury caused by the debtor's operation of a motor vehicle, vessel, or aircraft if such operation was unlawful because the debtor was intoxicated from using alcohol, a drug, or another substance;

(10) that was or could have been listed or scheduled by the debtor in a prior case concerning the debtor under this title or under the Bankruptcy Act in which the debtor waived discharge, or was denied a discharge under section 727(a)(2), (3), (4), (5), (6), or (7) of this title, or under section 14c(1), (2), (3), (4), (6), or (7) of such Act;

(11) provided in any final judgment, unreviewable order, or consent order or decree entered in any court of the United States or of any State, issued by a Federal depository institutions regulatory agency, or contained in any settlement agreement entered into by the debtor, arising from any act of fraud or defalcation while acting in a fiduciary capacity committed with respect to any depository institution or insured credit union;

(12) for malicious or reckless failure to fulfill any commitment by the debtor to a Federal depository institutions regulatory agency to maintain the capital of an insured depository institution, except that this paragraph shall not extend any such commitment which would otherwise be terminated due to any act of such agency;

(13) for any payment of an order of restitution issued under title 18, United States Code;

(14) incurred to pay a tax to the United States that would be nondischargeable pursuant to paragraph (1);

(14A) incurred to pay a tax to a governmental unit, other than the United States, that would be nondischargeable under paragraph (1);

(14B) incurred to pay fines or penalties imposed under Federal election law;

(15) to a spouse, former spouse, or child of the debtor and not of the kind described in paragraph (5) that is incurred by the debtor in the course of a divorce or separation or in connection with a separation agreement, divorce decree or other order of a court of record, or a determination made in accordance with State or territorial law by a governmental unit;

(16) for a fee or assessment that becomes due and payable after the order for relief to a membership association with respect to the debtor's interest in a unit that has condominium ownership , in a share of a cooperative corporation, or a lot in a homeowners association, for as long as the debtor or the trustee has a legal, equitable, or possessory ownership interest in such unit, such corporation, or such lot, but nothing in this paragraph shall except from discharge the debt of a debtor for a membership association fee or assessment for a period arising before entry of the order for relief in a pending or subsequent bankruptcy case;

(17) for a fee imposed on a prisoner by any court for the filing of a case, motion, complaint, or appeal, or for other costs and expenses assessed with respect to such filing, regardless of an assertion of poverty by the debtor under subsection (b) or (f)(2) of section 1915 of title 28 (or a similar non-Federal law), or the debtor's status as a prisoner, as defined in section 1915(h) of title 28 (or a similar non-Federal law);

(18) owed to a pension, profit-sharing, stock bonus, or other plan established under section 401, 403, 408, 408A, 414, 457, or 501(c) of the Internal Revenue Code of 1986, under--

    (A) a loan permitted under section 408(b)(1) of the Employee Retirement Income Security Act of 1974, or subject to section 72(p) of the Internal Revenue Code of 1986; or

    (B) a loan from a thrift savings plan permitted under subchapter III of chapter 84 of title 5, that satisfies the requirements of section 8433(g) of such title;

but nothing in this paragraph may be construed to provide that any loan made under a governmental plan under section 414(d), or a contract or account under section 403(b), of the Internal Revenue Code of 1986 constitutes a claim or a debt under this title; or

(19) that--

    (A) is for--

        (i) the violation of any of the Federal securities laws (as that term is defined in section 3(a)(47) of the Securities Exchange Act of 1934), any of the State securities laws, or any regulation or order issued under such Federal or State securities laws; or

        (ii) common law fraud, deceit, or manipulation in connection with the purchase or sale of any security; and

    (B) results, before, on, or after the date on which the petition was filed, from--

        (i) any judgment, order, consent order, or decree entered in any Federal or State judicial or administrative proceeding;

        (ii) any settlement agreement entered into by the debtor; or

        (iii) any court or administrative order for any damages, fine, penalty, citation, restitutionary payment, disgorgement payment, attorney fee, cost, or other payment owed by the debtor.

For purposes of this subsection, the term "return" means a return that satisfies the requirements of applicable nonbankruptcy law (including applicable filing requirements). Such term includes a return prepared pursuant to section 6020(a) of the Internal Revenue Code of 1986, or similar State or local law, or a written stipulation to a judgment or a final order entered by a nonbankruptcy tribunal, but does not include a return made pursuant to section 6020(b) of the Internal Revenue Code of 1986, or a similar State or local law.

(b) Notwithstanding subsection (a) of this section, a debt that was excepted from discharge under subsection (a)(1), (a)(3), or (a)(8) of this section, under section 17a(1), 17a(3), or 17a(5) of the Bankruptcy Act, under section 439A of the Higher Education Act of 1965, or under section 733(g) of the Public Health Service Act in a prior case concerning the debtor under this title, or under the Bankruptcy Act, is dischargeable in a case under this title unless, by the terms of subsection (a) of this section, such debt is not dischargeable in the case under this title.

(c)
- (1) Except as provided in subsection (a)(3)(B) of this section, the debtor shall be discharged from a debt of a kind specified in paragraph (2), (4), or (6) of subsection (a) of this section, unless, on request of the creditor to whom such debt is owed, and after notice and a hearing, the court determines such debt to be excepted from discharge under paragraph (2), (4), or (6), as the case may be, of subsection (a) of this section.
- (2) Paragraph (1) shall not apply in the case of a Federal depository institutions regulatory agency seeking, in its capacity as conservator, receiver, or liquidating agent for an insured depository institution, to recover a debt described in subsection (a)(2), (a)(4), (a)(6), or (a)(11) owed to such institution by an institution-affiliated party unless the receiver, conservator, or liquidating agent was appointed in time to reasonably comply, or for a Federal depository institutions regulatory agency acting in its corporate capacity as a successor to such receiver, conservator, or liquidating agent to reasonably comply, with subsection (a)(3)(B) as a creditor of such institution-affiliated party with respect to such debt.

(d) If a creditor requests a determination of dischargeability of a consumer debt under subsection (a)(2) of this section, and such debt is discharged, the court shall grant judgment in favor of the debtor for the costs of, and a reasonable attorney's fee for, the proceeding if the court finds that the position of the creditor was not substantially justified, except that the court shall not award such costs and fees if special circumstances would make the award unjust.

(e) Any institution-affiliated party of an insured depository institution shall be considered to be acting in a fiduciary capacity with respect to the purposes of subsection (a)(4) or (11).

APPENDIX C
Bankruptcy Forms

Chapter 7 Bankruptcy

U.S. Bankruptcy Forms 2023

https://www.uscourts.gov/forms/bankruptcy-forms

These forms are for educational purposes only. If you are planning on filing a Chapter 13 or Chapter 7 bankruptcy, please obtain a book or other materials that describe the process in detail. NOLO press has a number of fine books on bankruptcy. Visit them at: https://store.nolo.com/products/bankruptcy
What NOLO does not carry is a book (this book) on how to bankrupt student loans.

Form Number	Form Name	Category
B 101	Voluntary Petition for Individuals Filing for Bankruptcy	Individual Debtors
B 101A	Initial Statement About an Eviction Judgment Against You (individuals)	Individual Debtors
B 101B	Statement About Payment of an Eviction Judgment Against You (individuals)	Individual Debtors
B 103A	Application for Individuals to Pay the Filing Fee in Installments	Individual Debtors
B 103B	Application to Have the Chapter 7 Filing Fee Waived	Individual Debtors
B 104	For Individual Chapter 11 Cases: The List of Creditors Who Have the 20 Largest Unsecured Claims Against You Who Are Not Insiders	Individual Debtors
B 105	Involuntary Petition Against an Individual	Individual Debtors
B 106 Declaration	Declaration About an Individual Debtor's Schedules	Individual Debtors
B 106 Summary	A Summary of Your Assets and Liabilities and Certain Statistical Information (individuals)	Individual Debtors
B 106A/B	Schedule A/B: Property (individuals)	Individual Debtors
B 106C	Schedule C: The Property You Claim as Exempt (individuals)	Individual Debtors
B 106D	Schedule D: Creditors Who Hold Claims Secured By Property (individuals)	Individual Debtors
B 106E/F	Schedule E/F: Creditors Who Have Unsecured Claims (individuals)	Individual Debtors
B 106G	Schedule G: Executory Contracts and Unexpired Leases (individuals)	Individual Debtors
B 106H	Schedule H: Your Codebtors (individuals)	Individual Debtors
B 106I	Schedule I: Your Income (individuals)	Individual Debtors
B 106J	Schedule J: Your Expenses (individuals)	Individual Debtors

Form Number	Form Name	Category
B 106J-2	Schedule J-2: Expenses for Separate Household of Debtor 2 (individuals)	Individual Debtors
B 107	Your Statement of Financial Affairs for Individuals Filing for Bankruptcy (individuals)	Individual Debtors
B 108	Statement of Intention for Individuals Filing Under Chapter 7	Individual Debtors
B 113	Chapter 13 Plan	Individual Debtors
B 119	Bankruptcy Petition Preparer's Notice, Declaration and Signature	Individual Debtors
B 121	Your Statement About Your Social Security Numbers	Individual Debtors
B 122A-1	Chapter 7 Statement of Your Current Monthly Income	Means Test Forms
B 122A-1Supp	Statement of Exemption from Presumption of Abuse Under §707(b)(2)	Means Test Forms
B 122A-2	Chapter 7 Means Test Calculation	Means Test Forms
B 122B	Chapter 11 Statement of Your Current Monthly Income	Means Test Forms
B 122C-1	Chapter 13 Statement of Your Current Monthly Income and Calculation of Commitment Period	Means Test Forms
B 122C-2	Chapter 13 Calculation of Your Disposable Income	Means Test Forms
B 201	Voluntary Petition for Non-Individuals Filing for Bankruptcy	Non-Individual Debtors
B 201A	Attachment to Voluntary Petition for Non-Individuals Filing for Bankruptcy Under Chapter 11	Non-Individual Debtors
B 202	Declaration Under Penalty of Perjury for Non-Individual Debtors	Non-Individual Debtors
B 204	For Chapter 11 Cases: The List of Creditors Who Have the 20 Largest Unsecured Claims Against You Who Are Not Insiders (non-individuals)	Non-Individual Debtors
B 205	Involuntary Petition Against a Non-Individual	Non-Individual Debtors
B 206 Summary	A Summary of Your Assets and Liabilities (non-individuals)	Non-Individual Debtors
B 206A/B	Schedule A/B: Property (non-individuals)	Non-Individual Debtors
B 206D	Schedule D: Creditors Who Have Claims Secured By Property (non-individuals)	Non-Individual Debtors
B 206E/F	Schedule E/F: Creditors Who Have Unsecured Claims (non-individuals)	Non-Individual Debtors
B 206G	Schedule G: Executory Contracts and Unexpired Leases (non-individuals)	Non-Individual Debtors
B 206H	Schedule H: Your Codebtors (non-individuals)	Non-Individual Debtors
B 207	Statement of Your Financial Affairs (non-individuals)	Non-Individual Debtors
B 309A	Notice of Chapter 7 Bankruptcy Case – No Proof of Claim Deadline (For Individuals or Joint Debtors)	Meeting of Creditors Notices
B 309B	Notice of Chapter 7 Bankruptcy Case – Proof of Claim Deadline Set (For Individuals or Joint Debtors)	Meeting of Creditors Notices

Form Number	Form Name	Category
B 309C	Notice of Chapter 7 Bankruptcy Case – No Proof of Claim Deadline Set (For Corporations or Partnerships)	Meeting of Creditors Notices
B 309D	Notice of Chapter 7 Bankruptcy Case – Proof of Claim Deadline Set (For Corporations or Partnerships)	Meeting of Creditors Notices
B 309E1	Notice of Chapter 11 Bankruptcy Case (For Individuals or Joint Debtors)	Meeting of Creditors Notices
B 309E2	Notice of Chapter 11 Bankruptcy Case (For Individuals or Joint Debtors under Subchapter V)	Meeting of Creditors Notices
B 309F1	Notice of Chapter 11 Bankruptcy Case (For Corporations or Partnerships)	Meeting of Creditors Notices
B 309F2	Notice of Chapter 11 Bankruptcy Case (For Corporations or Partnerships) under Subchapter V)	Meeting of Creditors Notices
B 309G	Notice of Chapter 12 Bankruptcy Case (For Individuals or Joint Debtors)	Meeting of Creditors Notices
B 309H	Notice of Chapter 12 Bankruptcy Case (For Corporations or Partnerships)	Meeting of Creditors Notices
B 309I	Notice of Chapter 13 Bankruptcy Case	Meeting of Creditors Notices
B 312	Order and Notice for Hearing on Disclosure Statement	Bankruptcy Forms
B 313	Order Approving Disclosure Statement and Fixing Time for Filing Acceptances or Rejections of Plan, Combined with Notice Thereof	Bankruptcy Forms
B 314	Ballot for Accepting or Rejecting Plan	Bankruptcy Forms
B 315	Order Confirming Plan	Bankruptcy Forms
B 318	Discharge of Debtor in a Chapter 7 Case	Bankruptcy Forms
B 401	Petition for Recognition of Foreign Proceeding	Bankruptcy Forms
B 410	Proof Of Claim	Bankruptcy Forms
B 410A	Proof Of Claim, Attachment A	Bankruptcy Forms
B 410S-1	Proof Of Claim, Supplement 1	Bankruptcy Forms
B 410S-2	Proof Of Claim, Supplement 2	Bankruptcy Forms
B 411A	General Power of Attorney	Bankruptcy Forms
B 411B	Special Power of Attorney	Bankruptcy Forms
B 416A	Caption	Bankruptcy Forms
B 416B	Caption (Short Title)	Bankruptcy Forms

Form Number	Form Name	Category
B 416D	Caption for Use in Adversary Proceeding other than for a Complaint Filed by a Debtor	Bankruptcy Forms
B 417A	Notice Of Appeal And Statement Of Election	Appellate Forms
B 417B	Optional Appellee Statement Of Election To Proceed In District Court	Appellate Forms
B 417C	Certificate of Compliance With Rule 8015(a)(7)(B) or 8016(d)(2)	Appellate Forms
B 420A	Notice of Motion or Objection	Bankruptcy Forms
B 420B	Notice of Objection to Claim	Bankruptcy Forms
B 423	Certification About a Financial Management Course	Bankruptcy Forms
B 424	Certification to Court of Appeals	Appellate Forms
B 425A	Plan of Reorganization for Small Business Under Chapter 11	Small Business Forms
B 425B	Disclosure Statement for Small Business Under Chapter 11	Small Business Forms
B 425C	Monthly Operating Report for Small Business Under Chapter 11	Small Business Forms
B 426	Periodic Report Regarding Value, Operations, and Profitability of Entities in Which the Debtor's Estate Holds a Substantial or Controlling Interest	Bankruptcy Forms
B 427	Cover Sheet for Reaffirmation Agreement	Bankruptcy Forms
B 1040	Adversary Proceeding Cover Sheet	Bankruptcy Forms
B 1130	Motion, Notice and Order for Adequate Protection Payments and Opportunity to Object	Bankruptcy Forms
B 1310	Exemplification Certificate	Bankruptcy Forms
B 1320	Application For Search of Bankruptcy Records	Bankruptcy Forms
B 1330	Claims Register	Bankruptcy Forms
B 1340	Application for Payment of Unclaimed Funds	Bankruptcy Forms
B 2000	Required Lists, Schedules, Statements, and Fees	Bankruptcy Forms
B 2010	Notice Required by 11 U.S.C. § 342(b) for Individuals Filing for Bankruptcy	Bankruptcy Forms
B 2020	Statement of Military Service	Bankruptcy Forms
B 2030	Disclosure of Compensation of Attorney For Debtor	Bankruptcy Forms
B 2040	Notice of Need to File Proof of Claim Due to Recovery of Assets	Bankruptcy Forms
B 2050	Notice to Creditors and Other Parties in Interest	Bankruptcy Forms
B 2060	Certificate of Commencement of Case	Bankruptcy Forms
B 2070	Certificate of Retention of Debtor in Possesion	Bankruptcy Forms
B 2100A	Transfer of Claim Other Than For Security	Bankruptcy Forms
B 2100B	Notice of Transfer of Claim Other Than for Security	Bankruptcy Forms

Form Number	Form Name	Category
B 2300A	Order Confirming Chapter 12 Plan	Bankruptcy Forms
B 2300B	Order Confirming Chapter 13 Plan	Bankruptcy Forms
B 2310A	Order Fixing Time to Object to Proposed Modfication of Confirmed Chapter 12 Plan	Bankruptcy Forms
B 2310B	Order Fixing Time to Object to Proposed Modification of Confirmed Chapter 13 Plan	Bankruptcy Forms
B 2400A	Reaffirmation Documents	Bankruptcy Forms
B 2400A/B ALT	Reaffirmation Agreement	Bankruptcy Forms
B 2400B	Motion For Approval of Reaffirmation Agreement	Bankruptcy Forms
B 2400C	Order on Reaffirmation Agreement	Bankruptcy Forms
B 2400C ALT	Order on Reaffirmation Agreement (Alt.)	Bankruptcy Forms
B 2500A	Summons in an Adversary Proceeding	Bankruptcy Forms
B 2500B	Summons and Notice of Pretrial Conference in an Adversary Proceeding	Bankruptcy Forms
B 2500C	Summons and Notice of Trial in an Adversary Proceeding	Bankruptcy Forms
B 2500D	Third-Party Summons	Bankruptcy Forms
B 2500E	Summons to Debtor in Involuntary Case	Bankruptcy Forms
B 2500F	Summons in a Chapter 15 Case Seeking Recognition of a Foreign Nonmain Proceeding	Bankruptcy Forms
B 2530	Order For Relief in an Involuntary Case	Bankruptcy Forms
B 2540	Subpoena For Rule 2004 Examination	Bankruptcy Forms
B 2550	Subpoena to Appear and Testify at a Hearing or Trial in a Bankruptcy Case (or Adversary Proceeding)	Bankruptcy Forms
B 2560	Subpoena to Testify at a Deposition in a Bankruptcy Case (or Adversary Proceeding)	Bankruptcy Forms
B 2570	Subpoena to Produce Documents, Information, or Objects or to Permit Inspection of Premises ina Bankruptcy Case (or Adversary Proceeding)	Bankruptcy Forms
B 2600	Entry of Default	Bankruptcy Forms
B 2610A	Judgment by Default - Clerk	Bankruptcy Forms
B 2610B	Judgment by Default - Judge	Bankruptcy Forms
B 2610C	Judgment in an Adversary Proceeding	Bankruptcy Forms
B 2620	Notice of Entry of Judgment	Bankruptcy Forms
B 2630	Bill of Costs	Bankruptcy Forms
B 2640	Writ of Execution to the United State Marshal	Bankruptcy Forms

Form Number	Form Name	Category
B 2650	Certification of Judgment for Registration in Another District	Bankruptcy Forms
B 2700	Notice of Filing of Final Report of Trustee	Bankruptcy Forms
B 2710	Final Decree	Bankruptcy Forms
B 2800	Disclosure of Compensation of Bankruptcy Petition Preparer	Bankruptcy Forms
B 2810	Appearance of Child Support Creditor or Representative	Bankruptcy Forms
B 2830	Chapter 13 Debtor's Certifications Regarding Domestic Support Obligations and Section 522(q)	Bankruptcy Forms
B 3130S	Order Conditionally Approving Disclosure Statement	Bankruptcy Forms
B 3150S	Order Approving Disclosure Statement and Confirming Plan	Bankruptcy Forms
B 3180F	Chapter 12 Discharge	Bankruptcy Forms
B 3180FH	Chapter 12 Hardship Discharge	Bankruptcy Forms
B 3180RI	Individual Chapter 11 Discharge	Bankruptcy Forms
B 3180RV1	Chapter 11 Discharge for Individual Whose Plan was Confirmed under § 1191(a)	Bankruptcy Forms
B 3180RV2	Chapter 11 Discharge for Individual Whose Plan was Confirmed under § 1191(b)	Bankruptcy Forms
B 3180RV3	For Corporation or Partnership Whose Plan was Confirmed under § 1191(b)	Bankruptcy Forms
B 3180W	Chapter 13 Discharge	Bankruptcy Forms
B 3180WH	Chapter 13 Hardship Discharge	Bankruptcy Forms
B 4100N	Notice of Final Cure Payment	Bankruptcy Forms
B 4100R	Response to Notice of Final Cure Payment	Bankruptcy Forms
B 4170	Declaration of Inmate Filing	Bankruptcy Forms

Voluntary Petition for Individuals Filing for Bankruptcy

Form 101—Filing Form

Fill in this information to identify your case:

United States Bankruptcy Court for the:
_____ District of _____ ▼

Case number *(if known)*: _____

Chapter you are filing under:
- ❏ Chapter 7
- ❏ Chapter 11
- ❏ Chapter 12
- ❏ Chapter 13

❏ Check if this is an amended filing

Official Form 101

Voluntary Petition for Individuals Filing for Bankruptcy   04/20

The bankruptcy forms use *you* and *Debtor 1* to refer to a debtor filing alone. A married couple may file a bankruptcy case together—called a *joint case*—and in joint cases, these forms use *you* to ask for information from both debtors. For example, if a form asks, "Do you own a car," the answer would be *yes* if either debtor owns a car. When information is needed about the spouses separately, the form uses *Debtor 1* and *Debtor 2* to distinguish between them. In joint cases, one of the spouses must report information as *Debtor 1* and the other as *Debtor 2*. The same person must be *Debtor 1* in all of the forms.

Be as complete and accurate as possible. If two married people are filing together, both are equally responsible for supplying correct information. If more space is needed, attach a separate sheet to this form. On the top of any additional pages, write your name and case number (if known). Answer every question.

Part 1: Identify Yourself

	About Debtor 1:	About Debtor 2 (Spouse Only in a Joint Case):
1. Your full name Write the name that is on your government-issued picture identification (for example, your driver's license or passport). Bring your picture identification to your meeting with the trustee.	First name _____ Middle name _____ Last name _____ Suffix (Sr., Jr., II, III) _____	First name _____ Middle name _____ Last name _____ Suffix (Sr., Jr., II, III) _____
2. All other names you have used in the last 8 years Include your married or maiden names.	First name _____ Middle name _____ Last name _____ First name _____ Middle name _____ Last name _____	First name _____ Middle name _____ Last name _____ First name _____ Middle name _____ Last name _____
3. Only the last 4 digits of your Social Security number or federal Individual Taxpayer Identification number (ITIN)	XXX – XX – __ __ __ __ OR 9 XX – XX – __ __ __ __	XXX – XX – __ __ __ __ OR 9 XX – XX – __ __ __ __

https://www.uscourts.gov/forms/bankruptcy-forms

Debtor 1 _____ Case number (if known)_____
         First Name   Middle Name   Last Name

		About Debtor 1:	About Debtor 2 (Spouse Only in a Joint Case):
4.	Any business names and Employer Identification Numbers (EIN) you have used in the last 8 years Include trade names and *doing business as* names	☐ I have not used any business names or EINs. _____ Business name _____ Business name __ __ - __ __ __ __ __ __ __ EIN __ __ - __ __ __ __ __ __ __ EIN	☐ I have not used any business names or EINs. _____ Business name _____ Business name __ __ - __ __ __ __ __ __ __ EIN __ __ - __ __ __ __ __ __ __ EIN
5.	Where you live	_____ Number Street _____ _____ City State ZIP Code _____ County If your mailing address is different from the one above, fill it in here. Note that the court will send any notices to you at this mailing address. _____ Number Street _____ P.O. Box _____ City State ZIP Code	If Debtor 2 lives at a different address: _____ Number Street _____ _____ City State ZIP Code _____ County If Debtor 2's mailing address is different from yours, fill it in here. Note that the court will send any notices to this mailing address. _____ Number Street _____ P.O. Box _____ City State ZIP Code
6.	Why you are choosing *this district* to file for bankruptcy	Check one: ☐ Over the last 180 days before filing this petition, I have lived in this district longer than in any other district. ☐ I have another reason. Explain. (See 28 U.S.C. § 1408.) _____ _____ _____ _____	Check one: ☐ Over the last 180 days before filing this petition, I have lived in this district longer than in any other district. ☐ I have another reason. Explain. (See 28 U.S.C. § 1408.) _____ _____ _____ _____

Official Form 101   Voluntary Petition for Individuals Filing for Bankruptcy   page 2

Debtor 1 _____ Case number (if known)_____
         First Name   Middle Name   Last Name

Part 2: Tell the Court About Your Bankruptcy Case

7. The chapter of the Bankruptcy Code you are choosing to file under

    Check one. (For a brief description of each, see *Notice Required by 11 U.S.C. § 342(b) for Individuals Filing for Bankruptcy* (Form 2010)). Also, go to the top of page 1 and check the appropriate box.

    ❑ Chapter 7
    ❑ Chapter 11
    ❑ Chapter 12
    ❑ Chapter 13

8. How you will pay the fee

    ❑ **I will pay the entire fee when I file my petition.** Please check with the clerk's office in your local court for more details about how you may pay. Typically, if you are paying the fee yourself, you may pay with cash, cashier's check, or money order. If your attorney is submitting your payment on your behalf, your attorney may pay with a credit card or check with a pre-printed address.

    ❑ **I need to pay the fee in installments.** If you choose this option, sign and attach the *Application for Individuals to Pay The Filing Fee in Installments* (Official Form 103A).

    ❑ **I request that my fee be waived** (You may request this option only if you are filing for Chapter 7. By law, a judge may, but is not required to, waive your fee, and may do so only if your income is less than 150% of the official poverty line that applies to your family size and you are unable to pay the fee in installments). If you choose this option, you must fill out the *Application to Have the Chapter 7 Filing Fee Waived* (Official Form 103B) and file it with your petition.

9. Have you filed for bankruptcy within the last 8 years?

    ❑ No
    ❑ Yes. District _____ When _____ Case number _____
                                                  MM / DD / YYYY
            District _____ When _____ Case number _____
                                                  MM / DD / YYYY
            District _____ When _____ Case number _____
                                                  MM / DD / YYYY

10. Are any bankruptcy cases pending or being filed by a spouse who is not filing this case with you, or by a business partner, or by an affiliate?

    ❑ No
    ❑ Yes. Debtor _____ Relationship to you _____
            District _____ When _____ Case number, if known _____
                                                  MM / DD / YYYY

            Debtor _____ Relationship to you _____
            District _____ When _____ Case number, if known _____
                                                  MM / DD / YYYY

11. Do you rent your residence?

    ❑ No. Go to line 12.
    ❑ Yes. Has your landlord obtained an eviction judgment against you?

        ❑ No. Go to line 12.
        ❑ Yes. Fill out *Initial Statement About an Eviction Judgment Against You* (Form 101A) and file it as part of this bankruptcy petition.

Official Form 101   Voluntary Petition for Individuals Filing for Bankruptcy   page 3

Debtor 1 _____ _____ _____ Case number (if known)_____
         First Name   Middle Name   Last Name

Part 3: Report About Any Businesses You Own as a Sole Proprietor

12. **Are you a sole proprietor of any full- or part-time business?**

    A sole proprietorship is a business you operate as an individual, and is not a separate legal entity such as a corporation, partnership, or LLC.

    If you have more than one sole proprietorship, use a separate sheet and attach it to this petition.

    ☐ No. Go to Part 4.

    ☐ Yes. Name and location of business

    _____
    Name of business, if any

    _____
    Number   Street

    _____

    _____
    City   State   ZIP Code

    Check the appropriate box to describe your business:

    ☐ Health Care Business (as defined in 11 U.S.C. § 101(27A))

    ☐ Single Asset Real Estate (as defined in 11 U.S.C. § 101(51B))

    ☐ Stockbroker (as defined in 11 U.S.C. § 101(53A))

    ☐ Commodity Broker (as defined in 11 U.S.C. § 101(6))

    ☐ None of the above

13. **Are you filing under Chapter 11 of the Bankruptcy Code, and are you a *small business debtor* or a debtor as defined by 11 U.S.C. § 1182(1)?**

    For a definition of *small business debtor*, see 11 U.S.C. § 101(51D).

    If you are filing under Chapter 11, the court must know whether you are a small business debtor or a debtor choosing to proceed under Subchapter V so that it can set appropriate deadlines. If you indicate that you are a small business debtor or you are choosing to proceed under Subchapter V, you must attach your most recent balance sheet, statement of operations, cash-flow statement, and federal income tax return or if any of these documents do not exist, follow the procedure in 11 U.S.C. § 1116(1)(B).

    ☐ No. I am not filing under Chapter 11.

    ☐ No. I am filing under Chapter 11, but I am NOT a small business debtor according to the definition in the Bankruptcy Code.

    ☐ Yes. I am filing under Chapter 11, I am a small business debtor according to the definition in the Bankruptcy Code, and I do not choose to proceed under Subchapter V of Chapter 11.

    ☐ Yes. I am filing under Chapter 11, I am a debtor according to the definition in § 1182(1) of the Bankruptcy Code, and I choose to proceed under Subchapter V of Chapter 11.

Official Form 101   Voluntary Petition for Individuals Filing for Bankruptcy   page 4

Debtor 1 _____ Case number (if known)_____
           First Name   Middle Name   Last Name

Part 4: Report if You Own or Have Any Hazardous Property or Any Property That Needs Immediate Attention

14. Do you own or have any property that poses or is alleged to pose a threat of imminent and identifiable hazard to public health or safety? Or do you own any property that needs immediate attention?

    For example, do you own perishable goods, or livestock that must be fed, or a building that needs urgent repairs?

    ❑ No
    ❑ Yes. What is the hazard? _____
    _____

    If immediate attention is needed, why is it needed? _____
    _____

    Where is the property? _____
                          Number   Street

    _____

    _____
    City   State   ZIP Code

Official Form 101   Voluntary Petition for Individuals Filing for Bankruptcy   page 5

How to Bankrupt Your Student Loans, by Chuck Stewart, Ph.D. 2023   **APPENDIX C**   Page 241

Debtor 1 _____ Case number (if known)_____
         First Name   Middle Name   Last Name

Part 5: Explain Your Efforts to Receive a Briefing About Credit Counseling

15. **Tell the court whether you have received a briefing about credit counseling.**

    The law requires that you receive a briefing about credit counseling before you file for bankruptcy. You must truthfully check one of the following choices. If you cannot do so, you are not eligible to file.

    If you file anyway, the court can dismiss your case, you will lose whatever filing fee you paid, and your creditors can begin collection activities again.

About Debtor 1:	About Debtor 2 (Spouse Only in a Joint Case):
You must check one:	*You must check one:*
❏ I received a briefing from an approved credit counseling agency within the 180 days before I filed this bankruptcy petition, and I received a certificate of completion. Attach a copy of the certificate and the payment plan, if any, that you developed with the agency.	❏ I received a briefing from an approved credit counseling agency within the 180 days before I filed this bankruptcy petition, and I received a certificate of completion. Attach a copy of the certificate and the payment plan, if any, that you developed with the agency.
❏ I received a briefing from an approved credit counseling agency within the 180 days before I filed this bankruptcy petition, but I do not have a certificate of completion. Within 14 days after you file this bankruptcy petition, you MUST file a copy of the certificate and payment plan, if any.	❏ I received a briefing from an approved credit counseling agency within the 180 days before I filed this bankruptcy petition, but I do not have a certificate of completion. Within 14 days after you file this bankruptcy petition, you MUST file a copy of the certificate and payment plan, if any.
❏ I certify that I asked for credit counseling services from an approved agency, but was unable to obtain those services during the 7 days after I made my request, and exigent circumstances merit a 30-day temporary waiver of the requirement. To ask for a 30-day temporary waiver of the requirement, attach a separate sheet explaining what efforts you made to obtain the briefing, why you were unable to obtain it before you filed for bankruptcy, and what exigent circumstances required you to file this case. Your case may be dismissed if the court is dissatisfied with your reasons for not receiving a briefing before you filed for bankruptcy. If the court is satisfied with your reasons, you must still receive a briefing within 30 days after you file. You must file a certificate from the approved agency, along with a copy of the payment plan you developed, if any. If you do not do so, your case may be dismissed. Any extension of the 30-day deadline is granted only for cause and is limited to a maximum of 15 days.	❏ I certify that I asked for credit counseling services from an approved agency, but was unable to obtain those services during the 7 days after I made my request, and exigent circumstances merit a 30-day temporary waiver of the requirement. To ask for a 30-day temporary waiver of the requirement, attach a separate sheet explaining what efforts you made to obtain the briefing, why you were unable to obtain it before you filed for bankruptcy, and what exigent circumstances required you to file this case. Your case may be dismissed if the court is dissatisfied with your reasons for not receiving a briefing before you filed for bankruptcy. If the court is satisfied with your reasons, you must still receive a briefing within 30 days after you file. You must file a certificate from the approved agency, along with a copy of the payment plan you developed, if any. If you do not do so, your case may be dismissed. Any extension of the 30-day deadline is granted only for cause and is limited to a maximum of 15 days.
❏ I am not required to receive a briefing about credit counseling because of: ❏ **Incapacity.** I have a mental illness or a mental deficiency that makes me incapable of realizing or making rational decisions about finances. ❏ **Disability.** My physical disability causes me to be unable to participate in a briefing in person, by phone, or through the internet, even after I reasonably tried to do so. ❏ **Active duty.** I am currently on active military duty in a military combat zone. If you believe you are not required to receive a briefing about credit counseling, you must file a motion for waiver of credit counseling with the court.	❏ I am not required to receive a briefing about credit counseling because of: ❏ **Incapacity.** I have a mental illness or a mental deficiency that makes me incapable of realizing or making rational decisions about finances. ❏ **Disability.** My physical disability causes me to be unable to participate in a briefing in person, by phone, or through the internet, even after I reasonably tried to do so. ❏ **Active duty.** I am currently on active military duty in a military combat zone. If you believe you are not required to receive a briefing about credit counseling, you must file a motion for waiver of credit counseling with the court.

Official Form 101   Voluntary Petition for Individuals Filing for Bankruptcy   page 6

Debtor 1 _____ Case number (if known) _____
        First Name Middle Name Last Name

Part 6: Answer These Questions for Reporting Purposes

16. What kind of debts do you have?

16a. **Are your debts primarily consumer debts?** *Consumer debts* are defined in 11 U.S.C. § 101(8) as "incurred by an individual primarily for a personal, family, or household purpose."

☐ No. Go to line 16b.
☐ Yes. Go to line 17.

16b. **Are your debts primarily business debts?** *Business debts* are debts that you incurred to obtain money for a business or investment or through the operation of the business or investment.

☐ No. Go to line 16c.
☐ Yes. Go to line 17.

16c. State the type of debts you owe that are not consumer debts or business debts.

_____

17. Are you filing under Chapter 7?

Do you estimate that after any exempt property is excluded and administrative expenses are paid that funds will be available for distribution to unsecured creditors?

☐ No. I am not filing under Chapter 7. Go to line 18.

☐ Yes. I am filing under Chapter 7. Do you estimate that after any exempt property is excluded and administrative expenses are paid that funds will be available to distribute to unsecured creditors?

☐ No
☐ Yes

18. How many creditors do you estimate that you owe?

☐ 1-49
☐ 50-99
☐ 100-199
☐ 200-999
☐ 1,000-5,000
☐ 5,001-10,000
☐ 10,001-25,000
☐ 25,001-50,000
☐ 50,001-100,000
☐ More than 100,000

19. How much do you estimate your assets to be worth?

☐ $0-$50,000
☐ $50,001-$100,000
☐ $100,001-$500,000
☐ $500,001-$1 million
☐ $1,000,001-$10 million
☐ $10,000,001-$50 million
☐ $50,000,001-$100 million
☐ $100,000,001-$500 million
☐ $500,000,001-$1 billion
☐ $1,000,000,001-$10 billion
☐ $10,000,000,001-$50 billion
☐ More than $50 billion

20. How much do you estimate your liabilities to be?

☐ $0-$50,000
☐ $50,001-$100,000
☐ $100,001-$500,000
☐ $500,001-$1 million
☐ $1,000,001-$10 million
☐ $10,000,001-$50 million
☐ $50,000,001-$100 million
☐ $100,000,001-$500 million
☐ $500,000,001-$1 billion
☐ $1,000,000,001-$10 billion
☐ $10,000,000,001-$50 billion
☐ More than $50 billion

Part 7: Sign Below

For you

I have examined this petition, and I declare under penalty of perjury that the information provided is true and correct.

If I have chosen to file under Chapter 7, I am aware that I may proceed, if eligible, under Chapter 7, 11,12, or 13 of title 11, United States Code. I understand the relief available under each chapter, and I choose to proceed under Chapter 7.

If no attorney represents me and I did not pay or agree to pay someone who is not an attorney to help me fill out this document, I have obtained and read the notice required by 11 U.S.C. § 342(b).

I request relief in accordance with the chapter of title 11, United States Code, specified in this petition.

I understand making a false statement, concealing property, or obtaining money or property by fraud in connection with a bankruptcy case can result in fines up to $250,000, or imprisonment for up to 20 years, or both. 18 U.S.C. §§ 152, 1341, 1519, and 3571.

✗ _____   ✗ _____
  Signature of Debtor 1   Signature of Debtor 2

  Executed on _____   Executed on _____
              MM / DD / YYYY   MM / DD / YYYY

Official Form 101   Voluntary Petition for Individuals Filing for Bankruptcy   page 7

Debtor 1 _____ Case number (if known)_____
        First Name   Middle Name   Last Name

For your attorney, if you are represented by one

If you are not represented by an attorney, you do not need to file this page.

I, the attorney for the debtor(s) named in this petition, declare that I have informed the debtor(s) about eligibility to proceed under Chapter 7, 11, 12, or 13 of title 11, United States Code, and have explained the relief available under each chapter for which the person is eligible. I also certify that I have delivered to the debtor(s) the notice required by 11 U.S.C. § 342(b) and, in a case in which § 707(b)(4)(D) applies, certify that I have no knowledge after an inquiry that the information in the schedules filed with the petition is incorrect.

✗ _____   Date _____
Signature of Attorney for Debtor   MM / DD / YYYY

_____
Printed name

_____
Firm name

_____
Number   Street

_____

_____
City   State   ZIP Code

Contact phone _____   Email address _____

_____   _____
Bar number   State

Official Form 101   Voluntary Petition for Individuals Filing for Bankruptcy   page 8

Debtor 1 _____ Case number (if known)_____
         First Name Middle Name Last Name

For you if you are filing this bankruptcy without an attorney

If you are represented by an attorney, you do not need to file this page.

The law allows you, as an individual, to represent yourself in bankruptcy court, but you should understand that many people find it extremely difficult to represent themselves successfully. Because bankruptcy has long-term financial and legal consequences, you are strongly urged to hire a qualified attorney.

To be successful, you must correctly file and handle your bankruptcy case. The rules are very technical, and a mistake or inaction may affect your rights. For example, your case may be dismissed because you did not file a required document, pay a fee on time, attend a meeting or hearing, or cooperate with the court, case trustee, U.S. trustee, bankruptcy administrator, or audit firm if your case is selected for audit. If that happens, you could lose your right to file another case, or you may lose protections, including the benefit of the automatic stay.

You must list all your property and debts in the schedules that you are required to file with the court. Even if you plan to pay a particular debt outside of your bankruptcy, you must list that debt in your schedules. If you do not list a debt, the debt may not be discharged. If you do not list property or properly claim it as exempt, you may not be able to keep the property. The judge can also deny you a discharge of all your debts if you do something dishonest in your bankruptcy case, such as destroying or hiding property, falsifying records, or lying. Individual bankruptcy cases are randomly audited to determine if debtors have been accurate, truthful, and complete. **Bankruptcy fraud is a serious crime; you could be fined and imprisoned.**

If you decide to file without an attorney, the court expects you to follow the rules as if you had hired an attorney. The court will not treat you differently because you are filing for yourself. To be successful, you must be familiar with the United States Bankruptcy Code, the Federal Rules of Bankruptcy Procedure, and the local rules of the court in which your case is filed. You must also be familiar with any state exemption laws that apply.

Are you aware that filing for bankruptcy is a serious action with long-term financial and legal consequences?

☐ No
☐ Yes

Are you aware that bankruptcy fraud is a serious crime and that if your bankruptcy forms are inaccurate or incomplete, you could be fined or imprisoned?

☐ No
☐ Yes

Did you pay or agree to pay someone who is not an attorney to help you fill out your bankruptcy forms?

☐ No
☐ Yes. Name of Person_____.
    Attach *Bankruptcy Petition Preparer's Notice, Declaration, and Signature* (Official Form 119).

By signing here, I acknowledge that I understand the risks involved in filing without an attorney. I have read and understood this notice, and I am aware that filing a bankruptcy case without an attorney may cause me to lose my rights or property if I do not properly handle the case.

✗ _____   ✗ _____
Signature of Debtor 1   Signature of Debtor 2

Date _____   Date _____
     MM / DD / YYYY   MM / DD / YYYY

Contact phone _____   Contact phone _____

Cell phone _____   Cell phone _____

Email address _____   Email address _____

Official Form 101   Voluntary Petition for Individuals Filing for Bankruptcy   page 9

Application to Have the Chapter 7 Filing Fee Waived

Form 103B—Fee Waiver

Fill in this information to identify your case:

Debtor 1 _____ _____ _____
         First Name   Middle Name   Last Name

Debtor 2 _____ _____ _____
(Spouse, if filing) First Name Middle Name Last Name

United States Bankruptcy Court for the: _____ District of _____ ▼

Case number _____
(if known)

☐ Check if this is an amended filing

Official Form 103B

Application to Have the Chapter 7 Filing Fee Waived   12/15

Be as complete and accurate as possible. If two married people are filing together, both are equally responsible for supplying correct information. If more space is needed, attach a separate sheet to this form. On the top of any additional pages, write your name and case number (if known).

Part 1: Tell the Court About Your Family and Your Family's Income

1. **What is the size of your family?**
   Your family includes you, your spouse, and any dependents listed on *Schedule J: Your Expenses* (Official Form 106J).

   Check all that apply:
   ☐ You
   ☐ Your spouse
   ☐ Your dependents

   How many dependents? _____   Total number of people _____

2. **Fill in your family's average monthly income.**

   Include your spouse's income if your spouse is living with you, even if your spouse is not filing.

   Do not include your spouse's income if you are separated and your spouse is not filing with you.

   Add your income and your spouse's income. Include the value (if known) of any non-cash governmental assistance that you receive, such as food stamps (benefits under the Supplemental Nutrition Assistance Program) or housing subsidies.

   If you have already filled out *Schedule I: Your Income,* see line 10 of that schedule.

   Subtract any non-cash governmental assistance that you included above.

   Your family's average monthly net income

	That person's average monthly net income (take-home pay)
You	$ _____
Your spouse .... +	$ _____
Subtotal	$ _____
	− $ _____
Total	$ _____

3. **Do you receive non-cash governmental assistance?**
   ☐ No
   ☐ Yes. Describe.......... Type of assistance _____

4. **Do you expect your family's average monthly net income to increase or decrease by more than 10% during the next 6 months?**
   ☐ No
   ☐ Yes. Explain............ _____

5. **Tell the court why you are unable to pay the filing fee in installments within 120 days.** If you have some additional circumstances that cause you to not be able to pay your filing fee in installments, explain them.

   _____

Official Form 103B   Application to Have the Chapter 7 Filing Fee Waived   page 1

Debtor 1 _____   Case number (if known) _____
         First Name Middle Name Last Name

Part 2: Tell the Court About Your Monthly Expenses

6. Estimate your average monthly expenses.
   Include amounts paid by any government assistance that you $_____
   reported on line 2.

   If you have already filled out *Schedule J, Your Expenses,* copy
   line 22 from that form.

7. Do these expenses cover anyone   ☐ No
   who is not included in your family   ☐ Yes. Identify who .... [_____]
   as reported in line 1?

8. Does anyone other than you   ☐ No
   regularly pay any of these   ☐ Yes. How much do you regularly receive as contributions? $_____ monthly
   expenses?

   If you have already filled out
   Schedule I: Your Income, copy the
   total from line 11.

9. Do you expect your average   ☐ No
   monthly expenses to increase or   ☐ Yes. Explain .... [_____]
   decrease by more than 10% during
   the next 6 months?

Part 3: Tell the Court About Your Property

If you have already filled out *Schedule A/B: Property (Official Form 106A/B)* attach copies to this application and go to Part 4.

10. How much cash do you have?
    Examples: Money you have in
    your wallet, in your home, and on   Cash: $_____
    hand when you file this application

11. Bank accounts and other deposits   Institution name: Amount:
    of money?
    Examples: Checking, savings,   Checking account: _____ $_____
    money market, or other financial
    accounts; certificates of deposit;   Savings account: _____ $_____
    shares in banks, credit unions,
    brokerage houses, and other   Other financial accounts: _____ $_____
    similar institutions. If you have
    more than one account with the   Other financial accounts: _____ $_____
    same institution, list each. Do not
    include 401(k) and IRA accounts.

12. Your home? (if you own it outright or
    are purchasing it)   Number   Street   Current value: $_____
    Examples: House, condominium,   Amount you owe
    manufactured home, or mobile home   City   State   ZIP Code   on mortgage and $_____
                                                                                                liens:

13. Other real estate?   Current value: $_____
                                          Number   Street
                                                                                                Amount you owe
                                          City   State   ZIP Code   on mortgage and $_____
                                                                                                liens:

14. The vehicles you own?   Make:
    Examples: Cars, vans, trucks,   Model: Current value: $_____
    sports utility vehicles, motorcycles, Year: _____   Amount you owe
    tractors, boats   on liens: $_____
                                          Mileage   _____

                                          Make:
                                          Model: Current value: $_____
                                          Year: _____   Amount you owe
                                          Mileage   _____   on liens: $_____

Official Form 103B   Application to Have the Chapter 7 Filing Fee Waived   page 2

Debtor 1 _____ _____ _____   Case number (if known) _____
        First Name   Middle Name   Last Name

15. Other assets?
Do not include household items and clothing.

Describe the other assets:
[   ]

Current value: $_____
Amount you owe on liens: $_____

16. Money or property due you?
Examples: Tax refunds, past due or lump sum alimony, spousal support, child support, maintenance, divorce or property settlements, Social Security benefits, workers' compensation, personal injury recovery

Who owes you the money or property?
_____
_____

How much is owed?
$_____
$_____

Do you believe you will likely receive payment in the next 180 days?
☐ No
☐ Yes. Explain:
[   ]

Part 4: Answer These Additional Questions

17. Have you paid anyone for services for this case, including filling out this application, the bankruptcy filing package, or the schedules?

☐ No
☐ Yes. Whom did you pay? *Check all that apply*:
  ☐ An attorney
  ☐ A bankruptcy petition preparer, paralegal, or typing service
  ☐ Someone else _____

How much did you pay?
$_____

18. Have you promised to pay or do you expect to pay someone for services for your bankruptcy case?

☐ No
☐ Yes. Whom do you expect to pay? *Check all that apply*:
  ☐ An attorney
  ☐ A bankruptcy petition preparer, paralegal, or typing service
  ☐ Someone else _____

How much do you expect to pay?
$_____

19. Has anyone paid someone on your behalf for services for this case?

☐ No
☐ Yes. Who was paid on your behalf?
Check all that apply:
  ☐ An attorney
  ☐ A bankruptcy petition preparer, paralegal, or typing service
  ☐ Someone else _____

Who paid? *Check all that apply*:
  ☐ Parent
  ☐ Brother or sister
  ☐ Friend
  ☐ Pastor or clergy
  ☐ Someone else _____

How much did someone else pay?
$_____

20. Have you filed for bankruptcy within the last 8 years?

☐ No
☐ Yes. District _____ When _____ Case number _____
                                  MM/ DD/ YYYY

District _____ When _____ Case number _____
                              MM/ DD/ YYYY

District _____ When _____ Case number _____
                              MM/ DD/ YYYY

Part 5: Sign Below

By signing here under penalty of perjury, I declare that I cannot afford to pay the filing fee either in full or in installments. I also declare that the information I provided in this application is true and correct.

✗ _____   ✗ _____
Signature of Debtor 1   Signature of Debtor 2

Date MM / DD /YYYY   Date MM / DD /YYYY

Official Form 103B   Application to Have the Chapter 7 Filing Fee Waived   page 3

How to Bankrupt Your Student Loans, by Chuck Stewart, Ph.D. 2023   **APPENDIX C**   Page 248

Fill in this information to identify the case:

Debtor 1 _____ _____ _____
         First Name   Middle Name   Last Name

Debtor 2 _____ _____ _____
(Spouse, if filing) First Name   Middle Name   Last Name

United States Bankruptcy Court for the: _____ District of _____

Case number _____
(if known)

Order on the Application to Have the Chapter 7 Filing Fee Waived

After considering the debtor's *Application to Have the Chapter 7 Filing Fee Waived* (Official Form 103B), the court orders that the application is:

[ ] Granted. However, the court may order the debtor to pay the fee in the future if developments in administering the bankruptcy case show that the waiver was unwarranted.

[ ] Denied. The debtor must pay the filing fee according to the following terms:

You must pay...	On or before this date...
$_____	Month / day / year
$_____	Month / day / year
$_____	Month / day / year
+ $_____	Month / day / year
Total _____	

If the debtor would like to propose a different payment timetable, the debtor must file a motion promptly with a payment proposal. The debtor may use *Application for Individuals to Pay the Filing Fee in Installments* (Official Form 103A) for this purpose. The court will consider it.

The debtor must pay the entire filing fee before making any more payments or transferring any more property to an attorney, bankruptcy petition preparer, or anyone else in connection with the bankruptcy case. The debtor must also pay the entire filing fee to receive a discharge. If the debtor does not make any payment when it is due, the bankruptcy case may be dismissed and the debtor's rights in future bankruptcy cases may be affected.

[ ] Scheduled for hearing.

A hearing to consider the debtor's application will be held

on _____ at _____ AM / PM at _____
   Month / day / year   Address of courthouse

If the debtor does not appear at this hearing, the court may deny the application.

_____   By the court: _____
Month / day / year   United States Bankruptcy Judge

[Print] [Save As...] [Add Attachment]   [Reset]

How to Bankrupt Your Student Loans, by Chuck Stewart, Ph.D. 2023

Chapter 7 Income

Form 106I—Income

Fill in this information to identify your case:

Debtor 1 _____
         First Name   Middle Name   Last Name

Debtor 2 _____
(Spouse, if filing) First Name Middle Name Last Name

United States Bankruptcy Court for the: _____ District of _____

Case number _____
(if known)

Check if this is:
- ☐ An amended filing
- ☐ A supplement showing postpetition chapter 13 income as of the following date:
  _____
  MM / DD / YYYY

Official Form 106I

Schedule I: Your Income   12/15

Be as complete and accurate as possible. If two married people are filing together (Debtor 1 and Debtor 2), both are equally responsible for supplying correct information. If you are married and not filing jointly, and your spouse is living with you, include information about your spouse. If you are separated and your spouse is not filing with you, do not include information about your spouse. If more space is needed, attach a separate sheet to this form. On the top of any additional pages, write your name and case number (if known). Answer every question.

Part 1: Describe Employment

1. Fill in your employment information.

    If you have more than one job, attach a separate page with information about additional employers.

    Include part-time, seasonal, or self-employed work.

    Occupation may include student or homemaker, if it applies.

	Debtor 1	Debtor 2 or non-filing spouse
Employment status	☐ Employed ☐ Not employed	☐ Employed ☐ Not employed
Occupation	_____	_____
Employer's name	_____	_____
Employer's address	_____ Number Street _____ _____ _____ City State ZIP Code	_____ Number Street _____ _____ _____ City State ZIP Code
How long employed there?	_____	_____

Part 2: Give Details About Monthly Income

Estimate monthly income as of the date you file this form. If you have nothing to report for any line, write $0 in the space. Include your non-filing spouse unless you are separated.

If you or your non-filing spouse have more than one employer, combine the information for all employers for that person on the lines below. If you need more space, attach a separate sheet to this form.

	For Debtor 1	For Debtor 2 or non-filing spouse
2. List monthly gross wages, salary, and commissions (before all payroll deductions). If not paid monthly, calculate what the monthly wage would be.	$_____	$_____
3. Estimate and list monthly overtime pay.	+$_____	+$_____
4. Calculate gross income. Add line 2 + line 3.	$_____	$_____

Official Form 106I   Schedule I: Your Income   page 1

Debtor 1 _____ Case number (if known)_____
         First Name Middle Name Last Name

		For Debtor 1	For Debtor 2 or non-filing spouse
Copy line 4 here..→	4.	$_____	$_____

5. List all payroll deductions:

5a. Tax, Medicare, and Social Security deductions	5a.	$_____	$_____
5b. Mandatory contributions for retirement plans	5b.	$_____	$_____
5c. Voluntary contributions for retirement plans	5c.	$_____	$_____
5d. Required repayments of retirement fund loans	5d.	$_____	$_____
5e. Insurance	5e.	$_____	$_____
5f. Domestic support obligations	5f.	$_____	$_____
5g. Union dues	5g.	$_____	$_____
5h. Other deductions. Specify: _____	5h.	+$_____	+$_____

6. Add the payroll deductions. Add lines 5a + 5b + 5c + 5d + 5e +5f + 5g + 5h. 6. $_____ $_____

7. Calculate total monthly take-home pay. Subtract line 6 from line 4. 7. $_____ $_____

8. List all other income regularly received:

   8a. Net income from rental property and from operating a business, profession, or farm
      Attach a statement for each property and business showing gross receipts, ordinary and necessary business expenses, and the total monthly net income. 8a. $_____ $_____

   8b. Interest and dividends 8b. $_____ $_____

   8c. Family support payments that you, a non-filing spouse, or a dependent regularly receive
      Include alimony, spousal support, child support, maintenance, divorce settlement, and property settlement. 8c. $_____ $_____

   8d. Unemployment compensation 8d. $_____ $_____

   8e. Social Security 8e. $_____ $_____

   8f. Other government assistance that you regularly receive
      Include cash assistance and the value (if known) of any non-cash assistance that you receive, such as food stamps (benefits under the Supplemental Nutrition Assistance Program) or housing subsidies.
      Specify: _____ 8f. $_____ $_____

   8g. Pension or retirement income 8g. $_____ $_____

   8h. Other monthly income. Specify: _____ 8h. +$_____   +$_____

9. Add all other income. Add lines 8a + 8b + 8c + 8d + 8e + 8f +8g + 8h. 9. $_____ $_____

10. Calculate monthly income. Add line 7 + line 9.
    Add the entries in line 10 for Debtor 1 and Debtor 2 or non-filing spouse. 10. $_____ + $_____ = $_____

11. State all other regular contributions to the expenses that you list in *Schedule J*.
    Include contributions from an unmarried partner, members of your household, your dependents, your roommates, and other friends or relatives.
    Do not include any amounts already included in lines 2-10 or amounts that are not available to pay expenses listed in *Schedule J*.
    Specify: _____ 11. + $_____

12. Add the amount in the last column of line 10 to the amount in line 11. The result is the combined monthly income.
    Write that amount on the *Summary of Your Assets and Liabilities and Certain Statistical Information*, if it applies 12. $_____
    Combined monthly income

13. Do you expect an increase or decrease within the year after you file this form?
    ☐ No.
    ☐ Yes. Explain: _____

Official Form 106I   Schedule I: Your Income   page 2

Chapter 7 Creditors

Form 106E/F—Creditors

Fill in this information to identify your case:

Debtor 1 _____
        First Name   Middle Name   Last Name

Debtor 2 _____
(Spouse, if filing) First Name   Middle Name   Last Name

United States Bankruptcy Court for the: _____ District of _____

Case number _____
(If known)

☐ Check if this is an amended filing

Official Form 106E/F
Schedule E/F: Creditors Who Have Unsecured Claims   12/15

Be as complete and accurate as possible. Use Part 1 for creditors with PRIORITY claims and Part 2 for creditors with NONPRIORITY claims. List the other party to any executory contracts or unexpired leases that could result in a claim. Also list executory contracts on *Schedule A/B: Property* (Official Form 106A/B) and on *Schedule G: Executory Contracts and Unexpired Leases* (Official Form 106G). Do not include any creditors with partially secured claims that are listed in *Schedule D: Creditors Who Have Claims Secured by Property*. If more space is needed, copy the Part you need, fill it out, number the entries in the boxes on the left. Attach the Continuation Page to this page. On the top of any additional pages, write your name and case number (if known).

Part 1:   **List All of Your PRIORITY Unsecured Claims**

1. Do any creditors have priority unsecured claims against you?
   ☐ No. Go to Part 2.
   ☐ Yes.

2. List all of your priority unsecured claims. If a creditor has more than one priority unsecured claim, list the creditor separately for each claim. For each claim listed, identify what type of claim it is. If a claim has both priority and nonpriority amounts, list that claim here and show both priority and nonpriority amounts. As much as possible, list the claims in alphabetical order according to the creditor's name. If you have more than two priority unsecured claims, fill out the Continuation Page of Part 1. If more than one creditor holds a particular claim, list the other creditors in Part 3.
   (For an explanation of each type of claim, see the instructions for this form in the instruction booklet.)

		Total claim	Priority amount	Nonpriority amount

2.1

Priority Creditor's Name _____

Number Street _____

_____

City   State   ZIP Code

Who incurred the debt? Check one.
☐ Debtor 1 only
☐ Debtor 2 only
☐ Debtor 1 and Debtor 2 only
☐ At least one of the debtors and another
☐ Check if this claim is for a community debt

Is the claim subject to offset?
☐ No
☐ Yes

Last 4 digits of account number ___ ___ ___ ___ $_____ $_____ $_____

When was the debt incurred? _____

As of the date you file, the claim is: Check all that apply.
☐ Contingent
☐ Unliquidated
☐ Disputed

Type of PRIORITY unsecured claim:
☐ Domestic support obligations
☐ Taxes and certain other debts you owe the government
☐ Claims for death or personal injury while you were intoxicated
☐ Other. Specify _____

2.2

Priority Creditor's Name _____

Number Street _____

_____

City   State   ZIP Code

Who incurred the debt? Check one.
☐ Debtor 1 only
☐ Debtor 2 only
☐ Debtor 1 and Debtor 2 only
☐ At least one of the debtors and another
☐ Check if this claim is for a community debt

Is the claim subject to offset?
☐ No
☐ Yes

Last 4 digits of account number ___ ___ ___ ___ $_____ $_____ $_____

When was the debt incurred? _____

As of the date you file, the claim is: Check all that apply.
☐ Contingent
☐ Unliquidated
☐ Disputed

Type of PRIORITY unsecured claim:
☐ Domestic support obligations
☐ Taxes and certain other debts you owe the government
☐ Claims for death or personal injury while you were intoxicated
☐ Other. Specify _____

Official Form 106E/F   Schedule E/F: Creditors Who Have Unsecured Claims   page 1 of ___

Debtor 1 _____
First Name   Middle Name   Last Name

Case number (if known) _____

Part 1: Your PRIORITY Unsecured Claims – Continuation Page

After listing any entries on this page, number them beginning with 2.3, followed by 2.4, and so forth.

| | Total claim | Priority amount | Nonpriority amount |

☐ ___

Priority Creditor's Name _____

Number Street _____

_____

City   State   ZIP Code

Who incurred the debt? Check one.
☐ Debtor 1 only
☐ Debtor 2 only
☐ Debtor 1 and Debtor 2 only
☐ At least one of the debtors and another

☐ Check if this claim is for a community debt

Is the claim subject to offset?
☐ No
☐ Yes

Last 4 digits of account number ___ ___ ___ ___ $_____ $_____ $_____

When was the debt incurred? _____

As of the date you file, the claim is: Check all that apply.
☐ Contingent
☐ Unliquidated
☐ Disputed

Type of PRIORITY unsecured claim:
☐ Domestic support obligations
☐ Taxes and certain other debts you owe the government
☐ Claims for death or personal injury while you were intoxicated
☐ Other. Specify _____

☐ ___

Priority Creditor's Name _____

Number Street _____

_____

City   State   ZIP Code

Who incurred the debt? Check one.
☐ Debtor 1 only
☐ Debtor 2 only
☐ Debtor 1 and Debtor 2 only
☐ At least one of the debtors and another

☐ Check if this claim is for a community debt

Is the claim subject to offset?
☐ No
☐ Yes

Last 4 digits of account number ___ ___ ___ ___ $_____ $_____ $_____

When was the debt incurred? _____

As of the date you file, the claim is: Check all that apply.
☐ Contingent
☐ Unliquidated
☐ Disputed

Type of PRIORITY unsecured claim:
☐ Domestic support obligations
☐ Taxes and certain other debts you owe the government
☐ Claims for death or personal injury while you were intoxicated
☐ Other. Specify _____

☐ ___

Priority Creditor's Name _____

Number Street _____

_____

City   State   ZIP Code

Who incurred the debt? Check one.
☐ Debtor 1 only
☐ Debtor 2 only
☐ Debtor 1 and Debtor 2 only
☐ At least one of the debtors and another

☐ Check if this claim is for a community debt

Is the claim subject to offset?
☐ No
☐ Yes

Last 4 digits of account number ___ ___ ___ ___ $_____ $_____ $_____

When was the debt incurred? _____

As of the date you file, the claim is: Check all that apply.
☐ Contingent
☐ Unliquidated
☐ Disputed

Type of PRIORITY unsecured claim:
☐ Domestic support obligations
☐ Taxes and certain other debts you owe the government
☐ Claims for death or personal injury while you were intoxicated
☐ Other. Specify _____

Official Form 106E/F   Schedule E/F: Creditors Who Have Unsecured Claims   page ___ of ___

Debtor 1 _____ Case number (if known) _____
        First Name   Middle Name   Last Name

Part 2: List All of Your NONPRIORITY Unsecured Claims

3. Do any creditors have nonpriority unsecured claims against you?
   ☐ No. You have nothing to report in this part. Submit this form to the court with your other schedules.
   ☐ Yes

4. List all of your nonpriority unsecured claims in the alphabetical order of the creditor who holds each claim. If a creditor has more than one nonpriority unsecured claim, list the creditor separately for each claim. For each claim listed, identify what type of claim it is. Do not list claims already included in Part 1. If more than one creditor holds a particular claim, list the other creditors in Part 3. If you have more than three nonpriority unsecured claims fill out the Continuation Page of Part 2.

Total claim

4.1 _____
Nonpriority Creditor's Name

Number   Street

_____
City   State   ZIP Code

Who incurred the debt? Check one.
☐ Debtor 1 only
☐ Debtor 2 only
☐ Debtor 1 and Debtor 2 only
☐ At least one of the debtors and another

☐ Check if this claim is for a community debt

Is the claim subject to offset?
☐ No
☐ Yes

Last 4 digits of account number ___ ___ ___ ___

When was the debt incurred? _____

As of the date you file, the claim is: Check all that apply.
☐ Contingent
☐ Unliquidated
☐ Disputed

Type of NONPRIORITY unsecured claim:
☐ Student loans
☐ Obligations arising out of a separation agreement or divorce that you did not report as priority claims
☐ Debts to pension or profit-sharing plans, and other similar debts
☐ Other. Specify _____

$ _____

4.2 _____
Nonpriority Creditor's Name

Number   Street

_____
City   State   ZIP Code

Who incurred the debt? Check one.
☐ Debtor 1 only
☐ Debtor 2 only
☐ Debtor 1 and Debtor 2 only
☐ At least one of the debtors and another

☐ Check if this claim is for a community debt

Is the claim subject to offset?
☐ No
☐ Yes

Last 4 digits of account number ___ ___ ___ ___

When was the debt incurred? _____

As of the date you file, the claim is: Check all that apply.
☐ Contingent
☐ Unliquidated
☐ Disputed

Type of NONPRIORITY unsecured claim:
☐ Student loans
☐ Obligations arising out of a separation agreement or divorce that you did not report as priority claims
☐ Debts to pension or profit-sharing plans, and other similar debts
☐ Other. Specify _____

$ _____

4.3 _____
Nonpriority Creditor's Name

Number   Street

_____
City   State   ZIP Code

Who incurred the debt? Check one.
☐ Debtor 1 only
☐ Debtor 2 only
☐ Debtor 1 and Debtor 2 only
☐ At least one of the debtors and another

☐ Check if this claim is for a community debt

Is the claim subject to offset?
☐ No
☐ Yes

Last 4 digits of account number ___ ___ ___ ___

When was the debt incurred? _____

As of the date you file, the claim is: Check all that apply.
☐ Contingent
☐ Unliquidated
☐ Disputed

Type of NONPRIORITY unsecured claim:
☐ Student loans
☐ Obligations arising out of a separation agreement or divorce that you did not report as priority claims
☐ Debts to pension or profit-sharing plans, and other similar debts
☐ Other. Specify _____

$ _____

Official Form 106E/F   Schedule E/F: Creditors Who Have Unsecured Claims   page ___ of ___

Debtor 1 _____ Case number (if known) _____
         First Name   Middle Name   Last Name

Part 2: Your NONPRIORITY Unsecured Claims – Continuation Page

After listing any entries on this page, number them beginning with 4.4, followed by 4.5, and so forth.   Total claim

☐

| Nonpriority Creditor's Name _____ | Last 4 digits of account number ___ ___ ___ ___ | $_____ |

Number Street _____

City _____ State ____ ZIP Code ____

When was the debt incurred? _____

As of the date you file, the claim is: Check all that apply.
☐ Contingent
☐ Unliquidated
☐ Disputed

Who incurred the debt? Check one.
☐ Debtor 1 only
☐ Debtor 2 only
☐ Debtor 1 and Debtor 2 only
☐ At least one of the debtors and another

☐ Check if this claim is for a community debt

Is the claim subject to offset?
☐ No
☐ Yes

Type of NONPRIORITY unsecured claim:
☐ Student loans
☐ Obligations arising out of a separation agreement or divorce that you did not report as priority claims
☐ Debts to pension or profit-sharing plans, and other similar debts
☐ Other. Specify _____

☐

Nonpriority Creditor's Name _____

Number Street _____

City _____ State ____ ZIP Code ____

Last 4 digits of account number ___ ___ ___ ___ $_____

When was the debt incurred? _____

As of the date you file, the claim is: Check all that apply.
☐ Contingent
☐ Unliquidated
☐ Disputed

Who incurred the debt? Check one.
☐ Debtor 1 only
☐ Debtor 2 only
☐ Debtor 1 and Debtor 2 only
☐ At least one of the debtors and another

☐ Check if this claim is for a community debt

Is the claim subject to offset?
☐ No
☐ Yes

Type of NONPRIORITY unsecured claim:
☐ Student loans
☐ Obligations arising out of a separation agreement or divorce that you did not report as priority claims
☐ Debts to pension or profit-sharing plans, and other similar debts
☐ Other. Specify _____

☐

Nonpriority Creditor's Name _____

Number Street _____

City _____ State ____ ZIP Code ____

Last 4 digits of account number ___ ___ ___ ___ $_____

When was the debt incurred? _____

As of the date you file, the claim is: Check all that apply.
☐ Contingent
☐ Unliquidated
☐ Disputed

Who incurred the debt? Check one.
☐ Debtor 1 only
☐ Debtor 2 only
☐ Debtor 1 and Debtor 2 only
☐ At least one of the debtors and another

☐ Check if this claim is for a community debt

Is the claim subject to offset?
☐ No
☐ Yes

Type of NONPRIORITY unsecured claim:
☐ Student loans
☐ Obligations arising out of a separation agreement or divorce that you did not report as priority claims
☐ Debts to pension or profit-sharing plans, and other similar debts
☐ Other. Specify _____

Official Form 106E/F   Schedule E/F: Creditors Who Have Unsecured Claims   page ___ of ___

Debtor 1 _____   Case number (if known)_____
         First Name Middle Name Last Name

Part 3: List Others to Be Notified About a Debt That You Already Listed

5. Use this page only if you have others to be notified about your bankruptcy, for a debt that you already listed in Parts 1 or 2. For example, if a collection agency is trying to collect from you for a debt you owe to someone else, list the original creditor in Parts 1 or 2, then list the collection agency here. Similarly, if you have more than one creditor for any of the debts that you listed in Parts 1 or 2, list the additional creditors here. If you do not have additional persons to be notified for any debts in Parts 1 or 2, do not fill out or submit this page.

Name _____	On which entry in Part 1 or Part 2 did you list the original creditor?
Number Street	Line _____ of (Check one): ❏ Part 1: Creditors with Priority Unsecured Claims
	❏ Part 2: Creditors with Nonpriority Unsecured Claims
City State ZIP Code	Last 4 digits of account number ___ ___ ___ ___

Name _____	On which entry in Part 1 or Part 2 did you list the original creditor?
Number Street	Line _____ of (Check one): ❏ Part 1: Creditors with Priority Unsecured Claims
	❏ Part 2: Creditors with Nonpriority Unsecured Claims
City State ZIP Code	Last 4 digits of account number ___ ___ ___ ___

Name _____	On which entry in Part 1 or Part 2 did you list the original creditor?
Number Street	Line _____ of (Check one): ❏ Part 1: Creditors with Priority Unsecured Claims
	❏ Part 2: Creditors with Nonpriority Unsecured Claims
City State ZIP Code	Last 4 digits of account number ___ ___ ___ ___

Name _____	On which entry in Part 1 or Part 2 did you list the original creditor?
Number Street	Line _____ of (Check one): ❏ Part 1: Creditors with Priority Unsecured Claims
	❏ Part 2: Creditors with Nonpriority Unsecured Claims
City State ZIP Code	Last 4 digits of account number ___ ___ ___ ___

Name _____	On which entry in Part 1 or Part 2 did you list the original creditor?
Number Street	Line _____ of (Check one): ❏ Part 1: Creditors with Priority Unsecured Claims
	❏ Part 2: Creditors with Nonpriority Unsecured Claims
City State ZIP Code	Last 4 digits of account number ___ ___ ___ ___

Name _____	On which entry in Part 1 or Part 2 did you list the original creditor?
Number Street	Line _____ of (Check one): ❏ Part 1: Creditors with Priority Unsecured Claims
	❏ Part 2: Creditors with Nonpriority Unsecured Claims
City State ZIP Code	Last 4 digits of account number ___ ___ ___ ___

Name _____	On which entry in Part 1 or Part 2 did you list the original creditor?
Number Street	Line _____ of (Check one): ❏ Part 1: Creditors with Priority Unsecured Claims
	❏ Part 2: Creditors with Nonpriority Unsecured Claims
City State ZIP Code	Last 4 digits of account number ___ ___ ___ ___

Official Form 106E/F   Schedule E/F: Creditors Who Have Unsecured Claims   page ___ of ___

Debtor 1 _____   Case number (if known)_____
        First Name   Middle Name   Last Name

Part 4: Add the Amounts for Each Type of Unsecured Claim

6. Total the amounts of certain types of unsecured claims. This information is for statistical reporting purposes only. 28 U.S.C. § 159.
Add the amounts for each type of unsecured claim.

Total claim

Total claims from Part 1

6a. Domestic support obligations 6a. $_____

6b. Taxes and certain other debts you owe the government 6b. $_____

6c. Claims for death or personal injury while you were intoxicated 6c. $_____

6d. Other. Add all other priority unsecured claims. Write that amount here. 6d. + $_____

6e. Total. Add lines 6a through 6d. 6e. $_____

Total claim

Total claims from Part 2

6f. Student loans 6f. $_____

6g. Obligations arising out of a separation agreement or divorce that you did not report as priority claims 6g. $_____

6h. Debts to pension or profit-sharing plans, and other similar debts 6h. $_____

6i. Other. Add all other nonpriority unsecured claims. Write that amount here. 6i. + $_____

6j. Total. Add lines 6f through 6i. 6j. $_____

Official Form 106E/F   Schedule E/F: Creditors Who Have Unsecured Claims   page ___ of ___

Chapter 7 Expenses

Form 106J—Expenses

Fill in this information to identify your case:

Debtor 1 _____ _____ _____
           First Name   Middle Name   Last Name

Debtor 2 _____ _____ _____
(Spouse, if filing) First Name Middle Name Last Name

United States Bankruptcy Court for the: _____ District of _____

Case number _____
(If known)

Check if this is:

☐ An amended filing
☐ A supplement showing postpetition chapter 13 expenses as of the following date:
_____
MM / DD / YYYY

Official Form 106J
Schedule J: Your Expenses   12/15

Be as complete and accurate as possible. If two married people are filing together, both are equally responsible for supplying correct information. If more space is needed, attach another sheet to this form. On the top of any additional pages, write your name and case number (if known). Answer every question.

Part 1: Describe Your Household

1. Is this a joint case?

    ☐ No. Go to line 2.
    ☐ Yes. Does Debtor 2 live in a separate household?

        ☐ No
        ☐ Yes. Debtor 2 must file Official Form 106J-2, *Expenses for Separate Household of Debtor 2*.

2. Do you have dependents?

    Do not list Debtor 1 and Debtor 2.
    Do not state the dependents' names.

    ☐ No
    ☐ Yes. Fill out this information for each dependent..........

Dependent's relationship to Debtor 1 or Debtor 2	Dependent's age	Does dependent live with you?
_____	_____	☐ No ☐ Yes
_____	_____	☐ No ☐ Yes
_____	_____	☐ No ☐ Yes
_____	_____	☐ No ☐ Yes
_____	_____	☐ No ☐ Yes

3. Do your expenses include expenses of people other than yourself and your dependents?

    ☐ No
    ☐ Yes

Part 2: Estimate Your Ongoing Monthly Expenses

Estimate your expenses as of your bankruptcy filing date unless you are using this form as a supplement in a Chapter 13 case to report expenses as of a date after the bankruptcy is filed. If this is a supplemental *Schedule J*, check the box at the top of the form and fill in the applicable date.

Include expenses paid for with non-cash government assistance if you know the value of such assistance and have included it on *Schedule I: Your Income* (Official Form 106I).

Your expenses

4. The rental or home ownership expenses for your residence. Include first mortgage payments and any rent for the ground or lot. .... 4. $_____

    If not included in line 4:

    4a. Real estate taxes .... 4a. $_____
    4b. Property, homeowner's, or renter's insurance .... 4b. $_____
    4c. Home maintenance, repair, and upkeep expenses .... 4c. $_____
    4d. Homeowner's association or condominium dues .... 4d. $_____

Official Form 106J   Schedule J: Your Expenses   page 1

Debtor 1 _____ _____ _____ Case number (if known)_____
         First Name   Middle Name   Last Name

	Your expenses

5. Additional mortgage payments for your residence, such as home equity loans   5. $_____

6. Utilities:
   - 6a. Electricity, heat, natural gas   6a. $_____
   - 6b. Water, sewer, garbage collection   6b. $_____
   - 6c. Telephone, cell phone, Internet, satellite, and cable services   6c. $_____
   - 6d. Other. Specify:_____   6d. $_____

7. Food and housekeeping supplies   7. $_____

8. Childcare and children's education costs   8. $_____

9. Clothing, laundry, and dry cleaning   9. $_____

10. Personal care products and services   10. $_____

11. Medical and dental expenses   11. $_____

12. Transportation. Include gas, maintenance, bus or train fare.
    Do not include car payments.   12. $_____

13. Entertainment, clubs, recreation, newspapers, magazines, and books   13. $_____

14. Charitable contributions and religious donations   14. $_____

15. Insurance.
    Do not include insurance deducted from your pay or included in lines 4 or 20.
    - 15a. Life insurance   15a. $_____
    - 15b. Health insurance   15b. $_____
    - 15c. Vehicle insurance   15c. $_____
    - 15d. Other insurance. Specify:_____   15d. $_____

16. Taxes. Do not include taxes deducted from your pay or included in lines 4 or 20.
    Specify:_____   16. $_____

17. Installment or lease payments:
    - 17a. Car payments for Vehicle 1   17a. $_____
    - 17b. Car payments for Vehicle 2   17b. $_____
    - 17c. Other. Specify:_____   17c. $_____
    - 17d. Other. Specify:_____   17d. $_____

18. Your payments of alimony, maintenance, and support that you did not report as deducted from your pay on line 5, *Schedule I, Your Income* (Official Form 106I).   18. $_____

19. Other payments you make to support others who do not live with you.
    Specify:_____   19. $_____

20. Other real property expenses not included in lines 4 or 5 of this form or on *Schedule I: Your Income*.
    - 20a. Mortgages on other property   20a. $_____
    - 20b. Real estate taxes   20b. $_____
    - 20c. Property, homeowner's, or renter's insurance   20c. $_____
    - 20d. Maintenance, repair, and upkeep expenses   20d. $_____
    - 20e. Homeowner's association or condominium dues   20e. $_____

Official Form 106J   Schedule J: Your Expenses   page 2

Debtor 1 _____   Case number (if known)_____
         First Name   Middle Name   Last Name

21. Other. Specify: _____   21. +$_____

22. Calculate your monthly expenses.

    22a. Add lines 4 through 21.   22a. $_____

    22b. Copy line 22 (monthly expenses for Debtor 2), if any, from Official Form 106J-2   22b. $_____

    22c. Add line 22a and 22b. The result is your monthly expenses.   22c. $_____

23. Calculate your monthly net income.

    23a. Copy line 12 (*your combined monthly income*) from *Schedule I*.   23a. $_____

    23b. Copy your monthly expenses from line 22c above.   23b. –$_____

    23c. Subtract your monthly expenses from your monthly income.
The result is your *monthly net income*.   23c. $_____

24. Do you expect an increase or decrease in your expenses within the year after you file this form?

    For example, do you expect to finish paying for your car loan within the year or do you expect your mortgage payment to increase or decrease because of a modification to the terms of your mortgage?

    ❏ No.
    ❏ Yes.   Explain here:

Official Form 106J   Schedule J: Your Expenses   page 3

Reopening a Bankruptcy

Motion to Reopen Bankruptcy Sample 1

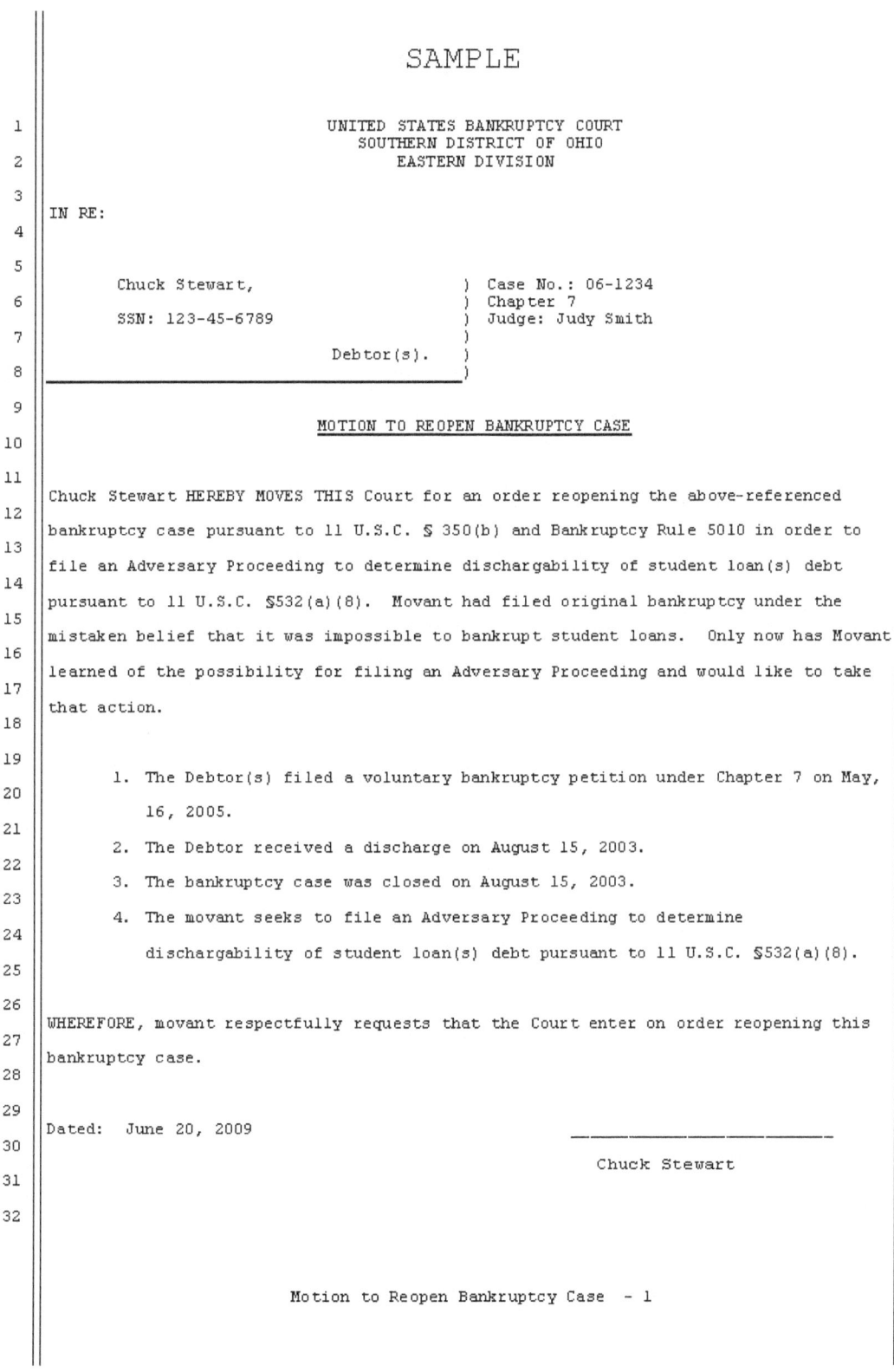

How to Bankrupt Your Student Loans, by Chuck Stewart, Ph.D. 2023

UNITED STATES BANKRUPTCY COURT
(Title of District)

IN RE:

_____,) Case No.: [Case number]
)
            Debtor(s).   ) Chapter
)
)
_____)

MOTION TO REOPEN BANKRUPTCY CASE

_____ HEREBY MOVES THIS Court for an order reopening the above-referenced bankruptcy case pursuant to 11 U.S.C. § 350(b) and Bankruptcy Rule 5010 in order to file an Adversary Proceeding to determine dischargability of student loan(s) debt pursuant to 11 U.S.C. §532(a)(8). Movant had filed original bankruptcy under the mistaken belief that it was impossible to bankrupt student loans. Only now has Movant learned of the possibility for filing an Adversary Proceeding and would like to take that action.

1. The Debtor(s) filed a voluntary bankruptcy petition under Chapter _ on _____.
2. The Debtor received a discharge on _____.
3. The bankruptcy case was closed on _____.
4. The movant seeks to file an Adversary Proceeding to determine dischargability of student loan(s) debt pursuant to 11 U.S.C. §532(a)(8).

WHEREFORE, movant respectfully requests that the Court enter on order reopening this bankruptcy case.

Dated: _____   _____
                                              [Movant]

Motion to Reopen Bankruptcy Sample 2

UNITED STATES BANKRUPTCY COURT
SOUTHERN DISTRICT OF FLORIDA
www.flsb.uscourts.gov

In re: Case No.
                                                                  Chapter 7

_____ Debtor   /

ORDER REOPENING CASE TO ADD OMITTED CREDITOR(S)

THIS CAUSE having come before the court upon debtor's Motion to Reopen Case pursuant to 11 U.S.C. §350, Bankruptcy Rule 5010, and Local Rule 5010-1(B) and the court having considered the motion and having determined that good cause has been shown, and being otherwise fully advised in the premises, it is

ORDERED:

1. This case is reopened. No filing fee is required to be paid to the clerk unless the debtor fails to comply with paragraph 3 of this order and the case is closed pursuant to paragraph 4. No trustee shall be appointed.

2. Within 15 days from the entry of this order, the debtor shall amend the schedules (and pay applicable amendment fee) to add the name(s) and address(es) of the creditor(s) previously omitted from the original schedules. A supplemental matrix of creditors as required by the "Clerk's Instructions for Preparing, Submitting and Obtaining Service Matrices" must accompany the amended schedules.

3. The debtor (or the debtor's attorney) is directed to furnish a complete and correct copy of this order to all affected parties, including the added creditor and a copy of the clerk's notice of meeting of creditors must also be served on the creditor as required under Local Rule 1009-1(D). A certificate of service must be filed as required under Local Rule 2002-1(F).

4. Within 15 days from the entry of this order, the debtor shall file an adversary proceeding(s) to determine whether the debt(s), subject to such amendment(s), is/are or is/are not dischargeable under 11 U.S.C. §523(a).

5. Upon the filing of the adversary case(s) by the debtor, or upon the debtor's failure to comply with this order, the case will be reclosed by the clerk's office.

###

Submitted by:

Copies to:
Debtor (or Debtor's Attorney)

Amendment to Schedule F Sample

SAMPLE

UNITED STATES BANKRUPTCY COURT
SOUTHERN DISTRICT OF OHIO
EASTERN DIVISION

IN RE:

    Chuck Stewart   ) Case No.: 07-12345
) Chapter 7
    SSN: 123-45-6789   ) Judge: Judy Smith
)
)
    Debtor.

AMENDMENT TO SCHEDULE F

CREDITOR HOLDING UNSECURED CLAIMS

The Debtor Amends Schedule F to add the following creditor, as described below:

Creditor	Description	Amount
U.S. Dept. of Education	Student Loan	$50,000.00
Direct Loan Servicing System	Date of debt: 2003	
PO Box 4609		
Utica, NY 13504-4609		

Dated: June 20, 2009

                                                      Plaintiff (sign your name)

Amend Schedule F - 1

Amendment to Schedule F Blank Form

```
                    UNITED STATES BANKRUPTCY COURT
                          (Title of District)


IN RE:


_____,  ) Case No.: [Case number]
                                 ) Chapter
                    Debtor(s).   ) Judge:
                                 )
                                 )
_____   )


                        AMENDMENT TO SCHEUDLE F
                   CREDITOR HOLDING UNSECURED CLAIMS


    The Debtor Amends Schedule F to add the following creditor, as described below:


    Creditor                Description              Amount
















Dated: _____              _____
                                        Plaintiff (signature)

                        Amend Schedule F - 1
```

APPENDIX D
Worksheets

Worksheets

Student Loan History

It is important to know the status of your student loans. The table below helps to organize that information. If you do not have current information, contact your lender for a complete printout of your loans.

Use additional copies of this table as needed.

	Loan 1	Loan 2	Loan 3	Loan 4	Loan 5	Loan 6
Name of Loan						
Guarantor						
Amount						
Date of Issuance						
Payment Status						
Amount Repaid to date						
Payment dates						

Current Income Status

This worksheet is used to establish your current income at the time of the adversary proceeding mediation or trial. Use *Chapter 7 Bankruptcy (Form B106I)— Schedule I-Your Income)* for data. Use additional sheets, as necessary.

Debtor's Marital Status:	DEPENDENTS OF DEBTOR AND SPOUSE	
	RELATIONSHIP	AGE
Employment:	**DEBTOR**	**SPOUSE**
Occupation		
Name of Employer		
How Long Employed		
Address of Employer		

	Col. 1	Col. 2	Col. 3	Col. 4
Instruction: In columns 1 & 2, write the numbers listed with your Chapter 7 bankruptcy form 106I. The 3rd & 4th columns are the numbers updated at the time the adversary proceeding mediation or trial.	At time of Chapter 7 filing	At time of Chapter 7 filing	Current Status (date)	Current Status (date)
Income: (Estimate of average monthly income)	Debtor	Spouse	Debtor	Spouse
Current monthly gross wages, salary, and commissions (prorate if not paid monthly)				
Estimated monthly overtime				
SUBTOTAL				
LESS PAYROLL DEDUCTIONS				
a. Payroll taxes and Social Security				
b. Insurance				
c. Union dues				
d. Other (specify)				
SUBTOTAL OF PAYROLL DEDUCTIONS				
TOTAL NET MONTHLY TAKE HOME PAY				
Regular income form operation of business or profession or farm (attach detailed statement)				
Income from real property				
Interest and dividends				
Alimony, maintenance, or support payments payable to the debtor for the debtor's use of that of dependents listed above.				
Social security or other government assistance (Specify) _____				
Pension or retirement income				
Other monthly income (Specify) _____				
(Specify) _____				
TOTAL MONTHLY INCOME				
TOTAL COMBINED MONTHLY INCOME				

Current Expenditure Status

This two-page worksheet is used to establish your current expenses at the time of the adversary proceeding mediation or trail and to compare these expenses to national norms.

INSTRUCTIONS:

FIRST: Go to the United States Department of Health and Human Services (https://aspe.hhs.gov/poverty-guidelines) and **download a copy** of the current Federal Poverty Guideline. This is also available at your local library. The table gives the Poverty level as related to family size. Look up your family size and fill in below:

      _____ : Size of your Family Unit
      _____ : Total Yearly Income (see your Current Financial Status worksheet)
      _____ : Yearly Income as specified by the Federal Poverty Guideline

Comment: If your Yearly Income is very different than what is established by the Federal Poverty Guideline, you need to explain the discrepancy. Most courts, rightly or wrongly, use the Federal Poverty Guidelines as a baseline for determining "undue hardship" when considering discharging federally guaranteed student loans. Very few courts have understood that undue hardship is to be evaluated at the middle-class level and reject the Federal Poverty Guidelines analysis. Thus, if your family income is more than 1 ½ time greater than that established by the Federal Poverty Guideline, be prepared to advocate the use of a more moderate middle-class analysis. See Chapter 8 for this discussion.

SECOND: Complete the Current Expenditure Status table on the next page.

Column 1— Use the data from your *Chapter 7 Bankruptcy (Form 106J)— Schedule J-Your Expenses* to fill in column 1.
Column 2 — If there have been any changes to your expenditures listed in column 1, make the changes in column 2.
Column 3 — These are national norms developed by the IRS. Go to the IRS website for Collection Financial Standards (https://www.irs.gov/businesses/small-businesses-self-employed/collection-financial-standards). Follow the links to the various standards. The boxes in column 3 represent values pulled from the IRS Collection Financial Standards. In most cases they represent a summation of a number of expenditures. Below is indicated which Collection Financial Standards are placed in the table and the expenditures they correspond. Samples of the Collection Financial Standards are in the Appendix.
    Box 1—Food, Clothing and Other Items (https://www.irs.gov/businesses/small-businesses-self-employed/national-standards-food-clothing-and-other-items) is the same as the sum of Food, Clothing, and Laundry and dry cleaning.
    Box 2—Housing and Utilities (https://www.irs.gov/businesses/small-businesses-self-employed/local-standards-housing-and-utilities) is the same as the sum of Rent, Electricity and Heating Fuel, Water and Sewer, and Telephone.
    Box 3—Transportation (ownership) (https://www.irs.gov/businesses/small-businesses-self-employed/local-standards-transportation) is the same as Installment payments—Auto.
    Box 4—Transportation (operating costs and public transportation costs) (https://www.irs.gov/businesses/small-businesses-self-employed/local-standards-transportation) is the same as Transportation (not including car payments) and Insurance—auto.
Column 4 — If your expenditures are significantly higher or lower than the national norm, then you need to write an explanation. For example, your housing costs are higher than the national norm because you live in a high rent area. A good explanation is that you live closer to work and thus save on transportation costs. Or, this places you closer to a grandparent who provided free daily childcare for your young children. Maybe your automobile expenses are higher due to higher insurance rates for those living in the city, or maybe they are very old cars requiring much repair.

Current Expenditure Status See Instructions for how to use this chart.	Col. 1 At time of Chapter 7 filing	Col. 2 Current Status (date)	Col. 3 National Norms	Col. 4 Comment
Rent or home mortgage payment (include lot rented for mobile home)			Box 2	
Are real estate taxes included? Yes ___ No ___				
Is property insurance included? Yes ___ No ___				
Utilities: Electricity and heating fuel				
Water and sewer				
Telephone				
Other _____				
Home Maintenance (Repairs and Upkeep)				
Food			Box 1	
Clothing				
Laundry and dry cleaning				
Medical and dental expenses				
Transportation (not including car payments)			Box 4	
Recreation, clubs and entertainment, newspapers, magazines, etc.				
Charitable contributions				
Insurance (not deducted from wages or included in home mortgage payments):				
Homeowner's or renter's				
Life				
Health				
Auto			Box 4	
Other _____				
Taxes (not deducted from wages or included in home mortgage payments) (specify) _____				
Installment payments (in chapter 12 and 13 cases, do not list payments to be included in the plan)				
Auto			Box 3	
Other _____				
Other _____				
Alimony, maintenance, and support paid to others				
Payments for support of additional dependents not living at your home				
Regular expenses from operation of business, profession, or farm (attach detailed statement)				
Other _____				
TOTAL MONTHLY EXPENSES				

Work Time Accounting Table

Goal: You want to show that your time working (jobs for which you receive money or expect to) and taking care of dependents exceeds approximately 60 hours a week—so that the court can't come back to you and insist that you get another job. If you are medically restricted to work fewer hours per week, make a detailed notation in the job description. Still, the goal is to show that your time is fully committed.

Make sure the work hours listed here match your income statement on your Chapter 7 bankruptcy—Schedule 106I. See the next worksheet: Financial Status to collaborate the numbers here. Create this table on your own paper.

Current Work Time Load	Hours Per Week
Job #1: Title and Company: Duties:	
Job #2: Title and Company: Duties:	
Job #3: Title and Company: Duties:	
Job #4: Title and Company: Duties:	
Dependents: (give names, ages, any medical condition)	
Dependents: (give names, ages, any medical condition)	
Total	

Income and Student Loan Payment

The purpose of this worksheet is to present your income tax reports for all years since obtaining your most recent student loan, determine if the income exceeded the Federal Poverty Guidelines, and if you made payments on your student loans.

Instructions:

1. Make a copy of the top page of your income tax filings <u>for every year from current, back to the year you last received a student loan</u>. The chart below shows you which lines of the Form 1040, 1040A and 1040 EZ apply. Fill in the <u>Income (Gross)</u>, <u>Total Income</u>, and <u>Taxable Income</u> in the marked columns in the large chart on the next page for each year.

Where to Find Tax Information by Form and Line Number

	Income (Gross)	Total Income	Taxable Income
Line Number Form 1040	7	22	36
Line Number Form 1040A	7	15	21
Line Number Form 1040 EZ	1	4	6
1040 SR	1	8b	11b

2. Go to the website of the United States Department of Health and Human Services (https://aspe.hhs.gov/poverty-guidelines) and download a copy of the Federal Poverty Guidelines (a copy of this homepage and document are in Appendix B) for all years since receiving your last student loan until now. If you do not have access to the web, your local library should have a copy of this government publication. Locate your size family in the Guidelines and write the income number in the column marked <u>Federal Poverty Guideline</u>. Indicate your family size.

3. Now compare your Total Income with the Federal Poverty Guideline. If your <u>Total Income</u> is greater than the <u>Federal Poverty Guidelines</u> for your size family, write the word "yes" in the column marked <u>Are You Above Poverty Level?</u>

4. Previously, you prepared the worksheet *Student Loan History*. From that worksheet, you should be able to tell which years you made payments on your student loans. In the chart below, indicate which years you made payments on your student loans by writing the dollar amount in the column marked <u>Student loan payments?</u> If your student loans were in forbearance or deferment, write the words "forbearance" or "deferment" as necessary in the <u>Student loan payments?</u> column.

5. If there are years in which you failed to make student loan payments or they were not in deferment or forbearance, AND your income was above the poverty level, you need to write some explanation.

Income Tax Report by Year (SAMPLE)

Year	Income (Gross)	Total Income	Taxable Income	Federal Poverty Guideline Family Size= 3	Are You Above Poverty Level?	Student loan payments?
(year you received your last student loan) 2016	15,000	14,000	13,500	14,150	no	deferment
2017	14,000	13,900	13,200	14,630	no	deferment
2018	15,000	14,500	14,500	15,020	no	deferment
2019	17,000	16,000	14,200	15,260	yes	no
2020	23,000	21,000	20,400	15,670	yes	$1,200
2021	17,500	17,000	16,500	16,090	yes	forbearance

Comments: _Example: In 2018, my family had large medical bills that made paying student loans impossible. In 2019, I got a new job that allowed me to make student loan payments. Unfortunately, I lost that job and got a new one at lower pay in 2020 due to the COVID-19 pandemic and had to delay paying my student loans._

Income Tax Report by Year

Year	Income (Gross)	Total Income	Taxable Income	Federal Poverty Guideline Family Size=	Are You Above Poverty Level?	Student loan payments?
(year you received your last student loan)						

Comments: _____

_____

_____

_____

_____

_____

_____

Worksheet Samples

Current Income and Family Status

On a blank piece of paper, write a similar letter using data from the *Current Financial Status* worksheet. **Use your own words**.

Name   SAMPLE
Date
Adversary Number [*omit if filing a Compromise or Write-Off*]

(Put the rest of this document in your own words. If you are not filing an adversary proceeding, remove all references to Chapter 7 bankruptcy and its forms.)

Current Income and Family Status
(use some other combination of terms for this title)

Since filing my Chapter 7 bankruptcy in (date), there have been changes in my income and family. My current income is $(amount).

The income I reported on Form 106I—Schedule I-Current Income of Individual Debtor(s) (give the name of the form used in your court), needs to be (increased or decreased) by ($ amount). This is due to (list reasons such as getting or losing a job, divorce or getting married, increase or reduction in federal benefits or alimony or child support, unemployment, etc.)

My family consists of:

Yourself. (Write about yourself, giving your age and medical condition. If you have medical conditions that limit your ability to work, give details about the medical conditions, how long you have had them, how it limits your ability to work, the prognosis, and include the name and contact information for your medical doctors.)

Spouse and Dependents. (Give their names, ages, how they are related, and whether or not they are working. If they have medical conditions, tell how they are disabled, how long they have been disabled, the prognosis, and detail how you support them. Be sure to tell if you have to limit work to care for a medically ill spouse or dependent. List the contact information for the medical doctors involved.)

(Medical note: If you or your spouse or dependents have medical conditions, <u>obtain a letter</u> from your physician that summarizes the problem and states the long-term prognosis.)

Current Expenditures and Minimalized Living

On a blank piece of paper, write a letter similar to that shown below using data from the *Current Expenditure Status* and the *Current Income Status* worksheets. Use your own words. This letter has three parts: (1) an update of your expense reported in your chapter 7 bankruptcy, (2) to demonstrate that all your expenses are reasonable and are kept to a minimum, and (3) it would be impossible to pay on your student loans without creating an undue hardship. Remember, you want to show that you live without extravagance, that all expenditures are necessary and minimal, and that your income just meets your expenses— thereby leaving no excess income available to pay toward student loan debt. In fact, you want to show that if you had to make student loan payments, then your family would drop to a sub-standard level of living. **Use your own words**.

Name   SAMPLE
Date
Adversary Number [*omit if filing a Compromise or Write-Off*]

(Put the rest of this document in your own words. If you are not filing an adversary proceeding, remove all references to Chapter 7 bankruptcy and its forms.)

Current Expenditures and Minimalized Living
(use some other combination of terms for this title)

Since filing my Chapter 7 bankruptcy in (date), there have been changes in my family expenses. The expenses I reported on Form 106J—Schedule J-Current Expenditure of Individual Debtor(s) (give the name of the form used in your court), needs to be (increased or decreased) by ($ amount). This is due to (list reasons such as divorce or getting married, moving, more medical problems, auto repair problems, the birth or death of a spouse or dependent, house repair, etc.)

My family lives at the Federal Poverty Level. (Write about how difficult it is to live so poorly). (Note: if you live well above the Federal Poverty Level, do not mention it here. You will address this later.)

My family expenses are kept to a minimum with no extras. (Write some more about how you save money buying used clothes at thrift stores, buying food in bulk at discount warehouse stores, that you almost never eat out or take in a movie or sporting event or other entertainment, and more. Be sure to mention if you do not have health insurance, bank savings, or any retirement funds. If medical expenses are a major problem, be sure to mention them.)

My family expenses just match (or exceed) my family income. If I were required to pay on my student loans, then my family would be pushed into a sub-minimal living standard, and this would be an undue hardship.

Work Time Accounting Statement

On a blank piece of paper, write a letter similar to the one shown below using data from the *Work time Account Table* worksheets. Explain in your own words why all your time is committed, and it would be impossible for you to take on another job. **Use your own words**.

Name   SAMPLE
Date
Adversary Number [*omit if filing a Compromise or Write-Off*]

(Put the rest of this document in your own words.)

Work Time Accounting
(use some other combination of terms for this title)

I currently work (quantity) hours a week as a (title) with (company name). With travel time included, (quantity) hours a week are devoted to paid employment. (If you have more than one paying job, expand this paragraph to list each one.)

I also work part-time for (company name) performing (sales, grant writing, etc.—something where you are only paid if you make a sale). This takes (quantity) hours per week, and I am only paid if I make the (sale, grant, promotion, etc.).

At home, I take care of (list dependents) for (quantity) hours per week. (If they have medical needs, list the problems).

Combining my time on the job and caring for my dependents, I am committed (quantity—should be more than a 40-hour week) each week. It would be impossible for me to take on any more work or responsibility.

Personal Limitations Statement

The purpose of this letter is to detail any <u>personal limitations</u> that may impact your ability to work and, therefore, service your student loan debt. This includes personal medical limitations, support of dependents (and their medical conditions, if applicable), and lack of useable job skills. These need to be described in detail and with supporting documents (like medical records). Your letter will probably be longer than one page.

Here are the guidelines for composing your letter:

• Medical Limitations
If you have medical problems that contributed to your bankruptcy, discuss the following:
1. How your medical condition contributed to your bankruptcy. Here you need to give a complete history of your medical condition and subsequent loss of work and income.
2. That your medical condition will continue into the future, most likely become worse, and that it will be impossible to make payments on the student loans. It helps to find a physician who will write you a letter claiming that you are disabled or partially disabled, and that it will persist for many years to come.

• Dependents
Courts are aware that dependents cause time constraints for debtors who otherwise could use the time for employment. Thus, the greater the number of dependents and the time involved in their care directly impact the debtor's ability to repay student loans.
1. <u>Children</u>: Courts make the assumption that children will leave home at 18-years of age. Thus, courts will calculate when the youngest child is expected to leave home and try to determine if the debtor would then be capable of resuming payments on his or her student loans. Extenuating circumstances would be if the child is disabled and will continue to reside with the parent.
2. <u>Spouse, Civil Union, or Domestic Partner</u>: Courts are sensitive to the situation where debtors provide financial and emotional support for medically ill spouses (whether by marriage, Civil Union, or Domestic Partnership). Unlike with children, there is no assumption the spouse will leave home. You are encouraged to combine the care of a medically ill spouse with other factors that will impact your future ability to make income.
3. <u>Elderly or Medically Ill Parents or Siblings</u>: There have been a number of cases where courts have shown themselves insensitive to debtors who take care of elderly or medically ill parents or siblings. The courts question why the debtor is taking care of these people. It may seem obvious to the debtor, but it is not to the court. Debtors need to make a strong case as to why it is they, and not their siblings, parents, or the government taking care of these people. If this is your situation, you may want to discuss your moral or religious convictions that have influenced you to be the caretaker of these people. Too often, courts take the position that the debtor should not take on this responsibility and, instead, focus on paying back student loans.

• Lack of Useable Job Skills
A good number of debtors filing bankruptcy have student loans from training programs they either did not complete, or the program was of such dubious value that the debtor gained no improved job skills. Courts have been sensitive to debtors who lack useable job skills. They are aware that without proper job skills, it is very difficult for debtors to obtain high-paying employment and, subsequently, be able to make student loan payments. In this situation, you are encouraged to forcibly show the court how your low job skills are preventing you from getting a good job. Of course, the court may respond by asking why you don't educate yourself further and get a better job. The best answer is to show working <u>and</u> taking care of dependents is consuming all your time making it impossible to obtain more education.

Use your own words.

Name   **SAMPLE**
Date
Adversary Number [*omit if filing a Compromise or Write-Off*]

(Put the rest of this document in your own words.)

Personal Limitations
(create your own title)

I have a number of personal issues that limit my future ability to work and earn sufficient income to service my student loan debt.

(Talk about yours and your dependent's medical conditions and how they will persist into the future.)

(Write about your dependents and how their care interferes with you obtaining higher income.)

(Explain how your low work skills are impacting your ability to work.)

These conditions affect my future ability to make sufficient income to service my student loans. There is no indication that I will ever earn enough to repay my student loans.

[Your letter should be much longer and in greater detail.]

Good Faith and Loan Repayment Statement

Instructions:

On a blank piece of paper, write a letter similar to the one shown on the next page. You will be blending the data you created on the worksheets *Income and Student Loan Payment* and *Student Loan History* with your own work and life history. The goal of the narrative is to show:
1. That you worked. If you were out of work or your income was too low, you sought work or had a legitimate medical disability.
2. Whenever your family income exceeded the Federal Poverty Guideline, you made payments on your student loans. If you could not make payments due to medical or other problems, you obtained deferments or forbearances on the loans.
3. If your family income dropped below the Federal Poverty Guideline, you obtained deferments or forbearances on the loans.
4. Ultimately, you want to show that it will be impossible to service your student loan debt.

In many cases, debtors will be deposition by the Department of Education attorneys regarding their work and family history. This can be nerve-racking. By writing this history in advance, you will be clear about details. You can take your time and accurately compile information without being under pressure. In fact, if you give this history to the other side before mediation, the deposition may be waived.

In your work and life history, include any and all topics below that apply):

Employments/ Job Firings
Dependents
Schooling and Career Choices
Changes in living conditions

Marriages/ Divorces
Discriminations
Medical Conditions
And more to show your struggles

Tell your story in your own words.

Name SAMPLE
Date
Adversary Number [*omit if filing a Compromise or Write-Off*]

(Put the rest of this document in your own words. If you are not filing an adversary proceeding, remove all references to Chapter 7 bankruptcy and its forms.)

Good Faith and Loan Repayment
(use some other combination of terms for this title)

My student loan debt of $(amount) represents about (quantity)% of my total debt being discharged through Chapter 7 bankruptcy. The last time I received a student loan was (how many) years ago.

I obtained my (degree or certificate) in (year), and it is the last year I received a student loan. I immediately looked for higher paying work. I applied for more than 200 jobs but did not get any new job (be sure you can verify the efforts to find work). I contacted my lender, who granted a deferment.

The next two years, I applied for hundreds more jobs but without success. I did get an additional part-time job that increased the family's income to just above the poverty level. However, my spouse experienced severe medical problems (specify in detail) that consumed all spare cash. Later that year, I lost my job and my student loans became due because of failure to make payment. Luckily, in early 2004, I got a well-paying job that increased our family income to almost $5,000 above the Federal Poverty Level. That year I paid $1,200 toward my student loans.

Two-thousand-five was a rough year. I lost my job but found another a few months later paying just above the Federal Poverty Level. My spouse is ill again, and we have no savings. I contacted my student loan lender and received a forbearance.

I have been diligent in trying to service my student loans, and there is no fraud in seeking their discharge.

(Your letter may be much longer and in greater detail than this sample.)

Income-Driven Repayment (IDR) Plans

On a blank piece of paper, write a statement similar to the one shown below. Use your own words. You are stating why any of the IDR plans are not an appropriate repayment plan in your situation.

Use your own words.

Name   SAMPLE
Date
Adversary Number [*omit if filing a Compromise or Write-Off*]

(Put the rest of this document in your own words)

Income-Driven Repayment Plans
(use some other combination of terms for this title)

The Income-Driven Repayment plans are not an appropriate repayment plan for my student loans. I am (over 50 years old, or living on federal benefits) and the tax liability after twenty-five years would prove an undue hardship. It will be impossible for me, because I will be living on a fixed and limited income to pay the income taxes on the discharged loans. As such, the IDR represents an undue hardship and cannot be implemented in my case.

(Your letter may be much longer and in greater detail than this sample. See the discussion in Chapter 8 Advocacy for many more arguments against the IDR Plans. Include as many of these arguments you feel apply to your case.)

APPENDIX E
Forms for Adversary Proceeding

This section of the Appendix contains all the legal forms needed to file an Adversary Proceeding. The forms are presented three ways—

- First, the forms are given with detailed **INSTRUCTION(S)** regarding their completion.

- Second, the forms are completed using fictitious names and data so you can see a finished **SAMPLE** form.

- Third, **BLANK** forms are provide for you to fill in with your specific information.

Forms—Instructions

This section of the Appendix gives detailed instructions for completing several of the forms needed for filing an adversary proceeding. Check with your local bankruptcy court for their forms. Although the forms are supposed to be standardized between all courts, they are not.

Blue Back

Many courts require all papers filed with the clerk to be assembled in what is termed a "blue back." How it is constructed is shown on the next page.

Adversary Proceeding Sheet (Cover)

The bankruptcy court where the adversary complaint is filed requires a cover sheet to be placed on top of the complaint. The federal form B1040 (12/15) has two pages. Both pages need to be completed along with a mailing matrix.

Adversary Proceeding Complaint

There are many variations for writing an adversary complaint. Here is shown a basic version that can be altered according to the needs of the court and whether or not you want to advocate for the abolition of §523(a)(8).

Summons

The court issues a summons for the first court hearing (otherwise known as a status hearing). The instructions here are for the federal form F 7004-1 page 1. Check with the clerk for one for your district.

Proof of Service

After serving the complaint and summons, the court needs documentation that the service was done appropriately; Federal form F 7004-1 page 2 fulfills that need.

Mail Matrix

Attached to the Proof of Service is the Mail Matrix.

Proof of Service Cover

To file the proof of service, a cover may be required by the court. A sample is given here.

Blue Back

All original petitions and pleadings must be "backed" to aid in easy identification of documents in case files. "Backing" is paper that resembles construction paper. The Court requires blue backs in the standard size of 9" wide by 11 ¾" in length with a ¾" top flap. You may obtain backing from any stationery store. The court does not sell nor is it obligated to provide blue backs. Staple the backing to the petition or pleading in the following manner:

- Mount original petition or pleading on backing, face side up and flush with the top, centered.
- Staple complete ORIGINAL petition or pleading on the left corner only.
- Hole-punch original petition or pleading by placing two standard size holes, centered 2 ¾" apart. A standard home/office stapler usually has adjustments to allow this spacing.
- Type a short title of petition or pleading on the lower right-hand corner of the backing. You may type this on a small label and place the label in the lower right-hand corner.

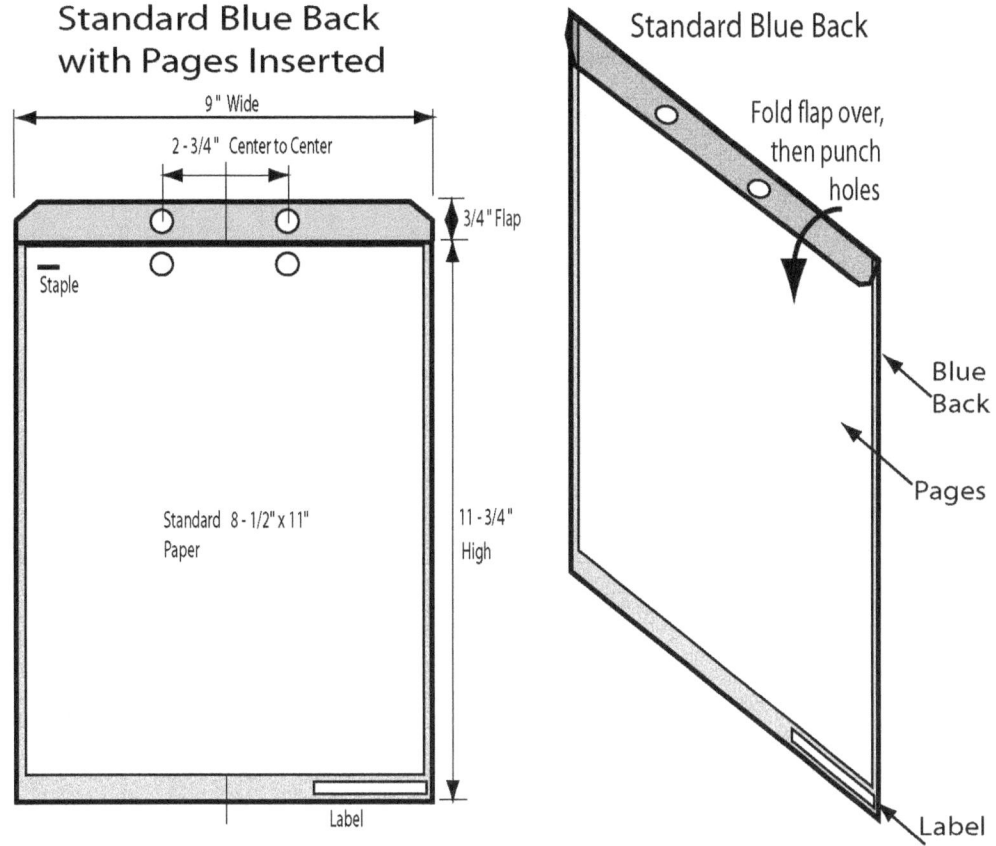

Who Handles My Loans?

https://studentaid.gov/manage-loans/repayment/servicers

The information contained on this page helps you identify your loan servicer. It can be very confusing who handles your loans as they are bought and sold between many companies and the U.S. government. Please conduct your research now to identify who owns your loans as that information is needed on the adversary documentation.

What Loan Servicers Do

A loan servicer is a company that we assign to handle the billing and other services on your federal student loan on our behalf, at no cost to you. Your loan servicer will work with you on repayment options (such as income-driven repayment plans and loan consolidation) and will assist you with other tasks related to your federal student loans.

Keep your contact information up to date so your loan servicer can help you stay on track with repaying your loans. If your circumstances change at any time during your repayment period, your loan servicer will be able to help.

Never pay an outside company for help with your federal student loans. Your loan servicer will help you for FREE. Contact your servicer to apply for income-driven repayment plans, student loan forgiveness, and more.

Identifying Your Servicer

The following are loan servicers for loans that the U.S Department of Education (ED) owns. To find out who your loan servicer is, call the Federal Student Aid Information Center (FSAIC) at 1-800-433-3243.

Loan Servicer	Contact
CornerStone	1-800-663-1662
FedLoan Servicing (PHEAA)	1-800-699-2908
Granite State – GSMR	1-888-556-0022
Great Lakes Educational Loan Services, Inc.	1-800-236-4300
HESC/Edfinancial	1-855-337-6884
MOHELA	1-888-866-4352
Navient	1-800-722-1300
Nelnet	1-888-486-4722
OSLA Servicing	1-866-264-9762
ECSI	1-866-313-3797
Default Resolution Group (also known as Maximus Federal Services, Inc.)	1-800-621-3115 (TTY: 1-877-825-9923 for the deaf or hard of hearing)

Whom to Contact for Loan Information

If your loan is for the current or upcoming school year, contact your school's financial aid office directly for information about
- loan status,

- the timeframes for cancelling all or part of your loan or loan disbursement, and
- loan disbursement amounts and timing.

Only your school's financial aid office can provide this information.

If your loan was disbursed in a past school year and you are still in school, keep your contact information up to date with your school and contact your loan servicer when you
- withdraw,
- graduate,
- drop below half-time enrollment, or
- stop going to school.

If you are no longer in school, contact your loan servicer when you
- change your name, address, or phone number;
- need help making your loan payment;
- have a question about your bill; or
- have other questions about your student loan.

Contact Information for Loans Not Owned by ED

If you have FFEL Program loans that are not owned by ED, contact your servicer for details about repayment options and tools. Not sure who your servicer is? Look for the most recent communication from the entity sending you bills for your loan payments.

If you have Federal Perkins Loans that are not owned by ED, contact the school where you received your Federal Perkins Loan for details about repaying your loan. Your school may be the servicer for your loan.

If you have HEAL Program loans and you are not in default, contact your loan servicer for help with account-related questions. Use the contact information your loan servicer provided to you. Not sure who your servicer is? Look for the most recent communication from the entity sending you bills for your loan payments.

If you have HEAL Program loans and you are in default, contact the Debt Collection Center for help with account-related questions:

For mail sent via U.S. Postal Service:
Accounting Services, Debt Collection Center
Mailstop 10230B
7700 Wisconsin Avenue, Suite 8-8110D
Bethesda, MD 20857

For mail sent via UPS or FedEx:
HHS Program Support Center
Accounting Services, Debt Collection Center
Mailstop Seventh Floor
7700 Wisconsin Avenue, Suite 8-8110D
Bethesda, MD 20814
Phone: 301-492-4664

Understanding Loan Transfers

In some cases, we need to transfer loans from one servicer to another servicer. If we transfer your federal student loans from one servicer to another servicer, your loans will still be owned by ED. The "transfer" to another servicer simply means that a new servicer will provide the support you need to fully repay your loans.

Here's what you should expect if your loan is transferred to a new servicer:
- You will receive an email or a letter from your assigned servicer to inform you about the transfer.
- You will receive a welcome letter from the new servicer after the new servicer receives your loans. This notice will provide you with the contact information for the new servicer and inform you of actions that you may need to take.
- All of your loan information will be transferred from your assigned servicer to your new servicer, but you may only be able to see online information that covers the period since your new servicer took your loans over.
- There will be no change in the terms of your loans.
- Your previous loan servicer and new loan servicer will work together to make sure that all payments you make during the transfer process are credited to your loan account with the new servicer.

After you receive the welcome letter from your new servicer, you should do the following:
- Begin sending your loan payments to your new servicer. If you use a bank or bill paying service to make your loan payments, update the new servicer's contact information with the bank or bill paying service.
- Follow the new servicer's instructions for creating an online account so that you can more easily communicate with the new servicer and keep track of your loan account.

Avoid Paying for Federal Student Loan Assistance

You don't have to pay to receive help with loan services such as consolidating your federal student loans or applying for an income-driven repayment plan.

If you are contacted by a company asking you to pay "enrollment," "subscription," or "maintenance" fees to enroll you in a federal repayment plan or forgiveness program, you should walk away.

These services and more can be completed by your servicer for **free!**

Want to learn more? Read our blog post called "Don't Be Fooled: You Never Have to Pay for Student Loan Help."

Adversary Proceeding Cover Sheet

The following page shows where you fill in the form. A finished sample is given in the next section of the Appendix. A blank form is given in the Appendix.

It is suggested that you type your response. However, the person who successfully had $225,000 in student loans discharged through bankruptcy hand printed his information in the forms. Obviously, you don't need to type these forms.

Instructions:

BOX MARKED AS—	ACTION
Page 1	
PLAINTIFFS	type your first and last name, address, city, state, and zip code
DEFENDANTS	type the name of the defendant along with their address. Most likely the defendant is the United States Department of Education Direct Loan Servicing. Verify this by contacting the Department of Education. See the previous page to help you locate who owns your loan. https://studentaid.gov/manage-loans/repayment/servicers
ATTORNEYS (under Plaintiffs)	type — *None*
ATTORNEYS (under Defendants)	type — *In Pro Per*
PARTY (Plaintiffs)	place check mark in first box — *Debtor*
PARTY (Defendants)	place check mark in second box — *Creditor*
CAUSE OF ACTION	type — *Plaintiff seeks dischargeability of debt pursuant to 11 U.S.C.A. §523(a)(8).*
NATURE OF SUIT	place check mark in box next to — *63-Dischargeability - §523(a)(8), student loan*
DEMAND $	type approximate amount of debt.
Page 2	
NAME OF DEBTOR	type your first and last name
BANKRUPTCY CASE NUMBER	type your bankruptcy case number
DISTRICT IN WHICH CASE IS PENDING	type the name of your district court
DIVISIONAL OFFICE	type the division the bankruptcy court is located
DATE	type the date the adversary proceeding is filed.
SIGNATURE OF ATTORNEY (OR PLAINTIFF)	sign your name.

B1040 (FORM 1040) (12/15)

ADVERSARY PROCEEDING COVER SHEET (Instructions on Reverse)	ADVERSARY PROCEEDING NUMBER (Court Use Only)
PLAINTIFFS (Your Name) (Your street, city, state, zip)	**DEFENDANTS** (Most likely this address: United States Department of Education Direct Loan Servicing PO Box 4609 Utica, NY 13504-4609)
ATTORNEYS (Firm Name, Address, and Telephone No.) None	**ATTORNEYS** (If Known) In Pro Per
PARTY (Check One Box Only) ☑ Debtor ☐ U.S. Trustee/Bankruptcy Admin ☐ Creditor ☐ Other ☐ Trustee	**PARTY** (Check One Box Only) ☐ Debtor ☐ U.S. Trustee/Bankruptcy Admin ☑ Creditor ☐ Other ☐ Trustee
CAUSE OF ACTION (WRITE A BRIEF STATEMENT OF CAUSE OF ACTION, INCLUDING ALL U.S. STATUTES INVOLVED) Plaintiff seeks dischargeability of debt pursuant to 11 U.S.C. §523(a)(8)	

NATURE OF SUIT

(Number up to five (5) boxes starting with lead cause of action as 1, first alternative cause as 2, second alternative cause as 3, etc.)

FRBP 7001(1) – Recovery of Money/Property ☐ 11-Recovery of money/property - §542 turnover of property ☐ 12-Recovery of money/property - §547 preference ☐ 13-Recovery of money/property - §548 fraudulent transfer ☐ 14-Recovery of money/property - other **FRBP 7001(2) – Validity, Priority or Extent of Lien** ☐ 21-Validity, priority or extent of lien or other interest in property **FRBP 7001(3) – Approval of Sale of Property** ☐ 31-Approval of sale of property of estate and of a co-owner - §363(h) **FRBP 7001(4) – Objection/Revocation of Discharge** ☐ 41-Objection / revocation of discharge - §727(c),(d),(e) **FRBP 7001(5) – Revocation of Confirmation** ☐ 51-Revocation of confirmation **FRBP 7001(6) – Dischargeability** ☐ 66-Dischargeability - §523(a)(1),(14),(14A) priority tax claims ☐ 62-Dischargeability - §523(a)(2), false pretenses, false representation, actual fraud ☐ 67-Dischargeability - §523(a)(4), fraud as fiduciary, embezzlement, larceny **(continued next column)**	**FRBP 7001(6) – Dischargeability (continued)** ☐ 61-Dischargeability - §523(a)(5), domestic support ☐ 68-Dischargeability - §523(a)(6), willful and malicious injury ☑ 63-Dischargeability - §523(a)(8), student loan ☐ 64-Dischargeability - §523(a)(15), divorce or separation obligation (other than domestic support) ☐ 65-Dischargeability - other **FRBP 7001(7) – Injunctive Relief** ☐ 71-Injunctive relief – imposition of stay ☐ 72-Injunctive relief – other **FRBP 7001(8) Subordination of Claim or Interest** ☐ 81-Subordination of claim or interest **FRBP 7001(9) Declaratory Judgment** ☐ 91-Declaratory judgment **FRBP 7001(10) Determination of Removed Action** ☐ 01-Determination of removed claim or cause **Other** ☐ SS-SIPA Case – 15 U.S.C. §§78aaa *et.seq.* ☐ 02-Other (e.g. other actions that would have been brought in state court if unrelated to bankruptcy case)
☐ Check if this case involves a substantive issue of state law	☐ Check if this is asserted to be a class action under FRCP 23
☐ Check if a jury trial is demanded in complaint	Demand $ (your debt amount)
Other Relief Sought	

B1040 (FORM 1040) (12/15)

BANKRUPTCY CASE IN WHICH THIS ADVERSARY PROCEEDING ARISES			
NAME OF DEBTOR (Your Name)		BANKRUPTCY CASE NO. (type in your bankruptcy case number)	
DISTRICT IN WHICH CASE IS PENDING (type in the name of your district court)		DIVISION OFFICE (type in the name of the division your bankruptcy court)	NAME OF JUDGE
RELATED ADVERSARY PROCEEDING (IF ANY)			
PLAINTIFF	DEFENDANT		ADVERSARY PROCEEDING NO.
DISTRICT IN WHICH ADVERSARY IS PENDING		DIVISION OFFICE	NAME OF JUDGE
SIGNATURE OF ATTORNEY (OR PLAINTIFF)			
DATE (Date of signing)		PRINT NAME OF ATTORNEY (OR PLAINTIFF) (Your Name)	

INSTRUCTIONS

The filing of a bankruptcy case creates an "estate" under the jurisdiction of the bankruptcy court which consists of all of the property of the debtor, wherever that property is located. Because the bankruptcy estate is so extensive and the jurisdiction of the court so broad, there may be lawsuits over the property or property rights of the estate. There also may be lawsuits concerning the debtor's discharge. If such a lawsuit is filed in a bankruptcy court, it is called an adversary proceeding.

A party filing an adversary proceeding must also must complete and file Form 1040, the Adversary Proceeding Cover Sheet, unless the party files the adversary proceeding electronically through the court's Case Management/Electronic Case Filing system (CM/ECF). (CM/ECF captures the information on Form 1040 as part of the filing process.) When completed, the cover sheet summarizes basic information on the adversary proceeding. The clerk of court needs the information to process the adversary proceeding and prepare required statistical reports on court activity.

The cover sheet and the information contained on it do not replace or supplement the filing and service of pleadings or other papers as required by law, the Bankruptcy Rules, or the local rules of court. The cover sheet, which is largely self-explanatory, must be completed by the plaintiff's attorney (or by the plaintiff if the plaintiff is not represented by an attorney). A separate cover sheet must be submitted to the clerk for each complaint filed.

Plaintiffs and Defendants. Give the names of the plaintiffs and defendants exactly as they appear on the complaint.

Attorneys. Give the names and addresses of the attorneys, if known.

Party. Check the most appropriate box in the first column for the plaintiffs and the second column for the defendants.

Demand. Enter the dollar amount being demanded in the complaint.

Signature. This cover sheet must be signed by the attorney of record in the box on the second page of the form. If the plaintiff is represented by a law firm, a member of the firm must sign. If the plaintiff is pro se, that is, not represented by an attorney, the plaintiff must sign.

Adversary Proceeding Complaint

The following pages show where you fill in the form. A finished sample is given in the next section of the Appendix.

The sample given here is for a <u>basic adversary complaint</u>. There are two variations of this form that are discussed below. Some courts may require you to give details in the initial complaint as to why you cannot repay the loan. In general, if you are going to be pushed into mediation, you can use the simpler basic form given below. During mediation and subsequent deposition, all the particular information about your dire condition will come out. So, before filling out this form, find out if you will be going to mediation. More than 90% of the bankruptcy courts will require you to go to mediation. Of course, you can always request mediation. If you need to include in the adversary complaint greater information about why you cannot repay your loans, look at the <u>Alternate Ending1</u> shown later in this Appendix.

The second condition that will alter this form is if you are going to advocate changing or rescinding the bankruptcy law 11 U.S.C.A. §523(a) (8). This is discussed at length in the book. If you want to include challenges to the law, there are additional items to include in the adversary complaint. These are detailed below as <u>Alternate Ending 2</u>.

Instructions:

It is suggested that you type your response. However, one debtor who had $225,000 in student loans, successfully discharged the loans through bankruptcy by simply whiting-out the appropriate sections of the form and hand printed his information. Obviously, you don't need to type these forms.

Use this instructional form and sample to show you how to type the complaint. Use legal paper as instructed by the court. Blank legal paper is provided in this book. Make copies of the blank paper. However, remember that every time you make a photocopy, it shrinks by 2% and typing on such paper may be difficult to line up in your typewriter. It is strongly suggested that you buy legal numbered paper at a stationery store.

If you look at the bottom of the form, you will see that a short title of the document is printed to the left of the page number and your name, address, and phone number is printed to the right of the page number. You do not need to include this kind of information in the footer. It is a convenience for the court. However, you must have the page number <u>centered in the footer</u>. Notice that the footer is below the last numbered line.

Copy the next page onto numbered legal paper. Items that are italicized are items that you need to fill in. The following table guides you in filling in the italicized items:

Line Number	Action
Page 1	
1.	type your first and last name, and that of your spouse if you are filing jointly.
2.	type your address.
2.5	type your city, state, zip.
3.	type your phone number.
4.	type — *In Pro Per*.
8.	type the name of the district bankruptcy court.
9.	type the name of the bankruptcy court division.
11.	type your first and last name.
12.	type your bankruptcy case number.

16.	type the name of the defendant. Most likely this is the *United States Department of Education*. This may include a guarantee agency and any other collection agency. See the section "Who Has My Loans?"
16.	type the date the complaint was filed.

At this point, you may want to make a few copies of the page so far. This "header" paper may be necessary for future filings (like filing the *Proof of Service* described later) and it will save you time and potential mistakes to use these copies. Now take one of your copies and continue copying and filling in from line 20 on down.

24.	type your first and last name.
26.	type your first and last name.
27.	type the date you filed your chapter 7 bankruptcy.
27.	type the name of your chapter 7 trustee.
Page 2	
2.	if you have dependents, include the line.
5.	type the name of the defendant.
6.	type the names of the educational institutions from which the loans were used. Indicated if a degree was attained.
10.	type the name of the defendant.
11.	type the address of the defendant.
21.	type the approximate amount of the debt.

Once your complete copying down to and including line 24, you will need to decide if you are going to use one of the alternate endings (changes to item 8). If you are filing the basic complaint, continue on. If you are using one of the alternate forms, see details below.

27.	type your pronoun.
Page 3	
1.	type your pronoun.
4.	type your pronoun.
8.	type the date.
12.	sign your name.
13.	type your first and last name.

Alternate Endings

Alternate Ending 1— If you are required to include details about why you cannot repay the debt, item 8 (line 25 page 2) of the basic adversary complaint needs to be expanded.

Follow all the steps above for pages 1 and 2, stopping at line 25 page 2.
Instead of items 8 and 9, we are expanding item 8 into 3 more items and renumbering item 9 as item 11. Copy the following onto your complaint. Italicized items need your input. Replace items 8 and 9 with the following:

  8. Based on the Debtor(s) current income and expenses, the Debtor(s) cannot maintain a minimal standard of living and at the same time repay (*his/her*) student loan(s). (*Now give details about your current income, the sources of your income, your employment, education, work skills, potential for work, personal and family health, and support obligations.*)
  9. The Debtor(s)' current financial status most likely will continue for a significant portion of the repayment period of the loan. (*Now give details about the conditions that are preventing you from getting more income. Examples would be poor health, care of dependents and more. You have developed your arguments in Chapter 8.*)
  10. The Debtor(s) has made a good-faith effort to repay on (*his/her*) student loans. (*Give details about your student loan payment history and other attempts to repay or reschedule the loans.*)
  11. The Debtor has filed for bankruptcy for reasons other than just to discharge (*his/her*) student loans.

Now finish the complaint and copy page 3 line 5 to 13, filing in the date, your name, and signing the document.

Alternate Ending 2 — If you want to include challenges to the bankruptcy law, you must list challenges in the Adversary Complaint. Chapter 8 discussed a wide range of deficiencies in the law that are open to legal challenges. We really advise you seek the help of an attorney to word your challenges correctly. Another approach is to seek the help of law students who need a special project for school and may take on the opportunity to help you in your challenge of the law.

Challenging the law may result in it being overturned. That would be a big help to so many other honest debtors. Challenging the law is also about the only avenue open to middle-class debtors who otherwise would not qualify for an "undue hardship" discharge.

(your name)
(address)
(city, state, zip)
(telephone)
In Pro Per

UNITED STATED BANKRUPTCY COURT
(name of district)
(name of division)

(your name)	) CHAPTER 7 BANKRUPTCY CASE
	) (bankruptcy case number)
PLAINTIFF,	)
	)
vs.	) ADV. NO.
	)
(name of defendant-- most likely	) COMPLAINT FILED: (date)
UNITED STATES DEPARTMENT	) DEPT:
OF EDUCATION),	) JUDGE:
	)
DEFENDANT	)

COMPLAINT TO DETERMINE DISCHARGEABILITY OF DEBT
PURSUANT TO 11 U.S.C. §523(a)(8)

(*your name*), Debtor and Plaintiff in the above captioned adversary proceeding, represents as follows:

1. (*your name*) filed a voluntary petition for relief under Chapter 7 of the United States Bankruptcy Code on (*date*). (*name*) is the duly appointed Chapter 7

trustee. This complaint seeks to determine the dischargeability of a student loan as it presents an undue hardship for the Debtor (*and his/her dependents*).

2. One of the unsecured debts owing by the Debtor and listed on Schedule F—Creditors Holding Unsecured Nonpriority Claims— is a student loan owing to (*most likely United States Department of Education*).

3. This loan was incurred to pay expenses at (*list colleges where debt was assumed and indicate if degree was obtained*).

JURISDICTION

4. Defendant (*most likely United States Department of Education*) maintains its (*address – most likely Direct Loan Servicing Center in Utica, New York*) (*verify this address*).

5. Jurisdiction exists under 28 U.S.C. §1334. Venue is proper under 28 U.S.C. §1409(a). The District Court has generally referred these matters to the Bankruptcy Court for hearing pursuant to 28 U.S.C. §157(a). This is a core proceeding within the meaning of 28 U.S.C. §157(b)(2)(I). This adversary complaint is brought pursuant to 11 U.S.C. §523(a)(8).

FIRST CAUSE OF ACTION [11 U.S.C. §523(a)(8)]

6. Plaintiff is indebted to the Defendant in the approximate sum of $(*amount*) for education loans made by Defendant to Plaintiff.

7. Requiring Plaintiff to repay these debts will impose undue hardship on the Debtor and the Debtor's dependents as contemplated under 11 U.S.C. §523(a)(8).

8. Based upon Plaintiff's current income and expenses, Plaintiff cannot maintain a minimum standard of living if forced to repay the loan. Plaintiff believes that (*his/her*) economic state of affairs is likely to persist for a significant

portion of the repayment period and (*he/she*) has made good faith efforts to repay the loans.

    9. The Debtor has filed for bankruptcy for reasons other than just to discharge (*his/her*) student loan.

WHEREFORE, the Debtor asks this court to enter an Order declaring the student loan debt to be dischargeable.

Date: (*date*).

                                                    _____
                                                    Plaintiff (*your name*)

PLAINTIFF'S COMPLAINT TO DETERMINE
DISCHARGEABILITY OF DEBT

YOUR NAME
ADDRESS
CITY, STATE, ZIP
TELEPHONE

Summons

You may or may not need to fill out this form before filing the adversary complaint with the bankruptcy clerk. Usually, you ask for the form from the clerks, they give you a blank one, you fill in the information, then get back in line to complete filing the adversary complaint. They fill out the rest and give you a conformed copy (stamped). Regardless, seeing the form here will prepare you for when you are given one. We suggest that you complete this form and take it with you even if you don't use it.

The form here is for the Central District of California. It will help in preparing your own form. Use the correct form specified for your bankruptcy court.

Instructions for *Summons and Notice of Status Conference — Page 1*:

BOX MARKED AS—	ACTION
ATTORNEY OR PARTY	type your first and last name, address, city, state, and zip code
ATTORNEY OR PLAINTIFF	type — *In Pro Per*
DEBTOR	type your first and last name
PLAINTIFF(S), VS. DEFENDANT(S)	type your first and last name alongside Plaintiff(s). type name of Defendant— most likely the *United States Dept. of Education Direct Loan Servicing*.
CHAPTER	type — 7
CASE NUMBER	type your bankruptcy case number

The clerk will assign:

- Adversary Case Number
- Status Conference:
    - Date and time of Hearing
    - Court Address indicating Courtroom and Floor

Attorney or Party Name, Address, Telephone & FAX Numbers, and California State Bar Number	FOR COURT USE ONLY
(name) (address) (city, state, zip) *Attorney for Plaintiff* In Pro Per	

UNITED STATES BANKRUPTCY COURT
CENTRAL DISTRICT OF CALIFORNIA

In re: (your name) Debtor.	CHAPTER __7__ CASE NUMBER (bankruptcy number) ADVERSARY NUMBER (adversary number)
(your name) Plaintiff(s), vs. (most likely United States Dept. of Education Direct Loan Servicing) Defendant(s).	*(The Boxes and Blank Lines below are for the Court's Use Only) (Do Not Fill Them In)* **SUMMONS AND NOTICE OF STATUS CONFERENCE**

TO THE DEFENDANT: A Complaint has been filed by the Plaintiff against you. If you wish to defend yourself, you must file with the Court a written pleading, in duplicate, in response to the Complaint. You must also send a copy of your written response to the party shown in the upper left-hand corner of this page. Unless you have filed in duplicate and served a responsive pleading by _____, the Court may enter a judgment by default against you for the relief demanded in the Complaint.

A Status Conference on the proceeding commenced by the Complaint has been set for:

Hearing Date: **Time:**   **Courtroom:**   **Floor:**

❏ 255 East Temple Street, Los Angeles   ❏ 411 West Fourth Street, Santa Ana
❏ 21041 Burbank Boulevard, Woodland Hills   ❏ 1415 State Street, Santa Barbara
❏ 3420 Twelfth Street, Riverside

PLEASE TAKE NOTICE that if the trial of the proceeding is anticipated to take less than two (2) hours, the parties may stipulate to conduct the trial of the case on the date specified, instead of holding a Status Conference. Such a stipulation must be lodged with the Court at least two (2) Court days before the date set forth above and is subject to Court approval. The Court may continue the trial to another date if necessary to accommodate the anticipated length of the trial.

Date of Issuance: _____

Clerk of the Bankruptcy Court

By: _____
Deputy Clerk

This form is mandatory. It has been approved for use by the United States Bankruptcy Court for the Central District of California.

Revised December 1998 (COA-SA)   **F 7004-1**

Proof of Service with Mail Matrix and Cover

Once the complaint has been filed and the court summons issued, the papers must be served on all parties and the court given proof that they were served. Here is an illustrative sample Proof of Service with Mail Matrix and Cover used in the California Central District. Check with your court for their forms. It is the person who performs the service that fills out these forms, not the debtor.

Before filling out this form, contact the Department of Education and the bankruptcy court to verify the names and addresses for service:

- Office of the U.S. Trustee in you bankruptcy district.
- Civil process clerk at the office of the United States attorney for the district in which the action is brought (local U.S. Attorney used to defend the case).
- The Attorney General in Washington, D.C.
- Particular agency named in or affected by the lawsuit (most likely the Dept. of Education).
- Your Chapter 7 bankruptcy trustee.

Samples of these forms are given later in the Appendix.

Instructions for *Summons and Notice of Status Conference – Page 2*:

BOX OR LINE	ACTION
IN RE	type your first and last name (name of debtor)
CHAPTER	type — 7
CASE NUMBER	type your bankruptcy case number
Under the box marked CHAPTER	type — *Adversary Number* (with your number)
STATE OF CALIF., COUNTY OF	type your county
1.	type your county
In space below item 1	type the business address of the person who is serving the notice.
2. (first line)	Check off box and type — *See Attached Service List*
2. (last line)	type name of city notice mailed from
3.	Check off box and type name of local U.S. Attorney.
4.	type name and address of local U.S. Attorney
4. (box)	Check off box indicating *Names and Address continued on attached page* (otherwise known as a Mail Matrix).
DATED	type date
TYPE NAME	Type the name of the person making the hand delivery and mailing the notices.
SIGNATURE	The person making the deliveries of these notices signs the form.

Instructions for *Mail Matrix* attachment:
See the Mail Matrix form. It is self-explanatory.

Instructions for *Proof of Service* cover: After the Summons and Complaint are hand-delivered and mailed to all parties, the Proof of Service is filed with the court.

When you prepared your Adversary Complaint, we asked that you make a few extra copies of the first page after completing the "header" but before writing the title or body. This provided you with "header" paper for future filings. Here is where we will use one of these copies. Simply type in the title *PROOF OF SERVICE OF SUMMONS AND COMPLAINT* on line 19.

For your reference, an instructional header is given two pages from here and given the title "Proof of Service of Summons and Complaint."

If you need to create a new header paper for this cover, here are the steps:

On lined legal paper type the following—

Line Number	Action
Page 1	
1.	type your first and last name, and that of your spouse if you are filing jointly.
2.	type your address.
2.5	type your city, state, zip.
3.	type your phone number.
4.	type — *In Pro Per*.
8.	type the name of the district bankruptcy court.
9.	type the name of the bankruptcy court division.
11.	type your first and last name.
12.	type your bankruptcy case number.
13.	type your adversary case number.
16.	type the name of the defendant. Most likely this is the *United States Department of Education*. This may include a guarantee agency and any other collection agency.
16.	type the date the complaint was filed.
17.	type the name of the presiding judge.
19.	type — *PROOF OF SERVICE OF SUMMONS AND COMPLAINT.*

Summons and Notice of Status Conference - *Page 2*　　　**F 7004-1**

In re (your first and last name), Debtor.

CHAPTER 7
CASE NUMBER (bankruptcy case number)

Adversary Number (your number)

PROOF OF SERVICE

STATE OF CALIFORNIA, COUNTY OF ___(county)___

1. I am employed in the County of ___(county)___, State of California. I am over the age of 18 and not a party to the within action. My business address is as follows:

    (address
    city, state, zip)

2. ☑ **Regular Mail Service:** On ___See Attached Service List___, I served the foregoing Summons and Notice of Status Conference (and any instructions attached thereto), together with the Complaint filed in this proceeding, on the Defendant(s) at the following address(es) by placing a true and correct copy thereof in a sealed envelope with postage thereon fully prepaid in the United States Mail at ___(city mailed from)___, California, addressed as set forth below.

3. ☑ **Personal Service:** On ___(name of local US Attorney)___ personal service of the foregoing Summons and Notice of Status Conference (and any instructions attached thereto), together with the Complaint filed in this proceeding, was made on the Defendant(s) at the address(es) set forth below.

4. Defendant(s) and address(es) upon which service was made:

    (name and address of local U.S. Attorney
    in the bankruptcy court district)

☑ Names and Addresses continued on attached page

I declare under penalty of perjury under the laws of the United States of America that the foregoing is true and correct.

Dated: (date)

(first and last name)
_____   _____
Type Name   Signature

This form is mandatory. It has been approved for use by the United States Bankruptcy Court for the Central District of California.

Revised December 1998 (COA-SA)　　　**F 7004-1**

(This is the *Mail Matrix* that is attached to the Proof of Service form.)

In re: (*debtor's name*)
Case Number (*debtor's bankruptcy case number*)

Regular Mail Service

Name and address (*office of the U.S. Trustee in you bankruptcy district*)

Name and address (*the Attorney General in Washington, D.C.*)

Name and address (*particular agency named in or affected by the lawsuit,* most likely the Dept. of Education)

Name and address (*debtor's Chapter 7 bankruptcy trustee*)

(This is the *Cover* used when filing the Proof of Service with the court.)

```
1   (your name)
2   (address)
    (city, state, zip)
3   (telephone)
4   In Pro Per
5
6
7              UNITED STATED BANKRUPTCY COURT
8                      (name of district)
9                      (name of division)
10
11
    (your name)                    )  CHAPTER 7 BANKRUPTCY CASE
12                                 )  (bankruptcy case number)
13  PLAINTIFF,                     )
                                   )
14  vs.                            )  ADV. NO.
15                                 )
16  (name of defendant-- most likely )  COMPLAINT FILED:   (date)
    UNITED STATES DEPARTMENT       )  DEPT:
17  OF EDUCATION),                 )  JUDGE:
18                                 )
19  DEFENDANT                      )
    _____ )
20
21          PROOF OF SERVICE OF SUMMONS AND COMPLAINT
22
23
24
25
26
27
28
```

PROOF OF SERVICE

- 1 -

(NAME)
(ADDRESS)
(CITY, STATE, ZIP)
(TELEPHONE)

Forms—Samples

This section contains samples of the following documents:

Adversary Proceeding Sheet (Cover)

Adversary Proceeding Complaint

Summons

Proof of Service

Mailing Matrix

Proof of Service Cover

Joint Status Report

Request for Documents from Department of Education

Stipulation

Adversary Proceeding Sheet (Cover) (Sample)

B1040 (FORM 1040) (12/15)

ADVERSARY PROCEEDING COVER SHEET (Instructions on Reverse)	ADVERSARY PROCEEDING NUMBER (Court Use Only)
PLAINTIFFS Bob Smith 3722 Anystreet #1 Los Angeles, CA 90034	**DEFENDANTS** United States Department of Education Direct Loan Servicing PO Box 4609 Utica, NY 13504-4609
ATTORNEYS (Firm Name, Address, and Telephone No.) None	ATTORNEYS (If Known) In Pro Per
PARTY (Check One Box Only) ☑ Debtor ☐ U.S. Trustee/Bankruptcy Admin ☐ Creditor ☐ Other ☐ Trustee	PARTY (Check One Box Only) ☐ Debtor ☐ U.S. Trustee/Bankruptcy Admin ☑ Creditor ☐ Other ☐ Trustee

CAUSE OF ACTION (WRITE A BRIEF STATEMENT OF CAUSE OF ACTION, INCLUDING ALL U.S. STATUTES INVOLVED)

Plaintiff seeks dischargeability of debt pursuant to 11 U.S.C. §523(a)(8)

NATURE OF SUIT

(Number up to five (5) boxes starting with lead cause of action as 1, first alternative cause as 2, second alternative cause as 3, etc.)

FRBP 7001(1) – Recovery of Money/Property
☐ 11-Recovery of money/property - §542 turnover of property
☐ 12-Recovery of money/property - §547 preference
☐ 13-Recovery of money/property - §548 fraudulent transfer
☐ 14-Recovery of money/property - other

FRBP 7001(2) – Validity, Priority or Extent of Lien
☐ 21-Validity, priority or extent of lien or other interest in property

FRBP 7001(3) – Approval of Sale of Property
☐ 31-Approval of sale of property of estate and of a co-owner - §363(h)

FRBP 7001(4) – Objection/Revocation of Discharge
☐ 41-Objection / revocation of discharge - §727(c),(d),(e)

FRBP 7001(5) – Revocation of Confirmation
☐ 51-Revocation of confirmation

FRBP 7001(6) – Dischargeability
☐ 66-Dischargeability - §523(a)(1),(14),(14A) priority tax claims
☐ 62-Dischargeability - §523(a)(2), false pretenses, false representation, actual fraud
☐ 67-Dischargeability - §523(a)(4), fraud as fiduciary, embezzlement, larceny
(continued next column)

FRBP 7001(6) – Dischargeability (continued)
☐ 61-Dischargeability - §523(a)(5), domestic support
☐ 68-Dischargeability - §523(a)(6), willful and malicious injury
☑ 63-Dischargeability - §523(a)(8), student loan
☐ 64-Dischargeability - §523(a)(15), divorce or separation obligation (other than domestic support)
☐ 65-Dischargeability - other

FRBP 7001(7) – Injunctive Relief
☐ 71-Injunctive relief – imposition of stay
☐ 72-Injunctive relief – other

FRBP 7001(8) Subordination of Claim or Interest
☐ 81-Subordination of claim or interest

FRBP 7001(9) Declaratory Judgment
☐ 91-Declaratory judgment

FRBP 7001(10) Determination of Removed Action
☐ 01-Determination of removed claim or cause

Other
☐ SS-SIPA Case – 15 U.S.C. §§78aaa et.seq.
☐ 02-Other (e.g. other actions that would have been brought in state court if unrelated to bankruptcy case)

☐ Check if this case involves a substantive issue of state law	☐ Check if this is asserted to be a class action under FRCP 23
☐ Check if a jury trial is demanded in complaint	Demand $ 55,000.00

Other Relief Sought

B1040 (FORM 1040) (12/15)

BANKRUPTCY CASE IN WHICH THIS ADVERSARY PROCEEDING ARISES				
NAME OF DEBTOR Bob Smith		BANKRUPTCY CASE NO. LA 04-19681-ER		
DISTRICT IN WHICH CASE IS PENDING Central District of California		DIVISION OFFICE Los Angeles		NAME OF JUDGE
RELATED ADVERSARY PROCEEDING (IF ANY)				
PLAINTIFF	DEFENDANT			ADVERSARY PROCEEDING NO.
DISTRICT IN WHICH ADVERSARY IS PENDING		DIVISION OFFICE		NAME OF JUDGE
SIGNATURE OF ATTORNEY (OR PLAINTIFF)				
DATE October 1, 2020				PRINT NAME OF ATTORNEY (OR PLAINTIFF) *Bob Smith*

INSTRUCTIONS

The filing of a bankruptcy case creates an "estate" under the jurisdiction of the bankruptcy court which consists of all of the property of the debtor, wherever that property is located. Because the bankruptcy estate is so extensive and the jurisdiction of the court so broad, there may be lawsuits over the property or property rights of the estate. There also may be lawsuits concerning the debtor's discharge. If such a lawsuit is filed in a bankruptcy court, it is called an adversary proceeding.

A party filing an adversary proceeding must also must complete and file Form 1040, the Adversary Proceeding Cover Sheet, unless the party files the adversary proceeding electronically through the court's Case Management/Electronic Case Filing system (CM/ECF). (CM/ECF captures the information on Form 1040 as part of the filing process.) When completed, the cover sheet summarizes basic information on the adversary proceeding. The clerk of court needs the information to process the adversary proceeding and prepare required statistical reports on court activity.

The cover sheet and the information contained on it do not replace or supplement the filing and service of pleadings or other papers as required by law, the Bankruptcy Rules, or the local rules of court. The cover sheet, which is largely self-explanatory, must be completed by the plaintiff's attorney (or by the plaintiff if the plaintiff is not represented by an attorney). A separate cover sheet must be submitted to the clerk for each complaint filed.

Plaintiffs and Defendants. Give the names of the plaintiffs and defendants exactly as they appear on the complaint.

Attorneys. Give the names and addresses of the attorneys, if known.

Party. Check the most appropriate box in the first column for the plaintiffs and the second column for the defendants.

Demand. Enter the dollar amount being demanded in the complaint.

Signature. This cover sheet must be signed by the attorney of record in the box on the second page of the form. If the plaintiff is represented by a law firm, a member of the firm must sign. If the plaintiff is pro se, that is, not represented by an attorney, the plaintiff must sign.

Bob Smith
3722 Anystreet #1
Los Angeles, CA 90034
555-000-0000
In Pro Per

UNITED STATED BANKRUPTCY COURT

CENTRAL DISTRICT OF CALIFORNIA

(LOS ANGELES DIVISION)

BOB SMITH	) CHAPTER 7 BANKRUPTCY CASE
	) NO. LA 04-19681-ER
PLAINTIFF,	)
	)
vs.	) ADV. NO.
	)
UNITED STATES DEPARTMENT OF EDUCATION,	) COMPLAINT FILED: 8/2/2004
	) DEPT:
	) JUDGE:
DEFENDANT	)

COMPLAINT TO DETERMINE DISCHARGEABILITY OF DEBT
PURSUANT TO 11 U.S.C. §523(a)(8)

Bob Smith, Debtor and Plaintiff in the above captioned adversary proceeding, represents as follows:

1. Bob Smith filed a voluntary petition for relief under Chapter 7 of the United States Bankruptcy Code on April 28, 2004. Alberta P. Stahl is the duly appointed Chapter 7 trustee. This complaint seeks to determine the

dischargeability of a student loan as it presents an undue hardship for the Debtor and his dependents.

2. One of the unsecured debts owing by the Debtor and listed on Schedule F—Creditors Holding Unsecured Nonpriority Claims— is a student loan owing to United States Department of Education.

3. This loan was incurred to pay expenses at California State University, Chico for a Secondary Teaching Credential, and University of Southern California for a Ph.D. in Education (both were attained).

JURISDICTION

4. Defendant United States Department of Education maintains its Direct Loan Servicing Center in Utica, New York.

5. Jurisdiction exists under 28 U.S.C. §1334. Venue is proper under 28 U.S.C. §1409(a). The District Court has generally referred these matters to the Bankruptcy Court for hearing pursuant to 28 U.S.C. §157(a). This is a core proceeding within the meaning of 28 U.S.C. §157(b)(2)(I). This adversary complaint is brought pursuant to 11 U.S.C. §523(a)(8).

FIRST CAUSE OF ACTION [11 U.S.C. §523(a)(8)]

6. Plaintiff is indebted to the Defendant in the approximate sum of $55,000 for education loans made by Defendant to Plaintiff.

7. Requiring Plaintiff to repay these debts will impose undue hardship on the Debtor and the Debtor's dependents as contemplated under 11 U.S.C. §523(a)(8).

8. Based upon Plaintiff's current income and expenses, Plaintiff cannot maintain a minimum standard of living if forced to repay the loan. Plaintiff believes that his economic state of affairs is likely to persist for a significant

portion of the repayment period and he has made good faith efforts to repay the loans.

9. The Debtor has filed for bankruptcy for reasons other than just to discharge his student loan.

WHEREFORE, the Debtor asks this court to enter an Order declaring the student loan debt to be dischargeable.

Date: August 2, 2004.

Bob Smith
_____
Plaintiff BOB SMITH

PLAINTIFF'S COMPLAINT TO DETERMINE
DISCHARGEABILITY OF DEBT

BOB SMITH
3722 ANYSTREET #1
LOS ANGELES, CA 90034
555-000-0000

Adversary Proceeding Complaint (Sample-Full)

(Note: this document is a "full" pleading— meaning that the rationale for allowing you to discharge your student loans in bankruptcy are given in full. Typically, that level of detail is not included in initial filing but are developed during interrogatories and mediation. Some courts have been asking for everything to be included in the initial pleading. That is what this document is, beside including advocacy to reject the "undue hardship" clause and the *Brunner* test. Decide which parts you need for your case. Perhaps the simpler pleading given earlier is sufficient.)

[Your Name]

3722 Anystreet #1

Los Angeles, CA 90034

555-000-0000

In Pro Per

UNITED STATED BANKRUPTCY COURT

CENTRAL DISTRICT OF CALIFORNIA

(LOS ANGELES DIVISION)

[Your Name]	) CHAPTER 7 BANKRUPTCY CASE
	) NO. [Your case number]
PLAINTIFF,	)
	)
vs.	) ADV. NO.
	)
UNITED STATES DEPARTMENT	) COMPLAINT FILED: [date}
OF EDUCATION,	) DEPT:
[may be a list of defendants]	) JUDGE:
DEFENDANT	)
_____	)

PLAINTIFF'S COMPLAINT TO DETERMINE
DISCHARGEABILITY OF DEBT

- 1 -

YOUR NAME
3722 ANYSTREET #1
LOS ANGELES, CA 90034
555-000-0000

COMPLAINT TO DETERMINE DISCHARGEABILITY OF DEBT
PURSUANT TO 11 U.S.C. §523(a)(8)

[Your name], Debtor and Plaintiff in the above captioned adversary proceeding, represents as follows:

1. [Your name] filed a voluntary petition for relief under Chapter 7 of the United States Bankruptcy Code on October 1, 2020. [Trustee name] is the duly appointed Chapter 7 trustee. This complaint seeks to determine the dischargeability of a student loan as it presents an undue hardship for the Debtor and his dependents.

2. One of the unsecured debts owing by the Debtor and listed on Schedule F—Creditors Holding Unsecured Nonpriority Claims— is a student loan owing to [name of corporation].

3. This loan was incurred to pay expenses at [name of college], [city] for a [degree], and [another college name] for a [another degree][keep listing all colleges and cities] [and tell if the degree was obtained].

JURISDICTION

4. Defendant [name of company that owns debt] maintains its Direct Loan Servicing Center in [city, state].

5. Jurisdiction exists under 28 U.S.C. §1334. Venue is proper under 28 U.S.C. §1409(a). The District Court has generally referred these matters to the Bankruptcy Court for hearing pursuant to 28 U.S.C. §157(a). This is a core proceeding within the meaning of 28 U.S.C. §157(b)(2)(I). This adversary complaint is brought pursuant to 11 U.S.C. §523(a)(8).

[perhaps you can't determine who has your loan; you could add this additional text if needed, otherwise this text is unnecessary]

6. I have been informed that Defendant [name of corporation] alleges that it is the 'owner' of the debt. I have requested verification that Defendant

[name] owns my debt but they have not provided any documentation to establish such a fact. I never borrowed any money from Defendant [name]. I do not know what Defendant [name] bases their claim upon. I do not know if Defendant [name] are valid creditors/debt holders. They should be required to prove the alleged debt.

[perhaps you disagree with the total of the alleged debt; you could add this text and more if needed, otherwise this text is unnecessary]

7. I do not know how Defendant [name] came up with the debt of $X. I borrowed approximately $X for student expenses and paid back $X. I've asked for a detailed explanation of the debt but Defendant [name] has failed to provide me with it. I dispute the balance claimed by the Defendant [name]. The creditor bears the initial burden of proving the debt exists. The amount of the debt is in dispute. The Defendants [name] should be required by this Court to prove their alleged debts.

<u>FIRST CAUSE OF ACTION:</u>

<u>[11 U.S.C. §523(a)(8)]:</u>

<u>PLAINTIFF IS ENTITLED TO DISCHARGE OF STUDENT LOANS</u>

<u>BASED ON UNDUE HARDSHIP</u>

[the purpose of this section is to plead the case in detail according to the *Brunner* guidelines]

8. Plaintiff may be indebted to the Defendant in the approximate sum of $X for education loans made by Defendant to Plaintiff.

9. Requiring Plaintiff to repay these debts will impose undue hardship on the Debtor and the Debtor's dependents as contemplated under 11 U.S.C. §523(a)(8).

10. Based upon Plaintiff's current income and expenses, Plaintiff cannot maintain a minimum standard of living if forced to repay the loan. Plaintiff believes that his/her economic state of affairs is likely to persist for a significant portion of the repayment period and has made good faith efforts to repay the loans.

[Insert a short summary: (a) your age and health status, (b) effort to obtain and maintain employment, and (c) a brief statement that you live frugally. A longer statement will be developed later in this document.]

11. The following are specifics applied to the *Brunner Test* adopted by this Court. Under the *Brunner Test*, a debtor seeking the dischargeability of student loan debt must show by a preponderance of the evidence that:

    i. Based on current income and expenses, the debtor cannot maintain a "minimal" standard of living for himself and his dependents if forced to repay the loans;

    ii. Additional circumstances exist indicating that this state of affairs is likely to persist for a significant portion of the repayment period of the student loans; and,

    iii. The debtor has made good faith efforts to repay the loans.

See *Brunner v. N.Y. State Higher Educ. Servs. Corp.*, 46 B.R. 752, 756 (S.D.N.Y. 1985), aff'd, 831 F.2d 395 (2d Cir. 1987).

12. Although I am clearly entitled to the discharge of my student loans under the *Brunner Test*, in my opinion, I also encourage this Court to consider the *Totality of the Circumstances Test* used in *Conway v. National Collegiate Trust*, 495 NB.R. 416 (8th Cir. BAP 2013), aff'med, 559 Fed. Appx. 610 (8th Cir. 2014). The Court in *Conway* asserted that bankruptcy income decisions must be based on the "totality of the circumstances" test which looks in part at "the debtor's past, present, and reasonably reliable future financial resources, the debtor's reasonable and necessary living expenses, and 'any other relevant facts and circumstances'." *Conway*, 495 B.R. at 419, quoting educ. *Credit Mgmt v. Jesperson. Corp*, 571 F.3d 775, 779 (8th Cir. 209).

<u>THREE PART *BRUNNER* TEST: PART I:</u>

<u>I CANNOT MAINTAIN, BASED ON CURRENT INCOME AND EXPENSES,</u>

A MINIMAL STANDARD OF LIVING
FOR MYSELF IF FORCED TO REPAY THE LOANS.

13. As set forth below, I cannot maintain, based on current income and expenses, a minimum standard of living for myself if forced to repay the loans.

[Here you give details about your age, income, expenses, medical conditions, and debt. You use the details that you laid out in the worksheets in preparation of the adversary.

    i. Current Income Status worksheet

    ii. Current Expenditure Status worksheet

    iii. Work Time Accounting Table worksheet

    iv. Income and Student Loan Payment worksheet

    v. Current Financial Status worksheet

Remember, the goal is to convince the court that you are poor and you've tried hard to maximize your income while at the same time minimizing your living expenses.]

BRUNNER TEST PART II:
ADDITIONAL AND EXTENUATING CIRCUMSTANCES EXIST
INDICATING THAT THIS STATE OF AFFAIRS IS LIKELY TO PERSIST
FOR A SIGNIFICANT PORTION OF THE REPAYMENT PERIOD

14. As set forth below, additional, and extenuating circumstances exist indicating that this state of affairs is likely to persist for a significant portion of the repayment of the loans.

[Here you give details developed in the worksheets including:

    i. Personal Limitations Statement worksheet

The goal is to show why, for at least the next ten years, you don't expect your financial status to change. This may include items such as your:

    ii. age and entering retirement before the end of the loan terms

   iii. deteriorating medical conditions

   iv. taking care of dependents—particularly disabled dependents

   v. your disability

   vi. discrimination based on age, race, national origin, sexual orientation, and more,

   vii. owning an old car that will require replacement soon

   viii. just the act of filing for bankruptcy may have repercussion on certain jobs now being off limit (it is legal for employers to discriminate against potential employees for the sole reason that such potential employee filed for bankruptcy, see *Rea v. Federated Investors*, 2010 U.S. App[. LESIX 25501, 3d Cir. 2010), and so much more.

   ix. If the amount they are asking you to pay on the loans does not service the debt and interest keeps increasing the total balance, emphasize how the increasing debt creates an undue hardship mental strain. "The law does not require a party to engage in futile acts," *Roth v. Educational Credit Management Corp, In re Roth*, 490 B.R. 908, 920 (9th Cir. BAP 2013).

   x. Although age was mentioned, you need to take it a step further. The federal government, pursuant to the Social Security administration's analysis using its 'grid rules', considers individuals aged 55-59 to be of "advanced age." 45 FR 55584, August 20, 1980, as amended at 56 FR 57944, Nov. 14, 1991; 68 FR 51164, Aug. 26, 2003; 73 FR 64197, Oct 29, 2008. Thus, the federal government recognizes that those over 55 years of age do not have a better future ahead of them than their current situation, and, therefore, the Social Security Administration is more likely to grant disability awards to those over 55 years of age, due to their age.

[If your loans are in default, this needs to be mentioned in this section.]

   xi. Upon filing for bankruptcy, I have also officially defaulted on my student loans. As a consequence, the repayment terms of the loans override the original repayment schedule with a demand for payment right now. The second *Brunner* prong states that "this state of affairs is likely to persist for a significant portion of the repayment period of the student loans." Since filing for bankruptcy indicates that I am in dire financial straits and this has lasted during the repayment period (now over), the second *Brunner* prong is satisfied. Student loans in default automatically satisfy the *Brunner* second prong. (*In re Rosenberg*, Case No. 18-35379 Bankr. S.D.N.Y. Jan. 7, 2020).

[You must spell this out in details. Don't assume they understand.]

BRUNNER TEST PART III:
I MADE A GOOD FAITH EFFORT
TO REPAY THESE STUDENT LOAN DEBTS.

15. As set forth below, I have made a good faith effort to repay these student loans.

[You need to demonstrate your efforts to make payments when you could afford to do so and that you were in contact with DOE when you could not. Use the worksheets to help develop your narrative:
    i. Income and Student Loan Payment worksheet
    ii. Student Loan History worksheet
    iii. Good faith and Loan Repayment Statement worksheet
Even if you did not make any payments, you can still demonstrate that you were responsible with your loans. For example, Roth never made a voluntary payment in over 20-years, yet the court accepted her claims since she demonstrated that she lived frugally and attempted to maximize her income (*In re Roth*, 490 B. R. 908 (9th Cir. BAP 2013)). Further, the Court stated, "[T]he law does not require a party

to engage in futile acts…and Congress could not have intended such a lengthy empty commitment as a requirement for determination of undue hardship." *Id.*]

FRESH START:

16. I seek access to the "fresh start" assured to all honest debtors afforded in the Bankruptcy reform Act of 1978. "Traditional bankruptcy policy has maintained that society benefits when honest and hopeless debtors are relieved of their debts and granted a fresh start." The Fresh Start Policy in Bankruptcy Law, 98 Harv. L. Rev. 3893, 1420 (1985).

[This next section "Second Cause of Action" is here only if you are wanting to advocate for the revocation of Section 523(a)(8) and/or the *Brunner* test for all debtors. You do not need this section for your personal case.]

SECOND CAUSE OF ACTION:
PLAINTIFF IS ENTITLED TO DISCHARGE OF STUDENT LOANS BASED ON PRINCIPALS OF EQUITY

17. In *In re Roth*, 490 B.R. 908 (9th Cir. BAP 2013), the Ninth Circuit Bankruptcy Appellate Panel drew on equity principles when applying the *Brunner* test to a student-loan bankruptcy case. "[T]he law does not require a party to engage in futile acts," the court ruled in a case in which was clear that forcing a student-loan debtor to make further student-loan payments would be futile. (*Id.* at 920). In the Ninth Circuit Bankruptcy Appellate Court's opinion, "Congress could not have intended such a lengthy, empty commitment as a requirement for a determination of undue hardship." *Id.*

18. In recent years, several bankruptcy court decisions in the Ninth Circuit have applied principles of compassion and practicality to student-loan bankruptcy cases in accordance with the equity principles expressed in *Roth*. See

In re Nys, 446 f.3d 938 (9th Cir. 2006); *In re Scott*, 417 B.R. 623 (Bankr. W.D. Wash., 2009); *Hedlund v. The Educ. Resources Inst., Inc. & Pa. Higher Educ. Assistance Agency*, 718 F. 3d 848 (9th Cir. 2013); and *In re Roth*, 490 B.R. 908 (9th Cir. BAP 2013).

19. In addition, in *Krieger v. Educational Credit Management Corporation,* 713 F.3d 882 (7th Cir. 2013), the seventh Circuit Court of Appeals ruled that a 53-year old debtor was entitled to bankruptcy relief and that her efforts to obtain employment had been futile. The Seventh Circuit implicitly acknowledged that the debtor's age was a disadvantage to her in finding future employment. (*Id.* at 884-85.)

20. Plaintiff believes that the facts set forth in this complaint and that will be further elaborated at trial entitle him to relief from his student loan debts under §523(a)(8) of the U.S. Bankruptcy Code as interpreted by equity principles as articulated by the Ninth Circuit Bankruptcy Appellate Panel in *In Re Roth* in its interpretation of the three-part *Brunner* test.

21. 11 U.S.C. §523(a)(8) is, itself, vague, legally unenforceable, and inherently discriminatory.

   i. As discussed by Andrew M. Campbell in "Bankruptcy Discharge of Student Loan on Ground of Undue Hardship Under § 523(a)(8)(B) of Bankruptcy Code of 1978," 144 A.L.R. Fed. 1 (1998), the bankruptcy code is applied unequally between different classes of debtors. For example, low-income debtors with chronic medical conditions and dependents have the highest rate of success at proving under hardship. Some could argue that the courts are recognizing the fact that debtors with dependents have a greater responsibility and greater need for debt relief. But, the low-income level from which the analysis is made is higher for those with dependents ($10,000 before 1990 and $15,000 in subsequent years) than those without ($7,000 before 1990 and $10,000 in subsequent years). In a sense, these are similar to the Federal Poverty Guidelines and the differences in income levels for those with dependents versus those without is reflected in the guidelines. Since the Guidelines adjust for the presence of dependents, <u>courts should treat single debtors without dependents exactly the same as those with dependents– taking in account that the income level cut-offs already accommodates for the difference.</u>

  ii. <u>Medical condition</u> also influences court decisions. Low-income debtors with medical conditions and dependents are one and one-half times more likely to achieve success at discharging their debt than similar debtors without medical conditions (77 percent vs. 48 percent). This effect is even more pronounced for low-income debtors without dependents where having a medical condition results in three times the success rate over similar debtors without a medical condition (55 percent vs. 17 percent). <u>Courts have shown an overwhelming bias toward debtors with medical conditions over those without.</u>

  iii. It may be argued that having a medical condition is strong evidence that a borrower will have little success with future employment and even less ability to repay student loans. This is often true, but there are many other factors equally important than medical condition related to a person's ability to find work. For example we live in an <u>ageist society</u> where it is next-to-impossible for older workers to find full employment at good wages. Expecting someone over sixty-five years of age to find a new job is ludicrous. There are many other social factors that impact just as severely the ability of healthy workers to find employment, as does a medical disability.

  iv. Courts seem to ignore factors other than medical conditions that impact debtors in their ability to secure employment. Courts seem to believe that if a debtor is healthy, then he or she should be able to get work, and, if he or she doesn't, it is the debtor's fault and the court denies the student loan discharge. Courts have shown a bias against factors other than medical conditions that present equal challenges to finding employment, e.g., higher level college degrees, race, ethnicity, sexual orientation, and more.

   v. Requiring a debtor who files for bankruptcy to then file an adversary proceeding against the government to determine if repaying the student loans create an "undue hardship" is, in itself, and "undue hardship." Debtors file bankruptcy due to lack of money. Some debtors represent themselves in Chapter 7 bankruptcies (some courts it is as high as 28 percent are *pro se*) because they can't afford an attorney. It is common knowledge (however a myth) that you can't bankrupt student loans. As such, virtually no one tries it on their own without an attorney. This means that poor debtors are not filing adversary proceedings to try and bankrupt their student loans since they don't have money for an attorney. Adding to the burden are the millions of debtors for whom English is not their primary language and they fear the idea of suing the government and speaking up in court. The lack of money and language barriers make the adversary proceeding an inherently discriminatory process for most debtors and should be abolished. The passage of §523(a)(8) was aimed at college-educated middle-class debtors but had the unintended impact of blocking large numbers of poor and English-as-a-second language debtors from obtaining a fresh start through bankruptcy. Debtors faced with bankruptcy should encourage courts to rescind or overturn §523(a)(8) because it has a disproportionate impact on poor, mostly minority, debtors.

   vi. Although §523(a)(8) renders student loans presumptively non-dischargeable, a review of the entire Bankruptcy Code reveals that the fresh start provision takes precedent over §523(a)(8).

   a. Congress stated in Section 507 of the Code which debts are given priority during liquidation or reorganization. Student loan claims are absent from Section 507, indicating Congress did not consider student loans to be among the most important kinds of debts considered during bankruptcy proceedings. The Bankruptcy Court in *Fox v. Pennsylvania Higher Education Assistance Agency* came to this same conclusion when it attempted to assess the priority repayment of student loans.

   b. The structure of §523(a)(8) shows that student loans are not required to be repaid, but rather, are prohibited from discharge. This is a significant distinction because if Congress desired repayment of student loans over all other bankruptcy objectives, it would have done so by enacting specific legislation to that effect. It did not.

   c. The undue hardship exception is included in §523(a)(8) to protect debtors, not creditors. As such, it functions to preserve the fresh start policy of the Bankruptcy Code.

   d. The Bankruptcy Code gives priority to repayment of student loans up to the point of impinging upon a debtor's fresh start. At that point, the fresh start policy predominates in the undue hardship analysis and allows for the discharge of student loans.

   e. The purpose of a fresh start policy is to allow debtors to afford the necessities of life at a quality and quantity expected within the mainstream American culture. Neither Chapter 7 nor Chapter 13 debtors are forced into poverty to achieve discharge of their loans. When Congress and the Bankruptcy Commission spoke of minimal standard of living, they meant a level of living that brings debtors back into society at the lower ends of the middle class.

  vii. Without going through a long review of court interpretations, most courts agree that the term "undue hardship" is extremely vague and left undefined by Congress. As such, the term has taken on a wide range of interpretations. This wide reading of *undue hardship* is evidence §523(a)(8) is bad law and should be rejected by courts.

For all these reasons, the very law, 11 U.S.C. §523(a)(8), should be abolished.

22. Each prong of the Brunner test is unenforceable, arbitrary, and should be rejected as a measure for determining the dischargeability of student loans through bankruptcy.

i. The first prong of the Brunner test requires a determination of a "minimal" standard of living for the debtor and his/her dependents if forced to repay the loans. Many early court tests used the Social Security's Federal Poverty Guidelines (hereinafter, referred to as Poverty Guidelines) to determine "minimal standard of living"; which were adopted by the Brunner Court. Even though the Bryant Court claimed that using the guidelines brought "objectivity" to the test, it did not (See *Bryant*, 72 B.R. at 915). The Social Security Administration developed the guidelines in 1964 by guessing the average family's total expenditure for food and multiplying it by a factor of three. (Even the federal government admits the official poverty level is subjective. See Bureau of the Census, U.S. Department of Commerce, Series P-60, No. 178, Workers With Low Earnings: 1964-1990, at B-3 (1992) (hereinafter Census II) ("The choice of a threshold for determining whether annual earnings are low or not low is necessarily subjective.") Cf. Teresa A. Sullivan et al., *Forklore and Facts: A Preliminary Report from the Consumer Bankruptcy Project*, 60 Am. Bankr. L.J. 293, 294, 312, 314 (1986) ("[A]ny inference from the data will still require a normative view about when repayment appears so onerous that the debtor 'can't pay'.") This number is updated yearly, but the basic definition has never been changed. The Social Security Administration's determination for a food budget was based on the **temporary or emergency** **dietary needs of a family, and not the cost for an adequate, sustainable diet**. (See Census II, supra note 241, at 9 ("[T]he USDA food budget that underlies the SSA index is at best a measure of temporary/emergency food needs and thus not appropriate as a long-run market basked.")

It is very indicative how inappropriate the Poverty Guidelines are when you consider that many other agencies of the U.S. Government reject the scale and use other government guidelines. For example, until 1985, the Bureau of Labor Statistics (BLS) calculated its own measure of poverty. The scale was designed to estimate a budget of minimum adequacy. Living below that level was considered to be <u>subminimal</u> existence. The BLS guideline was substantially higher than the Poverty Guidelines. (Winnick, Andrew J. (1989). *Toward two societies: The changing distributions of income and wealth in the U.S. since 1960* (p. 24-25). New York: Praeger.) Even though the BLS no longer produces these figures, the Department of Labor (DOL) updates the figures annually since they are used to measure eligibility for certain job training programs. (*See* Notice of Determination of Lower Living Standard Income Level, 59 Fed. Reg. 19241-46 (1994).)

Significantly, many federal and state need-based assistance programs do not use the Poverty Guidelines. (Salvin, Robert F. (1996). Student loans, bankruptcy, and the fresh start policy: Must debtors be impoverished to discharge educational loans? Tul. L. Rev. (71), 139, at 10.) The Department of Housing and Urban Development (HUD) links eligibility with the median income, not the Poverty Guidelines. For example, HUD classifies families earning between 50-80 percent of the median income as "Lower Income Families." Those earning less than 50 percent of the median income are "Very Low-Income Families." The HUD guidelines for low-income levels are higher than those of the Poverty Guidelines. The Legal Service Corporation (LSC) determined that people whose incomes do not exceed 125 percent of the Poverty Guidelines are poor enough to receive free legal services. In certain circumstances, this may extend up to 150 percent of the Poverty Guidelines. For tax determination, the Earned Income Tax Credits (EICs) are granted to families far above the Poverty Guidelines. EIC are characterized as a welfare payment made through the tax system to low-income families. Congress, in developing the EIC program, believed that families with incomes well above the Poverty Guidelines were entitled to the tax break to help lift them out of "poverty." (McGinley, Laurie. (March 31, 1993). Outline is given for expansion of a tax credit (supra note 298).

Wall St. Journal.) The Department of Education defines low-income as borrowers with incomes not exceeding 125 percent of the Poverty Guidelines. Such a designation qualifies them for extended repayment periods on direct education loans. (See 34 C.F.R. s 674.33(c)(2).) Finally, Aid to Families with Dependent Children (AFDC), does not set an income eligibility criteria at all, but rather leaves it up to each individual state to establish.

Linking the Federal Poverty Guidelines to undue hardship is, and has been, arbitrary. Neither Congress, the Bankruptcy Code, nor the Department of Education regulations require student debtors, who are subjected to an undue hardship analysis, to be evaluated against the Poverty Guidelines. The Poverty Guidelines is not an accurate measure of poverty and bear "no relationship at all to bankruptcy law or the fresh start policy." (Salvin, Robert F. (1996). Student loans, bankruptcy, and the fresh start policy: Must debtors be impoverished to discharge educational loans? Tul. L. Rev. (71), 139 at 11.) The use of the Social Security Federal Poverty Guidelines for determining "minimal" standard of living should be rejected. Debtors living conditions for the first Brunner prong should be evaluated at a middle-class level of living.

ii. The second Brunner prong requires the debtor to show that additional circumstances exist indicating that this state of affairs is likely to persist for a significant portion of the repayment period of the student loans. As so many courts have noted, this requires guessing the future income of the debtor for decades to come. This is impossible. Even the Brunner court stated that it was "problematic" to try to determine the ability of a debtor to make payments in the future; yet the court blithely proceeded to attempt to devise a method for doing exactly that (which failed). Some courts have advocated eliminating this part of the *Brunner* test. Yet, DOE continues to press the false narrative that the economic status of the debtor "should" get better and the courts should reject the debtor's claim.

What seems to be missing from court cases is the science behind making predictions. We can take a data set and fit a regression line (equation) that best fits the data. We can extend this line into the future to predict outcomes. This is called *statistical inference*. Predictability comes from past data. From this data we can predict future events within some level of probability. In our application, if a debtor has a decade or more of economic struggle due to lack of employment, disability, poor choices, cultural forces, illness, marriage, children, and so on, we can only predict the same conditions will continue into the future—regardless how much we think it "should" change. Courts trying to predict the ability of debtors to make future payments is magical thinking and not based on science. Predicting future earnings should be based on past earnings; nothing more.

     iii. The third Brunner prong requires debtors to prove they made good faith efforts to repay the loans. Tied to this prong is the Department of Education's claim that their income-driven repayment plans, like the Income Based Repayment (IBR) and Income Contingent Repayment (ICR) plans, make it impossible for debtors to bankrupt their student loans because "anyone can make a zero-dollar payment." There are a couple of issues to be addressed:

     a. The Barrett court rejected the use of IDR plans because the debtor would be "trading one nondischargeable debt for another" (*Barrett* 487 F.3d at 364); which is not the point of bankruptcy or adversary proceeding.

     b. Although the payment may be lower or zero on an IDR plan, the emotional consequences of having to report to DOE financial and other personal information every year are, in themselves, a hardship. A debtor who is entitled to and receives a hardship discharge does not have that additional burden. The DOE's "argument overlooks the psychological effect of having a significant debt remain[.]" [*In re Barrett.* at 365 n. 8; see *Balaski v. Educ. Credit Mgmt. Corp,* 280 B.R. 395, 400 Bankr. N.D. Ohio 2002)]

     c. DOE has claimed that debtors who do not enroll in an IDR plan are, by default, violating the "good faith effort" to repay students loans as required under the third prong of *Brunner*. DOE attempted this strategy to say that if debtors did not enroll in an IDR program, it would indicate that they were not acting in "good faith." Its position would create a *per se* rule requiring enrollment in the IDR program to satisfy the third *Brunner* prong and thus would, in effect, eliminate the discharge of student loans for undue hardship from the Bankruptcy Code. The court rejected this approach. (*In re Lamento*, 520 B.R. 667 (Bkrtcy. N.D. Ohio 2014)).

    d. DOE attempt to tie-in IDR plans with the concept of debtors making a "good faith effort" to replay student loans has been rejected. *In re Roth* (2013), the Ninth Circuit Court recommended abolition of the *Brunner* third prong requirement because it is of little utility in determining true undue hardship.

    e. As a matter of statutory construction, this "prong" of the test lacks any textual basis in the Bankruptcy Code.

    f. DOE has stated they wanted the debtor to pay "something" toward the debt by enrolling in IDR plans. But *In re Metz* (*Metz v. Navient Education Loan Corp and Educational Credit Management Corporation*, Case No. 12-13120 Adv. No. 17-5119, 589 B.R. 750 (2018)) the court believed that "something" should have a meaningful positive effect on the financial situation. In other words, the payment should be able to reduce the debt — not simply service it.

All three prongs of the *Brunner* test are poorly constructed and impossible to meet. The prongs have no basis in Bankruptcy Code nor help to determine "undue hardship" as required under 11 U.S.C. §523(a)(8). As such, the Brunner tests should be abolished.

[The pleading ends with these last statements. Be sure to write these two sentences regardless if you give the advocacy arguments.]

PLAINTIFF'S COMPLAINT TO DETERMINE
DISCHARGEABILITY OF DEBT

- 17 -

YOUR NAME
3722 ANYSTREET #1
LOS ANGELES, CA 90034
555-000-0000

23. The Debtor has filed for bankruptcy for reasons other than just to discharge his student loan.

WHEREFORE, the Debtor asks this court to enter an Order declaring the student loan debt to be dischargeable.

Date: October 1, 2020.

Your Name
_____
Plaintiff [YOUR NAME]

Summons (Sample)

Attorney or Party Name, Address, Telephone & FAX Numbers, and California State Bar Number	FOR COURT USE ONLY
Bob Smith 1111 Anystreet #1 Los Angeles, CA 90034 Attorney for Plaintiff In Pro Per	

UNITED STATES BANKRUPTCY COURT
CENTRAL DISTRICT OF CALIFORNIA

In re: Bob Smith Debtor.	CHAPTER __7__ CASE NUMBER LA 04-19681-ER ADVERSARY NUMBER AD04-02232
Bob Smith Plaintiff(s), United States Dept. of Education Direct Loan Servicing Defendant(s).	*(The Boxes and Blank Lines below are for the Court's Use Only) (Do Not Fill Them In)* **SUMMONS AND NOTICE OF STATUS CONFERENCE**

TO THE DEFENDANT: A Complaint has been filed by the Plaintiff against you. If you wish to defend yourself, you must file with the Court a written pleading, in duplicate, in response to the Complaint. You must also send a copy of your written response to the party shown in the upper left-hand corner of this page. Unless you have filed in duplicate and served a responsive pleading by _____, the Court may enter a judgment by default against you for the relief demanded in the Complaint.

A Status Conference on the proceeding commenced by the Complaint has been set for:

Hearing Date: Time: Courtroom: Floor:

☐ 255 East Temple Street, Los Angeles   ☐ 411 West Fourth Street, Santa Ana
☐ 21041 Burbank Boulevard, Woodland Hills   ☐ 1415 State Street, Santa Barbara
☐ 3420 Twelfth Street, Riverside

PLEASE TAKE NOTICE that if the trial of the proceeding is anticipated to take less than two (2) hours, the parties may stipulate to conduct the trial of the case on the date specified, instead of holding a Status Conference. Such a stipulation must be lodged with the Court at least two (2) Court days before the date set forth above and is subject to Court approval. The Court may continue the trial to another date if necessary to accommodate the anticipated length of the trial.

Date of Issuance: _____

Clerk of the Bankruptcy Court

By: _____
Deputy Clerk

This form is mandatory. It has been approved for use by the United States Bankruptcy Court for the Central District of California.

Revised December 1998 (COA-SA)   **F 7004-1**

Proof of Service (Sample)

Summons and Notice of Status Conference - *Page 2*   **F 7004-1**

In re: **Bob Smith**, Debtor
CHAPTER 7
CASE NUMBER LA 03-19681-ER

Adversary Number AB 04-022320ER

PROOF OF SERVICE

STATE OF CALIFORNIA, COUNTY OF ___Los Angeles___

1. I am employed in the County of ___Los Angeles___, State of California. I am over the age of 18 and not a party to the within action. My business address is as follows:

   2222 Anystreet #2
   Los Angeles, CA 90034

2. ☑ **Regular Mail Service:** On ___See Attached Service List___, I served the foregoing Summons and Notice of Status Conference (and any instructions attached thereto), together with the Complaint filed in this proceeding, on the Defendant(s) at the following address(es) by placing a true and correct copy thereof in a sealed envelope with postage thereon fully prepaid in the United States Mail at ___Los Angeles___, California, addressed as set forth below.

3. ☑ **Personal Service:** On ___Debra Hoffer___, personal service of the foregoing Summons and Notice of Status Conference (and any instructions attached thereto), together with the Complaint filed in this proceeding, was made on the Defendant(s) at the address(es) set forth below.

4. Defendant(s) and address(es) upon which service was made:

   Debra Hoffer
   1200 U.S. Courthouse
   312 N. Spring Street
   Los Angeles, Ca 90012
   For Defendant-Creditor
   U.S. Dept. of Education

   ☑ Names and Addresses continued on attached page

I declare under penalty of perjury under the laws of the United States of America that the foregoing is true and correct.

Dated: 9/21/04

Michael Hughes
_____
Type Name

Signature *Michael Hughes*

This form is mandatory. It has been approved for use by the United States Bankruptcy Court for the Central District of California.

Revised December 1998 (COA-SA)   **F 7004-1**

Mail Matrix (Sample)

In re: Bob Smith
Case Number LA 04-19681-ER

                                              Regular Mail Service

U. S. Dept. of Education
Direct Loan Servicing System
PO Box 4609
Utica, NY 13504-4609

Office of U.S. Trustee
725 S. Figueroa
26th Floor
Los Angeles, CA 90017

Attorney General
U.S. Dept. of Justice
10th Constitution Ave. NW
Washington, D.C. 20530

Jane Doe
Trustee
Law Offices of Jane Doe
221 N. Figueroa St. Suite 1200
Los Angeles, CA 90012

Proof of Service Cover (Sample)

```
1  Bob Smith
2  1111 Anystreet #1
   Los Angeles, CA 90034
3  555-000-0000
4  In Pro Per
5
6
7              UNITED STATED BANKRUPTCY COURT
8                CENTRAL DISTRICT OF CALIFORNIA
9                    (LOS ANGELES DIVISION)
10
11 BOB SMITH                    ) CHAPTER 7 BANKRUPTCY CASE
12                              ) NO. LA 04-19681-ER
13 PLAINTIFF,                   )
                                )
14 vs.                          ) ADV. NO.  AB 04-02232ER
15                              )
16 UNITED STATES DEPARTMENT     ) COMPLAINT FILED:   8/2/2004
   OF EDUCATION,                ) DEPT:
17
                                  JUDGE:              M.
18 DEFENDANT
19 _____ )
20           PROOF OF SERVICE OF SUMMONS AND COMPLAINT
21
22
23
24
25
26
27
28
```

PROOF OF SERVICE — - 1 -

BOB SMITH
1111 ANYSTREET #1
LOS ANGELES, CA 90034
555-000-0000

Joint Status Report (Sample)

Attorney or Party Name, Address, Telephone & FAX Numbers and California State Bar Number

Don Sing
U.S. Attorney Office
312 N. Spring St., Room 512
Los Angeles, CA 90012
213-555-5555

Attorney for **U.S. Department of Education**

FOR COURT USE ONLY

**UNITED STATES BANKRUPTCY COURT
CENTRAL DISTRICT OF CALIFORNIA**

In re: **Bob Smith**

Debtor.

Bob Smith Plaintiff(s).

vs.

United States Department of Education Defendant(s).

CHAPTER **7**
CASE NUMBER **LA 04-19681-ER**
ADVERSARY NUMBER **04-02232-ER**
DATE: **12/16/04**
TIME: **10:00 a.m.**
PLACE: **Crtrm 1568**

**JOINT STATUS REPORT
LOCAL BANKRUPTCY RULE 7016-1(a)(2)**

TO THE HONORABLE UNITED STATES BANKRUPTCY JUDGE:

The parties submit the following JOINT STATUS REPORT in accordance with Local Bankruptcy Rule 7016-1(a)(2):

A. PLEADINGS/SERVICE:

1. Have all parties been served? ☑ Yes ☐ No

2. Have all parties filed and served answers to the complaint/counter-complaints/etc.? ☑ Yes ☐ No

3. Have all motions addressed to the pleadings been resolved? ☑ Yes ☐ No

4. Have counsel met and conferred in compliance with Local Bankruptcy Rule 7026-1? ☑ Yes ☐ No

5. If your answer to any of the four preceding questions is anything *other* than an unqualified "YES," then please explain below *(or on attached page)*:

(Continued on next page)

Rev 1/01 This form is optional. It has been approved for use by the United States Bankruptcy Court for the Central District of California. **F 7016-1.1**

Joint Status Report - *Page 2* F 7016-1.1

In re: Bob Smith, Debtor.
CHAPTER 7
CASE NUMBER LA 04-19681-ER

B. **READINESS FOR TRIAL**:

1. When will you be ready for trial in this case?

Plaintiff	Defendant
January 2005	April 2005

2. If your answer to the above is more than four (4) months after the summons issued in this case, give reasons for further delay.

Plaintiff	Defendant
	Defendant belies a mediation conference may lead to settlement.

3. When do you expect to complete your discovery efforts?

Plaintiff	Defendant
January 2005	March 2005

4. What additional discovery do you require to prepare for trial?

Plaintiff	Defendant
None	Depositions, Requests for Admission, Interrogatories, Document Production

C. **TRIAL TIME**:

1. What is your estimate of the time required to present your side of the case at trial (including rebuttal stage if applicable)?

Plaintiff	Defendant
Two hours	One or two hours

2. How many witnesses do you intend to call at trial (including opposing parties)?

Plaintiff	Defendant
None	One or two

3. How many exhibits do you anticipate using at trial?

Plaintiff	Defendant
Twenty to fifty.	Ten to twenty.

(Continued on next page)

Rev 1/01 This form is optional. It has been approved for use by the United States Bankruptcy Court for the Central District of California.

F 7016-1.1

Joint Status Report - *Page 3* **F 7016-1.1**

In re	Bob Smith		CHAPTER 7
		Debtor.	CASE NUMBER LA 04-19681-ER

D. **PRE-TRIAL CONFERENCE:**

A pre-trial conference is usually conducted between a week to a month before trial, at which time a pre-trial order will be signed by the court. [See Local Rule 7016-1.] If you believe that a pre-trial conference is not necessary or appropriate in this case, please so note below, stating your reasons:

Plaintiff	Defendant
Pre-trial conference ✓ (is)/ ___ (is not) requested. Reasons: _____	Pre-trial conference ✓ (is)/ ___ (is not) requested. Reasons: _____

Plaintiff	Defendant
Pre-trial conference should be set *after*: (date) 02/04/05	Pre-trial conference should be set *after*: (date) 03/07/05

E. **SETTLEMENT:**

1. What is the status of settlement efforts?

2. Has this dispute been formally mediated? ☐ Yes ✓ No
   If so, when?

3. Do you want this matter sent to mediation at this time?

   Plaintiff ✓ Yes ☐ No   Defendant ✓ Yes ☐ No

(Continued on next page)

Rev 1/01 This form is optional. It has been approved for use by the United States Bankruptcy Court for the Central District of California. **F 7016-1.1**

	Joint Status Report - *Page 4*		**F 7016-1.1**
In re Bob Smith		CHAPTER 7	
	Debtor.	CASE NUMBER LA 04-19681-ER	

F. ADDITIONAL COMMENTS/RECOMMENDATIONS RE TRIAL: *(Use additional page if necessary.)*

Respectfully submitted,

Dated: 11/30/04

Dated: _____

United States Attorney's Office

Firm Name _____

Firm Name _____

By: _____

By: _____

Name: Bob Smith

Name: Don Sing

U.S. Department of Education

Attorney for: _____

Attorney for: _____

Rev 1/01 This form is optional. It has been approved for use by the United States Bankruptcy Court for the Central District of California. **F 7016-1.1**

Request for Documents from Department of Education (Sample)

This is a sample letter to be sent to the Department of Education requesting documents. The strategy is three–fold: first— to obtain information to prove your claim; second– to bring up issues the Department of Education does not want to be decided in court, and; third— to be an annoyance that will encourage them to settle in your favor before the trial.

In general, this letter is asking for information from the Department of Education to clarify and prove many of the issues brought forward in Chapter 8—Advocacy. 11 U.S.C.A. §523(a)(8) is bad law and should be overturned. Reread Chapter 8 to help you with your writing.

Remember, if you choose to write a letter like this, you **must** put it in your own words. Do not copy it as is.

Dear Department of Education,

This letter asks for data from the Department of Education for use in my own adversary proceeding.

A. I strongly believe the aggressive drive by the Department of Education to lower the student loan default rate has led to a terrible misreading of the law.

I've read many, many adversarial court cases and see a pattern of aggressive attempts to squeeze money out of destitute debtors. I've read many academic papers on the issue of student loan defaults and find virtually all writers in agreement that the current enforcement system is biased against debtors. This seems to stem from directives by Congress and the Department of Education to lower the default rates at all costs. What we see is the restructuring of loans in ways that make no economic sense, just to say that a loan is not in "default." For example, placing a 65-year-old debtor living at the poverty level on SSI with $50,000 in student loans on an Income-contingent Repayment plan makes no sense. Technically, the loan will not be in default, but, realistically, the person will NEVER be able to pay back the loan, much less keep up with the interest payments. The Department of Education will spend thousands of dollars over 25 years just maintaining the loan on the books and working with collection agencies. This is a loss to taxpayers and violates the reason to reduce default rates—that is to recover more money. Commercial banks understand that it is better to get 10 cents on the dollar than incur years of additional expense when collecting is near impossible.

I need more information to prove this point. **I request** copies of any internal directives, memorandums, position papers, strategy papers, and more since 1995 from the Department of Education about their efforts to lower default rates. For example, are there settlement goals employees are required to meet each month? Are employees trained to guide debtors who are in trouble with the ICR or other income-sensitive plans? I need Department level documents that can answer these questions.

B. I believe the Department of Education has consistently violated debtor rights during the adversary proceeding litigation.

Many attorneys told me that it is impossible to bankrupt my student loans. I conducted my own research and found that it was possible to bankrupt student loans but only through an adversary proceeding. When I contacted the Department of Education, I was never told about bankruptcy, or compromise, or write-off as possible ways to have my student loans discharged. There seems to be a concerted effort by the Department of Education to deny honest debtors relief through bankruptcy, compromise, or write-off.

There is also much evidence that the Department of Education fails to follow the Debt Reduction Act and pursues debtors whose debt cannot be recovered.

I need more information to prove this point. **I request** copies of documents spanning the past five years that provide the following information:
- Number of student loan defaults.
- Number of Chapter 7 filings in which student loans are listed
- Number of people filing an "adversarial proceeding" seeking discharge of student loans.
- How the adversarial proceedings were resolved, e.g.
    Number found in favor of the debtor
    How many settled before trial and their results
    How many go to trial and the final results
- Reports from the Department of Education on discharges of loans and adversarial proceedings.
- Reports, papers, analysis, recommendations, and guidance made by the legal department of the Department of Education detailing legal strategies surrounding the discharge of student loans through the adversarial proceeding process.
- Reports on how many debtors have debts that more than 10-years old, are living on government benefits, and the Department of Education is actively pursuing.

C. I believe the Department of Education has incorrectly employed use of the Federal Poverty Guidelines as a measure of "undue hardship."

Someplace in the history of defending against adversary proceedings, the Department of Education suggested to the court to measure "undue hardship" against the Federal Poverty Guidelines. I've never read any rationale as to why this happened and why the courts accepted the arguments. There seems to be no legislative guidance in this area. There are many other measures that could have been used, but the Federal Poverty Guidelines are the most restrictive measure of poverty The Federal Poverty Guidelines are based on temporary subsistence survival, not living. I believe this happened because the Department of Education was too aggressive in its defense against bankruptcy, and, unfortunately, the courts accepted their arguments.

I need more information to prove this point. **I request** copies of internal documents created by the Department of Education where it was decided to employ the strategy of using the Federal Poverty Guidelines as the measure of "undue hardship."

D. I believe the Department of Education discriminates against certain protected classes in its defense against student loan bankruptcies. I am in one of these classes.

A number of reports have pointed out that not all classes of debtors fair as well in their adversary proceeding. Those that fail most in securing a discharge of their student loans are racial minorities, single people, the well-educated, those living above the poverty level, those with limited English skills, and other classes.

I need more information to prove this point. **I request** copies of any studies, reports, memos, E-mails, or analysis that show the Department of Education is aware of its discriminatory practices, whether or not policies and programs have been established to assure the fair treatment of all debtors, and the results of these policies and programs.

E. I believe the Department of Education defense against the adversary proceeding has been too severe, so much so they violate debtor's "fresh start" policy of the United States Bankruptcy laws.

The Bankruptcy Code reveals that the fresh start provision takes precedent over §523(a)(8). The purpose of a fresh start policy is to allow debtors to afford the necessities of life at a quality and quantity expected within the mainstream American culture. It is consistent within the Bankruptcy Code and the fresh start policy for all debtors, including debtors with student loans, to have lifestyles approximating the middle class. The Bankruptcy Code legislative history supports this position. This is obvious if you review the impact bankruptcy has on debtors. Neither Chapter 13 nor Chapter 7 debtors are forced into poverty to achieve discharge of their loans.

But the history of debtors with student loans is different. With very few exceptions, debtors with student loans are unable to discharge their student loan debt unless they are at or below the Poverty Guidelines. The Bankruptcy Commission suggested that the undue hardship criterion meant debtors must observe a "minimal standard of living" during repayment. Does this require poverty levels of living? No. Poverty denotes "subminimal." When Congress and the Bankruptcy Commission spoke of a minimal standard of living, they meant a level of living that brings debtors back into society at the lower ends of the middle class.

I need more information to prove this point. I request copies of any reports, memos, E-mail, reports to Congress, guidance to attorney, or any other correspondence was made by the Department of Education where the issue of the Bankruptcy Code "fresh start" policy is considered in relation to student loan dischargeability or adversary proceedings.

F. I believe Congress failed to clearly define "undue hardship" in §523(a)(8). As such, the Department of Education must have devised policy and defense strategies to uphold "undue hardship."

I need more information to prove this point. I request copies of any reports, memos, E-mail, reports to Congress, guidance to attorney, or any other correspondence made by the Department of Education where legal strategy was developed to interpret 11 US §523(a)(8).

G. I believe the Income-Driven Repayment (IDR) plans are not appropriate for all persons with student loan debts. For certain classes of debtors, the income tax liability potential when the remaining debt is discharged poses a significant, if not impossible hardship. I believe the Department of Education fails to recognize the limitations of the ICR and fails to inform debtors of these limitations.

<u>I need more information to prove this point</u>. **I request** copies of any reports, memos, E-mail, analyses, reports to Congress, guidance to attorney, or any other correspondence made by the Department of Education that discusses the implementation of the IDR, including advisement to debtors.

I look forward to receiving these documents before my trial date.

Sincerely,

Your name.

Stipulation (Sample)

SAMPLE — Stipulation

1 Name 1
United States Attorney
2 Name 2
Assistant United States Attorney
3 Chief, Civil Division
Name 3
4 Assistant United States Attorney
5 Address 1
Address 2
6 City, State Zip
Telephone
7 Fax
Attorneys for Defendant
8 United States Department of Education

UNITED STATES BANKRUPTCY COURT

FOR THE CENTRAL DISTRICT OF CALIFORNIA

LOS ANGELES DIVISION

In re:
  Debtor Name,
        Debtor.
	Case No. XX-XX-XXXXX-XX
	Chapter 7
	Adv. No. XX-XX-XXXXX-XX

Debtor Name,
        Plaintiff,
vs.
UNITED STATES DEPARTMENT OF EDUCATION,
        Defendant.
	STIPULATION RE SETTLEMENT AND DISMISSAL WITH PREJUDICE; ORDER THEREON
	
	Pre-trial Conference:
	Date: XX XX, 20XX
	Time: XX AM/PM
	Courtroom: Address
	              City
	
	Hon. Name
	Bankruptcy Judge

This Stipulation is entered into by and between Debtor Name ("Plaintiff") and the United States Department of Education ("Education"), to settle Plaintiff's Complaint To Determine

SAMPLE — Stipulation

Dischargeability of Debt Pursuant to 11 U.S.C. § 523(a)(8) filed on DATE.

Plaintiff is indebted to Education, as of DATE, in the total amount of $(TOTAL DEBT)($ XX.00 in principal, and $ XX.00 in interest as of (Date Filed Adversary), as the result of a William D. Ford Federal Direct Loan made to Plaintiff by Education in DATE ("Debt").

Plaintiff and Education desire to resolve this dispute and terminate this adversary proceeding. The settlement memorialized by this Stipulation will allow Plaintiff to retire the Debt, by paying a reduced amount, if he abides by the terms herein.

Therefore, in consideration of the mutual covenants and conditions herein, the parties agree as follows:

1. Plaintiff shall pay Education $ XX.00 per month for X years (for a total of $ XXX.00). Payments shall be due by the end of each month, and they shall begin, at the latest, by DATE.

Plaintiff intends to set up a monthly electronic funds transfer to Education. In the event that Plaintiff does not make payments by way of electronic funds transfers, he should send payments, in the form of cashier's checks or money orders, to Education at the following address:

> U. S. Department of Education
> Payment Center
> P. O. Box 53260
> Atlanta, GA 30353-0260

Plaintiff must put his social security number on the face of all checks and money orders.

2

SAMPLE — Stipulation

2. If Plaintiff makes the payments required under Paragraph 1 above (a total of $ XX.00), the remaining amounts of the Debt will be considered by Education as discharged through Plaintiff's bankruptcy.

3. Plaintiff may pre-pay the $ XX.00 required under Paragraph 1 above, without penalty, and receive an earlier discharge, through bankruptcy, of the remaining amounts of the Debt.

4. If Plaintiff does not make the payments required under Paragraph 1 above, the remaining amounts of the Debt will not be considered as having been discharged through bankruptcy, and Education may use all available remedies to collect the remaining amounts of the Debt.

5. This Stipulation shall not affect Education's rights (or any other part of the federal government's rights) as to any other debts owed by Plaintiff, other than the Debt.

6. Except to the extent this Stipulation directly conflicts with the terms and conditions of the loan documents applicable to the Debt, the terms and conditions of the underlying loan documents remain unaffected.

7. The parties agree that this adversary proceeding be dismissed, with prejudice to refiling.

8. The parties shall bear their own costs.

///
///
///
///

SAMPLE — Stipulation

9. No modification of this Stipulation shall be effective unless made in writing and signed by the authorized representatives of the parties.

Respectfully submitted,

Dated: _____

Name 1
United States Attorney
Name 2
Assistant United States Attorney
Chief, Civil Division

_____
Name 3
Assistant United States Attorney

Attorneys for the United States
Department of Education

Dated: _____

_____
(Debtor's Name)

ORDER

Based on the foregoing Stipulation and for cause shown, **IT IS SO ORDERED** and the parties shall abide by this Stipulation. Adversary Proceeding No. XX-XX-XXXXX-XX is hereby dismissed, with prejudice.

Dated:

_____
HON. Name
UNITED STATES BANKRUPTCY JUDGE

///
///
///
///
///
///

Forms—Blank

This section includes:

Blank Legal (Pleading) Paper
    Your Local Rules will specify the maximum number of lines for the documents to be submitted. Most courts specify not more than 28 lines per page. The enclosed blank is for 28 lines. Although you are welcome to make copies of this paper for typing your own pleading, we recommend that you buy some at your local stationery store. This is because when you photocopy pages, they usually shrink by 2% or more each time, thereby making it difficult for a typewriter to line up.

For all forms listed below, check with your court to verify its correctness. If the form is not correct, obtain the correct form from the court clerk:

Adversary Proceeding Sheet (Cover)

Summons and Notice of Status Conference

Proof of Service

Joint Status Report

Adversary Proceeding Cover Sheet

B1040 (FORM 1040) (12/15)

ADVERSARY PROCEEDING COVER SHEET (Instructions on Reverse)	ADVERSARY PROCEEDING NUMBER (Court Use Only)
PLAINTIFFS	**DEFENDANTS**
ATTORNEYS (Firm Name, Address, and Telephone No.)	**ATTORNEYS** (If Known)
PARTY (Check One Box Only) ☐ Debtor ☐ U.S. Trustee/Bankruptcy Admin ☐ Creditor ☐ Other ☐ Trustee	**PARTY** (Check One Box Only) ☐ Debtor ☐ U.S. Trustee/Bankruptcy Admin ☐ Creditor ☐ Other ☐ Trustee
CAUSE OF ACTION (WRITE A BRIEF STATEMENT OF CAUSE OF ACTION, INCLUDING ALL U.S. STATUTES INVOLVED)	

NATURE OF SUIT

(Number up to five (5) boxes starting with lead cause of action as 1, first alternative cause as 2, second alternative cause as 3, etc.)

FRBP 7001(1) – Recovery of Money/Property
- ☐ 11-Recovery of money/property - §542 turnover of property
- ☐ 12-Recovery of money/property - §547 preference
- ☐ 13-Recovery of money/property - §548 fraudulent transfer
- ☐ 14-Recovery of money/property - other

FRBP 7001(2) – Validity, Priority or Extent of Lien
- ☐ 21-Validity, priority or extent of lien or other interest in property

FRBP 7001(3) – Approval of Sale of Property
- ☐ 31-Approval of sale of property of estate and of a co-owner - §363(h)

FRBP 7001(4) – Objection/Revocation of Discharge
- ☐ 41-Objection / revocation of discharge - §727(c),(d),(e)

FRBP 7001(5) – Revocation of Confirmation
- ☐ 51-Revocation of confirmation

FRBP 7001(6) – Dischargeability
- ☐ 66-Dischargeability - §523(a)(1),(14),(14A) priority tax claims
- ☐ 62-Dischargeability - §523(a)(2), false pretenses, false representation, actual fraud
- ☐ 67-Dischargeability - §523(a)(4), fraud as fiduciary, embezzlement, larceny

(continued next column)

FRBP 7001(6) – Dischargeability (continued)
- ☐ 61-Dischargeability - §523(a)(5), domestic support
- ☐ 68-Dischargeability - §523(a)(6), willful and malicious injury
- ☐ 63-Dischargeability - §523(a)(8), student loan
- ☐ 64-Dischargeability - §523(a)(15), divorce or separation obligation (other than domestic support)
- ☐ 65-Dischargeability - other

FRBP 7001(7) – Injunctive Relief
- ☐ 71-Injunctive relief – imposition of stay
- ☐ 72-Injunctive relief – other

FRBP 7001(8) Subordination of Claim or Interest
- ☐ 81-Subordination of claim or interest

FRBP 7001(9) Declaratory Judgment
- ☐ 91-Declaratory judgment

FRBP 7001(10) Determination of Removed Action
- ☐ 01-Determination of removed claim or cause

Other
- ☐ SS-SIPA Case – 15 U.S.C. §§78aaa *et.seq.*
- ☐ 02-Other (e.g. other actions that would have been brought in state court if unrelated to bankruptcy case)

☐ Check if this case involves a substantive issue of state law	☐ Check if this is asserted to be a class action under FRCP 23
☐ Check if a jury trial is demanded in complaint	Demand $
Other Relief Sought	

B1040 (FORM 1040) (12/15)

BANKRUPTCY CASE IN WHICH THIS ADVERSARY PROCEEDING ARISES			
NAME OF DEBTOR		BANKRUPTCY CASE NO.	
DISTRICT IN WHICH CASE IS PENDING		DIVISION OFFICE	NAME OF JUDGE
RELATED ADVERSARY PROCEEDING (IF ANY)			
PLAINTIFF	DEFENDANT		ADVERSARY PROCEEDING NO.
DISTRICT IN WHICH ADVERSARY IS PENDING		DIVISION OFFICE	NAME OF JUDGE
SIGNATURE OF ATTORNEY (OR PLAINTIFF)			
DATE		PRINT NAME OF ATTORNEY (OR PLAINTIFF)	

INSTRUCTIONS

The filing of a bankruptcy case creates an "estate" under the jurisdiction of the bankruptcy court which consists of all of the property of the debtor, wherever that property is located. Because the bankruptcy estate is so extensive and the jurisdiction of the court so broad, there may be lawsuits over the property or property rights of the estate. There also may be lawsuits concerning the debtor's discharge. If such a lawsuit is filed in a bankruptcy court, it is called an adversary proceeding.

A party filing an adversary proceeding must also must complete and file Form 1040, the Adversary Proceeding Cover Sheet, unless the party files the adversary proceeding electronically through the court's Case Management/Electronic Case Filing system (CM/ECF). (CM/ECF captures the information on Form 1040 as part of the filing process.) When completed, the cover sheet summarizes basic information on the adversary proceeding. The clerk of court needs the information to process the adversary proceeding and prepare required statistical reports on court activity.

The cover sheet and the information contained on it do not replace or supplement the filing and service of pleadings or other papers as required by law, the Bankruptcy Rules, or the local rules of court. The cover sheet, which is largely self-explanatory, must be completed by the plaintiff's attorney (or by the plaintiff if the plaintiff is not represented by an attorney). A separate cover sheet must be submitted to the clerk for each complaint filed.

Plaintiffs and Defendants. Give the names of the plaintiffs and defendants exactly as they appear on the complaint.

Attorneys. Give the names and addresses of the attorneys, if known.

Party. Check the most appropriate box in the first column for the plaintiffs and the second column for the defendants.

Demand. Enter the dollar amount being demanded in the complaint.

Signature. This cover sheet must be signed by the attorney of record in the box on the second page of the form. If the plaintiff is represented by a law firm, a member of the firm must sign. If the plaintiff is pro se, that is, not represented by an attorney, the plaintiff must sign.

Attorney or Party Name, Address, Telephone & FAX Numbers, and California State Bar Number	FOR COURT USE ONLY
Attorney for Plaintiff	
UNITED STATES BANKRUPTCY COURT **CENTRAL DISTRICT OF CALIFORNIA**	
In re: Debtor.	CHAPTER ____ CASE NUMBER ADVERSARY NUMBER
  Plaintiff(s), vs. Defendant(s).	*(The Boxes and Blank Lines below are for the Court's Use Only) (Do Not Fill Them In)* **SUMMONS AND NOTICE OF STATUS CONFERENCE**

TO THE DEFENDANT: A Complaint has been filed by the Plaintiff against you. If you wish to defend yourself, you must file with the Court a written pleading, in duplicate, in response to the Complaint. You must also send a copy of your written response to the party shown in the upper left-hand corner of this page. Unless you have filed in duplicate and served a responsive pleading by _____, the Court may enter a judgment by default against you for the relief demanded in the Complaint.

A Status Conference on the proceeding commenced by the Complaint has been set for:

Hearing Date:	**Time:**	**Courtroom:**	**Floor:**
☐ 255 East Temple Street, Los Angeles		☐ 411 West Fourth Street, Santa Ana	
☐ 21041 Burbank Boulevard, Woodland Hills		☐ 1415 State Street, Santa Barbara	
☐ 3420 Twelfth Street, Riverside			

PLEASE TAKE NOTICE that if the trial of the proceeding is anticipated to take less than two (2) hours, the parties may stipulate to conduct the trial of the case on the date specified, instead of holding a Status Conference. Such a stipulation must be lodged with the Court at least two (2) Court days before the date set forth above John Smith rt approval. The Court may continue the trial to another date if necessary to accommodate the anticip_____.

Date of Issuance: _____

JON D. CERETTO
Clerk of the Bankruptcy Court

By: _____
Deputy Clerk

This form is mandatory. It has been approved for use by the United States Bankruptcy Court for the Central District of California.

Revised December 1998 (COA-SA)

F 7004-1

Summons and Notice of Status Conference - *Page 2*   **F 7004-1**

In re	CHAPTER _____
Debtor:	CASE NUMBER

PROOF OF SERVICE

STATE OF CALIFORNIA, COUNTY OF _____

1. I am employed in the County of _____, State of California. I am over the age of 18 and not a party to the within action. My business address is as follows:

2. ☐ **Regular Mail Service:** On _____, I served the foregoing Summons and Notice of Status Conference (and any instructions attached thereto), together with the Complaint filed in this proceeding, on the Defendant(s) at the following address(es) by placing a true and correct copy thereof in a sealed envelope with postage thereon fully prepaid in the United States Mail at _____, California, addressed as set forth below.

3. ☐ **Personal Service:** On _____, personal service of the foregoing Summons and Notice of Status Conference (and any instructions attached thereto), together with the Complaint filed in this proceeding, was made on the Defendant(s) at the address(es) set forth below.

4. Defendant(s) and address(es) upon which service was made:

☐ Names and Addresses continued on attached page

I declare under penalty of perjury under the laws of the United States of America that the foregoing is true and correct.

Dated:

_____   _____
Type Name   *Signature*

This form is mandatory. It has been approved for use by the United States Bankruptcy Court for the Central District of California.

Revised December 1998 (COA-SA)   **F 7004-1**

Attorney or Party Name, Address, Telephone & FAX Numbers and California State Bar Number	FOR COURT USE ONLY
Attorney for	
UNITED STATES BANKRUPTCY COURT CENTRAL DISTRICT OF CALIFORNIA	
In re: Debtor.	
Plaintiff(s). vs. Defendant(s).	CHAPTER _____ CASE NUMBER ADVERSARY NUMBER DATE: TIME: PLACE:

JOINT STATUS REPORT
LOCAL BANKRUPTCY RULE 7016-1(a)(2)

TO THE HONORABLE UNITED STATES BANKRUPTCY JUDGE:

The parties submit the following JOINT STATUS REPORT in accordance with Local Bankruptcy Rule 7016-1(a)(2):

A. PLEADINGS/SERVICE:

1. Have all parties been served? ❏ Yes ❏ No

2. Have all parties filed and served answers to the complaint/ counter-complaints/etc.? ❏ Yes ❏ No

3. Have all motions addressed to the pleadings been resolved? ❏ Yes ❏ No

4. Have counsel met and conferred in compliance with Local Bankruptcy Rule 7026-1? ❏ Yes ❏ No

5. If your answer to any of the four preceding questions is anything other than an unqualified "YES," then please explain below (or on attached page):

(Continued on next page)

Rev 1/01   This form is optional. It has been approved for use by the United States Bankruptcy Court for the Central District of California.   **F 7016-1.1**

Joint Status Report - *Page 2* F 7016-1.1

In re		CHAPTER _____
	Debtor.	CASE NUMBER

B. **READINESS FOR TRIAL**:

    1. When will you be ready for trial in this case?
                 Plaintiff   Defendant

    2. If your answer to the above is more than four (4) months after the summons issued in this case, give reasons for further delay.
                 Plaintiff   Defendant

    3. When do you expect to complete your discovery efforts?
                 Plaintiff   Defendant

    4. What additional discovery do you require to prepare for trial?
                 Plaintiff   Defendant

C. **TRIAL TIME**:

    1. What is your estimate of the time required to present your side of the case at trial (including rebuttal stage if applicable)?
                 Plaintiff   Defendant

    2. How many witnesses do you intend to call at trial (including opposing parties)?
                 Plaintiff   Defendant

    3. How many exhibits do you anticipate using at trial?
                 Plaintiff   Defendant

(Continued on next page)

Rev 1/01 This form is optional. It has been approved for use by the United States Bankruptcy Court for the Central District of California. F 7016-1.1

Joint Status Report - *Page 3* F 7016-1.1

In re		CHAPTER _____
	Debtor.	CASE NUMBER

D. **PRE-TRIAL CONFERENCE:**

A pre-trial conference is usually conducted between a week to a month before trial, at which time a pre-trial order will be signed by the court. [See Local Rule 7016-1.] If you believe that a pre-trial conference is not necessary or appropriate in this case, please so note below, stating your reasons:

Plaintiff	Defendant
Pre-trial conference ___ (is)/ ___ (is not) requested. Reasons: _____ _____ _____ _____	Pre-trial conference ___ (is)/ ___ (is not) requested. Reasons: _____ _____ _____ _____

Plaintiff	Defendant
Pre-trial conference should be set <u>after</u>:	Pre-trial conference should be set <u>after</u>:
(date) _____	(date) _____

E. **SETTLEMENT:**

1. What is the status of settlement efforts?

2. Has this dispute been formally mediated?   ❑ Yes   ❑ No
   If so, when?

3. Do you want this matter sent to mediation at this time?

   Plaintiff   Defendant
   ❑ Yes   ❑ No   ❑ Yes   ❑ No

(Continued on next page)

Rev 1/01   This form is optional. It has been approved for use by the United States Bankruptcy Court for the Central District of California.   F 7016-1.1

In re	CHAPTER _____
Debtor.	CASE NUMBER

Joint Status Report - *Page 4* **F 7016-1.1**

F.   ADDITIONAL COMMENTS/RECOMMENDATIONS RE TRIAL: *(Use additional page if necessary.)*

Respectfully submitted,

Dated: _____

_____
Firm Name

By: _____

Name: _____

Attorney for: _____

Dated: _____

_____
Firm Name

By: _____

Name: _____

Attorney for: _____

Rev 1/01   This form is optional. It has been approved for use by the United States Bankruptcy Court for the Central District of California.   **F 7016-1.1**

APPENDIX F
Academic Articles

The articles in this section are illustrative, not exhaustive. In general, you will need to research the factors influencing your case.

The articles include:

- Almost Two-Thirds of All Bankruptcies Due to Medical Bills
- The Consequences of Age on the Ability to Repay
- Discrimination Based on Age
- Discrimination Against the Highly Educated
- Discrimination Based on Sexual Orientation
- Reverse Discrimination Based on Gender or Race
- U.S. Economy (2023)

Almost Two-Thirds of All Bankruptcies Due to Medical Bills

Dr. David Himmelstein, associate professor of medicine at Harvard Medical School, conducted research in 2004 into the relationship between medical problems and expenses and bankruptcy. As reported in the journal of *Health Affairs*, Dr. Himmelstein found that almost two-thirds of all bankruptcies in the United States were caused by soaring medical bills. Most of those affected were middle-class workers with health insurance. Dr. Himmelstein stated, "Most of the medically bankrupt were average Americans who happened to get sick. Health insurance offered little protection."[1]

The researcher got permission from bankruptcy judges of five states (California, Illinois, Pennsylvania, Tennessee, and Texas) to survey 1,771 people who filed for bankruptcy. Sixty-two percent (931) cited medical causes for their bankruptcy, which affected 1.9 to 2.2 million Americans (filers plus dependents). Of those who went bankrupt due to illness, the average out-of-pocket expenses were $11,854 since the onset of the illness.

He found that in the two years prior to filing for bankruptcy:
- 54% went without needed doctor or dentist visits because of cost
- 43% did not fill prescriptions because of cost
- 40% lost telephone service
- 19% went without food
- 15% had taken out second or third mortgages to pay for medical expenses

Immediately after completing the bankruptcy, Dr. Himmelstein found debtors experienced continued problems, including:
- 33% continued to have problems paying their bills following bankruptcy, including paying their mortgage/rent and utility payments
- 9% were rejected for car loans
- 5% were turned away on apartment rentals
- 3.1% were turned down for jobs

Dr. Himmelstein stated, "Even good employment-based coverage sometimes fails to protect families, because illness may lead to job loss and the consequent loss of coverage . . . [especially] when they are financially most vulnerable."[2]

George Cauthen, attorney for Nelson Mullins Riely & Scarborough LLP in Columbia, South Carolina, reviewed every bankruptcy petition filed in South Carolina from the years 1982 to 1989. He concluded that medical bills and divorce were the two leading causes of bankruptcy. He also found that less than 1% of all bankruptcy filings were due to credit card debt. Credit card debt causing bankruptcy is "truly a myth."[3]

TO THE READER: If you want to present information like this in your court case, you will need to update it with current statistics and more. <u>Do not copy the above article verbatim. Instead, paraphrase and update this article as needed.</u>

---

[1] Gox, Maggie (Health and Science Correspondent.) (Feb 2, 2005). Half of bankruptcy due to medical bills. *Reuters*
[2] Davis, Jeanie Lerche. (Feb. 2, 2005). Medical bills can lead to bankruptcy. *WebMD Medical News*.
[3] Gox, Maggie (Health and Science Correspondent.) (Feb 2, 2005). Half of bankruptcy due to medical bills. *Reuters*.

The Consequences of Age on the Ability to Repay

Often, the Department of Education acts as persons with student loan debts can always find employment—regardless of age. This article presents some of the research showing the relationship between aging and the ability to work and, hence, make student loan payments.

As common sense tells us, there is a direct correlation between a person's age and need for living assistance. Here are some numbers:

Social Security Benefits[1]
- 91% of people age 65 or over received SSI benefits in 2004
- For 34% of all SSI recipients, the SSI benefits represented 90% or more of their total income.
- For 31% of all SSI recipients, the SSI benefits represented 50-80% of their total income.
- For 21% of all SSI recipients, the SSI benefits represented 100% of their total income.
- Overall, almost 2/3 of all persons over age 65 and over depend on SSI benefits for most or all of their income.

Obviously, the older the debtor, the more likely he or she is dependent upon SSI benefits to live and generally have little discretionary income.

Disability[2]
- 16.1% of men and 14.7% of women ages 62-64 are severely disabled and unable to work.
- 22-31% of men age 62-67 have disabilities that limit their ability to work.

Again, it is obvious that older people have greater instances of disabilities that affect their ability to work and make income.

Participation in the Workforce by Age[3]
- Men 65 to 74 comprise 3.2% of the labor force.
- Men 75 and over, comprise 0.6% of the labor force.

Since the downturn of the economy, there have been many articles about the difficulties older workers have finding employment. For example, see Tiffany Hsu, April 10 2009, "Job Market is Especially Cruel for Older Workers," *Los Angeles Times*; "Older Workers Need Not Apply," April 12, 2009, *New York Times*; or Michael Luo, April 12, 2009, "Longer Unemployment for Those 45 and Older," *New York Times*.

Obviously, the older a person is, the less likely he or she works.

The purpose of the information is to show that reaching age 65 is a milestone in many ways. Financially, most people over age 65 are dependent upon SSI benefits and are unable to secure additional income through work due to disability, discrimination, and other reasons. As such, payment plans through the

---

[1] All statistics taken from the *SSA's FY 2004 Performance and Accountability Report*.
[2] All statistics are from the National Bipartisan Commission on the Future of Medicare, *Increasing the Medicare Eligibility Age*, 1998.
[3] Statistics from the Bureau of Labor Statistics, Office of Occupational Statistics and Employment Projections, *Table 11 – Distribution of the population and labor force by age and sex, 1980, 1990, 2000, and projected 2010*.

Department of Education for outstanding student loans need to be structured to end by the time the debtor begins to receive SSI—around age 65.

In reality, the Department of Education recovers very little from outstanding student loans from debtors over age 65. Poverty, disability, and other factors make it impossible for older debtors to pay towards old student loans. Plus, for persons on SSI who live at the poverty level, the loans are generally uncollectible. As the baby-boomers reach retirement, this issue will become more common, and a plan should be developed by the Department of Education to address the problem.

Forcing older debtors into the Income-Driven Repayment (IDR) Plan is non-productive and causes an undue hardship. The Department of Education needs to consider some realistic percentage-on-the-dollar settlement during the years in which older workers are employed.

TO THE READER: If you want to present information like this in your court case, you will need to update it with current statistics and more. Do not copy the above article verbatim. Instead, paraphrase and update this article as needed.

Discrimination Based on Age

Ageism is such an onerous problem in the American workplace that Congress passed the Age Discrimination Employment Act (ADEA) in 1967. Every state in the Union has a Department on Aging providing information, referral, and more, to persons over age 50. Most major cities also have social services aimed particularly at older workers. Despite all these efforts, "age discriminatory practices are thought to be so widespread in business that enforcement is difficult although not impossible."[1]

How bad is age discrimination in the workplace? "Age discrimination cases filed with the Equal Employment Opportunity Commission hit 19,921 [in fiscal year 2001]" – a more than 41% jump from 14,141 in 1999[2]. In 2002, age discrimination cases jumped another 14.5% from the previous year (EEOC, 2003). Workplace age discrimination "complaints make up one of the fastest-growing categories of workplace bias."[3]

Discrimination complaints actually filed are just the tip of the iceberg. Most workers or job applicants who experience age discrimination do not file formal complaints. Also, businesses have "gotten a lot smarter about how they [discriminate]."[4]

"In the past decade, downsizings, job insecurity, increased use of part-time and contract employees and greater reliance on automation have created what some researchers call a 'corporate culture of expendability' among older workers, the Administration on Aging says."[5] "Employers know the law. They do not any longer mention age in their ads. But they have other ways of getting the message across. The ad that begins 'Young, aggressive company' seeks 'bright, energetic' office manager, purchasing agent, engineer or secretary is sending a clear signal. Many companies, particularly in high technology, specify years of experience as a way of indicating what they want. It's usually two-three or three-five years, sometimes as many as ten-fifteen for executive spots. The implication is that no one with a twenty-five-year employment record need apply."[6]

Some companies have an acronym to sum up their view of older workers, "like TFO (for Too F****** Old). If you are over 50, or even over 45, and looking for a job, the attitude is all too familiar, and the fact that age discrimination is illegal doesn't matter."[7] A survey of members of ExecuNet (www.execunet.com) "found that 82% consider age bias a 'serious problem' in today's workplace, up from 78% in 2001" (Fisher, 2004). Of those members who were managers, "a startling 94%, almost all in their 40s and 50s, said that they believed their age had resulted in their being cut out of the running for a particular job."[8]

How bad is it for workers in their fifties once they have been laid off? Only one-half of men ages 55-61 found new jobs after being laid off[9]. In most cases, it was part-time employment. Further, "After being laid off, the older worker [over 50] has a 50 percent probability of taking a pay cut in future jobs,"[10] and this pay cut may be as much as 39%[11]. <u>Realize, this means that half of older workers NEVER find any kind of employment again for the **rest of their lives**</u>. "Once an older worker is out of the labor force for a full year, the probability of working the next year is minuscule."[12]

"It is difficult for many older workers to find a new job, and many become discouraged."[13] In fact, the term 'discouraged' is an official designation when used to count the number of persons unemployed (discussed in a later article). Discouragement comes not only from lack of landing a job but also from the societal condemnation toward the older unemployed worker. "To the public in general, and even to older people who aren't job hunting, the unemployed older worker evokes stereotyped reactions: If they had been any good to begin with they wouldn't be out of a job. They must be slowing down, out of date. Or, if it has been established that the older worker is the victim of a mass layoff or merger, they aren't looking hard enough; don't know how to present themselves (they oversell, undersell); or are too fussy. They want too much money, or they won't consider changing fields. They won't or can't develop new skills. Maybe they're unwilling to relocate."[14] Many older workers give up looking for work.

Some older workers try a number of coping mechanisms to overcome job application discrimination. "Candidates are omitting dates or work experience from their resume. Others are taking more drastic steps, such as coloring their hair or getting plastic surgery."[15] Yet, these strategies can backfire. "Scott Testa, chief operating officer at Mindbridge Software, stated, "We are seeing more and more prospective employees trying to hide their ages on resumes. That's one more reason to delete the resume from the pile. If they hide that, what else are they hiding?'"[16]

The problem with age discrimination in California mirrors those of the nation. "The California Employment Development Department showed in a 1998 report that while 82% of laid-off workers ages 25-54 landed new jobs, only 60% of those ages 55-64 secured new employment."[17] Likewise, unemployed workers 45 years of age and over averaged more than "twice the time to procure new employment [for those who landed a job] [as] their younger counterparts."[18]

No industry is immune from the problem of age discrimination. You would think engineering, the sciences, teaching, and similar fields would have less age bias considering that we constantly hear of shortages of scientists, engineers, and teachers. Yet, "age discrimination seems to be endemic to the entire aerospace industry."[19] The recent Shuttle disasters have called into question the loss of older, experienced personnel at NASA. Yet, NASA "fills out its positions with people who are 'fresh out,' meaning fresh out of college. In other words, the agency wasn't going to consider anyone who was middle-aged."[20]

What about job placement agencies? Few fee-charging agencies will represent older workers. These agencies are not in the do-good business but rather must make a profit by placing workers— and they know older workers are a liability. As one representative reported, "[Employers] want young people . . . We'd get job requisitions from well-know high tech companies saying no one over 40."[21] As such, these agencies rarely make an effort to represent older workers.

The nonprofit and free job-placement agencies are mostly supported through government programs. "Most clients who apply to these agencies are referred to openings that pay less than $6.00 an hour, many of them part-time."[22] Further, authors Brudney & Scott, in their research on job-placement agencies, found job fairs targeting older workers to "never succeed." There is a lot of hope, but significant job placement of older workers never happens.

The American Dream "promises that if you work hard, show initiative, don't make too many waves, and save your money, you will progress up the ladder and spend your later years in security. . . yet [older workers] experiences tell us that it's time to stop dreaming."[23]

This article is a brief overview of the problem of age discrimination in the workplace. There are thousands of books and articles on the subject. Federal and state aging agencies have produced thousands of pamphlets, opinion papers, and more. The problem is real and not going away.

TO THE READER: If you want to present information like this in your court case, you will need to update it with current statistics and more. <u>Do not copy the above article verbatim. Instead, paraphrase and update this article as needed</u>.

---

[1] Johnson, Elizabeth & Williamson, John. (1980). *Growing old: The social problems of aging.* New York: Holt, Rinehart and Winston.

[2] Fisher, Anne, (2004, February 9). Workplace: Older, wiser, job-hunting. *Fortune.*; Cohen, Adam. (2003, March 2). Too old to work? *New York Times.*

[3] Marshall, Samantha, (2003, May 12-18). Age bias complaints rise as the workforce grays. *Crain's New York Business.*

[4] Mille, Margaret. (2003, August 24). Ageism in the workplace. *Sarasota Herald-Tribune.*

[5] Ibid.

[6] Brudney, Juliet & Scott, Hilda. (1987). *Forced out.* New York: Simon & Schuster, Inc.

[7] Fisher, Anne. (2004, February 9). Workplace: Older, wiser, job-hunting. *Fortune.*; Cohen, Adam. (2003, March 2). Too old to work? *New York Times.*

[8] Ibid.

[9] Administration on Aging. (2002, January 17). *Age discrimination: A pervasive and damaging influence.* [Online]. Available: http://www.aoa.gov/factsheets/ageism.html [2002, October 15]

[10] Cohen, S. (2002, March 7). *How to fight age discrimination.* [Online]. Available: http://ww.kiplinger.com [2002].

[11] Joyce, E. (1999, March). *Age bias may thwart boomers.* [Online]. Available: http://www.ncoa.org/news/archives/abe_bias.htm [2002, November 13].

[12] Berkowitz et al. (1998). The older worker. *Industrial Relations Research Association.*

[13] Crampton, Suzanne & Hodge, John. (2003). *The aging workforce and age discrimination.* Hawaii International Conference on Business, June 18-21, 2003. Sheraton Waikiki Hotel, Honolulu, Hawaii, U.S.A.

[14] Brudney, Juliet & Scott, Hilda. (1987). *Forced out.* New York: Simon & Schuster, Inc.

[15] Armour, Stephanie, (2003, July 20). More job seekers try to hide their ages. *Money.*

[16] Ibid.

[17] Kleyman, Paul. (2004). Options needed for aging workers. *Aging Today.* [report available online at www.cchi.org.

[18] Ibid.

[19] Khol, Ronald. (December 18, 2003). NASA gets away with blatant age discrimination. *Machine Design.*

[20] Ibid.

[21] Brudney, Juliet and Scott, Hilda. (1987). *Forced out.* New York: Simon & Schuster, Inc.

[22] Ibid.

[23] Ibid.

Discrimination Against the Highly Educated

Many believe that a person with a master's degree, and in particular, a doctorate, should 'absolutely' be able to find a job. It is not true. Often a higher degree acts as an impenetrable wall against employment. This section reviews the research on the effect of higher education on employment.

The Effect of Higher Education on Employment:

It is a myth that a Ph.D. 'guarantees' employment. In a study done by the American Institute of Physics, one-third of its members who received their Ph.D. were unable to find permanent employment within the first year after graduation[1]. Even in the long run, some Ph.D.s are not able to find employment. The University of Washington Graduate School reports the rate of unemployment among Ph.D.s in 2001 to be 1.5%[2]; this is the unemployment rate within the first 10 years after obtaining the degree. Thus, a small number of Ph.D.s looking for work are still not able to land a job after ten years of effort. These findings are similar to an earlier study done by the National Science Foundation. It, too, found that 1.5% of Ph.D.s were unemployed in 1995[3].

Even Ph.D.s in Computer Sciences face a difficult future. "As of 1997, 6.1 percent of new computer science Ph.D.'s could not find stable, full-time employment. The rate was significantly higher than the jobless rate for the entire American workforce."[4]

Our society promotes education as the road to success. It is often reported that college-educated workers make significantly more income than non-college-educated—referred to as an education "income gap." "In June 2003, an estimated 1,286,000 Bachelor's degrees were conferred, along with 436,000 Master's, 80,400 First Professional, and 46,700 Doctoral degrees, as well as 633,000 Associates degrees. Degrees in all these categories are up substantially since the mid-1980s, as young people have heeded the advice given them to acquire more education."[5] But has all this effort and expense paid off? The income gap "has been shrinking since 1989, not growing. . . .[Further] between 1979 and 1992, the percentage of U.S. men holding B.A. degrees but earning poverty-level wages (about $13,000 per year) doubled, to 6 percent. A recent MacArthur Foundation study found that in Chicago, fully 9.2 percent of the working poor hold B.A.'s."[6] In January 2004, it was reported that "there were more unemployed workers 25 years or older with college degrees than there were unemployed workers without high school diplomas."[7] Any level of college education affords, on average, higher lifetime income over those with no college education. But, a college education does not automatically translate into higher levels of employment or greater financial prosperity.

The National Science Foundation study found a number of other correlates between obtaining a doctorate and employment. "Disruptions in full-time employment subsequent to receiving a doctorate" and working part-time prior to receiving the Ph.D. were associated with significantly higher unemployment rates[8].

Another correlate was the age of the recipient at the time the doctorate was awarded. As the National Science Foundation reported, "Age at completing the doctorate is strongly associated with unemployment. When controlling for other relevant variables, the unemployment rate ranged from 0.6 percent for those who received doctorates before age 26 to 5.8 percent for those who received doctorates at age 40 or older."[9] Shockingly, the unemployment rate for computer programmers over the age of 50 was an astounding 17 percent."[10] Thus, even those with higher college degrees and/or who work in technical fields are not sheltered from age discrimination.

The current official unemployment rate in the United States is about 5.6%. Notice that the unemployment rate for Ph.D.s over 40 years of age is similar or higher. This would indicate that, contrary to popular opinion, there is very little difference in employment rates related to the level of education. It is a myth that a doctorate 'guarantees' life-long, highly paid employment.

TO THE READER: If you want to present information like this in your court case, you will need to update it with current statistics and more. Do not copy the above article verbatim. Instead, paraphrase and update this article as needed.

---

[1] Chu, Raymond & Curtin, Jean. (1996, September). Underemployment among post doctorates 1994 Society Membership Survey. *American Institute of Physics* (AIP).

[2] The Graduate School, University of Washington. (2001, May). Ph.D. career paths at UW — An update. *Notes on Graduate Education*.

[3] Shettle, Carolyn F. (1997). *Who is unemployed? Factors affecting unemployment among individuals with doctoral degrees in science and engineering*. National Science Foundation, Division of Science Resources Studies, Special Report, NSF 97-336.

[4] Tonelson, Alan. (2000). *The race to the bottom: Why a worldwide worker surplus and uncontrolled free trade are sinking American living standards*. Boulder, Colo: Westview Press.

[5] Almeida, Paul. (2003, June 18). *On the globalization of white-collar jobs*. Testimony before the U.S. House of Representatives Committee on Small Business.

[6] Ibid.

[7] Gongloff, Mark. (2004, March 1). Outsourcing: what to do? *CNN/Money*.

[8] Shettle, Carolyn F. (1997). *Who is unemployed? Factors affecting unemployment among individuals with doctoral degrees in science and engineering*. National Science Foundation, Division of Science Resources Studies, Special Report, NSF 97-336.

[9] Ibid.

[10] Tonelson (2000).

Discrimination Based on Sexual Orientation

Although there has been progress in civil rights for LGBT, the United States is still a dangerous place for those who are open about their difference or who are perceived to be LGBT. One measure of this is antigay violence, which has increased steadily every year, and now is the number one hate crime reported to police each year[1]. Similarly, the numbers of antigay employment claims are increasing. Another measure is the firestorm consuming U.S. media and governmental meetings over the prospect of gay marriage. Antigay sentiments impact the work environment.

Contrary to public belief, LGBT have lower incomes than the general population. Lee Badgett has conducted the most accurate research on the economic discrimination LGBT experience. Besides many other correlations, she discovered "men with male partners earned 26% less than married men with the same education, location, race, age, number of children, and disability status did."[2] She states, "The findings for gay men strongly suggests the influence of workplace discrimination."[3]

TO THE READER: If you want to present information like this in your court case, you will need to update it with current statistics and more. <u>Do not copy the above article verbatim. Instead, paraphrase and update this article as needed.</u>

---

[1] Stewart, Chuck. (2003). *Gay and lesbian issues: A contemporary resource*. Boulder, CO: ABC-CLIO Publishers, p. 48.

[2] Badgett, M.V. Lee (1998). *Income inflation: The myth of affluence among gay, lesbian, and bisexual Americans*. Washington, D.C.: NGLTF Policy Institute.

[3] Ibid.

Reverse Discrimination Based on Gender or Race

This article is a true example of reverse discrimination based on gender or race; names have been changed to ensure confidentiality.

Dr. Smith received his Ph.D. in Women's Studies with an outside emphasis on Gay Studies. He applied for hundreds of jobs with universities throughout the world as either a Director of Women's Studies or Director of Lesbian and Gay Student Support. In his nine years of applying for work, he was never granted an interview. Upon investigation, he found that out of 671 departments[1] (NWSA, 2002) of Women Studies, only 7 had male directors. That means that women head 99% of Women's Studies Departments. Academically, both men and women may qualify as directors of such departments since Gender and Women's Studies are fields of knowledge either gender may learn. But the reality is that men are almost never hired for these positions. Similarly, Dr. Smith applied for every LGBT Resource Directorship. He was never granted an interview. According to the Lesbian, Gay, Bisexual, Transgender Resource Directory (2004) found on the web, there are 2 1/4 times as many women directors as there are men[2]. Men are rarely hired to head these departments.

Dr. Smith's degrees and professional writings qualify him to teach multicultural courses, and work in or be the director of Affirmative Action offices. He applied for hundreds of such positions over the years and never received a job. He was a member of the American Association of Affirmative Action (AAAA) and presented at their conferences. AAAA is overwhelmingly non-white, whereas Dr. Smith is Caucasian. In reality, college Affirmative Action offices restrict hiring to mostly non-white directors and usually women. Dr. Smith experienced reverse discrimination to such a significant degree that employment in his chosen field has not materialized.

TO THE READER: If you want to present information like this in your court case, you will need to update it with current statistics and more. Do not copy the above article verbatim. Instead, paraphrase and update this article as needed.

---

[1] *NWSA 2002 Updated Directory of Women's Studies Programs.* (2002). NWSA Women's Center, Georgia Institute of Technology, Rm 216, Student Services Building, 404-385-1563, yvette.upton@vpss.gatech.edu.

[2] *Lesbian, gay, bisexual, transgender Resource Directory.* (2004). www.lgbtcampus.org/cirectory.htm

U.S. Economy (2023)

This book was written during the early days of Covid-19 pandemic. At that time, more than 220,000 Americans had died from the virus. Approximately thirty-million[1] Americans were out of work due to quarantine orders from state and city authorities to specific industries where groups of people typically congregate. This represented almost half of the working population being out of work. Restaurants, theaters, sporting events, libraries, live theaters, large stores, schools, hotels, airlines, amusement parks, and other locations have been impacted, and many have permanently gone out of business. Some of the largest retail chains, malls, and restaurants have entered into bankruptcy. Many more businesses closed by Christmas 2020 and early 2021 from lack of business; and never reopen, preventing millions of Americans from returning to work. Regardless of the media hype or politician promises, the rate of infections and deaths caused by the virus is following simple mathematical exponential growth. The pandemic lasted well into 2021 and 2022. It is now known that even mild infections may create a long-lasting physical impact on major organs leading to an unknown level of life-time disability. The virus has crippling consequences for the economy.

It is expected that millions of Americans will face bankruptcy and evictions in the next few years. How awful. The personal toll will be large, and many people and families will not recover facing decades or lifetime challenges. The ability to repay student loans will suffer.

Some of the other economic factors that affect the ability to earn enough income to service student loans are endemic and structural to the U.S. economy. We have seen certain programs and policies that lead to job loss. Predicting these losses is like reading tea leaves. As stated in *CNN/Money* during the economic downturn in the early 2000s, "it's important to remember that economists have done a lousy job of predicting job growth lately; the consensus forecast for payroll growth has been overly optimistic in 9 out of the past 14 months."[2]

With the current economic downtrend, unemployment is rising monthly. However, this number represents only those who have made claims with unemployment. Many people either do not claim unemployment (and are not counted) or their unemployment has run out (and are no longer counted to be unemployed). The actual number of unemployed is typically estimated to be almost double the official number when the discouraged or those who have given up looking are included.

Because of the glut of qualified professionals on the market, "companies are being incredibly restrictive in how they look at people [for job openings]"[3]. This means that many highly educated and experienced workers cannot find employment.

Two governmental policies are having a strong impact on the U.S. job market—"guest workers" (H1-B and L-1 visa) and "outsourcing." These policies have the greatest impact on the highly educated. The H1-B and L-1 visa programs allow foreigners to enter the U.S. to work legally. The rationale behind the program is the claim made by some businesses that there is a shortage of U.S. talent in particular industries and that foreign workers are needed to fill the gap. In the early 2000s, over a million foreigners entered the U.S. as guest workers[4]. The computer, engineering, and medical industries have been the primary users of the program. Initially, it was claimed that the programs would not take jobs away from U.S. citizens and not depress wages within the respective industries. After many years of implementation, the U.S. Department of Labor reported in April 1996, "We found the program does not protect U.S. worker's jobs; instead, it allows aliens to immigrate . . . and then shop their services in competition with equally or more qualified U.S. workers without regard to prevailing wage . . . [and] the prevailing wage may be eroded over time."[5] Two recent private studies confirmed the U.S. Department of Labor report, which stated, "Heavy use of these H1-B workers is reducing the wages of computer and software workers in particular."[6] Thus, the guest worker program is reducing many jobs in the United States, particularly jobs requiring specialized education and training, and has impacted (depressed) the wages for those jobs.

Related to the guest worker program is the problem of "outsourcing" jobs to foreign workers. Here, U.S. companies find workers in other countries to fill jobs that otherwise would be performed in the U.S. (sometimes referred to as "offshoring"). As Paul Almeida (2003) discusses in his article, *On the Globalization of White-Collar Jobs*, "When manufacturing jobs started moving offshore, we were told not to worry, that the U.S. comparative advantage was in services and high technology. We were assured that the new global division of labor was both natural and benign: we would keep the high-paying, high-skilled jobs, while the developing countries would do the actual work of making things. For decades, American workers were told to simply acquire more skills and education in order to succeed in the U.S. job market. Now engineers with Ph.D.s and recent college graduates alike are hear that they are too expensive, that their job can be done more cheaply abroad. Meanwhile, the U.S. trade picture is also shifting in ominous ways."

A survey conducted by Deloitte Research found that the one-hundred largest financial services firms expected to "shift $356 billion worth of operations and about two million jobs [out of the U.S.] to low-wage countries over the next five years."[7] Not only financial services but other kinds of white-collar work—computer programming, "patent research, credit checks, tax return preparation, insurance claim processing, even the reading of CAT scans"[8]— (which use the telephone and Internet communication systems) are being transferred to low-cost countries. There is an "apparent wholesale flight of technology jobs like computer programming and technical support to lower-cost nations, led by India."[9] As a result, "The number of computer jobs in the United States dropped 10 percent in the past two years"[10] further impacting college enrollment in these fields. "The Computing Research Association's annual survey of more than two hundred universities in the United States and Canada found that undergraduate enrollments in computer science and computer engineering programs were down 23 percent this year."[11]

Bill Gates of Microsoft Corporation went on a speaking tour to encourage young people into computer programming and computer education programs[12]. Gates is aware of the negative sentiments which outsourcing has created for his business in the United States. Yet, Microsoft is one of the primary users of computer programmers in India. This schizophrenic behavior— moving highly skilled jobs out of the United States while at the same time publicly telling people they should seek higher education for jobs that are no longer in the United States— is not lost on students entering college. Students are voting with their feet by choosing other fields; obtaining college degrees in fields exposed to outsourcing is a dead end.

"Alan Greenspan and President Bush believed the best response to the movement of U.S. jobs offshore is the same thing it's always been: educating U.S. workers so they can get better-paying jobs. But some economists doubt education will fully ease the pain."[13] Talent pools in other countries are "massive"[14] and highly educated. Both Indian and Chinese cultures highly value education and have large numbers of highly skilled and educated workers. For example, India and China each graduate more Ph.D.s in computer science each year than the United States. Many economists believe higher education is not the solution to the lack of jobs caused by outsourcing[15].

Outsourcing to foreign workers has become a major political issue in the United States. Severe negative reactions by citizens occurred when a few government departments began outsourcing jobs that could be done locally. "The political reaction in the United States against such outsourcing has built rapidly in the last year; nearly two dozen states have voted on legislation to ban government work from being contacted to non-Americans. . . More recently, the United States Senate approved a bill aimed at restricting outsourcing of contracts from two federal departments."[16] Several major political figures challenged the outsourcing threat while other politicians within the administration embraced outsourcing. For example, on March 16, 2004 in New Delhi, India, Secretary of State Colin L. Powell "sought to assure Indians that the Bush administration would not try to halt the outsourcing of high-technology jobs to their country."[17] Earlier in 2004, Gregory Mankiw, chairman of the White House Council of Economic Advisors, called outsourcing a "long-term plus for the economy."[18] A great political outcry was stirred and the Bush administration claimed that it would work to train people for new jobs.

Many manufacturing jobs have moved overseas, and now high-technology white-collar jobs are also moving; the only jobs left are service jobs such as waiters, teachers, plumbers, electricians, construction workers, physicians, nurses, dentists, real estate, food service, auto repair and other skilled by labor-intensive jobs that require a live person to perform. These are the jobs of the future. "This is shattering news to the waiters, cashiers, home and health care workers, and tens of millions of other Americans toiling at jobs which often pay minimum wage or slightly higher— the very Americans being urged into all the reeducation and retraining programs that the optimists have promised the government or business one day will adequately fund and get right. No matter what careers they prepare themselves for, they will remain trapped in the race to the bottom."[19] Many economists believed the "trend is real, irreversible and another step in the globalization of the American economy."[20]

Conclusion: The United States was caught in a "no job growth" recovery from the recession of 2000-2001 and saw a severe economic slump after 2008. Now, the pandemic is causing an even larger economic crash, and millions of Americans are expected to be out of work for many years. There simply are not enough jobs for all those who are unemployed.

Economists are perplexed by the situation and have been consistently wrong in predicting new job growth. Both the guest worker programs and outsourcing of jobs to foreign workers are contributing to the problem— and mostly for the highly educated.

Most important for our current situation, the pandemic has destroyed millions of jobs. Many, if not most, jobs will return but after years of weathering unemployment and slow job creation. All of this impacts the ability of workers to service their student loans.

TO THE READER: If you want to present information like this in your court case, you will need to update it with current statistics and more. Do not copy the above article verbatim. Instead, paraphrase and update this article as need.

---

[1] Li, Yun. (June 29, 2020). "Nearly half the U.S. population is without a job, showing how far the labor recovery has to go. CNBC. https://www.cnbc.com/2020/06/29/nearly-half-the-us-population-is-without-a-job-showing-how-far-the-labor-recovery-has-to-go.html

[2] Gongloff, Mark. (2004, March 4). Job boom still a hope, not a fact. *CNN/Money*.

[3] Ibid.

[4] Almeida, Paul. (2003, June 18). *On the globalization of white-collar jobs*. Testimony before the U.S. House of Representatives Committee on Small Business.

[5] Tonelson, Alan. (2000). *The race to the bottom: Why a worldwide worker surplus and uncontrolled free trade are sinking American living standards*. Boulder, Colo: Westview Press.

[6] Ibid

[7] Almeida (2003, June 18).

[8] Donnelly, Francis & Ramirez, Charles. (2003, August 10). Michigan loses as tech jobs slip overseas. *The Detroit New Technology*.

[9] Lohr, Steve. (2004, March 1). Microsoft, amid dwindling interest, talks up computing as a career. *The New York Times*.

[10] Donnelly and Ramirez. (2003, August 10).

[11] Lohr. (2003, December 22).

[12] Ibid.

[13] Gongloff. (2004, March 4).

[14] Donnelly and Ramirez. (2003, August 10).

[15] Gongloff. (2004, March 4).

[16] Rai, Saritha. (2004, February 9). Indians fearing repercussions of U.S. technology outsourcing. *New York Times*.

[17] Weisman, Steven. (2004, March 17). Powell reassures India on technology jobs. *The New York Times*.

[18] Ibid.

[19] Tonelson. (2000).

[20] Lohr. (2003, December 22).

APPENDIX G
Resources

U.S. Bankruptcy Court Contacts

Please visit the *United Stated Courts—Court Website Links* website for active links to each court. From there you will learn addresses and contact information.
https://www.uscourts.gov/about-federal-courts/federal-courts-public/court-website-links#districtbankruptcy

U.S. District Courts	U.S. Bankruptcy Courts
Alabama Middle Alabama Northern Alabama Southern	Alabama Middle Alabama Northern Alabama Southern
Alaska	Alaska
Arizona	Arizona
Arkansas Eastern Arkansas Western	Arkansas Eastern & Western
California Central California Eastern California Northern California Southern	California Central California Eastern California Northern California Southern
Colorado	Colorado
Connecticut	Connecticut
Delaware	Delaware
District of Columbia	District of Columbia
Florida Middle Florida Northern Florida Southern	Florida Middle Florida Northern Florida Southern
Georgia Middle Georgia Northern Georgia Southern	Georgia Middle Georgia Northern Georgia Southern
Guam	Guam

U.S. District Courts	U.S. Bankruptcy Courts
Hawaii	Hawaii
Idaho	Idaho
Illinois Central Illinois Northern Illinois Southern	Illinois Central Illinois Northern Illinois Southern
Indiana Northern Indiana Southern	Indiana Northern Indiana Southern
Iowa Northern Iowa Southern	Iowa Northern Iowa Southern
Kansas	Kansas
Kentucky Eastern Kentucky Western	Kentucky Eastern Kentucky Western
Louisiana Eastern Louisiana Middle Louisiana Western	Louisiana Eastern Louisiana Middle Louisiana Western
Maine	Maine
Maryland	Maryland
Massachusetts	Massachusetts
Michigan Eastern Michigan Western	Michigan Eastern Michigan Western
Minnesota	Minnesota
Mississippi Northern Mississippi Southern	Mississippi Northern Mississippi Southern
Missouri Eastern Missouri Western	Missouri Eastern Missouri Western
Montana	Montana
Nebraska	Nebraska
Nevada	Nevada
New Hampshire	New Hampshire

U.S. District Courts	U.S. Bankruptcy Courts
New Jersey	New Jersey
New Mexico	New Mexico
New York Eastern New York Northern New York Southern New York Western	New York Eastern New York Northern New York Southern New York Western
North Carolina Eastern North Carolina Middle North Carolina Western	North Carolina Eastern North Carolina Middle North Carolina Western
North Dakota	North Dakota
Northern Mariana Islands	
Ohio Northern Ohio Southern	Ohio Northern Ohio Southern
Oklahoma Eastern Oklahoma Northern Oklahoma Western	Oklahoma Eastern Oklahoma Northern Oklahoma Western
Oregon	Oregon
Pennsylvania Eastern Pennsylvania Middle Pennsylvania Western	Pennsylvania Eastern Pennsylvania Middle Pennsylvania Western
Puerto Rico	Puerto Rico
Rhode Island	Rhode Island
South Carolina	South Carolina
South Dakota	South Dakota
Tennessee Eastern Tennessee Middle Tennessee Western	Tennessee Eastern Tennessee Middle Tennessee Western
Texas Eastern Texas Northern Texas Southern Texas Western	Texas Eastern Texas Northern Texas Southern Texas Western
Utah	Utah

U.S. District Courts	U.S. Bankruptcy Courts
Vermont	Vermont
Virgin Islands	
Virginia Eastern Virginia Western	Virginia Eastern Virginia Western
Washington Eastern Washington Western	Washington Eastern Washington Western
West Virginia Northern West Virginia Southern	West Virginia Northern West Virginia Southern
Wisconsin Eastern Wisconsin Western	Wisconsin Eastern Wisconsin Western
Wyoming	Wyoming

Glossary

Adversary proceeding: An additional lawsuit filed in conjunction with a bankruptcy. Adversary proceedings often ask the court to determine the dischargeability of a debt that is typically nondischargeable (such as student loans).

Bankruptcy Code: Title 11 of the United States Code (often abbreviated as 11 U.S.C) governs bankruptcy proceedings. Bankruptcy is a matter of federal law and is similar in every state.

Chapter 7: Is the most common form of bankruptcy and is available to individuals, married couples, corporations, and partnerships. It provides a quick discharge of debt.

Compromise: Policy of the Department of Education that accepts less than the total amount due on student loans to fully satisfy the conditions of the loan.

Consolidation: Combines a number of student loans into one loan.

Debtor: Person, partnership, or corporation (legal entity) that is liable for debts and who is the subject of a bankruptcy.

Deferment: Postponement of student loan repayment under various, specific circumstances during which interest are not charged.

Deposition: Testimony that is given under oath, especially a statement given by a witness that is read out in court in the witness's absence

Discharge: The legal elimination of debt through bankruptcy.

Dischargeable: Debts that can be eliminated through bankruptcy. In general, student loans cannot be discharged through bankruptcy unless an adversary proceeding is launched, and the court determines repaying the loans would cause an "undue hardship."

Dismissal: The termination of a lawsuit without either entry or judgment, i.e., the court does not record a discharge or denial of discharge.

Federal Poverty Guideline: The Social Security Administration developed the guidelines in 1964 by guessing the average family's total expenditure for food and multiplying it by a factor three.

FFEL: Federal Family Education Loan

Forbearance: Payments of student loans are temporarily postponed or reduced while interest is still charged.

Fresh start: A core feature of the U.S. Bankruptcy Code that acknowledges one of the primary reasons for bankruptcy is to allow debtors to wipe out most all debt to "freshly" start over.

Income-Driven Repayment (IDR) Plan: Plans that base monthly payments on the ability of the debtor to pay. It is the most flexible repayment plan offered by the Department of Education for Direct Loans. A complicated formula is used to calculate how much a debtor should be able to afford to make toward loan repayments (see Appendix A). If a debtor experiences hard times and his or her income drops, payments drops accordingly— sometimes to zero. The plan lasts for twenty-five years and any outstanding debt remaining at the end of the plan is discharged. However, debtors are liable for the taxes (income) on the discharged amount.

Interrogatories: Forms used by attorneys to gather information from witnesses.

Mediation: Informal meeting between the Plaintiff and defendant before a trial to try and come to some mutually agreed solution, thereby negating the need to go to trial.

Meeting of the creditors: The one and only bankruptcy court meeting where creditors may challenge debts held by the Plaintiff.

NELRP: Nursing Education Loan Repayment Program

Non-dischargeable: Debts that cannot be discharged through bankruptcy. The Bankruptcy Code list of non-dischargeable debts is found at 11 U.S.C.A. 523.

Offset: Taking some of your federal benefits to satisfy government debt.

Partial discharge: Some courts have approved discharging a portion of a student loan instead of taking an "all or nothing" approach.

Precedent: Court rulings that establish points of law. For example, when preparing your own case, you may want to find other similar cases that ruled a particular way so you can cite them as evidence of how your court should rule.

Trustee: A person appointed by the bankruptcy court to review debtor's schedules and to represent the interests of creditors in the bankruptcy proceedings.

Undue hardship: Congress did not clarify in §523(a)(8) the meaning of "undue hardship." Many courts have harshly and narrowly ruled that debtors cannot discharge educational loans unless they can demonstrate "a certainty of hopelessness" about their long-term financial condition.

Write-Off: Policy of the Department of Education to allow debtors who are unable to repay their student loans to completely eliminate their student loan debt.

Index

11 USC § 523. Exceptions to discharge 226
Administrative Offset of Federal Benefits 183
Adversary Complaint 138
adversary proceeding 127, 135
    Complaint 292
    Complaint to Determine Dischargeability 137
    filing fee 137
    going forward 19
    impossible to win 2
    Proceeding Sheet (cover) instruction and form 289
    time frame 136
    Who Handles My Loans 286
    who qualifies 3
Adversary Proceeding Complaint (Sample) 308, 311
Adversary Proceeding Sheet 136, 138
Adversary Proceeding Sheet (Cover) (Sample) 306
age
    impact on ability to repay 357
ageism 60, 108, 357, 359
Aid to Families with Dependent Children 114
Amend Bankruptcy Forms 6
Amendment to Schedule F 266
Amendment to Schedule F Sample 262
AmeriCorps Program 16
bad faith 106
bankruptcy
    caused by medical bills 356
    Chapter 13 40
    Chapter 7 40
    debt ratio 105
    fresh start 40, 110
    number of 42
Bankruptcy Act (1898) 40, 55, 110
Bankruptcy Code 108, 113
Bankruptcy Code (2005) 119
Bankruptcy Commission (1978) 111
Bankruptcy Reform Act (1978) 40, 45, 63
Bankruptcy Reform Act (1998) 51, 55, 103
Bankruptcy Review Commission (1973) 43, 44
Black Lung 18
BLS .... *See* Bureau of Labor Statistics
Blue Back 138, 139, 285
Brunner Test 51, 54, 56, 157
    first prong 54
    second prong 55
    third prong 55
Brunner v. New York State Higher Education Services Corp 54
Bryant Poverty Test 51, 53, 55
Bryant v. Pennsylvania Higher Education Assistance Agency 53
Bureau of Labor Statistics 114

certainty of hopelessness 51, 53, 104, 111, 115
Chapter 13 .... 40, 119, 127
Chapter 7 .... 135, 141
    Filing Fee Waived 246
    Form 106J Expenses 258
    Petition for Bankruptcy 237
    Sechedule 106 e-f Creditors 252
    Sechedule 106I Income 250
Cheesman v. Tennessee Student Assistance Corp 71
children 60
Civil Union 60
Collection Financial Standards 129, 150, 206
    Food, Clothing and Other Items 209
    Housing and Utilities 211
    Out-of-Pocket Healthcare (2023) 221
    Transportation Standards (2023) 217
Committee on the Judiciary 44
Complaint to Determine Dischargeability 137
Compromise 149, 155
    authority 16
    guidelines 16
    letter of authority 186, 193, 196
    who qualifies 3
Congressional Bankruptcy Commission (1978) 115
Conner v. Illinois State Scholarship Comm'n 68
Consolidation 10
Cornell 44
Courtney v. Gainer Bank 67
crime 110
Current Living Condition 58
DCIA .... *See* Debt Collection Improvement Act
debt
    collection 103
    partial discharge 112
    priority 110
Debt Collection Improvement Act 18
debtor
    African American 109
    American Indians 109
    independent students 108
    minorities 108
    partially disabled 109
    single parents 108
    white 109
Default 17, 180
Deferment 10
defrauded .... *See* fraud
Department of Housing and Urban Development 114
    Lower Income Families 114
    median income 114
    Very Low-Income Families 114
Department of Labor 114

dependents 60, 107
deposition.. 147
diligence.. 63
Direct Consolidation Loan Program..................................... 10
disability 14
discharge options
    military.. 16
    permanently disabled.. 59
Discharge Options 14, 167
discovery... 147
discrimination 61
    ageism 60, 62, 359
    disability 62
    ethnicity 62
    gender 62
    highly educated 61, 62, 108, 362
    income.. 108
    past terminations 62
    physical characteristics 62
    race 62
    religion 62
    reverse 62, 365
    sexual orientation 62, 364
    whistleblower 62
divorce 110
DOL .... *See* Department of Labor
domestic partner 60
Earned Income Tax Credits 114
economy... 366
educational value 115
Edward York... 44
EEOC .... *See* Equal Employment Opportunity Commission
Eighth Circuit Court in Andrews v. South Dakota Student
    Loan Assistance Corp 53
Equal Employment Opportunity Commission 62
Equal Protection Clause... 106
equitable powers 112
Ertel, Rep. Allen 43, 44
exceptional 55, 58, 61
Exceptions to Discharge 226
Extended Repayment Plan.. 12
external factors 61, 130, 151
extraordinary circumstances 53, 111
federal benefits
    seize 103
Federal Benefits... 18
    types 18
Federal Family Education Loan 10
Federal Poverty Guidelines 52, 53, 56, 58, 63, 107, 108, 111,
    114, 116, 129, 131, 150, 152
    description... 222
    development.. 114
Federal Student Aid Information Center 15
FFEL .... *See* Federal Family Education Loan
Forbearance 10
Ford v. Tennessee Student Assistance Corp...................... 69
forum shopping... 113
fraud 63, 106

fresh start 40, 42, 55, 110
furlough.. 144
General Accounting Office.. 105
General Accounting Office Study (1976).......................... 43
good faith 52, 106, 131, 152
    analysis.. 55
Good Faith 63
Goulet v. Educational Credit Management Corp 76
Graduated Repayment Plan 11
Gravante... 68
GSLP........................ *See* Guaranteed Student Loan Program
Guaranteed Student Loan Program.............................. 42, 45
Half of All Bankruptcies Due to Medical Bills 355, 356
Healey v. Massachusetts Higher Education....................... 68
Higher Education Act 44, 45
House Report on the Bankruptcy Law Revision (1977)..... 43
HUD....*See* Department of Housing and Urban Development
ICR .... *See* Income Contingent Repayment (ICR) Plan
Income Contingent Repayment (ICR) Plan...... 137, 142, 158
    description.. 14
    preparing response 131, 152
    tax consequence 117
Infancy 19
Innes v. Kansas State Univ 74
interrogatories 147
Interrogatories 127, 199
Johnson court 111
Johnson Test 51, 52, 55
    good faith 52
    mechanical analysis 52
    policy analysis... 52
Joint Status Report.. 136
Joint Status Report (Sample) 333
judicial lawmaking 112, 116
Kraft v. New York State Higher Educ. Servs. Corp 70
Laches 19
Lack of Useable Job Skills 60
Legal Service Corporation 114
Lehman v. New York Higher Educ. Servs. Corp................. 75
Local Bankruptcy Rules 136
Lower Income Families 114
Mail Matrix 139, 300
Mail Matrix (Sample) 331
Maxine Waters... 109
mechanical analysis 52
Mechanical Analysis.. 55
median income 114
Mediation... 142
mediator 146
medical condition.. 59, 107
Middle Income Student Assistance Act............................. 43
minimal standard of living.. 110, 111
minimized expenses 58
Modified Repayment Plans................................ 112, 113, 116
Motion to Reopen Bankruptcy......................... 6, 7, 261, 263
Motion to Reopen Bankruptcy Sample............................ 261
Myers v. Pennsylvania Higher Education Assistance Agency
    70

National Bankruptcy Review Commission Report (1997) 106
National Community Service Trust Act 10
National Defense Education Act (NDEA).......................... 42
National Defense Student Loan 42
NDSL ....*See* National Defense Student Loan
nondischargeable debt 44, 45, 110, 115
non-disclosure 145
Nursing Education Loan Repayment Program 16
Order 140
overturn law 105
parents 60
pariah 63
partial discharge 58, 112, 116
Partial Discharge 112
past terminations 62
Pena v. United Student Aid Funds....................................... 76
Pennsylvania Higher Education Assistance Agency v. Johnson 52
Perkins Loans 14, 42
permanently disabled 59
personal limitations 59, 130, 151
Playing the Game 142
policy analysis 52
Policy Analysis 55
Postponement 9
Postponing Repayments 167
poverty 114
    defined by AFDC 114
    defined by Bureau of Labor Statistics 114
    defined by Department of Education 114
    defined by Legal Service Corporation 114
    defined by Social Security Administration 114
    sociological definition 114
Pretrial Hearing 147
Pretrial Order 148
principle of uniformity 113
Proof of Service 136, 139, 300
Proof of Service (Sample) 330
Proof of Service Cover 139
Proof of Service Cover (Sample) 332
proprietary schools 109
Railroad Retirement Benefits 18
Reopening a Bankruptcy 6
Repayment Options 9, 163
Repayment Plans 163
representing yourself 2
reverse discrimination 62
Rivers v. United Student Aid Funds 73
Roberson 70
seize federal benefits 103
Senate Permanent Subcommittee on Investigations (1993) 109
service of process 139
Sheldon Steinbach 44
siblings 60
Skaggs v. Great Lakes Higher Educ. Corp 72
Social Security Disability 18
Social Security Retirement 18

sociological definitions of poverty 114
spouse 60
Stafford Loan Program 42
Standard Repayment Plan 11
Status Hearing 141
statute of limitations 18
Stebbins-Hopf v. Texas Guaranteed Student Loan Corp 72
stereotype debtor 108
stipulation 146
Stipulation (Sample) 340
student loan
    amount 43
    bankruptcy
        rate 105
        success 104
        threat 105
    default
        increase 43
        number 43
        rate 105
    discharge
        bankruptcy 14
        disability 14
        loans less than 10 years old 18
        loans more than 10 years old 18
        rate 43
        teacher 14
    fraud 106
    how soon trying to bankrupt 63
    infancy 19
    laches 19
    media hype 43
    ratio to total debt 63
    spending increase 45
    statute of limitations 18
Student Loan
    bankruptcy
        consequence of age 357
    cancellation ....*See* Student Loan: discharge
    Consolidation 10
    Deferment 10
    discharge
        options 14
    Extended Repayment Plan 12
    Forbearance 10
    Graduated Repayment Plan 11
    history 39
    Income Contingent Repayment (ICR) Plan 14
    Postponement 9
    Repayment Options 9, 163
    Standard Repayment Plan 11
subminimal living 110
subpoena 147
subsistence or poverty level 111
suicide 110
Summons 136, 138, 298
Summons (Sample) 329
Supplemental Security Income 18

teacher low-income 14
Totality of the Circumstances Test 51, 53, 56
   certainty of hopelessness 53
   external factors 61
Trial 147
trustee 137
Truth-in-Lending 19
typical debtor 109
U.S. Economy 61, 366
U.S. trustee 137
U.S.C. 31 §3716(e) 184
U.S.C. Chapter 11 §523(a)(8) 45
undue hardship 45, 51, 142, 157
   ageism 62
   Civil Union 60
   dependents 60
   Domestic Partnet 60
   exceptional circumstances 59
   external factors 61
   extraordinary circumstances 53
   failed to define 111
   job terminated 61
   lack of useable job skills 60
   mechanical analysis 52
   medical condition 59
   parents 60
   personal limitations 59
   policy analysis 52

siblings 60
spouse 60
U.S. Economy 61
whistleblower 61
Undue hardship 55
Undue Hardship 51
undue hardship tests
   Brunner Test 51, 54
   Bryant Poverty Test 51, 53
   Johnson Test 51, 52
   Totality of the Circumstances 51, 53
   wide variance 113
unique 55, 58, 61, 111
United States Attorney 136
unpleasantness 53
unscrupulous recruiters 109
Value of the Education 116
Very Low-Income Families 114
Walcott v. USA Funds, Inc 72
Wegfehrt 53
Wetzel v. New York State Higher Educ. Servs. Corp 73
whistleblower 61, 62
write-off 156
Write-Off 17, 149, 155
   guidelines 17
   letter of authority 186, 193, 196
   who qualifies 3

Notes

www.ingramcontent.com/pod-product-compliance
Lightning Source LLC
Chambersburg PA
CBHW081143230426
43664CB00018B/2786